The Dubious Spectacle

Herbert Blau

The Dubious Spectacle

EXTREMITIES OF THEATER, 1976–2000

University of Minnesota Press
Minneapolis / London

Published by the University of Minnesota Press
111 Third Avenue South, Suite 290
Minneapolis, MN 55401-2520
http://www.upress.umn.edu

Library of Congress Cataloging-in-Publication Data

Blau, Herbert.
    The dubious spectacle : extremities of theater, 1976–2000 / Herbert Blau.
        p.   cm.
    Includes bibliographical references and index.
    ISBN 0-8166-3812-8 (alk. paper)—ISBN 0-8166-3813-6 (pbk. : alk. paper)
    1. Theater—Philosophy.   2. Drama—History and criticism—Theory, etc.
    I. Title.
    PN2039 .B577 2002
    792'.01—dc21

                                                                    2001005080

Printed in the United States of America on acid-free paper

The University of Minnesota is an equal-opportunity educator and employer.

12 11 10 09 08 07 06 05 04 03 02   10 9 8 7 6 5 4 3 2 1

For Kathy
nothing dubious here

Contents

Introduction

These essays span just about a quarter of a century, from the mid-seventies to the millennium. They track certain mutations in my thinking about the theater, and by way of theater about education, politics, fashion, photography, and the other arts, as well as the more than residual modernism in the postmodern condition. As there are other writings I might have included (some from almost a quarter century before), this is not exactly a full-scale retrospective, but the collection moves through and around most of the issues that have engaged me over the years, some of them inexhaustibly. Although the essays are not organized in chronological sequence, they constitute by accretion in the conceptual back and forth a sort of intellectual history of a turning from theater to theory, charged as it was to begin with by the work I had done in the theater—which, elsewhere, I have defined as "blooded thought."[1] What was also there to begin with, in the theater as in theory, are certain elliptical habits of mind that may rub against the grain of the new historicizations, no less the often foregone conclusions in the heuristics of cultural studies or—in the ethnographic consciousness now prominent in the field—the more predictable liminalities of performance studies.

Now that it is pretty much orthodoxy to think of artistic and cultural practices through the quadrivium of social construction (gender, race, ethnicity, class), it may seem peculiar to encounter, from the opening essay on, a view of the theater so insistently ontological. If that remains the egregious reflex of a hopeless essentialism, the fascination of theater for me is still in the mystery of its emergence, whenever that happened to be or as it happens now, that is, the materialization of theater—not the institution but the *sensation,* the thing that's passing strange[2]—from whatever there was before, whatever name we give it (*was* it there before?) that we think of as other than theater. Is it *life*? is it *the real*? or the relations of production? or, in the ether of ideology, merely another appearance? As I have asked in other books, how seriously are we to take the persistent themes of the canonical drama, that all the world's a stage or that life is a dream or that, seek for truth as we may—in the metaphysical mist of seeming that won't seem to go away—it somehow always escapes us or is not what it appears to be, as if at the heart of the reality principle is the future of illusion? And why do we seem to forget that at the heart of the theater itself is a genetic distrust of theater, at least in the specular tradition extending from the bloody eyes of Oedipus through the ghostings and mousetrap of *Hamlet* to the incriminating gaze in Ibsen's bourgeois parlor, confounded by Pirandello and turned back upon the watchers in the mirrored brothel of Genet?

For a while it was claimed, in the vanity of critique, that the system of representation on which the tradition depends had not only been demystified, first by Brecht, then deconstruction, but was in a state of virtual collapse. One has only to look, however, at the plaintive end of Derrida's essay on Artaud, "The Theater of Cruelty and the Closure of Representation," to realize that even the shattered mirror sustains, in its myriad of replications, all scenarios ending in death, the appalling truth of a cruelty requiring in the beginning and refusing to end its own representation.[3] To be sure, resistance to that refusal sustains itself as well, with more or less fantasy of subversion through permutations of theory: from the uncathected notion of a libidinal economy without reserve through the "phantasmaphysics" of amniotic desiring machines to the current investment in "bodies that matter" in queering performativity. Defined by Judith Butler in terms of repetitive acts, the "drag" of performativity or its *"corporeal style"*—suggesting "a dramatic and contingent construction of meaning"[4]—is in parody and remonstrance a disavowal of theater, or the sort of embodied performance that endorses or perpetuates what representation conceals. Which returns us to the charge (another repetitive act) that it is a humanistic cover-up for invisible power.

If, by way of Foucault or Deleuze, critique of the system continues, so does the idea of performance unable to escape from theater, with its topography of appearance, always under suspicion, and the impossible prospect of ever relieving that—no more than a generation of anti-

Oedipus or the lure of performative bodies has relieved us of mortal flesh or the cruel fatality of it. To dwell on that, of course, has its liabilities, as we could see in the mania of Artaud or, in another register of denunciation, the refusal to pay tribute to an "irresistible force," as Brecht made clear in "A Short Organum," in his assault on "Shakespeare's great solitary figures, bearing on their breast the star of their fate. . . ." What Brecht disdained in those star-crossed, mesmerizing, vainglorious figures was not the mere subjective burden of this too, too solid (or squalid?) flesh but fatality as pandemic, the catastrophe beyond criticism: "Human sacrifices all round! Barbaric delights!"—while we "under cover of darkness . . . take part in the crescendos and climaxes which 'normal' life denies us," until the restoration of order (a mandate of the age) by "the dreamlike executioner's axe which cuts short such crescendos as so many excesses." Despite the crescendo here, it always struck me that the very fervor of recrimination, like that of the Puritans upon the theater in Shakespeare's day, almost validated "those dreamlike figures up on the stage."[5] So it was, too, though Brecht did everything he could to remove the fatal star from her breast, with the isolate image of Mother Courage still pulling her wagon at the end of the play. Chastening it may have been, but with every device of Alienation almost never as Brecht wanted. Out there in the void the image seemed existential. Or so it did back in San Francisco, in 1957, when I staged *Mother Courage* in its first American production. By the time, a few years later, I did a somewhat revisionist staging of *Galileo,* I had already, drawn to Beckett astride of a grave, been equivocating about Brecht and his critique of dramatic form that became second nature in theory. What was at stake is tragic vision, now thought of as disempowering, but which at the perceptual limit haunts my previous books, and which for better or worse, at least in certain passages, will be ghosting this one too.

As for "Flat-Out Vision," which I wrote for a conference on photography put together by film theorists, what is tragic is only implicit in "the intractable referent of the photograph, what it can't get rid of," the absence in the image, immobile, funereal, alluring as it may be, what caused Roland Barthes, in *Camera Lucida,* to speak of the seductive filmic flatness as a virtual theater of death. As I suggest toward the end of the essay, what Barthes says of the photograph might be describing Brecht's Baal, whose serial mortifications not only occur in quick exposures but, in the repetitive acts of his perverse, insatiable, then hypertrophic, rotting, excremental body—waste matter in the end, looking at the stars—"like an imprinted residue of the radiant flesh of the

world. . . ." What I meant by that is not so much the paradoxical sense
of transcendence one may feel in tragedy but rather a flat-out attesta-
tion to the powers of imagination, dismissed in recent years as a swol-
len conceit or transcendental signifier, with its pretentious claims to a
privileged vision that is merely ideological. What can one say? Here the
imprinted residue may be that of high modernism, where imagination
goes with conceptual rigor too, as in the photographic *Equivalents* of
Alfred Stieglitz, which appear to bring the senses with surpassing vision
where—surely on a flat surface—the senses do not go. But at the risk of
being sucked into the emptiness of the signifier, let me speak of one domain in which I feel some privilege.

I have spent a lot of years watching actors in every imaginable repetition, in every conceivable corporeal style, mimetic or ideographic, laid
back, ribald, wild, as if out of nightmare or, making drag innocent, in
eye-opening figurations that you could hardly imagine dreaming. There
were times, moreover, when there was sufficient imaginative daring that,
spellbound in looking, you almost had to look away, close as it was—in
the recombinant seeming of body parts, ear into heel, ass into mouth, a
breasted elbow in flowing hair, sperm, shit, spittle, an intestinal presence
in the all-seeing eye—to the "miraculated" schizophrenia of a "body
without organs."[6] At other times, in other ways, the body parts intact, as
if riveted or frozen or, in the body that matters, caressed into being,
there might still be the overpowering sensation that, even if it is being
repeated, in nuance or extremity, it is being taken to some limit never
seen before. How did it get there? by what energy or demiurge, will or
inspiration? and if not brainless, by what even conceived? Whatever one
wants to call it, that indescribable power, I sure as hell know it when I
see it and certainly when I don't—never mind in those who never had it,
but even with the finest of actors in the most unbearable of rehearsals, of
which (sitting there in the dark through the many years) I have watched
more than I care to remember. As for trying to do something about it, I
have known then, too, when imagination fails, and if you are directing,
as I have also been privileged to do, especially gifted people who at some
impasse of rehearsal want *you* to pick up the cue, there is nothing more
mortifying than not knowing what it is.

"Whither wilt thou lead me? Speak. I'll go no further." That is
Hamlet to the Ghost (1.5.1), having followed on the ramparts—"He
waxes desperate with imagination" (1.4.87)—to the perilous site of
what, if he can hardly believe his eyes, has never been heard before. Or
so, in its extremity, it has to be imagined. About performance, however,

literally at the extreme I had a chance to think again, quite recently, in a rather extraordinary context, where it was approached as psychophysical, athletic, genetic, neuroscientific, ophthalmic, and under medical or competitive circumstances as possibly fatal too. This was in a symposium at Stanford, actually titled "Limits of Performance: Sports, Medicine, and the Humanities," whose international participants were world-class athletes (with Olympic medals) and world-class surgeons (one with a Nobel Prize), a sports clinician from South Africa (who monitored for training at high altitudes long-distance runners from Kenya), the head coaches at Stanford (brainy one and all, in basketball, football, swimming, track), a member of the House of Representatives who is legendary not for his politics but for having broken when still in high school the four-minute mile, and a former coach at Stanford who when he was with the San Francisco Forty-Niners made himself eligible for the Hall of Fame by winning three Super Bowls. He and the other coaches were particularly caught up by a sequence in my talk—the only one about performance as we know it from the theater—that referred to high-pressure moments in practice or rehearsal when, doing things you are almost ashamed of to bring out a surpassing performance, coaching and directing seem alike. What I had to say there, which led to a lively interchange, is expanded here as the final piece in the volume, "Limits of Performance: The Insane Root." The essay that precedes it was already close to that root. Written for the issue on "Revisionism" (or the revision of revisionism) by *New Literary History*, it passes from reflections on the new historicism to questionable stagings of *King Lear*, with the remembrance of a performance, astonishing in its delirium, as if driven by the compulsion to exceed representation by annihilating the body and revising the abyss.

As with the two just mentioned, the essays were written for various occasions, which will be identified when particularly relevant—aside from remarks here—in the notes for these texts (dates at the end will signify when text was published, performed, or finished). Some of the texts are documented, some not, depending on the occasion. While I have made some minor emendations, I have not tried to update things, or revise the historical circumstances impinging on, abrading, or faceting certain ideas, like the "index futures" following Black Monday before the Japanese "bubble" burst. So, the first essay—"Afterthought from the Vanishing Point: Theater at the End of the Real" (written in 1993)—refers to the levees breaking down on the Mississippi and to the legislative elections in France that seemed, until the *cohabitation* of

Lionel Jospin with Jacques Chirac, to put the Socialist Party out of commission. Elsewhere in the collection Reagan may still be president or
Beckett still alive, and along with afterthoughts on earlier writings there
are references to projects under way, the study of photography (mentioned before) and a book on fashion (now published).[7] Both of these
were impelled by an unabating obsession with the ubiquity of appearance or, in a society of the spectacle, almost obscenely imaged, the appearance of appearance to an exponential power or—in the merger with
simulacra: mediatized, commodified, the real disappearing into an abundance of dispossession—as the accumulative form or apotheosis of capital itself, dominating everywhere and wholly immaterial.

As the society of the spectacle metastasizes into the society of information, where it is not a matter of repetitive acts but incessant repetition, the same might be said of noise, through which, in the cybernetic
feedback of its lucrative dominance, multitudinous meanings clamor for
recognition. There is money in noise, as dot-com routers and disc jockeys
know, and if there was once a music of the spheres, imparting harmony
to the universe, it commanded nothing like the income of a rap musician. The relation of noise and money in the political economy of music
initiates an essay on new music and theater, in which I speak of collaborating with musicians who, with next to no money at all, were engaged
in the "desperate enterprise of destroying music as a commodity" or, like
John Cage, fetishizing noise as a way of rescuing music from the concert
hall and reconceiving it entirely. The effect of what, to some, did not
seem music at all—whether emanating from aboriginal synthesizers or
prepared pianos, a car crash, screeches, the hum of fluorescence or a toi-
let flushing, butterfly wings, a heartbeat, even the blink of an eye—on
my own conception of theater is suggested in the essay "Noise, Musication, Beethoven, and Solid Sound." However solid the sound, it is subject to evanescence, like this too, too solid flesh, destined to disappearance, though Beethoven in a sonata (his last, in C minor) could draw it
out exquisitely, memorially, through attenuations of the ethereal, as it
were to a sonorous silence deferring the ending doom. As if it were still
sounding, there is an afterword to the essay, about music as "the art of
memory precisely because it disappears, an art which it shares with theater," which in its canonical absence (the insubstantial pageant faded)
never seems to forget.

The order of essays is such that, in the successions of thought, some
of what appears to follow was actually written before, as if an inciting
subtext had surfaced from its apparent realization. Sometimes the mate-

rial is arranged by theoretical juxtaposition, as issues bear on each other, sometimes in terms of subject matter, as with two essays on Renaissance drama—the neglected plays of John Fletcher and the rehearsing of *King Lear*—or the sequence on American playwrights. As for the one inclusion that is not quite an essay, the "analytical scenario" of *Elsinore*—a text generated from *Hamlet* in my work with the KRAKEN group—it might have followed what I say of *Lear,* in "'Set Me Where You Stand': Revising the Abyss," because *Elsinore* was in the derangements of its conception another case of such revision. It comes earlier in the book, however, because I felt the need—after rehearsing the condition of the American theater, with incidental thoughts about acting and alternative theater—to give something more than an allusive sense of what, just before I stopped directing, my later work was about. There is a kind of history, too, in some of the essay titles, like those that open the book, which may be pointing forward but are also looking behind.

"The Impossible Takes a Little Time" has as its implicit referent the many years of working on precisely that, the impossible and its impediments, back in San Francisco (and the book I wrote about it). To the question, asked in the eighties, "What's new in the American theater?" the answer was—considering the expectancies that came out of the sixties—not all that much, though the essay pays attention to what there was at the time, with the Wooster Group and Squat, the Mabou Mines, and the work of Wilson and Foreman. "Spacing Out in the American Theater" refers to the cross-country and psychic accounting of multiple levels of spatiality, from the mise-en-scène of the unconscious through the Cartesian proscenium arch to a fantasized theater up in the air for an audience in helicopters, in the course of which it also describes the various performance sites (sometimes three or more at once) in which our work occurred, as well as the cultural atmosphere of the watery twin-peaked city, lyricized by a local columnist as Baghdad by the Bay. In that regard, "From Red Hill to the Renaissance" is like an extended footnote. It not only describes where I lived, just above Haight when it was still straight, when our theater began as a workshop, but also situates what we were doing—as the Diggers showed up in Golden Gate Park and the Beat Generation in North Beach—around the mantras of the counterculture and through the developing momentum of dissidence that was eventually to be mythicized as the San Francisco Renaissance. Whatever the substance of the myth, in the visual arts and poetry (and there was a lot of poetic activity before the eruption of *Howl*), the view from Red Hill on theater was not what it should have been. Even now, "I wish I could say that as it was in poetry, so it was in theater, but it wasn't." That's at the start of the essay, but I said it in San Francisco, in a forum at the MLA (1987) celebrating the Renaissance, as a prelude to explaining—not exactly in a celebrative mood—how we struggled, for all the ferment, against a certain inertia or provincialism in that otherwise spectacular city, suddenly aroused by our presence, but too late to keep us when we were invited to go to New York.

The essay that follows, "A Dove in My Chimney," was written in response to a series of questions (partially prompted by Joseph Chaikin, who had been performing in Paris) for an issue of a French journal about the American theater and alternatives within it, including my own work, which had recently been suspended. If the title seems anomalous, it refers to the fact that while I was turning over the questions, there *was* a dove in my chimney, behaving like Gertrude Stein. With a redundancy never ceasing, yet beguilingly there, that "logorrheic bird" took over the last page, not only with thoughts of noise but in remarks about performance under the spell of Stein. To start with, however, the issue was political theater and its relation to what in the introspection of Method acting was the privilege of the personal (or in the rites of privacy its unspeakable "private moment"). The essay proceeds from there to some questions of its own, about acting method and roundabout by way of acting to implications for a politics of theater. These are questions to which in other books I have returned as to a catechism: first of all, what do we mean by acting? *act where? how? for whom?* under what conditions? and to what ideological end? as well as the potentially disheartening question: *what difference does it make?*

Whether or not it made a difference, those questions took on a phantasmaphysical aspect in the methodology of KRAKEN, a process we called "ghosting,"[8] which is how *Elsinore* was developed through numerous revisions over the course of a year. If what it was in performance has receded into memory with the Ghost's "Remember me" (1.5.91), the analytical scenario—which follows in the collection—may somehow summon it up. Combining analysis, dialogue, scoring, and a sort of visual poetry, it still conveys much of what was extraordinary about the work, mainly the group's rethinking of *Hamlet* or, as I suggest in an introductory note, *Hamlet*'s rethinking of us. In that process there was a kind of cerebral passion in the remarkable bodies of the actors, who—speaking of corporeal style—could literally perform standing on their heads or, with ideographic precision, acrobatically through the air. Situated where it is, the text is still in the reflective vicinity of "Afterthought from the Vanishing Point"—the vanishing of KRAKEN having been, as I explained in *Take Up the Bodies,* a considerable part of that point. Which is still very much the sticking point, the instance of (dis)appearance, now you see it now you don't, in my theorizing of performance.

As if the instance were imminent—some years later, sick in Paris with the flu—I wrote the piece that, here, comes soon after *Elsinore.* "A Valediction: Chills and Fever, Mourning, and the Vanities of the Sublime" is a self-commiserating long title for a short response to another series of questions, posed this time by *Performing Arts Journal* to performers, writers, directors who had created a "body of work" and a "body of knowledge" in the experimental tradition.[9] Collected under the title "Ages of the Avant-Garde," the responses were from those (you had to be fifty or older) who had made what happened happen, aging in it too, maybe more in thinking about it, as I had been doing for some time. But then, unexpectedly, before and after the flu, I found myself working in the theater again, commuting from Paris to Florida, New Mexico, and California, to develop an electronic opera (largely computer-generated) by my former music director, Morton Subotnick. As I thought about what we were doing, and ideas informing the work—once we were into it, mostly by reflex—it seemed a far cry from attitudes about the arts circulating in critical theory, with its ideological take on the status of the aesthetic, to which I turned at one point in responding to the questions.

About my collaborators on the opera, one thing is sure: their "bloodlines are decidedly of the avant-garde," which caused me to observe that—while hardly indifferent to politics, with transgressive credentials too—they would probably wince at current notions of art as (in the terms of a leveling discourse) "social praxis" or "cultural production." And I cannot imagine any of them announcing anything like a "subject position." "A Valediction" is brief and maybe a little testy, but what came through the chills and fever is what, at the risk of elitism but out of the trenches of theater, where one struggles to be an artist, I had also come to believe. If art can no longer be thought autonomous in the strict formalist sense, it can do without the enclosure of a ready Foucauldian rhetoric, nor will it be opened to material reality, the contested substance of it, by a fix of revisionist Marx, or whatever now-commonplace disposition to the antihegemonic. To say that art is about nothing but art, as in the insurgence of modernism after Baudelaire, never really meant that it had no other awareness, or intention, though that may come to awareness in the process of *making* art. Or, with the shock of recognition, amidst the flux of historical forces out of which art is made. Or, in valediction, a "devastation of value" that could become—back in the flux again, with an incursion of strangeness or estrangement of forms—a liberating source of energy or agency or capable imagination. What I am talking about here, off the animus of the essay, is an eruption of the aesthetic that validates it again. What still compels me in art is a logic of unsettled feeling, unsusceptible to any coding, at least for the historical moment, thus awaking possibility or, in the capacity to be confounding, stirring the social imaginary, unblocking social praxis or refining an identity politics in ways it had not foreseen.

As for a politics of performance, that may define itself, too, in unanticipated ways, as it did for me in San Francisco when in what appeared to be a vacuum (not only in San Francisco), I was trying to create a theater with a political conscience. There was a period when I directed, one after the other, plays by Brecht, Sean O'Casey, and Arthur Miller, all of them on the left, sufficiently so that we developed a considerable following among the labor unions and—with its newspaper, *The People's World,* giving us rave reviews—the Communist Party. It was not long, however, before they were somewhat disenchanted by our dramaturgical swerve to the disaffiliated, or what, as they said of the newer work, was "a meaningless avant-gardism." Whatever the meanings may have been, or not, it was then that I discovered that the apparently aimless, actionless, insular (for some, opaque), self-reflexive incapacities of Beckett's plays or the scabrous mystifications of Genet's—turning identity inside out, queering even the queer—*felt* more efficacious, because they were (as the saying went, moving into the sixties) *where the action is.* And that is, truly, where it was *at,* even if, as in *Waiting for Godot,* there was next to no action at all.

If not impelling social change these (so-called) absurdist plays gave a more stringent, tactile sense of the "deep structure" or the "power structure" (terms in usage then), as well as the "instituting discourse" with its "spirals of power" (familiar usage now) that with more or less vanity is still being struggled against. At that specific historical moment, when the key word was "relevance,"[10] the anti-drama of Beckett and the derisive spectacles of Genet seemed even more germane than the plays of Brecht, no less the allegorical anti-McCarthyism of Miller's *The Crucible,* with its transparencies of hysteria that (in an awful production that was a great success) edified the incapacities of our liberal audience. "If the audience is not altogether an absence, it is by no means a reliable presence," I wrote in the opening paragraph of *The Audience,*[11] with a lasting distrust of easy sentiment in the facsimile of a social body whose apparent unity is that of an essential separation, which Brecht accepted as an irreversible datum in the formulation of a method and which—in the desire to overcome the separation on behalf of "essential theater"— drove Artaud mad. One might have more mixed feelings about it all, but the symptoms that troubled me way back in the mid-fifties in the reception of *The Crucible* were still around, with the social problem updated, when I saw—in a seventy-five-dollar seat on Broadway—Tony Kushner's *Angels in America,* during much of which I thought, well, there has been some progress since the more closeted *Tea and Sympathy.*

That said, the sequence on American playwrights may be thought of as a sort of atonement. For it may be apparent here and there that since my earliest work in the theater I have not been very well disposed to American drama, though I have always intended to write a book in which I make the case for it against my inclinations. Back there at The Actor's Workshop of San Francisco (1952–65), which became notorious for its productions of utterly unknown or relatively unknown, now canonical European dramatists, survival was next to impossible without the production of Broadway plays. It was these that paid the bills for our more controversial repertoire. With the onerous task of keeping us solvent, my partner Jules Irving (too long gone and still lamented) would have preferred to do more, but the only ones I would agree to were, with a couple or so exceptions, by Eugene O'Neill, Tennessee Williams, and Arthur Miller—and even these with a certain reluctance.

In those days I felt that what was true of the American theater in general, and the people in it, was also true of its drama: no ideas or shallow ideas, rare complexity or power of mind, which appears recently to have surfaced, however, in the vicinity of Broadway. Just this morning, for instance, a review in the *New York Times* of a play called *Proof*—about father and daughter mathematicians—began with the sentence, "Have you noticed how many well-educated characters are holding forth on New York stages?" And then, calling attention to the physicists of *Copenhagen* (imported from England), the playwright of *The Real Thing,* and the literary types in *The Designated Mourner,* the reviewer goes on to say that "all are challenging, and charming, audiences with the force of intellect."[12] Welcome as this may be, it is not merely the IQ of characters I had in mind, nor is the new drama of ideas quite what we found so challenging in those first encounters back in the fifties and sixties with Brecht, Beckett, and Genet. To be sure, whatever their charms, Didi and Gogo,

Anna Fierling, Madame Irma were not exactly scientific or literary—and not exactly traditional characters—but the force of intellect was pervasive, a prior or formal cause, intrinsic to the dramaturgy, virtually metabolic, what I meant by blooded thought. And as ideas circulated from the deep structure into performance, they were, by more than indirection, sometimes virulently, critiquing the theater itself. What was strange, alienating, unsettling in those plays was also a productive ungrounding, thus energizing my own critique.

If I avoided, for the most part, writing about American drama, there are belated essays here on O'Neill and Williams (I have written about Miller elsewhere), and another recently on Maria Irene Fornes, who was also utterly unknown when in the early sixties I staged her first production. As for Williams, his *Suddenly Last Summer* was one of the first plays I ever directed, and early on, too, I staged his *Camino Real,* which, at a time when I was still proving myself as a director, was quite consciously chosen to certify a capacity for extravagant theatricality. (Given the reception in San Francisco, it apparently did so.) The essay here is not, however, about either of these plays, but was written, rather, for a volume on *Streetcar Named Desire.* Going into the sixties, I had done two of the more formidable plays of O'Neill, *The Iceman Cometh* and *A Touch of the Poet,* though, again, neither of these plays figures much or at all in the essay here, which focuses instead on *The Hairy Ape.* The essay was originally given as a talk at an international symposium on O'Neill in 1988, the centennial year of his birth, at Hosei University, Tokyo. My Japanese hosts wanted me to consider his work in the context of deconstruction, which was just making its way to the Far East.

While I was not much engaged by American drama, I was by the sorry condition of the American theater, and remained so, as recurrent fallout from my earliest book, *The Impossible Theater: A Manifesto* (1964)—which was just that, starting with a corrosive assault on the state of the art in the emergent period of the Cold War. There are many more theaters around ("regional theaters" then, "resident professional" now), outside of New York, than there were at the time (about three hundred now, I hear, as opposed to the handful then),[13] and I like to think that the book had something to do with that. But when it first came out, it certainly raised a lot of hackles, and an equal and opposite rage, not only among Broadway theater people or otherwise in the mainstream, but in the educational theater as well. Yet, over the years—as an example, no doubt, of preemptive tolerance—nobody that I know of has been invited for more keynote talks at the AETA (American Educational Theater

Association) and its current avatar, the ATHE (Association for Theater in Higher Education), on which occasions I would do variations on the same theme: the almost unregenerate backwardness of most of our theater departments.

There were intimations of that view in the earliest things I wrote for *Theater Journal,* and I am surely one of the oldest living contributors, going back to when it was *Educational Theater Journal.* Half a century ago (March 1952), I published an article in *ETJ*—my first on the theater—titled "The Education of the Playwright." (It was written, actually, in the year the Workshop started in San Francisco, while I was still commuting to Stanford, where I came as a graduate student—without any experience in theater but having written a couple of plays—after completing a degree at NYU in chemical engineering, with which I fully expected to continue. I won't recount the series of accidents that led to my writing the plays and kept me in the theater, but what I said in that essay came more from my study of literature than from anything in the theater program, which seemed to me, nearly illiterate as I was, anti-intellectual—little different from what I came to feel about the profession overall. That's why I stayed in the English Department after wandering into a class on modern poetry, with a teacher who turned out to be—I hadn't the faintest idea who he was—the redoubtable Yvor Winters, with whom, eventually, I did my dissertation.) That novice essay on playwriting, with the fervor of an aesthetic somewhat ahead of itself, is not included here, but many years later *Theater Journal* published the keynote I gave at the first convention (August 1987) of the new ATHE in Chicago: the talk was subtitled "Educating the American Theater." That text *is* here, the aesthetic fervor undiminished but with more sophistication, in the scoring of long reflections on the vicissitudes of the American theater and, beyond the theater, on education in the arts. As it turned out, I had to think about that concretely and expansively—as if any claims to knowing what art is, no less how to teach it, were being put to the test—in an unprecedented venture endowed (few could believe it then) by the late Walt Disney: the creation of California Institute of the Arts, a combination of the Bauhaus and Black Mountain in the arroyos northwest of Hollywood.

That experience—and, in another sort of ghosting, the figure of Walt, cryogenically preserved—informs "Fantasia and Simulacra: Subtext of a Syllabus for the Arts in America." If there is anything like a pedagogy that goes along with the syllabus, it is derived most specifically, however, from the acting methodology with which I experimented at

Cal Arts, while also serving not only as dean of the School of Theater and Dance but as provost of the Institute, with its four other schools: Art, Music, Film, and Design. It was only at Cal Arts that I ever taught in a theater program, which I had the opportunity to shape, however, from the ground up. So, too, with the nucleus of the KRAKEN group, its every reflex charged by the idea of performance as an activity of perception. At ground zero the work moved through "the teleology of an impulse," by which I meant the inescapable following through of any physical or vocal gesture, "even in silence or seeming stasis," at whatever behavioral level, "recognizably mimetic or utterly abstract" but moving, once committed, *"beyond exhaustion,"* toward the consummation of what, however indeterminate, was already there in the impulse as if it were ordained. I am quoting from "Deep Throat: The Grail of the Voice," which provides, after a discussion of its methodological grounding and theoretical implications, the text of the Vocal Sequence that eventually came out of this work, and which in its execution becomes a performance itself. The essay—written for a conference (in 1982) at the Center for Music Experiment, University of California at San Diego— is placed after the text of *Elsinore,* in which not only the vocal but the ideographic elements of the entire structure all came, in performance, out of the inscape of an impulse, as "an intense activity of mind, highly verbal, physically charged, like a kind of brain fever in the body, caught up almost acrobatically in the incessant ghosting of thought."

This would appear to be at some performative and conceptual distance from the Method that came out of the Group Theater in the thirties, but there is also an essay in honor of Harold Clurman, whose book *The Fervent Years,* about the Group, was the only inspiriting referent for the ideas I brought, years before *Elsinore* was a mote in the mind's eye, to the evolution of a company at The Actor's Workshop. Clurman was generously responsive to some of my earliest writings, and his encouragement as our theater developed in San Francisco (he came out to visit when he was reviewing for *The Nation*) made it all the more poignantly ironic when Jules Irving and I went to New York, displacing him, along with Elia Kazan and Robert Whitehead, as we took over the directorship of the Repertory Theater of Lincoln Center. One of the last times I saw Harold was outside the soon-to-be-completed Beaumont Theater, in which I was directing the inaugural production, *Danton's Death.* After an early dinner, in which he was tactful with advice about some of the actors we had inherited and the hazards of New York, Harold walked me back to the theater, the stage door closing him out as I went in to continue rehearsal. The essay is something more, I trust, than a delayed apology for that.

If what Harold and I shared, across different periods, was a sense of the "fervently impossible," there was a point in both of our lives where we had to assess whatever illusions we may have had about the social formation required in order to sustain a theater. When the Group suspended operations in 1941, Harold insisted that it was not because of a loss of vision or inspiration, but because—for all the talk of collectivity during the thirties—nothing like it persisted into the forties, and certainly not for the sake of theater, so that the Group felt isolated, vulnerable, unnourished by other groups. While the group idea was resuscitated in the sixties, the impetus and support for it had diminished through the seventies, bottoming out in the eighties. And now we increasingly wonder, in a globalized economy expanding through cyberspace, about what sort of collectivity can be imagined at all, despite all the hype about chat groups as new communities on the World Wide Web or the prospect of digitized performance on inevitability.com—which turns out to be one-stop shopping for all your tax and funeral needs. Inevitably, to be sure. As if the fatal drama, in hypertext, were coming up to speed, that would appear to be the scene of the dubious spectacle itself, where collective identity—once taxed by tragedy for its funeral needs—passes too into the realm of commodification.

Or so I suggest at the outset of this book's eponymous essay. "As for the scholarship that takes for granted that theater is the site of the social, or an affirmation of community, that appears to me now—though I believed it when I was younger—an academic ceremony of innocence, assuming as a reality what is, perhaps, the theater's primary illusion." Without rehearsing that illusion, about which I had written at length in *The Audience,* the essay goes on to consider the anthropological turn that has radically widened the parameters of performance studies, from the play that was once the thing to almost any kind of event or aspect of behavior, commonplace or hieratic, sexual or pornographic, political or fantastic, with attention in the process to remote and peculiar forms that have not only become increasingly familiar but seem part of the worldwide circulation of commodities. Meanwhile, as we look to other cultures for alternatives to the endemic aggressiveness, unappeased longing, and therapeutic urgencies of modern life, we encounter in every direction this unsettling truth: "those alternative or nonaggressive cultures were never what they seemed to be," in the hallowed gestures or ceremonial practices that, like the soft movements of the Tai Chi Chuan, have

been drawn into the orbit of performance in the West. We long for renewal and, with every incursion of strangeness, relapse again to the real,
or the "anxiety of an absence that we glut with representations," while
sometimes claiming to be bending, distorting, subverting, transgressing
the system of representation itself, with its ever beguiling tyranny of redundant signs.

    If performance seems to have taken on the properties of a fundamen-
tal need, traversing all aspects of our lives, from the recesses of the unconscious to the presentation of a self (or some facsimile of identity in a
singular being), what remains dubious through it all is the prospect of
collectivity, which when it does emerge is not—as during or after wars
of national liberation—the salutary thing we thought it to be. My own
thinking about this began years ago, around the notion of *théâtre populaire*, an idea of theater bringing together students, workers, intellectuals,
one of the great dreams of the modern era, which has been nowhere realized except for, beyond the dubious, the delusive historical moment. This
is not said with any cynicism or congenital disenchantment. That it
seems impossible is no reason whatever for it not to be thought again,
perhaps all the more reason why it *will* be, in some unanticipated venture or, relentlessly in performance, by some visionary seizure, as if from
the insane root. Indeed, as I read through these essays just after the millennium, I was relieved to see that in the equivocal and circuitous movement around the vanishing point, turning things over and over, there
are perturbations from that source and little in the disposition of the essays, their attitudes, tone, emotional bias, that was not there when I was
writing a manifesto to change things or, for that matter, in the best of my
theater work. I still like to feel, as I suggested in *Take Up the Bodies*, that
what I am doing in theory has something of the animus of that work before, against all will and desire, it unfortunately came to an end. Thus, if
there is in these essays—as in the reflections on the multiple manifestations of the dubious spectacle itself—any lasting conviction, or anything
like faith at all, it arises as it always did, I think, at the enlivening impasse of undeterrable doubt.

1. Afterthought from the Vanishing Point

Theater at the End of the Real

For some months recently I was, unexpectedly, equivocally, and rather amused at my reluctance, commuting from Paris to the United States, to direct a sort of opera, which opened in Philadelphia and was later seen in New York, before going on to France. It is a remarkable piece, actually, with remarkable collaborators, but putting that aside (a one-shot deal, I say), I had not been active in the theater for more than a decade, a terminal condition, it seemed, for which my friend Ruby Cohn has never quite forgiven me.[1] At the time I stopped my theater work, after more than thirty-five years of it, I wrote a book on the activating pretense (or enabling fantasy) that what, in the last phase of that work especially, had been happening on the stage was continuing on the page: a certain elliptical and circuitous density of performance, whose energy came from an obsession with disappearance, or the forms of disappearance, now you see it now you don't, the ghostliness of the referent, it all, it all, as Beckett might say, encapsulating thus the unspeakable whole truth of its fatal attraction—whatever *it* might be. So far as I understand that obsession, it arose from the grounds of impossibility out of unabating desire, in theater, now theory, to get as close to the thought of theater as theater would be if it were thinking about itself, crossing the critical gamut and teasing us out of thought. Ruby never quite approved of this either, especially when it seemed, as it did to her, that I was personifying the theater and presuming to speak for it. Perhaps so. It may not in any way appease her, but it should be apparent in what I have written

1

that if I were somehow speaking for the theater I did not always like what it said. Meanwhile, obsession being what it is, to some degree arising here again, I shall try to keep presumption in the subjunctive to allay if possible the still quite agile astringency of her doubt.

Thus: *if* the theater were thinking about itself it might be concerned, as a preface to any reflection on its cultural politics or the current state of the art, whatever it has come to be, with how it materializes to begin with from whatever it is it is *not*. That there is something other than theater, prior to it, by whatever name—life, reality, manifestations of social process or relations of production—is not in itself a foregone conclusion (no more than the staple of theater history that theater is derived from ritual instead of, possibly, the other way around). Not at least, it would seem, if we took seriously what troubles the theater, so far as that can be deduced from the canonical drama, with its long rehearsed suggestion that the theater, *which always needs to be watched,* has never trusted itself. That is a suggestion taken up in the work I did at the end (with the experimental group KRAKEN) and the book derived from it (dedicated to Ruby), which initiated, in a period suspicious of ontology, a sort of ontology of performance—or just this side of "essentialism," a subatomic physics. That book was titled *Take Up the Bodies: Theater at the Vanishing Point,* which is the originary text of all I have been thinking since, even when, presumably, I am not thinking about the theater.

The subtitle of the book also accounts for the title of this essay, whose subtitle—"Theater at the End of the Real"—will have more or less reality depending on your perspective or, for that matter, your critical view of perspective with its notorious vanishing point. For there we encounter the liability, even the vice, of representation, implicating the theater in the recessive economy of mystification that, according to much recent theory, supports the imperious logic of advancing capitalism, as if it came with the bourgeois enlightenment out of the blinded sockets of Oedipus's eyes as formed in Plato's Cave. Things have advanced so far, however, so fast, that in the vertiginous excess of the postmodern scene, its obscenity of image, we seem to be living a redundancy of theater, so much so that even the system of representation appears to be obsolete. Or it is possible to think, as it is now being thought, that where the real has ended the spectacle begins or that the commodification of the spectacle *is* the end of the real. Whatever the case may be, as distinguished from the real, the case is defined by the interaction of theater and the phenomena of photography, which from its foundational moment, by a man of the theater, was also obsessed with disappearance.

That accounts in some measure for the theoretical work I have recently been doing, first on photography, then fashion. I mean by fashion not only the commodification of style, what's in, what's out (not at all inconsequential) but the movement of contingency through value that, with the seeming precision of aleatoric perception, makes a seductive puzzle of "life," raveled as it is in appearance. The old metaphor of the Theater of the World was fascinated with the play of appearance, but if it now seems overloaded with the play within the play, that is because the dominion of appearance is facilitated and augmented by the random exactitude of the camera: not that *this* not this *that*, the metaphor suffused with metonymy. Yet, for all the instamatic adjustments in the high-speed film, it is as if there is still a kind of friction in the shifting signifiers. What appears to be life may be theater, but for all the dazzle of appearances even fashion carries with it, as in the erotics of makeup, its "natural look," the thought of something more authentic, dative, other than mere appearance. That there is an artifice to this dubious look does not necessarily diminish the thought, nor does the theoretical animus against anything like the authentic, with its suggestions of an irreducible core or the truth-claiming authority of an original, make the whole issue any the less fascinating. It is, of course, the fascination-effect that links fashion and theater, and both have gone through phases where they have also tried to resist it.

The puzzle has been made all the more seductive through the twentieth century, as fashion became a virtual creature of photography, in turn responsible for the anthropology of fashion, even while escalating its theatricality. In the incursion of fashion upon art there has been, with an accelerated blurring of genres, a radical testing of the parameters of performance and performance theory, along with the whole spectrum of supportable ways of looking at what through the entire history of modernism resists being reliably imaged because it is always subject to change. In this regard, the early history of photography, with its desperate measures *to fix the image,* seems the emblematic double of emergent modernism, with its objectification of subjectivity in strategies, techniques, configurations as diverse as the verbal icon or the ideogram or the Brechtian *gestus* or—as with Benjamin's "chips of Messianic time,"[2] arrested into a monad, pregnant with tensions—the radiant Image itself. When photography managed at last (*hypo*-thetically) to fix it, it had already become the referential problem lamented in Beckett—"It? *(Pause.)* It all"[3]—so that the grammar of being seemed to have broken down, the object itself dispersed into the activity of perception.

What we were left with, bereft, is the residue of an appearance with the look of being looked at. And by the time of Beckett's *Play,* so far as the human presence was concerned, not entirely sure of that: "Am I as much as . . . being seen?" (*Shorter Plays,* 157). The terror of *not* being seen, pandemic to the landscape of Beckett, had its inverse (or perverse) objective correlative in "the anguish of perceivedness" of *Film* (163), along with the paranoid symptoms of the syntactical variants, no *being* seen (no presence, that is), no being except *as seen.* There was also, long before Beckett, the anguish of perceivedness doubled or compounded if it ended up on film, as in the horror of photography expressed by Balzac and reported by Nadar. Balzac's paranoia was such that he saw every photographic portrait as a successive deprivation of being, each time the shutter closes a layer peeled away. What we seem to have confirmed, however, in a world now thoroughly photographed, saturated with exposure, is that in the fragility of a specious substance there was no being to begin with.

About this unnerving eventuality there might be, in the postmodern era, paranoia or *jouissance,* but all of it brought us back to the foundational anxiety of photography that is the ongoing problematic of its theory: the "emanation of the referent,"[4] as if photography were theater—which is what, in the bereaved (and belated) phenomenology of *Camera Lucida,* Roland Barthes said it was. The semiology of his book *The Fashion System* might have been a somewhat different thing had it been revised after *Camera Lucida,* with its affective experience of photography as a form of primitive theater, or *tableau vivant,* "a figuration of the motionless and made-up face beneath which we see the dead" (*Camera Lucida,* 32). The sacramental image in Barthes's book of the dead is that of his mother, whose Winter Garden photograph was preserved, as if it were a chip of Messianic time, only to his own view. Whatever the futureless radiance of the Image, he cannot risk its being seen. Whatever he adds to the photograph, engorged as it is with time, the principal anxiety is change. Any way *you* look at it the Image is troubled by sight.

There is much more to be said about the potential abrasion of presence by sight, through photography, in theater, which is brazened out on the catwalk, with the engendered problem of the gaze, in the world of high fashion with its spectacular *défilés.* The theater itself—explicit source of fashion in previous periods, or a function of it in a relation of reciprocity—has always, of course, been subject to change, which is its subject. I wrote of the theater long ago as a time-serving form, but with the insubstantial pageant fading, cybernetically, into the feedback systems, it is as if we are dealing now with an overwhelming accession of temporality that, in the proliferous imaging of the mediascape of the postmodern, collapses time (into) itself. If this seems to be the totalization of theater into the apotheosis of fashion, it is also a considerable nuance beyond what Benjamin meant when, distinguishing fashion from history, "whose site is not homogeneous, empty time, but time filled by the presence of the now," he described it, even in its avidity for the topical, as "a tiger's leap into the past" ("Theses," 263). What we think of now as "retro," with a refurbished subjectivity in the recycling of vintage clothes, is in its pastiched sense of history a tamer version of that leap.

What are we to make, however, in this context of the standard conception of the theater as a paradigm of society, on which I was asked recently to give a keynote address at a conference in England? Those attending were leftist theater directors and neomarxist scholars, brimming with cultural materialism, but given the British variety, with a strong disposition to think—just as tenaciously as the Conservative Party—of society, and thus the paradigm, as more than less intact. If, to say the least, the reflective paradigm needs some drastic revision, that is because, in the age of mechanical reproduction or, at the leading edge of advancing capitalism, digital image manipulation, the parameters of the social have also broken down—assuming that the social (contrary to Baudrillard) really did exist.

They were already breaking or broken down, of course, at the time of the emergence of the theater of the Absurd, when Ruby Cohn and I were assigned the same office at San Francisco State College (not yet a university) because of our common interest in Beckett, considered by some elitist and by others merely fashionable. Revered as he is now, Beckett was barely known then in the academic world, and people still resisted in the theater, when I first staged his plays, the bleak and discomfiting vision of an entropic universe, atoms whirling around us with aimless half-life energies and, as if the cosmos were claustrophobic, the most minimal life support. That was bad enough, but it's as if the cataclysm of value described in the participial present—"All faiths are tottering"—at the opening of Ruby's early book, on the comic gamut in Beckett, were now inarguably and devastatingly complete; in the semantics of the unnameable, all substantives emptied of value: "religion and science, personality and ideology, family and nation, freedom and imperatives, subject and object. . . ."[5]

Yet, with faith so foundering, will miracles never cease? For in its

exhaustive enumeration of the exhaustion of value, its apparently hap-
less mimicry of the incapacity to act, *Waiting for Godot* was about to become something like the ground rhythm of dissidence for the politics of
the sixties. That impotency could be so activist was, for some interested
in a political drama, as inexplicable then as it is today in much cultural
critique, particularly in the ideological assault on the paradoxes and tensions of modernist form, which, for all its antidrama, *Godot* still master-
fully represents, along with the elegiac remnants of a "disempowering"
nostalgia. What was also called fashionable then, though it seems rea-
sonably transparent now, was the "obscurity" of the play—which at
some performances at our theater sent certain spectators up the wall—
though some obscurity would seem to have been inevitable amidst the
contradictions of late capitalism with no principle of coherence and, in
the ceaseless metonymic slippage, everything falling apart.

The litany of tottering faiths consists, to be sure, of truisms about
modernity that, if second nature in art and thought, and the cataleptic
agenda of Beckett, were never quite admissible, certainly not in their entirety, to a party platform in any democratic society of the postindustrial
world. Yet, not long before the levees on the Mississippi were also breaking down (happening as I write), swelling the federal deficit and turning
western farmlands into a postmodern setting for Noah's Ark, we heard an
apocalyptic voice that did not, however, resonate with near derangement
as in the annals of marginality. The voice was formed, rather, in the
Cartesian tradition, and if there was a note of dispossession (to which
we will turn in a moment), it came from a region of established power
that had just been inundated by the same wide-spreading calamities—
economic and demographic, with joblessness breeding rage, and the
media surveying it all—that not only complicate the gridlock here but
make it increasingly difficult for any party to govern in any western(ized)
democracy. Among the calamities, on a geopolitical grid where nothing is
distant anymore, are the formerly totalitarian states released into the
atomic whirl, with fragmentation, tribal rivalries, and ethnic cleansing—
the monstrous free marketry of illusory liberation that, in still other
parts of the world, are making a compelling case for neocolonization.
That may be very hard to swallow in our cultural studies, with its politics of difference and, with certain reigning pieties, discourse of power.
History, it has been said, is the thing that hurts, but if we are really keeping up with that history it may also be time for a slight revision of the
protocol from Benjamin that has become a virtual doctrine in our anti-
aesthetics: if the monuments of culture are accompanied by a history of

barbarism, the history of liberation has been accompanied, more often than not carried away, by the momentum of barbarism, which also has its monuments—some of them obscene or grotesque by any standard, not only that of the older aesthetic, and not as valorized in the carnival-esque of Bakhtin.

What happened in all this to the socialist dream that still shapes the agenda of critical theory, as well as the fantasy text of dissident theater practice? It's as if for the sake of renewal in the detritus of the dream a kind of homeopathic violence were required, and that is exactly what the former prime minister of France Michel Rocard discerned when, after the debacle of the legislative elections, he prescribed a "Big Bang" for the Socialist Party in France. Rocard did so in language that might have been sifted from poststructuralist theory, or, with ideology battered all over the world, the repressed or begrudging awareness, if not the worst case scenario, of British cultural materialism. If not the end of the real, then the end of social class, and with that too (also hard to swallow) the end of collectivity, with lingering fantasies of it—plaintive legacy of the Left—for the utterly dispossessed. There would seem to be obvious implications for those of us in theater studies, where we have had, in a modified recycling of the participatory ethos of the sixties, much theorizing of a shift of power in which, with repositioned subjects, meanings would be determined, or "constructed," by the members of the audience. But what audience they would be members of, in any public sense (with scale), is as indeterminate as meaning itself in the metaphysical slapstick of Beckett. Speaking of cultural materialism, it was one of its tutelary figures, Raymond Williams, who foresaw against his disposition (and before Baudrillard) the dissolution of the social, in an unguardedly elegiac moment of an essay on the drama of a dramatized society: "Privacy, deprivation," he wrote. "A lost public world; an uncreatable public world."[6]

What was ironic at the time that Ruby Cohn and I were first drawn to the drama of Beckett is that despite the epistemological caveat of the plays and Beckett's own insistence that he was writing into a void, we could not quite believe that the possibility of a public world was entirely lost or, if so, uncreatable. But while disaster may create a provisional sense of community, as on the banks of the Mississippi during the floods, erosion seems much less ineluctable there than it does with the illusions of collectivity at the end of the real. That end may merely be, if not its foundation myth, the most mordant master narrative of the postmodern; but if the real returns as ubiquitously as ideology—whose end has also been frequently declared—the cost of its return is, with an increase of entropy, further subtraction from the body politic, or in Rabelais's essentialist phrase, its "substantific marrow." What we are confronted with all over is the difficulty of a feasible politics in the insatiable suction upon the social, which collapses the ground of a public life. If we should desire to re-create it—whether at the utopian horizon of postmodern thought or out of modernist nostalgia for the world in which it appeared to exist—where would we find, in the absence of supportable value, any credible figure of authority as an armature for possibility? As for socialism's die-hard prospect, the chiliastic notion of class warfare, it is, according to the autocritique of Rocard, like centrist, technocratic management of the economy, a concept ready for the ash bin of history.

The Big Bang may need to be bigger than he dreams, and in the immediate pathos of history Pierre Bérégevoy, Rocard's successor as socialist prime minister, gave us the bang with a human face when he committed suicide, shooting himself after the legislative elections. Nobody, of course, knows exactly why, though subsequent allegorization of the suicide saw it as his either taking responsibility for the crushing defeat of socialism or a sacrificial act impelling it into the future. As the parable dissipates in the appalling fact, what Rocard said of France seems true of all those industrialized countries "where the sentiment of belonging to a class, or a collective movement, is no longer perceived as a reality, where change is effective only if it touches the individual."[7]

The notion of class may remain, despite all, obdurate in the English theater, its last-ditch referent, without which, perhaps, its dramaturgy would fall apart. And there is in France, as there is not in the United States, the last-ditch insistence of its Communist Party, though in the general state of dispossession some of its waning percentage points are going over to the reactionary/racist politics of Le Pen and the National Front. So much, so far, for residual collectivity. The rest is a national scandal (more or less extreme, depending on the nation), with ecology as a last resort (though it did woefully in the French elections). As Rocard said—with nobody in the Socialist Party having yet come up with an answer—"When the French can no longer find their identity in a social class, in a religion, a profession, a generation, or the amount of money they make, what is left for them to identify with?" (*Herald Tribune*, 4). They have, of course, the perennial figures of a national theater, but if the Comédie Française is, when not merely regressive, a mecca for tourists, like the Royal Shakespeare Company or Stratford-on-Avon in Britain, the theaters at the Maisons de la Culture in the *banlieues*—where the workers live on streets still named Lenin or Aragon—are patronized for the most part, as the Berliner Ensemble once was, by liberal and leftist intelligentsia from elsewhere. It is, I think, a familiar story, this desire for a populist theater in an urban space where the locals remain indifferent. So it was with Joan Littlewood when I saw her work at the end of the fifties in the Jewish quarter of London East. With its ebullience and strategic optimism it was, as we might expect, a success on the West End, before Littlewood turned to other populist projects, and disappeared from the theater.

Not everybody disappears, but the paradoxes remain, with disheartening complexities in the American theater, on which I have written extensively before. As for the illusions of *théâtre populaire,* they first brought me to Europe in the fifties, because it seemed the correlative of what we were trying to do then in my theater in San Francisco, fulfilling in a city with a strong labor tradition, and the still-vivid memory of a General Strike, what still amounts to a socialist dream: to create an audience of workers, students, and intellectuals. (There were several members of our company from the old San Francisco Labor Theater, and our stage manager then seemed an incarnation of the dream: a marvelous man named Kershaw, formerly a steward in the teamster's union, a self-taught Marxist who seemed to move behind the scenes, implacably, like History itself.) Calling for a revolution, *The Impossible Theater: A Manifesto* (published in 1964) was a testament to the dream with, however, an existential turn of mind, conscious that any apparent unity in the theater was, irreparably, in the reality of fracture, an essential rupture, for which the idea of community itself has always been a cover-up, as Euripides knew in his critique of the festival of Dionysus, the theater's foremost illusion. Why did we pursue it? *Because* it was impossible.

This paradox might be further defined around the concept of the audience, which is not so much, for me, what exists before the play, a congregation of people gathered before the curtain, but the thing about to happen in the subjunctivity of performance. I must add, however, that what happens more often than not is not always for the best. If this is a somewhat Beckettian idea, it is not construction theory. Whatever construction you put upon it, give an audience a chance, it will inevitably be wrong. A statement to that effect, from *The Impossible Theater,* is probably the most inflammatory I ever wrote, though it appears to be the recurrent subject of the play-within-the-play, which appears now to be culture itself, confounded by theatricality or—in the vision running from *The Bacchae* to *The Balcony,* which I staged in the early sixties—constituted by it. Perhaps I should have left it at that, but many years later I published a very long book titled *The Audience,* which ramified the subject, with no polemic, and by gathering into the concept of the audience, as heuristic principle, just about every issue that besets performance, from questions of power and authority to the vicissitudes of perception to the secretions of theater into the rhetoric and psychopathology of everyday life.

The book has nothing to do with reception theory and very little to do, though it draws on psychoanalysis, with current views of, say, the gendered spectator. It does reflect, however, on "gradients of the gaze," and begins with a woman's voice: " 'No audience. No echo. That's part of one's death,' wrote Virginia Woolf in her diary at the start of World War II. She was working on *Between the Acts,* in which the audience, 'orts, scraps and fragments like ourselves,' is brutally and equivocally mirrored in its dispersion. Her dread over 'this disparition of an echo' . . . is a conspicuous deepening of one of the major anxieties in the history of modernism, extending into the indeterminacies of the postmodern. If the audience is not altogether an absence, it is by no means a reliable presence." In the first chapter, and elsewhere, I examine the various ways in which the appearance of a gathered public has been looked upon with scorn or distrust by seminal practitioners in the theater, like Brecht and Artaud, and by social and critical theorists, like Gramsci, whose dramatic criticism was even more caustic than Brecht's about the culinary audience. The harshness of their judgments may be attributed to the urgencies of the period or the necessities of an insolent politics, but the gathering need not be quite so soporific or anesthetized to seem, as I wrote many years later, in the last decade of the century, "like the merest facsimile of remembered community paying its respects not so much to the still-echoing signals of a common set of values but to the better-forgotten remains of the most exhausted illusions."[8]

As it turns out, *Between the Acts,* with its parodistic history of English drama, written and directed by the lesbian Miss La Trobe, culminates in a sequence that, in mirroring the audience—orts, scraps, and fragments like ourselves—anticipates various modes of performance that, in an incessantly shattered mirror, and more or less brutally, have been seeking alternatives to the exhausted illusions. Were we to look back on the course of such developments since the fifties and the sixties, it might be with a recognition of something at the heart of theater that, despite all de-mystifications, has persisted in practice and been dispelled by no theory: whatever the alternative modes of performance, either by reducing the scale to local forms of intervention or by widening the parameters of what we think of (as) theater, either as it was or may be—as a paradigm of society or a model of power relations or an access to subjectivity and transsexual possibility or, in a body without organs, the prophetic voice of the wide world dreaming, anti-oedipally, on things that are yet to come—we are still caught up in the future of illusion. Which remains, and ever will, what all ideological struggle is about.

That is the burden of the last book I have published, *To All Appearances*, which moves from ontology to ideology and (as in Marx's camera obscura) its inseparability from performance, whose powers are often invoked, without much tactile knowledge of it, in the vanities of critique, dreaming on subversion or transgression if not a Big Bang.

To attempt the impossible, I always thought, could be more or less realistic, but there seems to me in much academic discourse—whose political desires I mostly share—a muscle-flexing rhetoric making very tenuous claims. The same may be true of performance. Yet, some alternative modes of performance have, with varying intensities, actually *felt* subversive or transgressive, and brought on the censors or a prison sentence. Some have been more or less theorized. Some, with the best intentions, remain psychosexually callow and politically banal, whether or not the censorship is alarmed. As for the audiences of the alternative theater scene, feminist, ethnic, gay, whatever, it becomes increasingly apparent that they can be, if anything, even more predictable, manipulable, or responsive to banalities and stereotypes, than the bourgeois audience that, according to now standard analysis, was ready to support a theater reproducing its own image, even when that image, as in Ibsen or Strindberg or Pirandello, was next to appalling and in no way edifying at all.

The liability of automatic response remains with any mode of performance, but when I speak of alternatives I mean for the most part the wide spectrum of events and practices that have already reformed, or will, our notions of theater by departing from the theater, or ignoring it to begin with. This has certainly been troubling to those with uninterrupted allegiance to the institutional forms of theater and, with whatever allowance for diverse experiment, the dramaturgy that goes with it. During the sixties the term *performer* was given an honorific turn in contradistinction to the actor who, according to the theorization then, was subservient to that dramaturgy, the playwright, the director, and the whole repressive apparatus of the theater as we had known it. There were, within the orbit of this critique, performances within the theater that borrowed from or elided with performance in the other arts, and that continue to this day (Wilson, Foreman), along with the ideological dispensation of apparently dissident forms that have not resolved their relationship—in acting method, dramaturgy, visual design—to the old repressive apparatus, counting on a new content, or parody, to do it in. Of those alternative modes, however, outside the structure of theater— from the emergence of the happening out of the scene of action painting to the situationist *dérive* and its critique of commodity culture to various manifestations of autodestruction or the aesthetics of the orgastic in Viennese actionism, as well as the new technological order of performance heading through interactive video towards virtual reality—what has been of most compelling interest to me were the variants of body art, with its conceptualized masochism and, through the sometimes unbearable silence of a perverse endurance, its glossolalia of pain.

Here we may come through the most repellent extremities of an apparent indifference back to the sticking point of any serious thought about the theater. (Body art was an offshoot of the presumably impersonal conceptual art of the seventies, but if its major figures are now doing other things, whether sculpture or photography or video art, that work is—like the return of figuration in painting—still inhabited by performance, and there are any number of variants of body art on the international scene today, markedly so, it now appears, on the mutilated landscape of Eastern Europe.) In a chapter of *The Audience* on "Repression, Pain, and the Participation Mystique," I rehearse in a fabric of association with body art the immanence of pain in the texts of classical theater, as something more than a ritual paradigm or pretext for catharsis, as something so unbearably present that, even in hearing about it, it seems to have destroyed the codes. "Slave as I am to such unending pain," says Oedipus at Colonus.[9] I mean pain and not a metaphor of pain, though even as metaphor unnegotiable—Philoctetes' cry, Medea's screams—persisting in the theater, as in history, with more or less displacement or repression, though so intolerable in certain periods that it presses to the surface again, as it does in *King Lear,* "where the subject of pain is the subject that disappears *into* the pain" (*Audience,* 180). So it is in Beckett's *Endgame,* that virtual model or manual or theory of body art, the consummation of a theater that at its excruciating limit, too painful to be watched, out of sight but not of mind (something dripping in the head), really impossible to perform, is almost embarrassed to be theater.

And what about its politics? "Use your head, use your head, can't you, you're on earth, there's no cure for that!"[10] What is peculiar about such theater is that, cutting to the brain, its vision can be empowering.

The same might be said of Artaud's vision of the theater of cruelty, which shares a certain embarrassment at being theater, where the body is the merest spectacle cannibalized by representation. Which may account for Artaud's own ravenous interest in radiophonic art, ultimate site of no-body, or of an alchemical theater, with its "meticulous and unremitting pulverization of every insufficiently fine, insufficiently matured form. . . ."[11] The laminations or overlays of amplified feedback might be, as he could only dream then, a pulverizing force, working on any last insufficiency in what Barthes called the grain of the voice, which seems in Artaud—as in the performance art of Diamanda Galas—to tear itself out of the throat. And when that occurs, it is as if, the language lined with flesh, the body is nothing but *voice,* reversing thus the denial in poststructuralist thought of the unfailing complicity between voice ("whose phenomenality does not have worldly form"),[12] and an idealizing metaphysics, with the delusional dignity of transcendence.

Various body artists were, to be sure, influenced by Artaud, and in their work—as in his last harrowing performance at the Vieux Colombier[13]— it is a virtual ethical principle to literalize the pain. So it is in the performances of Stelarc today, still striving to transcend the body, making it obsolete, the pure radiance of the (corporeal) Image suspended with fishhooks through its flesh. For Stelarc, however, swaying with stretched skin over street or ocean, it is not merely a matter of masochism as epiphany in the high modernist sense. It may very well be that his performances are that, too, but they are conceived as a way of forcing technology back to the body in a world assaulted by the information explosion, which he sees as the dead end of evolutionary process and a compensation for our genetic inadequacies. The fishhooks are, in their testing the limits of the genetic, the primitive technology of another genesis. Without the meditative refuge of a mind-altering state, he deflects the glut of information gathered through the hooks into the astonishment of knowledge, the pain disappearing, as if through Barthes's *punctum* (the rip, the tear, the wound) into "a kind of subtle *beyond*" (*Camera Lucida,* 59). Such art may appear to be, like the depilation of Vito Acconci or the vomitings of Gina Pane or the mummification of Rudolf Schwarzkogler, merely perverse or solipsistic, and whatever the inflictions upon the body, an aesthetic mystification. Maybe so. While there are few who can even look at photographs of Stelarc's suspensions, no less the actual event, without wincing, it is certainly possible, if you can bear the pain at a distance, to see his performances as exquisite or beautiful in an older romantic sense, like much of the meditative work, however perilous, of Ulay and Abramović. Yet, whatever the aesthetic or antiaesthetic or, in Foucault's terms, self-assumption of the body as a "subject of knowledge," what we also have is the art of risk in a state of emergency, presenting the body as a form of resistance.

We also know that there are bodies all over the world, as in Bosnia or Rwanda or Bangladesh today, that have no option of resistance. Which may make a mere vanity of body art. Still, it has its political correlative, when there happens to be an option, in putting one's body on the line. There have been various body artists with specific political intent, and despite its arising from the rather elitist context of the conceptualism of the seventies, it was absorbed very rapidly into the politics of identity, as in the early confessional modes of feminist performance. Yet the conceptual power of the practice seems proportioned to its pure gratuitousness, which is, as in modernist poetry, almost a moral choice. And the most challenging part of its legacy corresponds, I think, to the unavoidable movement in theory, and now in history, back to ethical questions, intersecting our politics, for which the most comprehensive paradigm remains the tragic form. It is surely to be expected that, along with theory's turn back to ethics and aesthetics, tragedy itself—shameful site of Oedipus in the critique of phallogocentricism—will also have to be reassessed, for it remains the paradigm of the body in a state of violation taking responsibility for that state, though not yet, perhaps, in possession of its meanings.

Violating the body is, in the paradox of performance, a testament to the human: not only the sign of its endurance but, in either the implacability or mania of self-determination, an inviolable respect. The resisting body is the subject of performance, and always has been, even in conventional theater, even when the body is absent, as Beckett perceived in "the instant of recorded vagitus" of his synoptic *Breath* (*Shorter Plays*, 211), haunted to begin with by disappearance. With all the theoretical emphasis on historically constructed bodies—the woman's body, the black body, the gay body, the myriad bodies of ethnic identity—it is the body in pain that invariably returns us to the emblooded logic of the vanishing point itself, *the essential body*, which is the thing that hurts if history hurts, crossing the politics of difference at the living end of the real.

If we see the body of the performer today flattened into a photograph, as in the case of Cindy Sherman, it is in a sense both living and dead, and the degree of its living depends not only on who is looking but on the emulsified prospect of a residual presence (something grittier than a trace?), the emanation of the referent as well. Sometimes you look and there seems to be nobody there, not the no-body of radiophonic art but the correlative of a cultural theory whose critique of presence, and fear of the hierarchical, has flattened or leveled the heuristic substance of what it deconstructs. That is what it did, it seems, with the figure of Oedipus, who disappeared into a narrative so rich and inexhaustible that, in the critique of representation, the third play is rarely remembered. The new historicisms remind us that the myth, and the tedious burden of its unending pain, is merely culture bound, but what are we to make of theatrical paradigms that, put off as they may be by the representation of fate, make very little provision for the fate of representation, baseless as it may be, its gratuitous necessity, not merely as a sign but as an agency of the real—as Derrida had to concede, with almost tragically poignant resistance, at the end of his essay on Artaud's theater of cruelty and the closure of representation. What is at stake here is something else again than conforming representation to some newly forced perspective (call it a subject position) or, in camp and masquerade, the illusions of multivalency in the ideology of desire.

The score is not in on whether, in the blade-running prospects of our time, we shall develop a better culture or something other than culture, though it should be clear enough—since the fall of the Berlin Wall and, after the euphoria, the demoralization of Europe—that with all the presumptions of recent discourse about the operations of power, the nature of power still eludes us, and we ought to be chastened by that. Overdosed on Foucault, we are callow about power and how to distinguish it from appearances, particularly from certain appearances we happen to convey ourselves when, in whatever minor genres, we acquire something like power. On this issue, nothing whatever in our cultural critique seems to me on a level with our canonical drama, or for that matter the theatrical pathos of history itself. "Kto Kovo? Who Whom?" asked Lenin in a conundrum about the Bolshevik Revolution. Who is the subject or guiding force of history and, with no punctuation between, who is the object? With the toppling of the statues of Lenin, it is as if once again history has refused the (Brechtian) punctuation, leaving us, amidst the prospects and terrors of exponential difference, with the object disappearing into the subjectivity of perception.

Which is not to make the case for, as they say, "releasing subjectivity." If subjectivity is going to be released, it is into a field of cross-purposed metastasizing claims where, with whatever impaired perception, we are not released from the grievous task of making finer distinctions, about difference (we want it and we don't want it, or only want it so much), about the subject (particularly the subject who—with a quite valid claim, and in an electoral process, the vote—happens to disagree with us), and about the uses and abuses and indeterminacies of power, and what we would do with it if we had it, since what it means to have it is (as we can see with Bill Clinton or Boris Yeltsin, or soon Nelson Mandela) also part of the problem. One might prefer to forget in all this, though history won't and Büchner didn't, the utter derangements of power, or its surreptitious perversions, in those who come to it (in a drama about revolution and fashion) through the most admirable idealisms. It is not an easy problem because, speaking of virtual reality, it is virtually insoluble— which appears to be why, if there was anything real to begin with, the tragic myth in all its inadequacy came into being itself, with the illusion of collective identity and the devastating prospect of its own critique.

That can be painful, so painful that, as if pain were its very emblem, there is no certainty but doubt, which is the one inheritance of the theater metaphor we can hardly do without. Critical theory came on the scene with disdain for that metaphor, and the dispensation of mimesis, as if it were the agency that instead of alleviating pain, sustained and reinforced it. There is something to be said for that, and Brecht said it, though he could no more do without it than can any appeal or demand made on behalf of the marginal or disadvantaged. Even now, as theory passes into cultural studies, with an increasing assumption of power in our graduate schools, it remains somewhat schizophrenic in its view of (the) theater, rejecting the institution with its oedipal history while moving off the datum of play inherited from the sixties into more or less appropriation or displacement of the idea of performance. Under the pressure of theory, approaches to theater history and dramatic literature have changed and diversified, more radically so than at any time during the career of Ruby Cohn, with the adamant boundaries of its impeccable scholarship (not at all pleased with the incursion of theory). Recently, there have been various books and theater journals concerned with new attitudes toward history and the consequences for methodology, not only crossing genres but epistemological disciplines, a commendable ambition with a crisis of qualification.

What, meanwhile, is the object of our study? As I see it—with or without the dramatic texts or performance texts, as in the recovered evidence of historical practice—that remains what it always was: the precipitation of theater from whatever it is it is not, which like the mystery of difference itself may be indecipherable. If I speak here for myself, it is with the unpurged assumption that released subjectivity is always subject to oedipal blindness. Appearance, and then again, appearance: for the rest, take up the bodies, what else is there to say? except that not to say it *then* is to start thinking about power.

(1993)

2. The Impossible Takes a Little Time

One of the more memorable passages, for me, of *The Playwright as Thinker,* the book that made Eric Bentley an enfant terrible, was the one in which he referred to a production of *Rosmersholm* at the Yale Drama School and said that when it was over the students talked about the lighting, costumes, directing, everything in fact but what was being lit, costumed, directed—"Ibsen's lines and Ibsen's meaning"—as if it didn't matter what the play meant. The students at Yale were by the end of the book just summing up the general scene. That was, of course, about forty years ago, a little before I started working in the theater. Given the emergence of regional theaters in the fifties and the radical activism of the sixties, I suppose the meaning matters now somewhat more, although one is never quite sure in America where or how it matters, to whom, since it never seems to matter very long.

Where it does not seem to matter at all—*Ibsen's* lines and *Ibsen's* meaning—it is not necessarily anymore because the playwright is not a thinker, but because he is, and because the actor has become something of a thinker too, encouraged by Brecht and then Grotowski to confront a text and, if it goes against his/her conviction, to change the lines and the meaning s/he doesn't like. Meanwhile, the thought of Ibsen and the major modernists has emptied itself into history like a seismic shock, or the avalanche in his last play among the awakened dead. As Rilke saw, thinking of Ibsen, that avalanche was always there, running through the capillaries of the canonical text as if the accelerated slide were language itself. Where that ruptured consciousness exists, expelling meaning, the theater often seems paradoxically more meaningful than it was before, shifting us through the arbitrariness of the signifier into a period of post-Brechtian post-structuralist thought with its *bricolage* and deconstruction and, assuming the death of the author even when he is alive, the production of meaning by the perceiver and a preemptive view of performance.

Certain of the authors, dead or alive, whose consciousness turned us almost inevitably to the performative dismantling of texts, want to do the preempting in precisely their own way. Brecht left behind his model books, and Beckett directs his own plays like musical scores, with unyielding rigor. But as far back as his essay on Proust, not to mention the disorienting rhythms of his texts, he was telling another story, like Brecht's Epic depredations upon the texts of older plays. It has been quite a while since we could insist on any theoretical grounds that the actor, who has become the living source of meaning's dissemination, its *dispersal,* be absolutely faithful to the text, *line perfect,* as I was taught to say, because the playwright is God and the director his surrogate in a world fixed by Cartesian coordinates in the recessions of a proscenium stage, which is if you think about it—not like Eric Bentley but Roland Barthes—a model of repressive power and a sneaky theological space. It is even sneakier when the stage is presumably liberated into a thrust or in the round, reinscribing the logocentrism with the same old oedipal drama.

But such theory is far from the thought of the American theater, which has next to no theory at all. That is so despite a period in which the *rehearsal,* with its visions and revisions that a minute might reverse, became something more than a preliminary to performance, trying this trying that, sending out inquisitive feelers, then doing *it* again (what was it?), the emancipated site of meaning's interrogation and deferral, what Derrida calls a "pregnancy without birth" and a virtual model of what we used to call—though the pregnancy might have been false—Alternative Theater. At the moment in the American theater, as in American politics, there isn't much alternative around. (That needn't bring us, however, to the political foolishness that minimized the differences, say, between Walter Mondale and Ronald Reagan, as the Left did, in the delusion of meaning that went through Watergate, with Humphrey and Nixon too.)

The dissidence and experiment that were in the period of improvised politics never entirely thought through have their major legacy now, after the impact of the American counterculture abroad, in a kind of theatricalized theory, a doubly sublimated reflux from the continent that came back to America as an eroticized abstraction in a discourse of desire (inflected from psychoanalysis to radical feminisms to the "desiring machines" of Deleuze). Abstruse as it is, it has become a determining force in our thinking about the visual arts, music, and especially film, and the artists are no more indifferent to such thought—after a period of conceptual art—than were Truffaut and Godard, who were critics to begin with, as they began to make their own films. As we can see in the career of Godard, it is attached to the larger discourse on Marxism that is by no means irrelevant in Europe, with its Socialist and Communist parties, not to mention the paranoia that arose from the Red Brigades and the Baader-Meinhof group (which in a curious repercussion had its effect on the theater, when Klaus Peymann—one of the more innovative German directors—was dismissed at Stuttgart for staging a benefit performance so that the Baader-Meinhof people could get dental work in prison). After the aberrations of the sixties, it makes us nervous, in or out of the theater, to think of such things at all, as if when Stanislavski told the actor not to come into the theater with mud on his feet, it was because the mud would be tracking in politics, which of course it eventually did.

At any rate, ideology isn't supposed to be our suit in America, since the pluralism is ideological enough. When it came, however, in the recycling of the polymorphous sixties through high European theory, as deconstruction or a libidinally inflected cultural materialism, an incursion of revisionist Marx with an admixture of revisionist Freud, no wonder that it unsettled our universities as it has seduced our best students and may—in cyclical, sluggish, and trickle-down time—have some effect on our theater as well, as it has had, directly or indirectly, in Germany and France, on Stein, Gruber, Mesguich, Chéreau, Zadek, and Pina Bausch. It has already, actually, had an effect on young practitioner/theorists like Matthew Maguire and Daryl Chin or dance theatricians like Kenneth King, as it did earlier on Richard Foreman, who has always been French-connected, which is why he had been doing—until the Socialist government withdrew his subsidy—about half of his recent work in France, as Robert Wilson has been doing most of his in Germany. Foreman would prefer to do most of it or all of it in France, or at least so he says, because he dislikes the present atmosphere at home, though he does some of it now too, when he is not at Joe Papp's, in a very occasional gig at a regional theater, where he deploys his collage and freeze-frame methods on classical texts.

What mostly remains, however, of the older alternative promise—the communitarian utopianism having burned itself out, with nothing approaching the realistic adaptations of the Green Party in Germany—is a certain restiveness and indeterminacy, a sort of anxious spillover into the psyche of the anaerobics of the postmodern whose deferrable prospects, like annuities, have been picked up by the galleries as the energy of performance has gone into the other arts and—where the prospects are enormous, measured in gold—onto video discs as well. What avails the theater when Michael Jackson is the culture hero on both stage and screen, in glittered tunic and single glove? "I love you all, I love you all," he coos with every Emmy to the adoring of all ages, his talent indisputable, the desperado of *Thriller* embraced by our cowboy president, in another break dance of consciousness that is in some of its video manifestations also brainless to boot, though there is also David Bowie, who is quite another trick. Bowie mediates ambiguously and androgynously between mass culture and high culture, between what Elias Canetti wrote of in *Crowds and Power* and the pathos of the avant-garde, with its dwindling "aura" and coterie, what Walter Benjamin projected in his now classical essay on "The Work of Art in the Age of Mechanical Reproduction." What is left of the avant-garde, in our theater at least, cannot make the momentum go the other way even when, as in The Wooster Group's *Route 1 and 9,* there is, without the charisma, something like Bowie's conceptual and performative force. The little attention it got came largely from charges of racism when the actors did black-face routines. As we continue to dream of the marriage of high culture and popular culture, we have nothing in our theater today comparable in both avant-garde credentials and public presence to what we see in dance, with Merce Cunningham, Paul Taylor, and Twyla Tharp, whatever concessions Taylor and Tharp may have made to public accessibility.

Route 1 and 9 is, however, in the drift of recent thought, a critique of the systems of representation and power, and the theater apparatus itself, its delinquent institutions, as well as a further chapter in the ongoing lament over the loss of simpler value in the degradation of language. In the process it gets a certain mediated emotional mileage from the nostalgic excerpts from Thornton Wilder's *Our Town,* performed on videotape. The scenes from *Our Town,* which look and play like soaps with archaic sentiments, are shown on monitors in front of a beam-and-guy-wire erector-set version of what could be Ronald Reagan's "little house on a hill," as if the domesticity were designed by a Nazi in disguise at the Bauhaus. There is another videotape of unidentified persons fucking in what is, I have heard, the bed of the director's parents in New Jersey, so that the conception has a subtextual affiliation, unspoken in this case, with the confessionals of Spalding Gray in his Rhode Island trilogy, where he dealt with his mother's suicide, in the group's previous work. The romance and familial warmth of Wilder's world appear, then, a rather mordant citation of redoubled plaintiveness between the quasi-porno film and the atomized and nearly berserk volatility of the black-faced assault on the sexual and social perversions of the American dream. In the manic aggressive patter, delivered at high unrelieved pitch, there is an implicit commentary on another arbitrary shift of the signifier, from Negro to black, which is refused in spades as an essence and not at all beautiful in this work. As with the cross-purposed allegiance of the Reverend Jesse Jackson to the Muslim Louis Farrakhan, the historical necessity of it is exposed as a corrosive linguistic construct that abrades upon itself.

Which is perhaps a more significant reason for blacks to have been outraged by the work, which does manage to do—obscenity and nakedness worn-out—what the avant-garde now finds hard to do, and that is to produce outrage. The trouble is the blurring of the target in the general abuse. Given the history of the group, I thought the charges of racism were boorish if not outrageous, but there was something ethically questionable about, say, an actual onstage phone call in black face and black jive to a fast-food counter in Harlem, ordering chicken to be delivered at the Performance Garage in SoHo—the blacks at the other end never knowing that it was a put-on by whites. It is the sort of ethical queasiness, along with a quotient of virulence, you sometimes have at performances of Squat, the dissident social-surrealist group from Hungary that has taken up residence in a storefront near the old quirky Chelsea Hotel in New York. The brutal zappiness of its images erupts onto the street, startling the passersby, who look through the plate-glass window at a salacious sexuality or they can't imagine what. Along with the mixed-media heavy-metal guignol manifestos of Squat, *Route 1 and 9* is among the very few theater pieces of recent years with an affective residue of political fervor that subsided with the sixties. It is a far more disturbing and sophisticated piece than *Viet Rock* or *America Hurrah* or *Commune* or almost anything done back then, except maybe moments of the Living Theater, and the Ontological-Hysteric Theater of Foreman, in his high and narrow loft over Broadway.

But Foreman was a mere apolitical eccentricity for a while, marginal to the theater scene and closer to the happenings and minimalist-conceptual activity of the artists in SoHo. There is another aspect of that narrowness, a sort of double distancing through the Alienation-effect of Brecht and the phenomenology of Merleau-Ponty, as well as the landscape plays of Gertrude Stein, which in its ontological insistence attenuates Foreman's work, giving reason to those who think it emotionally vapid or effete. There are no characters to speak of, not even Rhoda-who-is-Kate Mannheim who is a function in the plays of Foreman's interests and desires, not her own, his reading, his headaches, his fantasies, his manifestos, his associations of ideas—not at all uninteresting so far as I am concerned, repetitive but inventive, and with an acutely visual wit. But if there are no characters to identify with, our retrograde addictions, of which Foreman disapproves, look then to the performers, but they are busy being functions in—to use a term of Barthes's—a sort of "structuralist activity" without any voice of their own or, even if they have them, evidence of social concerns. Foreman has them but seems indifferent himself, despite his indebtedness to Brecht, which is more aesthetically than politically engaged. So there is something missing in the metabolism of the thing that keeps his theater from having not only what Yeats called "the emotion of multitude," an effect of symbol, but a palpable amplitude, the widening affinity of a social world even when he is outside the narrow loft and on a bigger stage—something that even in Yeats's plays leaked through the aestheticism of the occult and the curtained ideograms in Lady Gregory's drawing room.

Where there is something like the emotion of multitude, as with Robert Wilson's images soporifically on the edge of trance, it lacks the social extension despite the public figures in his titles. Where it has the extension, as in Lee Breuer's *Oedipus at Colonus,* done with Bob Telson and black gospel singers, it seems to me at worst spurious and at best misleading, since the choir itself could with any liberal audience arouse the same emotions, as I have seen such choirs do, getting them dancing in the aisles—which is saying something else about Oedipus and our relationship to power. Still, there is no work I admire more, overall, than that of the Mabou Mines, of which Breuer was the founding director before it diversified authority and gave the women a turn. The Mabou Mines emerged or caught attention somewhat later than Foreman. Like him, it is also attuned to the conceptual art scene, funkier, shrewder, West Coast, Beckettian, and perhaps from the contagion of that last-ditch humanism it modulates its own cool. There is a savviness in the group that does adroit maneuvers with the conventional emotions as if they were art objects, but, like the art of some painters, art objects in a dead time, art itself in danger of dying, what therefore makes the making of it impossible and necessary to do. It is as if they are recycling the emotions just in case, for another improbable time, with as much character as they need, although they cannot quite believe in it because character is a ruined convention, more *bricolage,* or shards of makeshift behavior for another shaggy dog. Yet even when they are super-technological and to all appearances post-humanist—as in the monodrama *Haaj* or the holographic Beckett that Ruth Maleczech has just done, *Imagination Dead Imagine*—they are interested in the cognitive assets of empathy even as they are siphoned into parody or stasis to return in another form.

It is an alert and eclectic work, not only ripping off mimesis and minimalism, but Brecht, Grotowski, Bunraku, and rock, and they do it with a collective intelligence that really deserves the name and is not merely catching up. Moreover, there is a rich, hip, and allusive poetry to Breuer's writing that spares no symbolism either, though well aware that in these deconstructive and new expressionist times symbols are polysaturated nothings, relics of history, and ideology is the synonym of myth. By contrast, the language of Foreman articulates the emptiness of the signifiers, obsessively dry, iterative, flat. That also contributes to the feeling—even among those who admire it—that there is something antiseptic in his theater, for all the magpie Magrittism and orchestrated hysteria. Still, when the perceptual bells are ringing funnily, the mise-en-scène like a puzzle box or, as in the recent *Egyptology,* like a crypt of the cradle of culture encoded, the sound deafening, it can also be one of the more beguiling theaters we have. In its cybernetic and immaculate excitement it is something like the Atari game of the avant-garde, as Wilson's operas are in the sonorous streaming of their autistic images, knee-jerked, like a computer printout of the Wagnerian *Ring.*

Astonishing as some of Wilson's images are, and majestic in scale, the concentration of *Route 1 and 9,* as directed by Elizabeth LeCompte, had another kind of promise with its spastic and hyperventilated Pigmeat Markham routines, with the augur bite of American culture in its schizo-analytic critique. It is a theater work that also—like Foreman and the Mabou Mines and not too much else of consequence in our theater—knows what's what in the other arts, including those other modes of performance with something lethal at the heart. It is the point at which an aesthetic, in a vertigo of distance, becomes a subculture of its own. There was something in the performance that seemed crazed. It was like the now-abated fury of punk in its attack upon everything in sight, but with a strict barrier in front of the audience. The actors pumped up their imposture like an abscess, not as if there were vermilion but razors in their hair, black face to black bile, their mouths spewing scorn and filth. This was in contrast to the unsullied language of the young lovers of Grover's Corners, which seemed anomalous on the video screen, where sincerity is always a lie. What we had in Wilder's lines, here untampered with, preserved, was the emotional memory of an ingenuousness that is—since the culture industry is also postmodern—an artifact to be reproduced, not mechanically but electronically, a ruined fantasy with use value, a commodity fetish of the family romance, as if our social reality that is only a surface were nothing but summer stock. *Our Town* is still being done by nearly every high school in the land whose students, watching an average of four or five hours of television a day, lose the language with their innocence as they are processed into a system that reverses the sentiments and, with more or less awareness, feel their lives becoming a lie.

The Wooster Group is a saving remnant of the Performance Group originally directed by Richard Schechner, who is exiled from it now and jaundiced about the avant-garde. If the work of the group since *Route 1 and 9* were an index, he would surely have grounds for believing that something was over and irrecoverable, and that their next plunge into *North Atlantic* was merely the end of the line. The recent pieces have seemed to me shallow, unaccountably scatterbrained and merely strident, as if they didn't know where to go when the linearity of the 1 turned back into the 9. Perhaps they were exhausted by a critique that in its pure exacerbation could, like the celebrations of the sixties, only go so far. Beginning with *The Cocktail Party*—and what for T. S. Eliot was there in a beginning in which they could hardly believe—the group has in a series of works been taking off from well-known plays that one or another has acted in before he or she joined the group. They are usually presented with quasi-academic lectures, as was done with *Our Town* too, the lectures growing increasingly schizophrenic and gradually falling apart. I cannot remember for the moment whether they lectured about Arthur Miller's *The Crucible*, to which they contributed nothing and derived nothing that I could pay attention to in one of the recent works, because of the amplified hysteria that is, in Miller's play, the substantial but already excessive content. Neither video nor a black masque, nor the high sloping battlement that they have used in other pieces, could help them to frame it, the ontological-hysterical blood vessels of intelligence having burst, I hope temporarily.

But turning back to the curve into the 9: seen within the history of the group and the history of the theater since the sixties, what a falling off was there! For it seems like the entropic decay of the ecstasies of '69, the era of Dionysus. It also corresponds, in the infolded consciousness of its reflexivity, to the solipsism that now dominates much of the solo performance and performance art that, in its psychosexual and tautological circling, is mostly in a rut. If the circling is the illusory path of a deadening end, I still think the theater has something to learn from the conceptual disposition of such work, including the various species of body art, and the decentering effects of its ontological risks. I say that perhaps because the solipsistic temptation was—after years of trying to create more institutional forms of theater with another public scale at both ends of the continent—the outside danger of my own most recent work with the KRAKEN group, its viral and obsessive subject, before it stopped. It didn't stop, I think, because of the solipsism, but that may have been a matter of time.

I started with Bentley's critique of the absence of meaning in the general scene, and I have been curving back to the mainstream through the experimental theater and its hybrids that were not even a shadow of possibility then. Years ago, before Bentley, who also put us on to Brecht, it was hard to find out where anything innovative was happening in the theater if it was happening at all, and it did not seem then as if it was happening in our country, which is why, with some desperation I first went to Europe. But I have written about that elsewhere, in *The Impossible Theater*, whose view of the American theater I was asked to more or less update for this occasion. Things have changed in these twenty years. Now even the most unregenerate squares have at their disposal anything they care to know about the theater almost anywhere. We have some journals we did not have then, everybody travels, so they do know about it and have even gone to see it when it hasn't come to them, not only the idiosyncrasies of Squat, which was something of a myth before it came to New York, or the scandalous body works of a Joseph Beuys or Vito Acconci, parodied by John Belushi on *Saturday Night Live,* but just before I came abroad this time, Pina Bausch from Wuppertal by way of the Olympics, and then in Los Angeles the Kabuki versions of Shakespeare by the Théâtre du Soleil. Now we've seen it all, even the more remote, less adulterate, and exotic forms of other cultures, even before they've come as they've come in recent years out of the temples or the bush. Things have changed, but the impossible takes a little time.

So if we turn to the theater proper, there seems to be, if not a solipsistic redundancy, a demoralized biding of time, without risks, an inability to develop from its own stalemate any of the suggestive tendencies of the experimental generation or any scale for its best intuitions. That is partly because there was very little transfer of energy or ideas across the echelons of our theater, though a few of the avant-garde directors—Breuer, Foreman, Serban—have done stints in the regional theaters, and despite a couple of large-scale conferences, with impossible constituencies, funded by the foundations. Not since André Gregory was ousted from Philadelphia, in the early seventies, and before that my own failure at Lincoln Center, has anyone from our more dissident forms of theater moved, as it often happens abroad, into the directorship of the now established civic theaters, although Liviu Ciulei, Serban's teacher, is now heading the Guthrie, and a young man, Peter Sellars, has just been selected by Roger Stevens for the Kennedy Center in Washington. That's promising, but unlike Breuer, who has struggled every inch of the way and is ready to move in a larger orbit, it is not entirely clear what Sellars represents as yet except his virtuosity, which is more than we usually have. Breuer also has the virtuosity, but when it fails—as it did in *The Tempest* for Joe Papp—it is hard to get, through a long-standing offbeat reputation, a second chance.

What is, however, really troubling—what amazes directors from other countries and has always depressed me—is that there is no natural discourse among practitioners in this presumably social art, no ideational framework for it, and sometimes, it seems, no desire. As for the inspiriting years of experiment—whose end was recently announced by Schechner to grim retorts from others who never took up the issues and misunderstood the history—it suffered as it happened, and, to this day, from an inadequate criticism, an untheorized practice and, through the incurable anti-intellectualism, even among the intellectuals, lapses of memory (which could be seen even in the mania of *Route 1 and 9,* with the identification of the mental and the repressive, and no verbal language to speak of except from Wilder). It is enough to make you want to say with Brecht's Galileo: "I believe in the brain!" For what I am speaking of now is the incessant amnesia of the American experience in which, unable to assess and sustain ideas, the best of them seem to get lost and we start all over again. Some of our best people also tend to get lost, but I will come back to that in a while.

What develops, then, in our theater is more like the picture puzzle at the end of the first act of the new musical *Sunday in the Park with George,* a chancy pointillist affair, this event, that event, but so far no collective or single genius, no Georges Seurat, to pull the loose ends of its randomness into an enlivening accomplishment of any magnitude that becomes, as *La Grande Jatte* did, part of the discourse of modern art that has been reflecting critically upon itself up through the conceptual work of Gilbert and George. Since we have no activating interchange in our theater, no tradition of interior reflection, we cannot quite expect what happens in Sondheim's *coup de théâtre*, when the painting is completed like a child's game of statues, imagine! by the master mind—a visualization raved about that seems to me pure cliché—the cast bursting after the dissonance into its first song of magical harmony.

Unfortunately, the dissonance persists. This is a period of local initiatives at best, in theater and politics, but when I was out in San Francisco in the fifties and sixties, what we were doing seemed part of a grand design, in art and politics. We thought the energies released then would not only reverse the repressive course of Tributary Theater—that is, Broadway as the fountainhead from which everything flowed, and to which in many blighted careers everybody paid tribute. We thought it would lead to some eventual fusion of the decentralized theater and the forces at work in the underground. There was eventually some seepage into the mainstream, like that combination of Brecht and environmental theater that turned up in *Cabaret* or the dancer's autobiographies that were, as in our workshops, improvised into *A Chorus Line*—both of which, of course, with more or less ass-kissing style ingratiated the audiences that the techniques were designed to alienate. Nor is it much different at the regional theaters, whose overall mediocrity everybody now worries about, along with the new tendency to pay tribute, although it looks reversed, by replacing Boston and New Haven as the places of out-of-town tryout of new plays for Broadway that are to begin with Broadway plays. As for the infusion of new ideas or seminal energies, there was a similar seepage, but it never went down to the roots, possibly because there are no roots.

Thus, despite some token productions at the regional theaters, the estranging concepts of Brecht, attached to his politics—the gist of the *gestus*—never took hold. We went through a period, remember, where we dealt with his politics like Tolstoy's view of history, as if it were an aberration transcended by his art. In both cases there was history passing us by, leaving behind what I started with here, the problem of meaning. What we mean by meaning, I suppose, is what we accept as history— some narrative of the career of truth—or what we *think* of history, or *that* we think of it at all. And the more we think of it, the more it is read and thought, the more it seems like a fantasy text of a future that is nothing but a past, in America a past we keep forgetting, or denying that we had, but still the nightmare from which—as all of modernism has followed Marx in saying—we are trying to awaken. That accounts for the scream that, arising from the ancient theater, is almost iconic in modern drama, from the end of Ibsen's *Ghosts* through the replays of Pirandello to Hamm's scream, Mother Courage's scream, or the myriad self-mocking screams in Genet. Or for that matter, the virulence at the edge of a scream like a legacy of the form at the beginning of two current plays by young dramatists in New York, John Patrick Shanley's *Danny and the Deep Blue Sea* and Dennis McIntyre's *Split Second,* which I single out because they are there or were when I was writing. Neither quite dares the scream because the author does not quite know what to do with it (which Pirandello foresaw) since the behavioral psychology that is the formulary psychology of the American theater is simply not adequate to the wincing complexities of reversed racial hatred (which Melville and Faulkner saw, though they did not write for our theater) or to the breaking of the incest taboos, upon which Artaud insisted in *The Theater and Its Double,* where he denounced the psychology and the actor formed in its image who has forgotten how to scream.

There is something in the postmodern that simply wants to forget it and get on with it, although there were a lot of primal screams in the sound/movement exercises of the sixties and early seventies, rising with a dying fall into the apathy and conservatism of the eighties. Meanwhile, in our theater, the cerebral discipline of Artaud never took hold either. I mean the effort to think at the overstretched scars and fugitive ganglia of thought, "by sheer force of destructive analysis," bursting with the ideas that escape us into states of "intellectual being" so intense and absolute as to require the redoubling of "this labor at the incandescent edges of the future. . . ." No major figure of the theater speaks so unremittingly and exactingly about *Ideas,* as if he were resurrecting Platonic forms in their nubile and murmurous outpouring realization. Certainly he was bound to fail, but we ignored in the alchemy the intellectual passion of Artaud, *les pensées sauvages* of alchemy, its science, rarely getting past the sonorous streaming, the lights noise postures chant, the immemorial incantations in the air and the bogus Myth and fake languages and the percussion, the ubiquitous and interminable percussion, cut with acid rock, which drowned out any kind of analysis and disguised every vacuity, including the shopping-mall shamanism.

Well, it is no wonder the established theaters wanted no part of it, after some responsive overtures to the seductions of body language like, in a new order of meaning under Robert Brustein, André Gregory's version of *The Bacchae* at Yale. Nor do they want any part of it now that it has turned into an intellectual passion—the whole "carnal stereophony," as Barthes says of the pleasure of the text, its bliss or *jouissance*—and, in the anti-oedipal ethos of advanced critical thought, into an ideology of desire with its libidinal economy and, by way of Artaud's body without organs signaling through the flames, into radical forms of feminism as well. Which does not mean they are not interested in women, far from it, women are getting a lot of attention these days, including two of three recent Pulitzer Prizes for exactly what you might expect (one of the recent prizes going to a black, also for what you might expect), a very conventional sort of play. The more radical women are not unpleased with this, at least not all of them, but they do want it recognized, as Colette Brooks said in a recent issue of *PAJ*, that to rank Marsha Norman with Beckett or Chekhov, "as the culture industry is on the edge of doing, . . . is to engage in a kind of hyperbole that only serves to reduce to meaninglessness the useful notion of modest virtues."

To return to the libidinal economy and the passions of the semiotic flux, which is a little like being on *Cloud 9*. The semiosis is, however, after Artaud, a good deal more destructively analytical, as if obeying, too, Marx's call for "a ruthless criticism of everything existing." Ruthless it may be, but little of it has taken hold in our theater. And that may be—for some, and in the eyes of God, not to mention the bourgeois economy—a saving grace. But the trouble is that no serious view of meaning or its absence, or of history or its absence, or of politics or its absence, or of ideology and its presence, which is most powerful in its absence, ever took hold either. Since Jan Kott and Peter Brook, we have had a discreet quota of revisionist productions and, recently, a pious backlash against them by the Moral Majority of critics who are now protecting Holy Writ.

But that is not in the dynamic of history what Bentley, who gave us not mere chronology but historical consciousness, meant by meaning after World War II. And the reason I am remembering his remark—aside from recent echoes of it in what little discourse we have, *within* the theater—is that if meaning has come to matter here and there it does not matter all that much, no more than our theater or its absence matters all that much in American culture, with its early Puritan tradition and the later dominion of film, as if it existed somehow on allowance, against the American grain. Most of us know it and try to forget it. And as we hang in there against the grain, what Bentley said is still the congenital objection of thinking people to the theaters they work in, not to mention the preponderant number, thinking or unthinking, who are not as usual working at all, making the normally alarming statistics about unemployment look utopian, a mere inflection of discontent in the Laffer Curve that guides the economic policy of our nation down route 1 and 9.

It is a policy that—leaving to the bounty of the "private sector" our established culture, the ballets and orchestras that, along with some regional theaters, already get most of the money from the government and foundations—has contributed to the draining of funds from much of what was worth thinking about in our theater. But while the absence of money in the shadow play of bourgeois exchange is the absence of meaning, I do not really want to make an issue of that here. More often than not the absence of money does not appear in the minds of theater people as a theoretical sign, the genotext of ideology—which is money of the mind—but rather a mere excuse. We have had a generation of young people whose aspirations have been unfortunately curtailed, before anything of consequence was done, no less the impossible, by the lapsed expectation of instant grants.

That cannot be said, however, about the aspirations of a talented playwright, Richard Nelson, in a couple of current essays on the non-profit regional theater in which he has worked as a dramaturg—a position still somewhat in left field—and for which he is trying to formulate an ideological position and an alternative practice. Nelson begins a section with an epigraph from the German director Peter Stein, in which he talks of the "scientific methodology in the preparatory work" of his theater, the detail, precision, and intellectual seriousness of everyone involved "in the process of conscious development." Envious and frustrated, Nelson writes of his own experience as if history had retracted forty years, the major difference being that the regional theaters to which he refers were not around to complain about, a mixed blessing to which I will return, having been a major polemicist for their establishment in the fifties and sixties: "After eight years," he says, "of working in many of our best non-profit theaters, after participating in over thirty productions as either playwright or adaptor, I doubt if I have ever been asked what my work means, why I wrote it, or even more importantly, what I believe. And I would think," he adds, "that most playwrights have had similar experiences in our non-profit theater."

So, what's new? Aside from surface changes, I am not entirely sure, not where it is heading, for the deep structure of a kind of emptiness or aimlessness seems to remain intact, with the same general indifference to meaning that has spanned a lot of years. What distinguishes the worst of architects from the best of bees, said Marx in *Capital,* is that the architect raises his structure in the imagination before he erects it in reality. Marx is putting the stress on conscious activity in preference to the indeterminacy of the unconscious or to animal instinct, like Brecht later. But as we look around our cities, it is not hard to believe, even with a little bit of history sitting coyly atop the AT&T in Manhattan, that all kinds of structures have been erected in reality by the very worst of architects who had no imagination to begin with, or by talented people who have somehow gone very wrong. I used to feel this way about the proliferation of activity in the American theater. When a case is made for its improvement, we are usually told that more theater is being done than ever before. I will not cite the statistics that make that dubious, and it is the same argument I have heard these many years. Some time ago I wrote that if nine-tenths of what is being done were to disappear overnight that might be an improvement in American culture. People who could once be counted upon to grow apoplectic over such a statement are, nowadays, saying pretty much the same thing. But before I come to that, let me review more or less in conclusion the primal scene—which is to say, for all the decentralization, New York.

When I was in there recently, the most moving event in the theater, on or off Broadway, was the memorial ceremony for the director Alan Schneider, who was killed, as you may know, in an accident in London. At the same time, the most distinguished plays on or off Broadway were the two revivals, Eugene O'Neill's *Moon for the Misbegotten* and Arthur Miller's *Death of a Salesman,* and a new play that is a sort of an abrasive sequel to *Salesman,* of shorter conceptual shrift—with something of the length and scope of Miller's *Memory of Two Mondays*—but aroused by a logorrhea of manic aggression to a kind of corrosive rage. The play was first done in England, David Mamet's *Glengarry Glen Ross.* It is as if the real estate hype had imploded in Mamet—with his Montgomery Ward catalog of Chicago speech—like a ruptured eardrum. The splenetic discharge of self-contempt by those whose lives are mortgaged, with almost no fringe benefits, to wheeling and dealing through the illusory exchange of money and language, might once have been thought more suitable to off-Broadway. But no, when you think it over, it is also precisely what it is, what they used to call an electrifying Broadway play in the older serious vein, with an intellectual threshold to its bloodletting but the dividend of accessible power—like O'Neill, Miller, and Williams—overcoming the aversion to seriousness by the force of its dramaturgical, social/critical, confessional, or lyrical gifts, unremittingly empathic, in what was and is and will forever be—despite Brecht, who they knew was un-American—a "culinary theater." It is a theater in which the wheeler-dealers, confronted with their most appalling image, can still sleep it off or, as in Mamet's play, laugh it off with a bellyful of preemptive tolerance, though it is unlikely for quite a while, on the supply side of its debased currency, to have anything like a surfeit of such revivals or a repletion of such drama.

But to return to the memorial for Alan Schneider, an old friend with whom I had my ups and downs. His death was the occasion for heartfelt tributes to his services in the theater, the ebullience and fervor of it, indefatigable, though in his heart of hearts he knew it had deprived him, as it did almost everybody of self-respecting intelligence, of a more substantial and self-articulated career. There are many good things I could say about him, but this is not another memorial, and what I particularly remember in this context was a moment, somewhat habitual for Alan, of belittling candor at his own expense that, though funny in the delivery, struck my hubris at the time as mortifying in its truth about him. He was out in San Francisco, directing a production at my theater, whose repertoire and continuity he encouraged and envied. He described himself one night as "a poor man's Tyrone Guthrie" who went from one place to another doing, if chance agreed, the best work he could, but despite the Beckett and Pinter—to whom he was dutiful to the end, not at all like Tyrone Guthrie—often doing much less, his standards going up and down, since for all his notorious stubbornness it was not always a matter of choice.

"I feel I've dealt with a lot of wasting circumstances as best I could, but I've had to waste my time defending my space, so to speak." That is not Alan, it is Arthur Miller. He did not speak at the memorial, but if he had, he might have been speaking for them both. He made the remark—if the interviewer is accurate—after the revival of *Death of a Salesman* made possible by Dustin Hoffman, to whom Miller feels grateful though the circumstances were "humiliating," knowing that it was hit or miss even with a superstar and despite his own status, "thrown back," as he said, "into the marketplace," a little like Willie Loman. "Had there been a working theater, it could have been or might have been otherwise. . . . We have no real theater. We have shows, which isn't really the same thing." The geography if not influence of Alan Schneider's activity—on Broadway, off Broadway, in the regional theaters and universities—was, despite *Salesman* in Beijing, wider than Arthur Miller's, whose primary focus is Broadway. The optimism about which everybody spoke might have kept Alan from agreeing. But Miller knew what he was talking about, and Schneider was quick enough to know that the people who did speak—from Broadway, the foundations, the regional theater, nothing experimental—had forgotten for the occasion what some of them knew too, that for all his activity it was not much of a theater they were talking about. The memorial, not exactly by the way, was held at the uptown Circle in the Square, where one of our most powerful actors who is mostly wasted, George C. Scott, was directing some of our more promising actors who will be wasted not only because it was a revival of Noel Coward.

If I labor the depressing part of the familiar scene, it is not because I want to repeat *The Impossible Theater*. But if shows and real theater are not the same thing, what is pretty much the same thing is what Miller is saying today and what was being said by directors and actors and playwrights and in the newspapers and on and off Broadway even before I wrote *The Impossible Theater,* in which I thought I was merely summing up in those notorious opening chapters what almost everybody took for granted. But I was much younger then and did not know that even worse perhaps than being told I told you so is to be told that you said it first not me, proving again that you don't mind saying yourself what you don't like to hear. "Okay," says the solipsistic antihero of a play, *Chucky's Hunch,* by a very gifted woman, Rochelle Owens, who never made it up there with all her queer imagination, along with Wendy Wasserstein and Beth Henley, "so you and I cut through some of those lies twenty years ago. . . . That's cool. My message to you now is"—he is addressing his ex-wife in a monologue of never-answered letters—"who are YOU talkin to?" I don't know. That is what makes it impossible, wasting so much time, we do not really know WHO, on or off Broadway or in the outlying regional theaters where we began way back in the fifties, with good liberal presumption, to "educate an audience" that, if and when it materialized, would not quite be the audience we wanted, as in America it almost never is.

Nothing to be done, we take it as it is. That wasn't a bad idea, as it came to us from *Waiting for Godot* in the middle of the fifties, since the waiting seemed the bottomless source of possibility, as insufficient as it seems at the moment. I do not mean to underestimate the work that was done in the twenty years between my particular presumption, which did (I think) spur some of it on, and Chucky's hunch, which seems the bitter end. Some of that work was suggestive and promising, some of it audacious, some of it with a lasting impact, for better or worse, on the

European theater; for instance, the apocalyptic adventures of the Living Theater, whose recent return to the United States did seem, however, in performance, like the pathetic bottoming out of a state of mind, not only anachronistic but plain dumb. If that is over, what still remains distressing in the United States—where not only *PAJ* but even the *New York Times* has been writing that the theater is next to hopeless, that "there is a widespread perception that American plays simply do not matter anymore," that theater seems to be "a special interest, occupying a ghetto on the cultural landscape"—are those theaters on the landscape all around the country that we worked so hard to establish, never mind the absence of a national theater, which is, in the sprawling logic of the American continent, a consummation I am not sure anymore we should wish because it seems like a contradiction in terms.

Anyhow, for better or worse, there are the theaters that were not there before. (They were never, as Nelson declares in his first article, revolutionary in design or impulse, The Actor's Workshop in San Francisco having been perhaps the most dissident, but still bourgeois; and The Group Theater was oriented to Broadway.) We have, as always, innumerable gifted people. And what cannot be denied to the Living Theater and the experimental groups of its period is that—whatever they amounted to in the raising or delusion of consciousness—they did extend the usable grammar of our theater.

Now, every technique is available, every sort of theater knowledge. We have the lore and suggestiveness of other cultures, the example of their disciplines and praxis. We are aware of alternative space and empty space and multiple possibilities of staging. We have seen a spectrum of acting behaviors, as well as all kinds of variations on the convention of character or fractions of character—roles and transformations, masks, personae, shadows, doubles, quoted increments and accretions of character—or unmediated character, the actor in his/her own person (and the attendant ambiguities of selfhood). We have grown used to frank artifice or utter naturalism, ideographs and recycled realism, all the imaginable forms of play and pretence, and the resistance to pretence, every possible articulation of those old platitudes about the illusion of reality and the reality of illusion and the illusion of the reality of illusion, etc., and thus the future of illusion. If we learned about cooling it from Brecht, it is now possible to move through states of empathy or alienation or all the orders of representation between. There is even the passion to end representation, Artaud's passion, one of the most powerful motives in the history of theater, which may be the deepest conceivable subtext (or is it fantasy text?) of the form.

It is this motive (or fantasy) that the theories of deconstruction are very much obsessed with in the critique of the "phallogocentric" tradition of power. Since, however, the desire to end representation is very unlikely to succeed anywhere—theater abolishing theater in its self-deceit—we can only hope that the theaters we have in America, our institutional theaters, no longer an illusion, can awaken to the new resources and manage to give them all meaning, so that those who come to undo it, as I trust they will, are not so much dealing with what they can do without, but are up to the mettle of the meaning to be undone, thus reforming those theaters too. It is a dynamic that we have long envied in the civic theaters of Europe. It may no longer be impossible, but I think it will take a little time.

(1984)

3. Spacing Out in the American Theater

I will eventually move on, in an American way, to speak of space through my own experience, but let me take off from French theory, which seems at times to have picked up the idea of *spacing*—the breach, the break, the effraction, the transgressive interval that, leaving only a trace, constitutes memory—not from Freud but from the American sixties, which, in the self-conscious activity of transgression called *spacing out,* seemed to have lost it. What *it?* It may not have been memory. It may have been consciousness. Or the self. To be spaced out was, as we know (perhaps from experience), associated with the drugged end of the counterculture. What exactly it lost may still be arguable, but if it was not quite memory, that's because—as the image goes, and the reality of the sixties—Americans, particularly young Americans, were never big on memory.

We have, of course, other surpluses, but the shortage of memory, like the famous eighteen minutes of Nixon's missing tape or Reagan's video-taped testimony on the Iran/Contra scandal, still remains a material reality of our national culture, and a political liability, though America can no longer plead innocence or that it is still coming of age. Putting aside the aging and failing memory once in the White House, the census appears to be telling us that while senior citizens accumulate in the Sun Belt and in the midst of Miami Vice, the median age in America is now over forty. Aside from the fact that we Americans thought of ourselves until recently as relatively young, and still insist on youth beyond middle age, the problem of memory is that it is also a function of space. Even on a computer, memory is spoken of in terms of space or, in the binary conception of bits, *spaces,* like the breaches or effractions, the emptiness required, the break in time or interval, for depositing information. But there is also a problem with too much space, which becomes a form of *motion,* almost without interval, mere spacing out with a sense of impermanence, leaving things behind.

I will return to some of those things, but meanwhile in the materiality of the unconscious where, for better or worse, everything is remembered, there is "a topography of traces, a map of breaches," as Derrida says, a detailed itinerary of psychic space. That is mostly, I think, what Foucault had in mind when, obsessed as he was with binaries, he wrote of something more or other than physical space: "A whole history remains to be written of *spaces*—which would at the same time be the history of *powers....*" His essay is titled "The Eye of Power," and the image suggests a relation of power to theatricalized space. That is the only space, it appears, *the space of appearance* in which (now you see it now you don't) there is a manifestation or semblance of power, the visible evidence of that which, not there, invisible, determines the evidence.

When I said they lost it in the sixties, an interval of history that was itself a theatricalized space, I meant they may have lost what they thought they had found, power (even those who were not on drugs), by making it all theater: education, politics, fashion, therapy, everyday behavior that was called "lifestyle." If that's now been appropriated by the commodity fetishism of material culture—*Penthouse,* the baby boomers, presidential candidates—there was a time when the spectacle of the Movement seemed to have taken its cue from the opening of *The Eighteenth Brumaire,* where Marx—with his remarkable consciousness of the mise-en-scène of history—speaks of revolution taking place in theatrical dress. *"The whole world is watching / the whole world is watching,"* they chanted in Chicago at the Democratic convention of 1968, as Lincoln Park and its environs became a playing space, with a multiplicity of costumes in a sort of Bakhtinian carnival, art spilling into life, as it appeared to do more recently at the Berlin Wall. Since a large part of the world *was* watching, it seemed a not altogether utopian illusion to think of performance as substantially changing American politics, though a better understanding of theater might have warned, as Brecht tried to do before, that the power of theater comes in the scenography of history, in keeping a certain distance from life by resisting itself as theater.

The distance Brecht had in mind was another sort of spacing, or historicizing, the interruption or arrest that is the space of Alienation. But the revival of Brecht in the fifties was overtaken by a participatory period of improvisational method and instant gratification. There was not much patience with theory, and besides—as professionals in the theater know—theatrical ambition grows quickly as it feels the pulse of power (as it does in academia, where we now talk of superstars). We had seen during this period innumerable kinds of theater in the streets, but who cared about agitprop or slow-moving pageants of larger-than-life puppets or even the quick hits of guerrilla theater when theatricality could be appropriated almost on its own terms: the pure Imaginary, the media, the fantasy-making apparatus itself that, disguising myth as information, was the real source of power. You know the scene—if you are old enough, you may have been there—this carnivalized space of performance with blue jeans and acid rock and that other American export, the notion of spacing out that, when the revolution subsided, was absorbed with the "polymorphous perversity," the libidinal economy of the idea of performance itself, into the ideological debates in continental thought. When in the recycling process of the postmodern it came back to us here, all of this was doubly sublimated—that is, repressed as behavior, reified in theory—in the more radical modes of deconstruction, feminism, or, through the anti-oedipal critique of Deleuze and Guattari, the flows and intensities of schizoanalysis.

Meanwhile in America, we have learned again—moving on to Bill Clinton from the staking out of Gary Hart—that not only does *being-watched* not give power, but that while every other space is now vulnerable, under surveillance, the media have taken over the function of the eye of power, sustaining its invisibility in the commodification of the spectacle, which remains inviolable in its own eye. As we narrow the gaze down to specific theatrical spaces, do we not have a sense that the dominion of theater, the spectacle, is by satellite transmission and the power of silicon chips, spacing out all over the world? While the Japanese are moving ahead of us in the technology of dissemination, microchips and superconductors, here is the major space of theater, the image-repertoire itself, which should have been copyrighted as American.

Now that we have the larger picture, the American space of fantasy (of which Disneyland in Tokyo is only a minor form), let us narrow by stages down, though after many years in the theater I am pretty well convinced that when you talk of space in the theater, it is mainly psychic space—all the more when, as in the American theater, you have to struggle to stake it out. I have been alluding to a period when, as theatricality took over the psychopathology of everyday life, people working at theater in America and abroad were growing indifferent to the established *institutions* of theater with their conventional playing spaces. There was a particular animus against the frame of the proscenium in which, plotted or encoded in the sight lines of perspective, there was the legacy of a theological vision, which Americans always have mixed feelings about. Blessed be the binaries of French thought, but the argument against the picture frame stage, which is Cartesian space, is that it conduces to a form of theater that, so far as it is "geometral vision," as Lacan says, "is not in its essence visual." It is rather a mere trick of perception passing itself off as metaphysical substance or psychological depth. It has been passing itself off as such elsewhere, but what is peculiar to the condition of theater in the United States, and our disposition toward playing spaces, is that the distrust of institutional theater, the proscenium, and conventional stages developed *at almost the same time* that the idea of an institutional theater—which could never be taken for granted, *because there was none*—had started to take hold.

Some years ago I was living in Paris on the rue de Richelieu, between the Bibliothèque Nationale and the Comédie Française, in what they told me was the apartment of Molière's sister. Aside from the fact that a space smaller than one floor of our three-story house in Milwaukee feels perfectly adequate in Paris, it may suggest what I mean by an institution and its psychic effect on space. I am not, obviously, talking of Broadway, which was actually once, when not a nervous condition, something of an institutional space, though by the time I am referring to it had become a kind of pari-mutuel betting establishment or at best a brokerage firm, already as unstable as our economy in the age of arbitrage. That was the fifties, when Jules Irving and I were starting our own theater in San Francisco, in a narrow room above a judo academy, which later became the vestry of the Ebenezer Baptist Church, confirming, perhaps, what I said about theological vision in America, if not the ancient connection between theater and religion, since by that time we had moved to a former automobile warehouse, which had been converted by the Ford Motor Company, though before it had been a church.

To me, these connections seem as significant as the freeway that virtually passed over our theater and, just before the Ferry Building, was cut off in midair. Out there in San Francisco, we felt similarly cut off. Yet some of us were already thinking about non-theater spaces, and I always wanted to do a performance, as if in midair, at the place where the freeway stopped. As it turns out, that was very near the Golden Gate Development where—when our company was invited to move to New

York—the city administration that had mostly ignored us wanted to build us a theater to keep us in San Francisco. This may remind us, as we place theater space within the larger space of America, that in the early fifties San Francisco was not the (most European) sophisticated city it appears to be now, but a sort of beautiful backwater by the Bay, with what they called "brown money"—money that aged in the bank, unrefreshed by circulation, and certainly not spent for art. It was a city already laid back, taking pleasure in itself, but not yet sufficiently embarrassed, in the continental tilt, by the absence of an endowed and established culture that, with whatever liabilities, was institutionalized in Europe. So it was, moreover, with every major city outside of New York, even Chicago, and New York was embarrassed, as Washington was, by not having a national theater. Which is in any case a strange concept to localize in America, as they tried to do at Lincoln Center—the place we went to in New York—and then with the Kennedy Center in Washington, that complex that is the national theater of anonymous suburban space.

But, as we used to say in the fifties, things were starting to happen and have happened since. From the fringe benefits of the dynastic families, Ford and Rockefeller, the foundations appeared on the scene, and *Time* magazine began to speak of the Cultural Revolution. As the notion of institutional or "regional theaters" started to take hold outside of New York, partially bankrolled by Ford, they did so with the model of another stage in mind, the so-called "thrust stage." This was first tested out in Stratford, Ontario, and then brought by Sir Tyrone Guthrie to Minneapolis, as if in one double transplant, certified by English knighthood, the American theater would be decentralized, and in that phallic form, the thrust, sticking it to the audience, we would shatter the metaphysical dominion of the proscenium and be back in the Sacred Grove.

What has still not been adequately considered, however, as we talk about new stages or alternative stages or the restorative datum of an empty space, is the staying power of perspective, the introjected authority of the proscenium frame, its determining presence as an obdurate state of mind. One can see it and feel it in whatever architectural space: ogive, ovoid, slant, trapped, or in the round; and so it is in the Globe Theater in San Diego, with its Shakespearean stage, or the black box in Seattle or the Arena Stage in Washington or the Alley Theater in Houston or on the adjustable thrust stage of Cincinnati's Theater-in-the-Park. And I say that descriptively rather than in judgment, because what I am talking about is an accretion of history that is a powerful scheme of thought. It may seem at times as if it is just there, without any thought at all, but as we think out space in production, it will inevitably insist on its own premises and psychic rights unless, in the dialectic of appearances, it is examined, watched for, challenged, understood as instrumental, and deployed as conceptual space. Which is not, for the most part, what happens in these theaters—as it does, say, in painting at the shaped edge of the picture plane.

"It is surprising," says Foucault, "how long the problem of space took to emerge as a historico-political problem." Among the reasons he gives for the deferral of a politics of spaces are the achievements in theoretical and experimental physics at the end of the eighteenth century, which dislodged philosophy from an ancient right to reflect on finite or infinite space, deflecting it to the problem of time, while both political technology and scientific practice staked out the ground of privileged space. Yet when we start thinking historically of space in America, this formulation holds and does not hold. For while political technology and scientific practice were delineating the ground of privileged space—and we were surely developing privilege despite all principle—we were privileged to begin with more space, it seemed, than could ever be staked out. As I have suggested, that accounts in some measure for the failures of memory, as it does for what people forget about the American theater—that it came belatedly into a culture that was itself an afterthought. To talk of space, then, in the American theater is in a sense a non sequitur. For there is a sense in which "America" is a non sequitur because of space. Seen from any distance, historicized, it is the history of a *geography*, or rather—until we reached land's end, not far from San Francisco, where they *started* spacing out—geography as history, which is not events in time, sequential or retrospective, but restless self-canceling and agitated space. "Some men ride on such space," said the poet Charles Olson, in his book on Melville, "others have to fasten themselves to a tent stake in order to survive." That is pretty much the history of space in the American theater, which, to the extent we can take it seriously, has been a history of survival. Or to adapt at the tent stake the poetic phrase from Watergate, "twisting, twisting in the wind."

For the theater was not only unacknowledged in the Bill of Rights as the source of any self-evident truth, but even when it appeared to be part of a social movement, as in the thirties, it never achieved the status, as in Germany, of something like a public utility. We must remember, on the contrary, that the theaters were closed in England in 1642 by ordinance of the Puritans. Not long after, banned themselves, more of them came to Plymouth Rock, where there were already clapboard meeting houses, which, as places of ritual, in its performance element, represented the sort of "poor theater" that if it could, would have abolished representation as an agency of the Devil. If our first plays were de-eroticized imitations of Restoration comedy, by the time the theater developed a reasonable facsimile of sexual maturity it was not only competing with the movies—not all that mature but still our major form—but was mixed up with show business, which, even before Ronald Reagan, became the major form of our politics. Whatever in our telegenic president was diminished by the scandal of laundered money to the contras, it was certainly not the proliferous space of the media, by which America remains at the center of the global expansion of the society of the spectacle. That, it would seem, is the outside limit of the dispossessed space of the American theater—aside from those worldwide "theaters of operation" for which, in the dramaturgy of diplomacy, Richard Nixon and Henry Kissinger were very conscious of working out a "Doctrine of Credibility" in the Aristotelian tradition. That doctrine has not entirely disappeared in the postmodern performance of the Bush administration that followed upon the breach, the break, the effraction in the Berlin Wall, with the subsequent expedition to the Gulf, under the auspices of the United Nations, after a dubious policy with Saddam.

But to reduce the scale again: there was not much theater of any consequence in America until about the 1920s, despite the entrepreneurial actor-managers in New York and occasional touring actors, of which the King and the Duke, in *Huckleberry Finn,* are the threadbare models. And the best of it ever since has been largely dispossessed, not always able to survive even barely. This is not the only reason Eugene O'Neill— by reluctant consent our greatest playwright—called his last will and testament, the saga of those long-brooding final plays, *A Tale of the Possessors Self-Dispossessed.* That is a spatial conception, a matter of real estate, just as much as with Willie Loman digging at night in the yard and trying to put roots in the ground. "I feel I've dealt with a lot of wasting circumstances as best I could, but I've had to waste my time defending my space, so to speak." That is not Willie Loman, but Arthur Miller himself (an interview in the *New York Times*), who once thought that a radical change in architectural space would revolutionize the stage, but who has just about realized that's a non sequitur as well, since a conception of a radical architecture would require in history a revolutionary stage.

This is not to imply that we have seen many innovative spaces, for all the new theaters in major cities. Some years ago the Ford Foundation published a book of designs for six ideal theaters, in which Miller expressed his positive view of architectural change. Most of these were versions of architectural ideas going back to the Bauhaus and other high modernist forms; they were great forms, but in theater space almost never used. When we think, however, that it was Gropius himself who designed the massive atrocity of the Pan Am Building that strides Park Avenue like a colossus, smothering the old Grand Central Terminal, one has a sense of the preemptive forces that prevail against an alternative architecture for theatrical space. Offhand, there are only three fairly innovative spaces I can think of that have actually been built, two of them in Texas. One was designed by Frank Lloyd Wright in Dallas. Those who have used it have complained about it since it was built, which does not convince me, however, for reasons I shall explain, that it is really an inadequate space. Actually, the circling ramps of Wright's Guggenheim Museum on Fifth Avenue, arguable as a space for showing paintings, are a rich conception of theatrical space, attractive to performative modes of postmodern art; and I have seen Meredith Monk and Dick Higgins, not your ordinary theater artists, use the space effectively. The other theater in Texas was designed by Paul Baker at Trinity College, near San Antonio. It is a large space with levels all around and swivel seats, meant to accommodate Baker's interest in simultaneous stagings.

The other unusual theater space is one I conceived in collaboration with the lighting designer Jules Fisher, with money provided by the late Walt Disney for the new California Institute of the Arts, in the foothills north of Los Angeles. Actually, it is a versatile syncopation of a space that was *given*, a rectilinear enclosure, but now with a modular floor that can be lifted by compressed air, and removable wall panels, also modular and sound porous, with adjustable baffles behind to focus the sound in any direction. With lightweight portable winches in a comprehensive grid, it is possible to situate any object imaginable, including actors and audience, at any point in space. But there is no point at all in space if you have no ideas to inform it, for the notion of manifest destiny is only an illusion of space. The disadvantage of being able to do almost anything in a theatrical space is that it can be intimidating, though it is no surprise that choreographers do better than directors with the Modular Theater.

But let me return to Arthur Miller and the issue of psychic space. Miller made the remark about defending his space when, after some years in which his plays were neglected, there was a revival of *Death of a*

Salesman. The revival was made possible by Dustin Hoffman, who wanted to play Willie Loman, and Miller felt grateful to him though the circumstances were, as he said, "humiliating." Knowing that it was hit or miss even with a superstar and despite his own distinction, Miller felt "thrown back into the marketplace" of Broadway, which somewhat sadly sums up his view of the American theater. Despite his aversion to what they have come to represent, his heart is in the old Broadway houses, built by the Schuberts and the Erlangers in nineteenth-century European style. But Miller's nostalgia is like Willie Loman's feeling about the human quality of the old railroad trains with their Indian names and solacing whistles, which are also a thing of the past. For most of these theater spaces have been or are being razed or, as on 42nd Street, are showing porno films. One exception was a recent play by Mac Wellman in the old Victory Theater, which searching out the space, from behind the teasers and tormentors to the motes in the mind's eye, summoned up the ghosts of its lamented past.

Meanwhile, there has been a kind of holding action against further rapacity as the city gears up for the rehabilitation of Times Square. Some of the theaters may eventually be restored, but it will not quite be gentrification. While the great theatrical space of Times Square is still illuminated at night, it is like a scene out of *Blade Runner,* a futuristic fantasy of miscegenated reality and polyglottal danger. As the old theaters have disappeared, some new ones are being built in the total environments like walled fortresses, the Marriott Hotel or the Uris Building, which, as a token of culture improving the real estate, may also provide a playing space. If you can afford the ticket, you can conveniently approach these spaces, without danger from the ethnic hordes. This is not, to keep things in perspective, what you can think of as real depth. "Had there been a working theater," Miller said, "it could have been or might have been otherwise. . . . We have no real theater. We have shows, which isn't really the same thing."

To stay with New York a moment: there are also, though Miller is understandably too jaundiced to mention them anymore, off-Broadway, which quickly became an adjunct of Broadway, and off-off-Broadway and even farther off, moving from TriBeCa to the Battery and Tomkins Park. There you can still find—in lofts and basements, galleries and converted garages, in abandoned public schools made into art spaces, in multimedia discos scaled down from the Palladium or the Danceteria—offbeat events, experimental work, nontheatrical performance or, in schlocky neopsychedelic venues in the far East Village, lesbian theater groups or a new breed of solo performers, particularly women, who seem to have tuned into Lenny Bruce through Deleuze and Guattari, as they pour out streams of manic aggressive filth on the whole shitty logocentric scene. If you go past Chinatown over the Manhattan Bridge to Atlantic Avenue in Brooklyn, you can escape this scene, maybe, at BAM— though most people who live in the neighborhood never go to the theater (as I never went when I grew up farther out on Atlantic Avenue). BAM is the staid and musty, once unused Brooklyn Academy of Music, with its old opera house and new open space; in both of these you can see the international New Wave, whose older generation, Robert Wilson or Pina Bausch, has been around for a while, or the newer wave, such as Anne-Teresa de Keersmaeker from Belgium or Hideki Noda from Japan. Manhattan is a volatile village with enough happening here or there that, if you look for it, you can probably find it, in some space or other: anything, however, except a space of continuity. Which as long as I can remember, they have been longing for in New York.

That's also what we were looking for in San Francisco, trying to put roots in the ground, when we gathered to do our first play in that workshop with rat shit under the staircase and, even during performance, banzai shouts coming up from below. That was when the notion of "Tributary Theater" was abroad in the land as a kind of natural truth, before it was named "decentralization." That truth had a double meaning in the ecology of the American theater. Whether one thought of the tributary of a river or the necessity of paying tribute, New York was the oceanic source and fountainhead of power. The doctrine of Tributary Theater had been promulgated throughout the country in the old yellow-covered *Theater Arts* magazine, which, however, also presented an unintended contradiction for us who read its earlier issues. For at the same time as it was preparing the territories for ideological subservience to New York in the twenties and the thirties, it was also recording from around the country what we can now see—like sexual freedom and feminism in the same period—as one of those premature revolutions that, if it wasn't merely aborted, has come round in a different form. I mean the lively growth of little theaters and community theaters in which amateur actors and directors—some of whom had gone abroad— were actually doing some experimental stagings derived from the European avant-garde, which *Theater Arts* was also reporting.

This may correct somewhat any wrong impression in what I have said: there were theaters before the fifties spread out in all that space.

But as they were, like other revolutionary prospects out of the thirties, waylaid and deflected by World War II, they were the late result of a retarded culture that, in the arts outside of New England, hardly took root until after World War I. When the university theaters first developed, they occupied a special place on the American landscape. Their developers were very conscious of fulfilling a social function. The theaters came about in the West and other remote regions after the establishment of the land grant colleges that later became the great state universities. After agriculture and the basic sciences came humanistic education and with it, eventually, the desire to make music, write, act, and to provide a local culture. The logical places to start were the universities themselves, with something of a constituency and a semblance of facilities. After that, one of the remarkable developments in American education, the early extension programs, or what we now call "outreach," was initiated. When they reached, they brought the theater with them in early versions of regional theater that fused with a burgeoning populism. The university where I now teach, in Wisconsin, was a leader in this development, literally sending people in snowshoes to direct plays in the rural areas. Thus, theater departments sprouted in North Carolina, Texas, Iowa, and upstate New York, and with them invigorating ideas out of surrealism, futurism, and expressionism brought back from the European capitals (in no doubt more innocent forms) ended up in the virgin forests. You will find to this day in North Carolina the sylvan amphitheater in which Paul Green created his epic historical dramas, optimistic pageants of American life, some of which, or dramas like them, were still being produced there until quite recently.

Somewhere, though, we made a mistake, for if you go now to the state universities, you will find some of the best "theater plants" and opera houses in the country, with huge stages, fly space, and the latest theater technology, but you are unlikely to find the early attitude of adventure and only minor gestures of outreach to the urban ghettos. This accounts for the fact—since many of those departments are now sending people into the job market—that even when there are new theaters in our cities, they quickly level to mediocrity or a mythologized professionalism, with the vaguest aesthetic and an invisible politics; when you think of what it might have been, all those nice theaters once not there, you almost want to start all over again with the empty spaces. You could trace the devolution of similar promise into symptoms of vacuity, and occasional senility, in the little theaters and community theaters that once flourished near the bayous of Louisiana or in the badlands of

Dakota. These, at least, had the excuse in these remote untutored places that they were isolated and not on great university campuses where Nobel prizes were being won in biochemistry or nuclear physics, while the theater departments were doing rehashed Broadway plays with *a* Shakespeare or *a* Chekhov and, maybe, in the new black box, a "collective creation" out of the sixties or a belated version of an absurdist play. That is one of the reasons why, to this day, though such departments can be very large and heavily budgeted, their programs are still looked upon with academic suspicion. As for the little theaters and community theaters that once abounded, many of them are disappearing as the landscape is suburbanized, and you can now go to a shopping mall and see something like *The Fantasticks* at a dinner theater.

Back again to land's end, where the particulars of my own experience will extend the view of the overall scene. When we started our work in San Francisco, in 1952, there were many little theaters performing up and down the Peninsula but, after a failed attempt at the end of the forties to establish one, no professional theater except what came from New York. There were a couple of "road houses" in the city, the Geary and the Curran, used for traveling musicals and the most brainless Broadway plays. We could hardly afford to rent such a theater to certify our professionalism, nor did we have an audience to fill it. This was the usual pattern in other American cities with aspiring groups and similar theaters, and to some extent this remains so to this day. The Geary and the Curran are still in San Francisco, one of them now used by the American Conservatory Theater, which replaced us not long after we went to Lincoln Center in 1965. There was a point, however, when we wanted to move "downtown." It was not so much that we had outgrown our automobile warehouse—a high-beamed, open, and flexible space— but with the freeway cut off, they were going to run a new one through our theater. And besides we wanted to "turn Equity"; that is, the actors would be unionized, and we would be recognized as professional, which had nothing to do with the quality of our work but only with an authorized space and the granting of a union card. I should add that we were almost unique in America in those years for attempting, against impermanence in the profession, to build a company, with continuity among the actors and, in the dynamic of the repertoire, the method of working; so, too, with the space in which we worked, though we continued to move about.

We eventually discovered a theater of 640 seats, whose balcony, pitched close to the stage, actually contributed to a sense of intimacy. It was on the second story of the Marines Memorial Hotel and had indeed been built for marines returning from the Pacific between the two wars. We liked performing there, but the character of the hotel caused a problem when the repertoire swerved, as it did, into the European avant-garde, which was relatively new and strange even in Europe. If there were anything like a censor, it would have come down hard, and the reviewers did on occasion behave like Jesse Helms. Here we are reminded that once space is socially constituted, and not an abstraction of traveling desire, it represents other problems. Thus, one night during a particularly lurid sequence in a brothel of Genet, a woman staying at the hotel who had unwittingly bought a ticket went screaming out of the balcony, calling out to the world, and the police, that we were criminally obscene—and that did cause something of a civic fuss even in a city that was on the verge of becoming the most sexually permissive in the United States.

It was also at the Marines Memorial Theater that the personal meaning of space came together with other issues in a single spontaneous gesture by the actor Robert Symonds, who was then playing Gogo in *Waiting for Godot*. Symonds is relatively well off today from things like *Dynasty* and other soaps, but when he was playing Gogo, he would have been starving to death, professional as we were, if he hadn't worked nights in the produce market, after rehearsal or performance. At the time he had an underground reputation as one of the best actors in the country, though he had chosen to stay out of New York. That was a gutsy thing to do in those days for somebody so talented, and he must have been feeling the strain of his idealism. You may remember the moment in the play when Gogo—speaking of failures of memory—cannot remember where they were, where they are, if this is the same tree, or what happened a moment before, and who says, when Didi keeps badgering him about it, "I'm not a historian!" All he knows, in the indeterminate space of Beckett's landscape, marked by that forlorn tree like a tent stake, is that he wants another carrot. At which point Symonds, summoning up the history of his own dispossession, the desire, the rage, a vertiginous impulse of self-assessment that could not be sustained in the space, burst beyond the staging and struck the proscenium with all his might, exclaiming for himself and Gogo, "I'm hungry!" as if he would, in order to appease that complicated hunger, abolish the theater itself. He was not only defending or staking out his space; he was, with that single blow of his fist, driven by desperation, virtually trying to remake it. I have seen a lot of theater and next to nothing like it since. The proscenium at the Marines Memorial Theater is about thirty feet high, solid concrete; needless to say, it did not fall.

We did, however, over the fourteen years we were in San Francisco, manage to extend the space. We performed in the auditorium of a high school near Fisherman's Wharf, a huge inhospitable place with a fore-stage the size of a basketball court and bad acoustics. We also performed on a basketball court and in more exotic places, like the mess hall of San Quentin (1,200 inmates there), the first time a theater production had ever played in a maximum security prison. There was a period, too, when we did a series of plays at the Bella Union Theater on the old Barbary Coast, reimmortalized by the Beats as North Beach. The Bella Union was the sort of place you might have expected to see in San Francisco before the earthquake of 1906—which it antedated—with Clark Gable and Spencer Tracy in the stalls. It had been a vaudeville house in its time and a whorehouse as well, and it is now showing Chinese movies. Down the hill from the Marines Memorial we had another theater for quite a few years, the Encore—a former nightclub in a long narrow basement, with a restored cable car as its lobby. Even though we played at one juncture in five such places simultaneously, and in the parks, on the beaches, in the aquarium, and even, once, on the Golden Gate Bridge, it was hard to think of The Actor's Workshop as an institution in the same sense as the German civic theaters that are, in dimensions inconceivable to us, subsidized by the state.

But to come back again to Symonds's gesture: if its magnificent impotence proved nothing else, it served to remind us that the primary architectural space of the theater is and always has been the body of the actor, subject as it is to the dematerializing power of the gaze that dissolves all space into itself. It is, of course, a transient architecture with a breathing skin, subject at any instant to the corrosions of time, the future in the instant constructed over a fault (as my own theater was in San Francisco, ontology doubled by geography, over the San Andreas Fault). A carnal space to begin with—blood, bone, tissue, muscle, nerves—the stage, the loft, the pit, the wings, the entire institutional superstructure of the theater hangs upon a breath, as the deepest sensation of performance seems to occur when an entire audience, for the moment, is not breathing at all. There is hardly a discipline of performance or acting method that does not center itself in breathing, and in the extremity of performance, literal to a fault, actor and spectator breathe each other. (If, however, we smell a fault in the theater, the fact is that it

"stinks of mortality," which is only more devastatingly than usual confirmed in *King Lear.*) They used to say, architecturally speaking, that all
you needed for the theater is two boards and a passion, but the truth of
the passion is such that you do not even need the boards, just the shadow of consciousness in every breath. The theater is (as I defined it some
years ago) the ocular site of "blooded thought." Any way you look at it,
what bleeds upon the boards if you have them is the inconsolable body
in its divisions. The actor out there, literally dying in front of your eyes,
reveals the space that is never seen. "We give birth astride of a grave,"
says Pozzo in Beckett's play, pointing in his blindness to the gravity of
that space. What is there is there even if the actor isn't, as she or he isn't,
inconsolably, in Beckett's *Breath.*

These are the not too concealed premises of all I have said about
space in the American theater. Sometimes, however, the actor is where
you expect nobody to be. Whereupon, let us raise our eyes from Pozzo's
grievous vision and observe another space. Some years ago, if you were
walking in lower Manhattan, you might have seen some bodies descending from the top of a building, as if they were walking there. What you
would have been seeing, if so, was one of Trisha Brown's "suspension
pieces," which occurred in various spaces, and with varying degrees of
existential jeopardy. There is a quotient of risk involved in the reconcep-
tion of space, not only in *Star Wars,* though it may take an escalation of
risk to make us see it. The dramatist Heiner Müller has been very much
influenced by such experiments and other aspects of dislocated space in
postmodern art and performance. When Müller was asked, a while before the reunification of Germany, where he would prefer to see and direct his plays, he picked a site in America, at the doubled omphalos of
the marketplace of the world: "I would like to stage Macbeth," he said,
"on top of the World Trade Center for an audience in helicopters." It is
not a bad concept, though perhaps a little extravagant, requiring not
only official permits but a fairly considerable budget.

So let us take another approach. When the French equilibrist Philippe
Petit stretched a line in the middle of the night and, virtually without an
audience, walked between the two towers of the World Trade Center, it
was as if he had lifted to its meridian dispossession itself, the notion of a
"public solitude" (Stanislavski's term) that had receded with unstable
identity and the costliness of space and production into the meditative
or solipsistic element of "solo performance." Up there in the awesome
draft, what you would have seen if you saw was a body so adept it hardly seemed carnal; it was more like an ideograph of the mind aloft at its

extremity. And while we hardly see such theater every day, it is very close, I think, to the solitary discipline and rigor of desire that (with a certain feeling for gravity) materializes culture, high culture, in the vertigo of a theater space.

(1993)

4. From Red Hill to the Renaissance

Rehearsing the Resistance

Lest performance turn out to be misrepresentation, I want to advance the terminal date of our subject, the San Francisco Renaissance, by a few years and narrow the perspective to my own experience. Public as it was, and relatively expansive, this experience of my theater work in San Francisco is actually narrower (in what may be the perversity of my own mind) than the much more hermetic experience of my later work, which intersects the much wider range of performance, in and out of the theater, that may be seen on the landscape now. But then, while history may repeat itself, it ought not to leap ahead of itself. I wish I could say that as it was in poetry so it was in theater, but it wasn't. So, as it was then, the lay of the land:

I remember Buena Vista Park when it was sylvan, idyllic, unoccupied, and the incline from which it rose still known as Red Hill, the name it was given out of the politics of the thirties. During most of the years of The Actor's Workshop, I lived beside the park—more or less the mathematical center of the city—just above Haight Street when the Haight was still straight. The Actor's Workshop began a short walk away, in a loft behind a judo academy on Divisadero Street, a long narrow room with a fireplace and rat shit under the stairs that later became the vestry of the Ebenezer Baptist Church. From my study in the basement of our house on Red Hill—where my partner Jules Irving and I often planned our seasons and argued policy—there was a magnificent view of the city toward the bridge spanning the bay. But so far as performance was concerned, the landscape was very different then, the closets still closed, no gays, no feminists, nothing known as performance art, no spectacles on the beaches or theater in the streets. But as Clov says in Beckett's *Endgame*, something was taking its course, and it soon became apparent that there was within the circumference of The Actor's Workshop, in its later years especially, various kinds of experiment that prepared the ground for the newer kinds of performance.

Some of that was inherent in the productions, and some of it we did after-hours, moonlighting in our own theater, since the production schedule (at various times in three theaters simultaneously) was over-committed, to say the least. Some of those involved were not from The Workshop, but from the San Francisco Art Institute or the Tape Music Center (that also started in the fifties); and some of those from the company, actors and directors, are now part of the history of experimental theater.

In a book I published in the early sixties—a manifesto on behalf of decentralization, based on the first ten years of our work in San Francisco—there was an epigraph from a poem by Kenneth Rexroth, one of the tutelary figures of the emergent renaissance. I first met Kenneth at the Hungry I, where he was performing his poetry with a jazz combo, as a kind of warm-up for Mort Sahl. If I am remembering correctly, the lights for the performance were being run by Alvah Bessie, who had faded into obscurity as one of the Hollywood Ten. We were just coming out of the McCarthy era, at one end of which—as a young instructor at San Francisco State College—I had worked for the repeal of the loyalty oath known as the Levering Act, and at the other end of which—aging fast at The Actor's Workshop—I had staged Arthur Miller's *The Crucible,* a play about witch-hunting with a dubious analogue, though it aroused the liberal Left in San Francisco as it had not done in New York.

The poem from which I took the epigraph was not on the program that night, but there was a riff of old protest in Kenneth's performance, as if eroticizing the Wobblies, whom in his populist mode he had always admired. Gyrating, perspiring, he assailed the banality of the age of Ike with its Silent Generation and gray-flanneled emotion that seemed to make everybody old before his time and, in the libidinal economy of pre-Esalen California, seemed like the bottom line before the dissidence to come. At the End of Ideology, there was something more than nostalgia. Kenneth was talking art, he was also talking politics, and to all those who had sold out the imagination, Kenneth was unsparing: "Who killed the bright-headed bird?" he wrote. "You did, you son of a bitch."

These lines became the epigraph for a chapter of *The Impossible Theater* titled "The Iron Curtain," and the structural rhythm of the book was mainly developed around the imagery and rhetoric of the Cold War, in which the state of our theater seemed written, as if it were the Energy Crisis that haunted the psyche long before the price-fixing of OPEC and the mining of the Persian Gulf. Belated to begin with, the theater in America was, so far as I could see (having come to it belatedly), a history of frustration and incapacitated vision, a laying waste of powers, hypocrisy, feebleness, careers in ruin, and the repeated betrayal of every promise of collectivity. At the heart of that was the self-defeating behavior of those who worked in the theater who, even when three thousand miles from Broadway, kept measuring their talent and achievement against what was happening there. Which—so it seemed to me then, as it still does now—wasn't very much. Certainly it wasn't much in the most basic material sense, since over 92 percent of the actors were unemployed, and those who were employed were employed ignominiously, in jobs that mostly insulted their intelligence.

"Stay here," I used to exhort them, "things are happening in San Francisco." "I love San Francisco," they would say, the last strains of idealism up against the wall. "If you could only pay me a living wage—." "If we could pay you a living wage, we wouldn't need you!" Things were happening in San Francisco, but they would go anyhow. Not all of them, but enough to undermine morale, undo a season, and keep us unstable. That is why, even before the epigraph from Rexroth, there was, in the first chapter of the book, titled "Fallout," an outburst of my own against everything in the theater that seemed to divest us of possibility in the stalemate of the Cold War. It may seem, in the trickle-down passions of the eighties, mediated and deconstructed, a little intemperate and not at all postmodern, but—as I wrote in the opening paragraph of the book—"I may as well confess right now the full extent of my animus: there are times when, confronted with the despicable behavior of people in the American theater, I feel like the lunatic Lear on the heath, wanting to 'kill, kill, kill, kill, kill!'"

There were in the Bay Area, at the time, others who went about their theater work in a milder register. There had been, actually, while I was a graduate student at Stanford, a good deal of community and little theater activity on the Peninsula, from the Hillbarn in San Mateo right up to the Sierras. And in San Francisco itself a group of Quakers and pacifists, some of whom had been conscientious objectors in World War II, started the Interplayers, from which the Playhouse later broke off and did plays ranging from Cocteau to James Broughton in a theater adjacent to the Buena Vista Café. The old Interplayers had done a repertoire of new, boulevard, and classical plays (with the most elegant theater programs I have ever seen in America, and I was glad to hear recently that Adrian Wilson, who designed them, received a MacArthur Award for the books he has done since[1]). These theaters were active in a relatively collegial way as The Workshop developed, but they had nothing of our combativeness, nor the actors we managed to keep (some of their best defecting to us), nor finally our more Faustian ambition that, for better or worse, led us to up the ante on the scope of our productions, to articulate a repertoire as if it were a mission, and to relate the plays to each other in a dialectical way. That is why if you saw our production of *King Lear,* you might or might not have liked it, but you would have known, if you had thought it over, and had seen other things, that it could not have been done as it was done, or looked the way it did, without our production of *Endgame* and the work we had done on Genet.

We wrestled with issues of acting method and theatrical style that we never quite solved, and there were turbulent arguments about them. Yet some of the more questionable things we did—like the hypertrophy of image and petrification of motion in the ballroom scene of *Galileo* or the solipsistic repetitions and overextension of play, the sinking figures of the actors on the silent foam-rubber stage of our second version of *Waiting for Godot,* with its toadstool mound made of auto parts and see-through curtain that could never get it up—anticipated ideas of performance that we are more familiar with today. So we came to be familiar, through the "polymorphous perversity" of the sixties, not only with the nudity but the B&D and S&M, in our productions of Genet. Some of the things we did with music, like laminating the stage with sound so that it seemed either immense or its contours virtually changed, suggested possibilities that have hardly been followed up.

At the same time, with the circuit of regional theaters beginning to develop as a faint facsimile of the state theaters in Europe, we were reconceiving our purposes ideologically on a national scale. It was on that scale that something lethal in me took over when, incessantly on the edge of bankruptcy, I thought about the prospects of The Workshop, the resistance within it to the best ideas we had, and—compared to other countries—the humiliating profession of theater in America.

It was the murderous side, as it is in *Lear,* of the "howl howl howl

howl howl," the impotent rage of "the best minds of the generation" as the postwar period subsided into an "armed madhouse." That was, as you may recall, Allen Ginsberg's description of the military-industrial complex with its policy of a Balance of Terror, which was—as we founded The Workshop in 1952—about to be somewhat unbalanced in the first of our undeclared wars, a queer sort of "shooting peace" in Korea. But while my own theater developed to some extent off the threshold of that rage, it was—for most of the actors, who were apolitical—more of a melodramatic function of a paranoid imagination, namely mine, which they more or less indulged as an impetus to cohesion, so long as the reviews were good. (I might add that one of the reviews of *The Impossible Theater* in San Francisco—by a drama critic who thought himself supportive but whom, with consummate tact, I had publicly declared a fool—compared it to *Mein Kampf.*) Despite the emerging fervor of an ideological position and a developing repertoire of what were, then, offbeat plays that are, now, part of the canon of modern drama, The Workshop was always an ambivalent organization. Even when taking risks, it was divided against itself, a theater becoming a civic institution associated with the avant-garde.

When the continent began to tilt, and money flowed out of corporate headquarters in New York for the first pump priming of the regional theaters, this issue was always troubling to the Ford Foundation, which gave us the money but found us strange. You might find it strange, but when we received the first of our grants, for half a million dollars, there was a big controversy in the company as to whether we should accept it—the older people who had been starving to death awaiting it with elation and the younger people who had fully identified with the more dissident thrust of The Workshop arguing that if we took it we would be selling out. There was a political axis from these younger members of The Workshop to the protest movement developing in Berkeley, and some who had shown up in San Francisco to be with The Workshop also felt an immediate affinity with the Beats. This was a division within the theater that persisted until Jules Irving and I were invited to take over the directorship of the Repertory Theater at Lincoln Center, and a large part of the company left with us for New York, whereupon some, like Ronnie Davis—who had founded the San Francisco Mime Troupe as an offshoot of The Workshop—were convinced that we had sold out.

Those of us who started The Workshop, as just that, a studio for actors, were not part of the Beat Generation. Yet for some years, in our scene shop in the Mission District, there hung high over the rehearsal area a collective portrait of various of the major Beats who lived then in San Francisco. They were at tables in the Polk Street cafeteria, conversing, reading, or writing, with a solitary figure seated to the side in the foreground, faced into the canvas, observing. The painting was done by Robert LaVigne, one of the most talented artists of that generation (perhaps the most diversely gifted), who eventually became our scene designer, and when he was in his perfect mind, the best scene designer in America. He was also in the portrait; but the solitary figure, that was me, though I never hung out in the Polk Street cafeteria. It was LaVigne's notion that I should be there, but positioned, it seemed, with the specular ambivalence of a superego. And there was a kind of truth or poetic justice in that. For while I did testify at the *Howl* trial, as an "expert witness" for the defense, Allen Ginsberg and I—who became acquainted through LaVigne (who had lived with Peter Orlovsky and had painted the famous portrait of him with which Allen reportedly fell in love)— would have disagreed as to who were really the best minds of the generation. I not only preferred another kind of poetry, but the fact of the matter was that while our scene shop in the Mission eventually became one of the centers of drug traffic in San Francisco, wildly experimenting with LSD, most of those in the company were—in what they were beginning to call "lifestyle"—a good deal more bourgeois than Beat, and very much oriented to the New York theater.

That, when we began, was virtually the state of the art. Which was why, when experiment began to occur within the company as a sort of subversive momentum that corresponded to my own interests, there was always a certain resistance. And in the years when The Workshop was becoming more embattled—partially for the obscurity of the plays, sometimes with charges of obscenity, or for politicizing the theater— some of the most gifted actors in our company had very mixed feelings. As we think of the theater's relation to the San Francisco Renaissance, that has to be understood, because I am talking about some of the best actors in the city (a few of whom are still performing there and still considered among the best). No matter how we justified this experiment or that, they were trying to overcome a history of timorousness and subservience that was a legacy of their profession. The term isn't used any more, but even into the fifties there was still the notion of Tributary Theater, promulgated in the twenties by the (then) rather elegant, sometimes art nouveauish *Theater Arts* magazine. Whatever was happening in the other arts or in the culture at large, that was in the theater still the law of the land. We were tributary in a double sense: to New York as the creative source and fountainhead of power, to which all the rivulets and streams of theater activity around the country, the little theaters and community theaters and university theaters (there was no such thing yet as the present regional theaters) would in turn pay tribute by imitation.

San Francisco should have been, it seemed, too prideful or sophisticated for that. With what was at the time—we forget this in the age of AIDS—the highest alcoholic and suicide rate in the United States, this landlocked harbor with its lyric bridges, this golden boomtown grown urban on a fissure, with its labor tradition and autodidactic dockworkers, its Bohemian Club and Barbary Coast, was celebrated by a local columnist as "Baghdad by the Bay." But as with the laid-back dominion of psychedelia, the reality of its sophistication was yet to come. The reputation was in part a transitional illusion. As I used to tell the members of our company who—counting the empty seats for some of the best work we ever did—complained that we were dealing with a myth, we were far ahead of those cities that had no myth to live up to. Where the arts were concerned, there were stirrings. There were unrecognized prospects about to be tapped. There would soon be dropouts from all over the country, bringing some talent with them. But at the time I am speaking of we were not always sure that the illusion had a future, and the problem was to some extent the amenities of the city itself. For the living truth of the living theater was that while San Francisco was on the brink of something, it was a rather somnolent place with a topographical splendor so comfortable to stay at home in that it hardly needed a culture, though it seemed to remember having had one, including a colorful history of old stock companies that had, along with some old theater houses, like the Alcazar, disappeared.

Meanwhile, it was acquiring a worldwide reputation for the culture it did not quite have, for it was still without the public means to make good on the myth. One of the reasons was what they called at the time "brown money," that is, money that does not circulate, Nob Hill money, discolored for want of use, at least not for the arts, which is why many of the better artists from the area headed for Los Angeles. For even more obvious reasons, so did the better actors, when they did not go to New York. One of the city's mayors, during the period of The Workshop, was an enlightened milkman who shared Kruschev's feeling about abstract art and who wondered, after our theater had operated in the city for eleven years and had developed its own international reputation for rather innovative work, what we had done to deserve a handout from the hotel tax. One of the things that, in fact, gave some scale to the city's thought about the arts was our leaving it—when there was a public furor to build us the theater we had always asked for, in order to keep us there.

That was the scene, as we knew it in San Francisco, before the Haight was theatricalized and they started "making the scene." The Beats were beginning to occupy North Beach shortly after we started, but like the freeway that had been stopped by the environmentalists just short of the Ferry Building, it was a city in suspension then, or in abeyance, and with all its natural assets a little cut off. Certainly for our purposes, in the theater. But then, cut off from what? I was much more engaged with what was happening in literature, poetry, and the other arts. I eventually profited much from working in our productions with painters and sculptors (e.g., aside from LaVigne, Lee Romero, Judy Davis, Robert Hudson), and nothing in the theater seemed as valuable to me as my long collaboration with Morton Subotnick, who had founded the Tape Music Center and was our music director in San Francisco and subsequently in New York, and later joined me in the conception of Cal Arts. I had not quite realized yet the degree to which my own instincts were moving, along with our younger directors (e.g., Davis, Lee Breuer, Ken Dewey, André Gregory), toward alternative modes of performance, but in the late fifties I told Jules that I had to get away, that there was nothing to be learned in San Francisco nor in America for that matter, not about the theater, and that is when I first went to Europe.

I returned imbued with the idea of *théâtre populaire,* a term associated with the Avignon festivals of Jean Vilar, but which also applies to a movement that includes the work of Planchon, Strehler, Littlewood, and the Berliner Ensemble of Bertolt Brecht, to which—after we did the American premiere of *Mother Courage*—I had been invited. It was an idea of theater that would—as in the modernist dream of a unity of socialism and surrealism—create an audience of students, workers, and intellectuals. For various reasons that I have written about elsewhere, the theaters abroad never really developed such an audience, and we never even approached it here. I don't think anything like it is possible in the United States, nor a genuine renaissance, so far as it carries along with it the image of great cities and, by whatever questionable means, the institutionalization of artistic powers, the civic endorsement by which you are both unburdened and unembarrassed.

When I returned from Europe, people were talking about the Cultural Explosion, another myth. And the animus of my book, that manic aggressive outburst, was not only an indictment of that myth with the theater at large, but a sort of internal monologue with the recalcitrant in our company who resisted just about every experiment that eventually made our reputation—as well as the indifference of a city that only took us seriously, no matter what we did, to the extent that we were confirmed in New York. That happened with increasing frequency, but even a review in the *New York Times* made only a temporary dent in the provinciality.

We developed a loyal following over those years, or we would never have survived at all (though some of the leftists who liked *The Crucible* were either puzzled or betrayed when we started doing things like *Waiting for Godot;* some of them never came back). When we left, however, in 1965, the public dismay was such, and the publicity, that when ACT set up on our premises at the Marines Memorial Theater, it had, before it began, a subscription about five or six times larger than what we had managed to develop in roughly fourteen years in San Francisco. Whatever ACT was or became, I don't suppose it is associated with what came to be known as the San Francisco Renaissance. We were there for its beginnings, and it was despite all a very exciting time—but if there was anything like a renaissance in the most authentic sense, it was finally accomplished in our absence.

(1988)

5. A Dove in My Chimney

Political theater and private problems:[1] so far as I can see, political theater was never at anything but a low ebb in this country. There was certainly an admirable fervor and wide-spreading participatory promise in
the Federal Theater of the thirties before it succumbed to war mobiliza-
tion and charges of creeping socialism. The Group Theater had (divided) political sentiments but no real politics, and its better aspirations
were bifurcated by Broadway. Who can say, retrospectively, that there is
very much worth preserving in the textual remains? What was called the
Third Theater of the sixties and seventies has since been renounced as
inadequate by those (like Robert Brustein) who avidly named it when it
was around. I think it was one of the major delusions of that period.
Much of it was sponsored by people who might have known better except for the way we were all damaged mentally by Vietnam. While it
provided a certain factitious relief from the established theater, think
how shallow (callow?) it all was politically, when you compare it with
mature political thought in the theater, from Büchner (young as he was)
to Brecht, in Planchon or Mnouchkine; or in what may be the greatest
play on politics in the century (though I have never seen a production
worthy of it, not even Blin's at the Odéon, charged by the Algerian War),
Genet's *The Screens,* which is most revolutionary in its exposure of the
political illusion. But then it is possible to suffer from what you expose,
as Genet did when he came over to Chicago and, for less reliable reasons, simpered over the Black Panthers.

I still think the most powerful political statement in the theater since World War II was *Waiting for Godot,* though it had no political intentions whatever. What it did was to anticipate the most effective strategy of activist politics—the one renounced when the rage took over—and that was an instrumental passivity or negative capability. There is still a crucial difference between the posturing and the politics, and what went on in the theatrical orbit of the Movement had no political theory, of which there is very little in American thought and even less in the theater. What we are left with, today, is vague participatory residues. What else is there to do when the public sphere is insufferably baffling? Then, the economic problems: even the small groups are now finding it hard to survive, with foundation money playing it closer to the vest, and the universities with stripped budgets. Then look at the nature of the public problems, like the core of the reactor at Three Mile Island. Alarming as it is, we guess about the dangers. The locus of complaint is not what it became with Vietnam. The indecisiveness of Carter is our public image. He may be better than what we deserve, and I hear nothing from his opponents, or the remains of the radical Left, that knows any better.

The privacy in the theater that still has to do with working out problems, getting in touch with yourself, learning how to share and support, is as boring as it always was, though in private life quite as necessary. I would rather leave it to counseling, that insipid legacy of encounter theory. For myself, I care only for that mode of privacy in performance that is the sheerest edge of a confession—but of the kind Marx spoke of in his essay "For a Ruthless Criticism of Everything Existing," the nature of criticism itself, which is *to be confessed;* that is, to understand where you are complicit, no bullshit, conspiring with that in which you disbelieve. That privacy is an ungrounding from which to proceed—ground zero: *what are we acting for? for whom? where?* and what difference does it make? since if you say anything important nobody is likely to be listening. It means parsing out inside the personal ingredients of action, an *incidence,* when everything socially prevails against it. I suppose it comes to remembering that when action goes out of the window, the readiness is all. The liability is solipsism, the self-canceling subject of my own work.

I am not quite sure what Chaikin meant by his being without a course. Nothing programmatic? taking things as they come? perhaps returning to a kind of problem solving? There is some of that in what I was doing, the pragmatism congenitally American; but if I have no course at present, it is because my work has been suspended. (The reasons are too complex to describe here, though I may have alluded to them when I was in Paris. Meanwhile, surely, "Something is taking its course," as in the enigma of *Endgame.*) I do not know if that represents some necessary recuperation from the shellshock of its sheer difficulty or a final abandonment of the theater after more than thirty years. Or perhaps I should reverse it, for the theater may be abandoning me. We may have been working at some untenable limit of the form, still wanting to *be theater* and not, as with Grotowski, having recourse to some paratheatrical alternative. In any case, the work was far more hermetic and, I think, heuristic, than what most of the other groups were doing, narrowing the terms of its possibility, including a possible audience. That had nothing to do, however, with wanting more private performance or reducing the scope to a solo, although the writing I am doing now may amount to something like that. For I did say in a book recently finished—which derives a theory of theater from the work with KRAKEN—that if none of that work ever existed, if I were simply making it up on the page as I go along, the theory would be no less true. I do not really believe that, but—with a kind of psychic marginality that is eminently theatrical—very nearly so. I have in fact been thinking of a series of stagings that would take place solely in consciousness. (There is a quite venerable tradition, as you know, to support that, particularly in Shakespearean criticism: what cliffs of fall, say, for Gloucester's suicide, as devastatingly perilous, in any production, as that which exists in the privacy of mind?) But I check myself there with a criticism like that by Marx of the young Hegelians, who took everything back into consciousness that they could not alter in the world.

Well, as Kafka reminds us, in the battle between you and the world, back the world. The world is pretty stubborn, and the problem for our better practitioners with larger public instincts is how to find out there a suitable apparatus for performance that will keep them out of the closet. Wilson seems to have managed it, at least in Germany, with an entrepreneurial brilliance matching his visual gifts. Then there is Germany's predilection for operatic musication. To use your terms, I don't think (for myself) it is so much a refusal of long-term goals as not having the means any longer for the scale on which I would like to work, and not seeing any institutional resource out of which it might come. Nor are many of us willing to continue doing what we have done for so many years to sustain a group as the people in it grow older and are constrained to think more sensibly of neglected aspects of their lives, the attritions that go with theatrical survival. (I heard a very dedicated actor speak recently with something like rage, after seeing a doctor he could not afford, about the fact that he is approaching middle age without a medical plan.) Nor do we have the sustaining versions of community to accommodate the groups that were once striving for it. Now, too, belated ambition is also taking over, the desire to get one's just deserts after years of unrewarded sacrifice. Some of us just run out of ideas, although I would like to believe I am inexhaustible myself.

The forms of theater that interest me are those that bear upon the self-reflexive problems of my own work. There are (as you suggest) resemblances in, say, Richard Foreman, but remote. His thought processes are too distanced for my nature from the self-determining powers of the actor. In the theater that I value the actor is still the rudimentary force. I rather prefer, then, the work of the Mabou Mines, because while it is equally sophisticated about the art world and its minimalist and conceptualist trends, there is still an ongoing allegiance to the last-ditch humanism of Beckett. Lee Breuer was an assistant of mine for some years at The Actor's Workshop in San Francisco. He was always inventive and knew where the action was in the other arts, but he came to us thinking about Dostoyevsky, who could never abide our post-phenomenological glee over the disappearance of man (or his represented image) into impersonal structures. If you think them over, the participatory structures of the New Dance and New Theater were, for all the ethos of non-authoritarianism, very tyrannical indeed. Presumably nonprofessionals could participate; that siphoned out inhibiting old skills. It also siphoned out discriminating judgment. The participatory experience was a rather cheap substitute for choice and investigation by the actor. The old bourgeois authority was displaced and disguised in those structures, not too disguised at that. One of the emblematic images is Foreman at his sound-and-light console ringing the bells and blowing the whistles within a prefabricated scheme where the actors, such as they were, behaved like puppets. It is a very intelligent scheme, and I respect the work. I never complained about authority when it had a good mind. But I was looking for another sort of intelligence in the theater, while experimenting with my own gifts of authority (*wanting* to give it up, no easy thing to do). I mean the intelligence of the thinking body, not mere body language (what they meant by that), but intelligence first of all. Speaking of the participatory illusion, I still think it is one of the major experimental issues in the theater, as it is in political life.

The trouble with its assertion before—that is, a participatory theater— is that its intelligence was taken for granted. There was the idea that if you bring many heads together, in exercised bodies, and in performance letting the audience in, you will come out with a better form of theater and politics. Forgive my unregenerate elitism, but that is patent nonsense. You cannot take the collecting of intelligence for granted at all. There may be good reason, as in democracy, for settling for less, but in either democracy or art, what we are really after, or should be, is no mere function of numbers. As for my own natural instincts, they invariably trust the single intelligence over the group (and with skepticism about the degree of intelligence in any case). Put a lot of heads together and they usually knock themselves into insensibility, as they often did in the Movement and the theater of that period. I cannot tell you how many actors I have known whose intelligence I have respected offstage, who seemed to me plain stupid onstage. But, as an experimental proposition: how to make a group think better than a single mind? Ah, that is a consummation devoutly to be wished, and well worth the going after. But there must be method to the madness. It is what we wanted to achieve in KRAKEN, where a kind of ruthless criticism was inseparable from the methodology of the collective process. It put the screws to loose thinking. What we did in, say, *Elsinore,* whatever its virtues or faults, I could not have even vaguely imagined on my own. I would not have believed I could have thought some of what it eventually thought, and to this moment I am not sure I can really think it all without that acting body of thought before the mind's eye.

You notice how much emphasis I am putting on *thought.* I mean it, too, in the specular way that, psychoanalytically, if elusively, was defined by Lacan. Or perhaps it is better to think of it as precise but indefinable. However you think of it, the theater is *speculation*; if it is not that, I am not personally interested. Which is why there is not much here that, so far as I can see, *needs* to be seen to *be thought.* The desire *to see*—right on the edge of what, perhaps, cannot be seen, or should not, or has to *be thought* before seen—that is what I look for in the theater. Who is looking like that? Not many: the few names I have mentioned—Wilson, Breuer, Foreman—differentially; less known or hardly known at all, Joe Dunn and Irja Koljonen. Their virtually disappearing conceptual pieces would seem to be from the art world but are, rather, exactingly from the theater, where the actor's labor, even if nearly invisible, is with unwavering rigor the uncentering locus of thought.

I can understand the turn to the classics in France, not only the ancients but the canonical modernists. Every now and then I find myself talking about Chekhov with a warmth one reserves for old love or cherished memory. There are any number of things from other forms that I would like to see in the theater. I would like to do something, for instance, with Rilke's *Duino Elegies* or *The Notebooks of Malte Laurids Brigge,* which by the way has an account of the capillary action in Ibsen, more indiscernible than a subtext, that resembles the perceptual tracery of our own thought—and that would, in its alchemical intensity, satisfy Artaud, who hated Ibsen. I cannot imagine myself, however, returning to the classics straight up. It would have to be through the alembic of this more labyrinthine work I have been alluding to. The irony, maybe, is that it was anticipated years ago by the production, say, of *King Lear* we did in San Francisco, which came out of early investigations of Beckett and Genet. So it would be like turning and turning in a widening gyre. . . .

The operatic emotion does not mean much to me in itself. The operatic work of Wilson is quite another matter, and hardly emotional in the climactic sense of the other operatic tradition that Chaikin seems to be referring to. Years ago I spoke of "risking the baroque" and did productions on that crazy premise (unbelievably extrapolated to the edge of collapsing, which they some times did). Yet I have always distrusted larger-than-life aspirations, not because I do not like magnitude. Thrones Dominations Principalities Powers—the Faustian ambition is still there, but it is the shadow of a magnitude that really attracts. To be clearer: emotion does not impress me, which is not to say that an alienating cool does either. It all depends on what emotion, what for. As I often said to the actors in KRAKEN, emotion is cheap. And as we see it in the theater, it mostly is easily producible. I saw Pavarotti giving a demonstration recently on television. Whenever he was asked how he could approach a certain note or technical difficulty, he simply pressed his finger into his temple and said it was a matter of brains. Réjane had the right idea about emotion when asked how she could cry on cue: *"C'est mon métier."* So, what else is new? What I am after is the shape and cost of emotion, the neural surge of its afterthought, every minuscule pulse of its elusive meaning, like the slippage of the signifying chain. One of the fiercest emotions of a piece we did recently, a theatrical essay on Shakespeare's sonnets, came out of the line "Ah, thought kills me that I am not thought." When I think of it, it virtually tears me apart emotionally.

The idea of a totally unmusical theater seems like a loaded question. Aristotle told us in the *Poetics* that one of the parts of theater is music, meaning more than we mean by a part. The idea of a theater approaching, as with the Symbolists, the condition of music has been around for a while—now one might think of the disappearance of the actor as Mallarmé thought of the elocutory disappearance of the poet. There would then be nothing but an incantation before the eye. To reverse that process and evaporate the music? Unimaginable, but worth imagining. There is nothing new about a Theater of Images, although we know well that there is theater that is more or less iconic or ideographic, and in which you are made more conscious of progression by images, as with Wilson or Foreman, than you are in the finest performance of Chekhov, where to be conscious of the image as an image is, in the appropriateness of the playing, to divest the image of its surreptitious power. The same is true of its music. Is there anything more musically cadenced in Wilson than the perambulating baby carriage at the end of *The Three Sisters,* which you can hear more profoundly than the military band? "Balzac was married in Berdichev." That disjunct line from the newspaper, another music, posing as prose. Systole. Diastole. Even when the stage is empty, that music is there, if there is anybody looking, and something to see. Brook's notion of the empty space was a naive reduction. The stage is filled so that it may be silenced. Still, there is music and music.

Still life. Rigor mortis. If the theater gives birth astride of a grave, it is manic with motion, to which photography thought, for an instant of history, it might bring a halt. That illusion was put in its place by Ibsen, quite early, when he set the habitat of the wild duck behind the photographic studio. All these problems—including the primacy of music and image—are problems of dispossessed motion, the sense that life is running away from (by) itself, and maybe needs a fix, but keeps moving, and it nearly drives us mad, like Troilus, "Instance, O instance" (I may be quoting a little wrong), but you get the panic-making idea that photography has now, by giving us the illusion of fixation, compounded. I just wrote a long essay on theater and cinema—and the "scopic drive"— which places the field of action between the curtain and the screen. There has been in recent years a lot of theorization of the screen, but since the Romans invented the *aulaeum,* never much about the curtain—a strange phenomenon (about which I have written elsewhere), its appearance to begin with, then its rising, falling, parting, draping; full curtains, half-curtains, and then its disappearance.

There is a dove in my chimney behaving like Gertrude Stein.[2] It is the subspeech of a solo performance for which actors would be superfluous. That is not exactly true of Stein's theater pieces, but she does have more than one thing in common with that logorrheic bird. It is a vestibulary theater taking place in the inner ear, where you want to *watch out,* because that is where you can really lose balance, if you mistake the song of spring for the murmur of history. That is not the reason, however, why Stein was the patron saint of the Judson Church during the camp shows of the sixties. She was part of a series of slapstick caprices that were in-groupy occasions for showing off. It was fun but not much, nor anything everlasting. It would be like having my neighbor, a Chinese psychiatrist from Singapore, come over and listen to the dove—except we would have moved through the seventies to a more private kind of theater. We went through the winter without a damper on the chimney, cold comfort, which nevertheless kept us warm. That is more like Stein.

Stein would have preferred to draw the curtain, but which way (open or closed) you can never really be sure. Which is what I should probably do now. She should probably hold her peace because the implication of her writing is that she is being produced all the time. But then we live in a world of information systems in which redundancy is the order of the day. To get through the noise, like that of this typewriter—a paradigm of the issue of continuity and discontinuity. (There goes the dove.) Who can help but be interested? It is happening to me.

(1980)

6. *Elsinore*

An Analytic Scenario

In the fall of 1975, the KRAKEN group started on a project that gathered momentum from the work already in progress, which was not, however, progressing very far. It was rich and strange but tautological, circling back upon itself—not really an impasse, but a proliferation of questions at the unnerving ends of thought, not coming to a conclusion but driving us to distraction. We were really looking for a subject, and months of rehearsal seemed to collect in a state of mind that caused us to turn to *Hamlet,* not because we wanted to do that play in any conventional sense, but because the play, we thought, was somehow rehearsing us. When we defined the state of mind, asking ourselves where we were, we said we were in Elsinore. When we described the way we worked, we called it *ghosting.* We found ourselves thinking through *Hamlet* as if *Hamlet* were thinking through us, and as if without the play we could not think at all. The play had become a language preempting what we thought.

The actors were never assigned roles in the Shakespearean text, but they knew it in its entirety, all the words words words. In the self-reflexive investigations that continued for about a year, the *whole play* was always present at any moment of thought like the whole structure of language in every single act of speech. If, as the work came into performance, you looked around for Hamlet, he seemed to have disappeared into the structure. You could not identify him with anyone (or more) of the actors at any given moment, but only as a transformational presence in a gravitational field. He was out there in the structure as an energizing source, identifiable only as a skein of vanishings, or the principle of indeterminacy in the spoor of thought. The actors in KRAKEN were, for all this emphasis on thought, extremely adept with their bodies. They could act, literally, standing on their heads. The performance was, thus, volatile and verbal, charged in body and mind, like an ideographic charting of the fever in the brain.

The following text was prepared, with the assistance of James Eigo, out of the improvisational studies done by the actors. The images were recorded during rehearsals, analyzed, and sorted out, but none of the writing was done until after about six months of work. I have left the scenario pretty much as it was, a dialectical incitement to the actors. What they encountered on the page mirrored and deflected what they had been doing, questioned or provoked it further, abraded the edge of an image, changed its contours. Sometimes they could barely recognize what they had done, which became an issue in the work; sometimes they wanted desperately to repossess it against the "authority" of the text, or the seemingly arbitrary placement of a personal image in an impersonal structure. They continued, however, to work through these and related images (which seem to have disappeared but are still subliminally there) over an additional period of about five months, and then through the final *scoring* of the performance. There were further improvisations around the early versions of this material, which was always meant to be provisional, an ongoing aspect of the work-in-progress, not a script to be performed. The rehearsals were associational, allusive, cryptic, and open-ended, but the eventual work was never meant to be anything but impeccably performed, unalterably *there,* legible if difficult, with the desire for the impossible perfection of the circle of accomplishment that is mentioned in the text.

Here the guiding text is in the form of an analytic scenario; other texts we have developed looked and read at the end more like a play script, though none of them can be easily deciphered on the page by those who were not immediately engaged in the work, since there are within the texts elliptical and coded messages to the actors named that would have to be translated to others. When, for instance, we did make a replacement in *Elsinore,* it took several months to find the right person, to brief her on the structure of the piece and train her in the techniques by which it was developed, the process of ghosting and its shadow text.

The initials in the scenario refer to the following actors: Julie Augenstein, Peter Ferry, Tom Henry, Karen Schwab Henry, Denise Koch,

Jackson Phippin, and Margaret Roiphe, who was eventually replaced by Ellen Parks. Since the scenario was originally addressed to the actors, I have tried to clarify various things by additional comments in brackets. The words actually spoken in performance are, as another increment of textuality, placed here in italics, and the words on tape in another typeface.

Scenario

Each major image is separated into its elements, with commentary on themes and motives. The text is either specified or suggested. The outside reflections and the political mapping will be developed in rehearsal as a further aspect of the thinking through. The sequences are named:

T'have Seen What I Have Seen

Actors standing at the walls: neutral to will and matter; observed of all observers. The audience, entering, is also observed. A tape is heard when they are seated:

> KAR: I saw a player rise from a group of players and walk
>   slowly out to the center of the circle.

The actors are reimagining at some time in the past what they have done at some time in the past to tell the story that, known, comes obscured through history. What was being seen, told now in the present, is motive and cue of its own future, since it is being heard now by the actors who are about to act, already acting in the act of fear. (What was seen may later, after being played, be told again, playing and telling no longer the same. The retrospective may be taped or told right there.) The actors move toward the playing space. Action of describing a perfect circle. The circle has traditional connotations of unity, order, perfection, truth in the center, unhidden. Its edge is a smooth body. The actors shift ground in respect to each other, always an imperfection: in nature? a particular fault? They gaze at the space, which invites an unfolding. They contemplate each other. "Who's there?" Always: otherness, doubleness, strangeness, rue. The watching are being watched. "I'll have grounds more relative than this."

[Actually, the tape—which continues through the circling and seating of the actors and the rising of the actor, below—started with my voice, recorded while giving directions to the actors during the taping of the following sequence. What I said—partly audible, partly not—was about the cadence of perceiving, seeing and being seen. It just happened to be on one of the many recordings we made and was spliced into the front of the tape during the final rehearsals. Karen's voice continues:]

> I saw each step he took, each foot raised, fearfully.
> At the center I saw the player softer:

DEN: Saw shoulders, chest, arms, hips, thighs.

JAC: The player saw—

KAR: I saw the player's knees lock.

JAC: —and turned away.

DEN: I saw what he did not want to see.

KAR: I saw the player arch back, eyes open, face whiten

JAC: Running running, saw—

PET: —saw the forms, moods, shapes of grief.

KAR: —mouth open, flailed from side to side, I saw him
    wrenched back.

PET: I saw a near perfect circle.

KAR: I saw him wrenched back again,
    Then I saw him dip down and come up with an older face,
    a monster face.

MAR: I saw a circle made and made again.

KAR: I saw the player turn.

MAR: I saw the King.
    And saw in his hands the power that wields my life.
    And saw the strength in that body and what it meant.
    I saw I was afraid.

TOM: I saw two woman; two woman. I could see no more,
    I saw one woman, I looked at her face. It was drawn and tight.
    I saw many others. I felt, felt, felt they would turn
    against me.
    Certainly I saw my pride,

KAR: I saw a woman on her knees, She tried
    reaching forward with her knees, but as if she were
    unstrung inside—

JAC: I thought I saw the ground move,

KAR: —kept falling forward.
    I saw her face was a great rock.

PET: I saw the unseen wall.

KAR: I saw her trying to form the sound and pointing.
    She would smash that rock!

PET: I saw a tongue flicking and flashing inside her mouth!
       I saw teeth closing. In the beginning, I saw the Word.

JUL: I saw silence.

MAR: I saw venom.

KAR: With her fallen limbs rising I saw her accuse.

TOM: I saw the circle, inscrutable—the thing run from, foolish.
       I saw a crab going backwards.

DEN: I saw myself making a mouth of my eyes.

JUL: A woman examined herself in front of me quite nakedly.
       I saw it really meant nothing,

MAR: I saw a knavish speech sleep in a foolish ear.

JAC: I saw a blade of many faces.
       I saw it mirror the poison I must defeat
       and the poison I must become.

DEN: In my dream I saw the body of my father,
       full and fat and black from the waist down.
       Layer on layer, I saw his flesh hang.

PET: I saw one enter, entered, transformed, transform
       again, hesitate, and leave.

[The others have already come from the walls into the playing space.
Peter is only now in the corner, about to enter the forming circle.]

JAC: I saw how quickly the flesh grows old.

DEN: I saw the blackness my mouth drew out of this man.
       With every bite, I saw his sores are my grief:
           they break my skin.
       I saw this body enter my body.
       I saw too much.

[Each of the lines exists in several dimensions: relative to the source-
play, as an act of confessional self-consciousness, as an intimation of
what is to be performed, and as a reflection upon the actors' relationships with each other—here, for instance, Denise shifting the image to
Jack, Jack reflecting on play, self, image, and Denise:]

JAC: I saw a grave too narrow for my mind.

KAR: I saw Hamlet in grief, I saw Hamlet caring,
           passionate and foaming.

PET: I saw nakedness clad with distance.

MAR: I saw the voice wears masks.

[The actors are by now seated in the circle, and during the following lines Tom rises for the sequence described below.]

DEN: I saw the ghost of the Ghost, rising.

KAR: I saw my body—

TOM: —the hollow skull, the wind.

KAR: —and saw how I couldn't get out of it:
      my father was at my back!

JAC: I saw the beauteous majesty of Denmark.

KAR: Following the blood to my heart, circling, I saw it beat there,
      walking slowly to the center of the circle, backwards.

TOM: Two heartbeats, wrapped in a single coil:
      I saw an almost smooth body.

JUL: I saw a very futile attempt.

DEN: I saw the sponge of my weakness take up those sores
      and drop them on everyone around me.

TOM: I saw myself choke back my pain, harden against
      the softening and lose my will.

JUL: I think I'm afraid there were times, I'm afraid there were
      times when I was too busy to see.

PET: I saw a wheel whose rim is in the center, and
      the head on top took turns being crushed.

DEN: At the innermost point of my brain I saw a Court.

MAR: I saw dirt, soil.
      I saw I was fascinated by it.

TOM: I saw a Crown.

JAC: I saw for a fleeting moment two players seeing:
      it was painful to see.

My Offense Is Rank

1) Tom moves to the center, infolded in thought. He does not take on "character"; he is "himself":

TOM: My offense is rank:
It hath the primal eldest curse upon't—

He reverses the key words:

It hath the eldest primal curse . . .

Jack ghosts the words.

Bow, stubborn knees.

The stubborn knees which won't bend, buckle through sheer force of will. The prayer which won't go up, goes down. The body is virtually torn apart in resistance to an atonement which, wanted, cannot in principle be grounded. The reversal of words already indicates that there will be an analytical tendency in the performance, with a short circuit from head to gut. The "O" before "My offense" [in the text of *Hamlet*] is eliminated because there is the explicit personal assumption of fault, the particular fault (*My* offense) and the fault in nature—inherited, inherent, first and agèd cause, before time ageless, primal. The action is a symptom of the act of fear and a raging denial of it; it is also a demonstration (active/passive? torn apart, tearing itself apart). The actor (Claudius? Hamlet? nephew/uncle) withdraws from the space [after the ideograph of tearing-himself-the self-apart] and returns to the edge, sitting.

2) As Tom moves center [above], Jack pivots out, squatting. He sees in the mind's eye the knees buckle and the body torn. He breaks into a run circling the audience, after ghosting Tom's words and crying "Lights! Lights!" As he runs, Tom sings out wildly, when still in the center:

> *Why, let the stricken deer go weep,*
> *The hart ungallèd play.*
> *For some must watch, while some must sleep;*
> *Thus runs the world away.*

There is a contrast, conceptual and personal, between Tom's broken willfulness and Jack's obsessive flight, which is both an avoidance and a response. The running (pursuing the Ghost? delirious to the closet? a figure of the figure of the stricken deer?) is an act of fear which, paradoxically, stabilizes visually the strange eruption in the state: Tom's tearing-the-self-apart. The circle is adhered to even though it's been broken. There is a declension of energy as he runs, entropic, a leak in the universe. Maimèd rites. Mortal coil.

3) On Tom's buckling, all except Jack speak these lines from the soliloquy:

> *O that this too too solid (sullied?) flesh would melt,*
> *Thaw, and resolve itself into a dew;*
> *Or that the Everlasting had not fix'd*
> *His canon 'gainst self-slaughter. O god, god.*

The words are just audible. ["Solid" and "sullied" were variables.] This is one side of the dialectic of which Julie's response is the antithesis. Extinguish the Self or murder the Other? It is the verbal cognate of the diminished energy in Jack's circling: melt, thaw, resolve into a dew; regressive. Dynamics: actions which are hard, willed, *yang*, contrasted to those which are soft, yielding, wanting to go inert, *yin*. [An important discipline of the group, with an intrinsic figuring of the yin and yang, was the Tai Chi Ch'uan.]

4) Julie has watched with horror but insists on naming the truth hid in the center. The word seems to draw her voice from its bowels: *MURDER!* As Tom leaves the space, she builds to a scream enveloping the nothingness at its center, first naming, then demanding: *MURDER!* It is a response, the opposite of the soliloquy's, to the primal eldest curse; it *is* the eldest primal curse. Whether born to it or victimized by it, it can drive you mad.

5) Peter, in response to Julie's *MURDER!* exclaims: "Long live the King!" (After the second or third *MURDER!* depending on how that is developed by Julie. Repeat??) The tone is indeterminate. The words signify a desire for continuity, as in Jack's run. But what does one mean by King? And who is that? Peter's (own) sense of irony is relevant here.

A Grass-Green Turf

1) *"Murder! Muurrder! Muuuurrrderr!"* Within the structure of Julie's image—vocally, then her movement—a continuum, hard/soft, yin/yang, thus: T'have seen what I have seen is to go mad. The brain splits in the scream. Whoever it was, that voice, Julie is now suggesting Ophelia, crossing the empty space. She is singing:

> *He is dead and gone, lady,*
> *He is dead and gone;*
> *At his head a grass-green turf,*
> *At his heels a stone.*

(Sing first stanza too?— *"How should I your true-love know . . ."*) As she crosses, she raises her hands and focuses on the imagined center through a cross-hatch web of fingers, her body oscillating in the crossing.

2) Denise gives a pure empirical description of the crossing, as Julie goes, thus: "Left foot, right foot . . . to the edge of the circle etc."

3) In the transition from *Murder!* to *"How should your true-love know,"* Peter narrates, his lines orchestrated with the song and Denise's descriptive following:

> *The King, elected, assumes the throne.*
> *The mourning Queen undoes her hair.*

The Prince is summoned from Wittenberg.
Ophelia is asleep in her chamber.
Laertes, the brother, sails from France.
The old man floats in the ground headdown.
Fortinbras shouts his orders.
An unnamed captain lies bleeding.
Two friends of Hamlet arrive in Court.
Horatio calculates his next move.
The King calculates.
The Queen weaves.
Fortinbras rides off.

4) The slight tone of mockery in Julie's song becomes more grieving. Lowers hands as she reaches the other side of the circle, turns and speaks into the space:

JUL: *Why, look you now, how unworthy a thing you make of me! You would play upon me, you would seem to know my stops, you would pluck out the heart of my mystery.*
DEN: *Seems, madam? Nay, it is. I know not "seems."*

Julie's tone changes again, a green thought in a green shade:

JUL: *Lord, we know what we are, but know not what we may be.*

5) Karen has risen and is moving center. Julie sits in Karen's place. Karen lies down, motionless. Julie's full image shows the implications of the curse. The terminals of psychic transformation—as an acting process—illuminate and frame each other: fresh death, fresh madness. A grass-green turf: Karen's bald fulfillment [below] of the requirement for a dead body focuses again on the act of acting. It establishes, too, the cross-sexual technique of the piece. *He* is dead and gone but he's a *she.* Julie's closing line, above, transcends and comments on the murder/madness. It anticipates themes to come: divinity shaping ends; providential sparrow; ignorance of final things: *do* we know what we are? Julie foreshadows a later shift, on one structural emotion, from Ophelia to Gertrude—the self (mad) telling its story through the Other.

6) "*. . . we know what we are . . . .*" To Julie's line, Denise's "*Seems, madam? Nay, it is. I know not 'seems.'*" That determination is represented, first, in the plain insistence of her phenomenological description of Julie's crossing. How do we know what we are if we can't see what we see? Counterpoint of Denise's description and Peter's narrative: what's *there* (the eye is the law) and the mythicizing of what's there (the mind's

eye). Giving audience to the act: to see in both dimensions, out-there, in-here. In the act of observing, of all observers, Denise's "nature" is relevant [she always bristled at the idea of having a nature]. Her concern for the "truth" in a realm of seeming, seeming. The sequence of images, disjunct but thematically joined, is a congealing and conjuring of the dreamscape of *Elsinore*. Forms, moods, shapes: Julie is after all shamelessly *acting* in her grief. To her shame. A passing show. We shall presently see Denise passing, reaching for the truth hid in the center, beyond the center, all the way out there: Is there a divinity that shapes our ends? She will ask that question explicitly, later.

So Like the King

1) Before she lies down after moving center, Karen stands there and removes her jersey, baring her body. In the manner of a demonstration, she runs her fingers along the side of her rib cage and over her chest. *"No marks of abuse, she is innocent."* She does the same on the other side. *"No signs of struggle, she is guilty."* She says these lines to the audience as dispassionately as possible. She then sits, center. *"Out of this soil,"* she says, *"violence will spring."* She lies down, ceremoniously placing the jersey over her bare chest.

2) Peter calls across the space of the dead body: *"Who's there?"* Jack, who has stopped abruptly on Julie's song: *"Nay, answer me. Stand, and unfold yourself."* The exchange returns us, "dramatically," to the "actual" ramparts. It is also, as compared to Karen's dispassionateness, a motive and cue for passion. (Add another: *"Long live the King!"*)

3) To which, in "a figure like your father," Karen responds. From supine lifelessness, neutral to will and matter, she gradually materializes the Ghost, breathing harshly, growing louder, larger, hyperventilated, spasms of limbs infused by some daimonic force. The magnitude of the materialization in Karen's very small body, an issue. At the crest, outcry of the sheeted dead (which did "squeak and gibber in the Roman streets") transposed to: *"I—am—thy—father's—spirit."* Which, as related to the process of acting, makes sense. *She* is. An act of unfolding, fearful, impelled by the primal eldest curse. The line squeaks and gibbers. As she rises, Margaret tolls: *Be now be now be now be now etc. . . .* Karen's action, a conceptual piece (overall), starts by further estranging the view of Ophelia we have had with Julie. We have seen the murder infuse the conventional madness (Julie's crossing should be composed of the "remembered" Ophelia). Now we are asked to understand it by seeing it askew. In Karen's observations on her body, *presented,* the issue is brought forward, too, by the suggestion of rape and the distressing

question of how the woman is supposed to respond to it or how she is judged in terms of her response. Hamlet's abuse of Ophelia is a kind of rape, as her serving as an instrument of Polonius is a betrayal. The dead body, motionless, is both material and immaterial (in the realm of evidence); that is Hamlet's "machine." But it also becomes, "this soil," sullied, the grass-green turf. The sweater marks the sheeted dead. When she rises, the breasts will be bared again, and to the degree the Ghost is oracular there should be suggestions of the breasted prophet (cf. Tiresias), giving an eerier cast to *"I am thy father's spirit."* It emphasizes, too, the motherliness of the Ghost ("Father and Mother are one flesh"), as well as providing a maenadic image for the weaving in Purgatory [below], contributing to the Walpurgisnacht. The whole image, from the conceptual presentation on Ophelia to the ideographic resurrection of the Ghost, contributes to the graded perception of the acting process, the varieties of play within the play. One final thing: the cool impersonal presentation of the evidence will, most probably, deepen the felt presence of Ophelia's madness (it's weirder than the "real" thing as usually performed) and contrast with the hyperventilated passion of the Ghost's rising. He has come from her grave, in the maimèd rites.

In the Blossoms of My Sin

1) Karen moves to the periphery, "fasting in fires." Jack crosses diagonally, Ophelia's ghost. Hand on loins ("o'erteemed"), hand on breast, spiraling. His tongue flickers, Eve and Serpent at once (lascivious source of the words words words); suggestion of the Garden, the primal space, site of the curse. He coils off. The surround is Purgatory.

2) Denise follows an impeccable line, extruded, in the opposite direction, arm stretched taut and reaching into the abyss, a distended and hallowed sound, like some desperate sounding of the distance from nature to eternity. In the tension between these passings, the undiscovered country from whose bourn . . . .

3) Karen, having risen from the dead, weaves on the circumference [behind the audience] the sound of Purgatory. Her voice moves from the low loud notes of the grave to the top of her compass, a high pure shriek, but controlled. A sound-abstraction forms around Karen, all the actors; then a tonal allusion to the ramparts, snatches of "rampart calls": frightened, lyric, frantic, baffled, singsong, fierce, birdlike. *"Stay, illusion."* Cockcrow and bird of dawning. Come, bird, come. A text for Purgatory:

KAR: *I—am—thy—fath-er's—spi-rit.*

She moves to the periphery on a shrill crest of Hamlet's name, weaving through the circumference. Margaret, crouched and sibylline, has been tolling: *Be now be now be now etc.*—"the bell then beating one!"—on Karen's ascension. Jack and Denise are crossing on the same diameter: expulsion from the Garden in a mortal coil; a reaching from nature to eternity, the undiscovered country between them fusing with the purgatorial image. As his tongue flickers, her mouth is wide open, calling from some bourn in the body, as if tongueless.

The sequence that follows is rapid and rhythmic, distant and cadenced, a kind of singsong. The cockcrows, bird of dawning, and the braying out are developed between lines and sustained with variations, which means that each actor must score an almost continuous line of words and sounds. As if in one breath:

MAR: *Be now*

PET: *Stay*

TOM: *Speak*

JUL: *Looks he not like the king?*

PET: *Most like*

MAR: *Not now*

TOM: *Like the king that's dead*

JUL: *Speak*

PET: *The king is a thing*

TOM: *Staayyy*

PET: *Illusion*

MAR: *If it be not now*

PET: *Stay*

JUL: *Like the king that was*

TOM: *Most like*

MAR: *Yet*

TOM: *Like the king that's dead*

JUL: *Come, bird, come!*

PET: *Speak*

MAR: *If it be not to come*

TOM: *Come*

PET: *Like the king*

JUL: *Stay*

(together)

TOM: Illo

MAR: Be not now

PET: Like the king that's dead

JUL: Illusion

(ghosting)

TOM: Illusion

(Peter with Julie, but a distant echo:)

PET: Illuuuuuuuu

MAR: It will come

PET: Stay

TOM: Illo illo

JUL: Illu

MAR: Hic, et ubique

TOM: Come, bird, come

JUL: The king is a thing

PET: Boy!

MAR: If it be not now

JUL: Illo illu

(together)

PET: illu

TOM: Boy!

JUL: Speak

PET: Like the king that was

JUL: Was

(together, but differently pitched)

TOM: And is

JUL: Most like

MAR: 'Tis not

TOM: Illuusionnn (tolling)

MAR: Yet it will come

They have been crouching, turning this way and that. They now rise and move abruptly, here and there, chasing the Ghost, Karen alone holding the circle.

PET: Come?

JUL: Illo illu

(together)

TOM: Illoouuuu
ALL: Stay
JUL: 'Tis here
TOM: 'Tis here
PET: Like the king that's dead
JUL: Illo illo illu

(together, Tom's voice distant)

TOM: Illu illu illo
PET: 'Tis gone (brays)
MAR: Now

4) Karen is still weaving, like fate. The other women are now hud-
dling together, a ghosting chorus, coming out of the purgatorial fires, as
Jack—who has passed to the other side—spirals backward to "removèd
ground." There is a scurrying over the playing space, Tom moving swiftly, Peter crossing: pursuit of the Ghost.

5) As Denise is passing off, Peter is alone in the center, confounded,
looking into the dark, after calling, *"O, answer me!"* He stops. His hand
moves into the light, as if disembodied, not his. He sees it. Suddenly, it
slaps him, hard. Then again and again and again. He slaps himself to the
periphery, braying, crossing Tom, Jack recoiling, the women gathering.
The following chorus is an extension of the previous sound texture, still
playing with the paradoxes, another weaving, the Fates, be now be now,
come come come etc. receiving stress, as their faces assume masks of the
elementary figures of the Great Mother, watching Jack perform, as if in
an instant of time, the forms, moods, shapes of Hamlet. In the whole sequence leading up through Jack's performance, there is something like a
Walpurgisnacht, a wassailing, a braying out around the permutations of
providence. The readiness is not yet. The swaggering upspring reels. The
ground is constantly shifting in the center, as in the rhythms of this chorus. On the outside, from the actors, reflections (narrative, political,
etc.) keeping madness in reason.

[Each word of the chorus comes exactly in the spacing indicated, the
whole composition being a unity and yet each voice maintaining its own
line and inflection:]

JUL:	*If*	*If*		*If it bé not to come*
MAR:	*If it be now*			*If it be nót to come*
DEN:	*If*		*tis not to come*	*If it be not to cóme*

JUL: *If*   *It will be now*   *If it be not now*   *It will come*
MAR: *If*   *It will be now*   *If it be not now*   *yet*
DEN: *If*   *It will be now*   *If it be not now*   *It will come*

JUL: *If*   *now*   *If it be*
MAR: *If it be now*   *come*   *If it be not*
DEN: *If*   *'tis not to come*   *If*

JUL: *If*   *not*   *come*   *it will be now*   *If*   *yet*
MAR: *come*   *If it be not now*
DEN: *If it be not to come*   *now*   *If*   *yet*

JUL: *it will come*   *yet*   *now If*   *yet*   *now*
MAR: *If*   *If it be*   *If it be now*   *if*
DEN: *it will come*   *now*   *yet*   *If*   *now*   *'tis not*

JUL: *come*   *if it be not to come*   *it will be now*   *yet*
MAR: *yet*   *not*   *now it will*   *come*
DEN: *to come*   *if*   *not*   *come*   *it will be*   *now*

JUL: *not*   *if it will come*   *if it be*
MAR: *if it be*   *not now yet*   *if*   *if it be not*
DEN: *yet*   *if it will come*   *if*

JUL: *yet*   *If*   *now*   *come not*   *if*   *If it be now*
MAR: *if*   *it will come*   *now*   *If it be*
DEN: *if it be now*   *come yet*   *if*   *If it be now*

JUL: *come*   *if it be not now*
MAR: *'tis not to come*   *it will be now*   *yet it will*
DEN: *come*   *if it be not now*

JUL:
MAR: come *If it be now, 'tis not to come; if it be not to come, it will be*
DEN:

MAR: *now; if it be not now, yet it will come.*

[In the first three lines above, I have indicated the kind of permutated stress that occurs throughout the piece, which is itself a reflection of the thought process of the entire structure of *Elsinore*.]

All My Smooth Body

1) Jack, having passed into darkness, has recoiled into the light. He spirals backwards to "removèd ground," out of the collective pursuit of

the Ghost. On him "all forms, all pressures past," male/female, Hamlet and Ghost, Jack regressing, the spinning Eve become Serpent coiling still. (The spinning also continues the motif of weaving in the Fates; all the circling and spinning is a premonition of "the massy wheel.") A passage of intuition between Father and Mother, the two becoming one. Jack should choose his lines from such as these: *"Seems, madam? Nay, it is . . . Thou com'st in such a questionable shape . . . Meet it is I set it down / That one may smile, and smile. . . ."* The lines are tumbling out, delivered at high speed. He is raking his genitals, back and side, up the belly, babbling, "good mother." (The women, through the chorus, are making facial masks.) He is sinking down, like the drowning Ophelia, another coil. But the lines are Hamlet's: *" 'Tis not alone my inky cloak, good mother."* Gouging himself on the belly: *"IN MY TABLES!"* Tables of the Law, inscribed on his body, the commandment. *"Say, why is this? wherefore? what should we do? Ha, ha, boy, say'st thou so? Go on, I'll follow thee."* The coiling momentum takes him head to ground, as if beating the commandment into the brain: *"O most pernicious woman! O villain, smiling damnèd villain. . . . Ay, thou poor ghost, while memory holds a seat in this distracted globe."* He has been rehearsing in swift succession all the motives and emotions of Hamlet, now whimpering like an infant in the regressive coil. *"Still am I called. These indeed seem. . . . O, wonderful. I'll go no further."* He subsides, in a fetal position. Backside of the act of fear.

2) The purgatorial fires have enveloped Jack. Counterpoint of the ghosting chorus. As that concludes and he curls up, thawed, the solid body regressed, Denise rises and approaches. Infant and sleeping King. A woman's voice (Julie's) is heard as Denise moves toward him:

> JUL: *'Tis given out that, sleeping in my orchard,*
> *My custom always of an afternoon,*
> *A serpent stung me. So the whole ear of Denmark*
> *Is by a forgèd process of my death*
> *Rankly abused.*

Here now is "the leperous distilment." Denise kneels beside Jack. She whispers simply, tenderly, pouring hebona in his ear: *"To be or not. to be etc. . . ."* There is no venom in her voice (on the contrary, it may sound like words of love), but the question is the vile and loathsome crust. It is a nightmare to Jack. (Lear: "When we are born into this world / We wawl and cry.") As she reaches the "undiscovered country," he twitches and thrashes like Tom in his buckling, repeating the figure of the self tearing itself apart. "Fie upon't, foh, about my brains." He bolts into the far corner. There, he becomes the Ghost. He had melted, thawed, re-solved psychologically into a dew (knowing only too well, personally, the desire of not-to-be); now he is armored.

The Rivals of My Watch

1) Regression/Assertion: the Faustian side of *"I'll go no further."* Tom leaps at the center as Jack runs away: *"Unhand me! I'll make a ghost of him that lets me."* He falls to his knees and claws not at himself but at the ground (frantic image of Margaret's boisterous grave digging later). Equal and opposite of Jack's complete regression—out of rage and self-flagellating irony—into the mortal coil. The final fetal position was an infolding of the self, not only thawed but clenched, holding himself there—like one clenches the teeth in sleep. It was a hiding, an act of fear, a wound-up-coil, teased back to thought by Denise's whispered words in the ear, and released now into the fury of Tom, whose flailing Jack had brought back to the scene before bolting from the stage. Thus, a contin-uous figure, one body to the other. Tom digs furiously. It's as if the ques-tion were to be answered by tearing the Father out of the grave, not a fantasy of a father but in all its rotting gravity the corporeal remains. Julie is pointing gleefully at Margaret, both arms extended: *"The skull! the skull! the skull!"* As Jack went, above, into the fetal position, Margaret had begun to quiver, her whole body jiggling. The hebona *("To be or not to be")* turns her into a shaking image of Yorick's skull. Julie has named the skull as she had named the murder. There is something of a Dumb Show in Margaret's action. Julie and Karen are spectators to the event, Julie's response suggesting a childish naïveté, almost delight, in the transformation, as if the thing thrown out of the grave (by Tom's digging, by the questioning) is a plaything—and, indeed, that's what Peter proceeds to do with it, the skull. He shakes Margaret, manipulates her like a puppet, from behind. This sequence follows:

2) Peter brays. He licks and ogles Margaret. She is on her knees, but moving as in a courtly procession, grotesquely regal.

TOM: *I'll have grounds more relative than this!*

He has dug up a skull, grasps it. Karen laughs. Peter brays. He is leading Margaret, as if they were King and Queen, across the space. The feeling is of a medieval Death's Head masque. Julie circles like a courtesan, in the procession, laughing emptily. Tom is still over the grave, glaring at the skull's blank eyes.

TOM: *Abuses me to damn me.*

Jack speaks from the corner, ghosting:

> JAC: *Who's there?*
> TOM: *Me! Me! Me!*

He is speaking fiercely to the skull. Julie laughs. Peter brays. Wassailing.

> JAC: *Mark me.*

Karen is narrating: telling the story from the death of old Hamlet.

> TOM: *I have rights of memory in this kingdom!*

Laugh. Bray. Peter ogles Margaret, who smirks; like Hamlet's worst fantasy of the funeral baked meats. The narrative continues, orchestrated: what Karen sees, in the mind's eye.

> JAC: *I am thy father's spirit.*
>   *Doomed for a certain term to walk the night . . .*

At first, the actor playing the Ghost, the voice conventionally sepulchral, but the convention disappearing into the ghosting, as it must penetrate through Tom's ferocious will-to-know.

The kingdom fragments around Tom. Denise rises to assert another principle and restore another kind of order, to bring the action into another mode, lest it lose the name of action. [Tom's momentum is that of the unaxled massy wheel, almost unstoppable, what was severely troubling to Denise during the improvisations.] Again—as in the reaching toward eternity—she follows a resolute straight line through the turbulence of the circling, the eruption in the state. Tom is torn between grave and Ghost.

> DEN: *But who, ah woe, had seen the mobled queen?*

She is playing the Player Queen—broad, Delsartian, yet tender and elegant. She touches his head lightly as Peter and Margaret parade in front of him.

> TOM: *Foh, about my brain!*
> JAC: *But that I am forbid*
>   *To tell the secrets of my prison house,*
>   *I could a tale unfold whose lightest word*
>   *Would harrow up thy soul, freeze thy young blood,*
> DEN: *Our wills and fates do so contrary run*
>   *That our devices still are overthrown;*
>   *Our thoughts are ours, their ends none of our own.*

In a gracefully executed exchange, Denise has taken Peter from Margaret, who continues on her knees, now frothing at the mouth.

> JAC: *. . . make thy two eyes like stars start from their*
>   *spheres . . .*
> MAR: *Eyes without feeling, feeling without sight.*

She keeps repeating the line. Denise and Peter have swung around to the end of the playing space furthest from Jack. They are now in Court, she the "real" Queen.

> TOM: *O my prophetic soul!*
> DEN: *Sleep rock thy brain.*

3) Tom's focus is divided now between the Court and the Ghost, playing with both at once. Margaret's lines diminish in volume, dissolving into no-feeling, as she returns to the circumference of the circle. Tom is alone now in the center. The others rise to form the Court. Swiftly:

> DEN: *Hamlet!*

She is firm but motherly, no deceit. So, too, with Peter, or so it appears.

> JAC: *If thou didst ever thy dear father love—*
> TOM: *O God!*
> DEN: *. . . cast thy nighted color off.*
> JAC: *—revenge his foul and most unnatural murder.*
> TOM: *Murder?*

> (Echoed by Julie, her sound.)

> JAC: *Murder most foul, as in the best it is,*
>   *But this most foul, strange, and unnatural.*
> PET: *Though yet of Hamlet our dear brother's death.*
>   *The memory be green . . .*
> DEN: *. . . let thine eye*
>   *Look like a friend on Denmark..*
> PET: *Your father lost*
>   *A father, that father lost, lost his.*

> (Overlapping *lost* and *list*)

> JAC: *List, list, O, list!*
> DEN: *Thou knowst 'tis common. All that lives must die,*

> *Passing through nature to eternity.*
> TOM: *Ay, madam, it is common.*
> DEN: *If it be,*
> *Why seems it so particular with thee?*
> TOM: *Seems, madam? nay it is! I know not seems.*
> *I have that within which passeth show.*
> PET: *'Tis a fault to heaven,*
> JAC: *a fault against the dead,*
> TOM: *Ha, ha, boy, say'st thou so?*
> DEN: *a fault to nature,*
> JAC: *Now, Hamlet, hear:*
> TOM: *Art thou there . . .*
> PET: *Hamlet!*
> TOM: *. . . truepenny?*
> PET: *To reason most absurd,*
> TOM: *You hear this fellow in the cellarage.*
> DEN: *whose common theme*
> JAC: *Swear!*
> DEN: *is death of fathers.*
> TOM (harshly to Peter and Denise): *Consent to swear!*
> MAR: *So lust, though to a radiant angel linked,*
> *Will sate itself in a celestial bed*
> *And prey on garbage.*
> TOM: *Well said, old mole!*
> JAC: *O, horrible! O, horrible! most horrible!*
> TOM: *Canst work i'th'earth so fast?*
> JAC: *All my smooth body.*
> TOM: *O, horrible! O, horrible! most horrible!*

He slaps at his ear, wildly. He moves as if his body were burning.

> *The leperous distilment . . . in the porches of my ears. . . . Curd.*

> (He screams.)

> *Swift as quicksilver! Vile and loathsome crust. Ah!*
> *Cut off . . .*
> JAC: *. . . even in the blossoms of my sin,*

> (Tom ghosts the following line.)

> *Unhouseled, disappointed, unannealed.*

PET: *From the first corse till he that died today:*
DEN: *This must be so!*
PET: *Think of us as of a father.*

The crossfire (of hell and association) speaks for itself. Margaret, whored and nauseated, has summed up the lust at the center, the psychosexual grounds for nausea. The most dramatic scene has its own associative pattern. The deepest fault is seeming, the very process compounded by the performance. The claim of something within, an interior self, that cannot find its outward form, mood, or shape may itself be one shape of the curse. Truepenny, then, combines self and Ghost. Are you there? So, too, with the death of fathers. The father who victimizes is also the victim. A further collapse into seeming. Then: transfer of roles, whose voice is whose? Tom assumes at the center the suffering of the Ghost (one form of atonement). The Ghost's words inscribed on his brain and smooth body drive him mad. He becomes the Ghost, there (never quite Hamlet, and never not Tom), as Jack before became the Ghost and as Peter at the end of the sequence becomes the Ghost, or will in a moment, when Tom attempts to leave the space. (Recall the rehearsal where Peter refused to let him leave, kept throwing him back.) The cellarage is already in the Court. It is all ghosting, the shifting ground is where the Ghost walks, in no single figure.

What Would Your Gracious Figure?

1) Tom, repelled by the Uncle-Father, starts out of the space. The Ghost pursues. The message must sink in, the commandment. Peter leaps after Tom and throws him down. Tom scrambles toward the edge of the circle. Peter touches him with a finger and, as if all power were concentrated there, throws him back. Tom rolls away. He goes again, crawling; Peter throws him back. Repeat.

PET: *Be ruled.*

Tom, enraged, leaps at Peter, high, as against a wall, impregnable. He falls back. They struggle. Mortal coil, mortal combat. They stalk each other, as on the dark of the ramparts, blindly at first, as if in total darkness; actually, Peter seeing, toying with him. Then they engage, lock, grapple. They fight silently.

2) Over the silent struggle, a tape plays: "I saw. . . ." It entered below the level of consciousness, not a projection of what's to come, as with the opening tape, but a reflection on what is being seen, and has been

seen in the performance so far. The action moves forward, memory moves back, but the memory is recorded time, prior memory, expanding back in a geometric ratio with accelerating speed of mind. In the struggle, several struggles: combat between Father and Son; altercation in the grave; the Duel. Wrestling with the Angel. As they reflect upon each other, there are, now, in the time warp between what is seen and what is remembered, suggestions of other struggles: Hamlet and Fortinbras, Pyrrhus and Priam. They part, suspended, breathing hard. The tape [text below] subsides. Peter speaks:

> PET: *Mark me.*
> TOM: *Whither wilt thou lead me? . . . Answer me!*

Peter does not answer. Tom is aroused, ready to leap.

> KAR: *What if it tempt you to the flood, my lord?*
> TOM: *I do not set my life at a pin's fee.*

Peter beckons him, courteously.

> DEN: *You will lose this wager, my lord.*

Tom rushes at Peter. They roll to the ground in an embrace. The tape is audible. They struggle.

> TOM: *And for my soul, what can it do to that?*
> *Being a thing immortal as itself?*

They fight silently, deeply. The tape continues, memory leaping back, widening the abyss between the scene and the source, illimitably back, as if it were a story with no beginning, behind even the curse.

   3) Peter throws Tom and holds him down, Tom choking with rage, the sound like a cockcrow. The form of the combat is like an initiation rite, relentless but ceremonious.

> PET: *My hour is almost come.*

Tom throws him over. They face each other on their knees, panting.

> TOM: *Speak. I am bound to hear!*
> PET: *So art thou to revenge, when thou shalt hear.*
> TOM: *What?*

Only the tape answers. Peter throws himself at Tom. They fight until they can hardly move. The fight is perilous, but like a dance, parts of it utterly suspended, slowed, an endurance.

[The phrases from *Hamlet* in the recorded text also give us the narrative backwards, eventually coming out the front end of the "known" play, into the myth of the myth, imagined origins. But that comes later. The tape was made as one uninterrupted sequence, but it is segmented into three parts that occur at intervals in the structure. The first part:]

TOM: I saw: will in the beginning.

KAR: I saw the soldiers shoot.

MAR: A cruel blow. I saw it lash out, bite, recoil.

PET: I saw them take up the bodies.

JAC: I saw them fight and one said, Well! I was born to fight.

DEN: I saw the King drink to Hamlet, a jewel I saw bleeding.

JUL: I saw them bleeding on all sides.

MAR: I saw hands and arms in the air.

PET: I saw the King is a thing.

DEN: Is she dead? Is she sleeping? I saw the Queen
    with her lion-red body, her wings of glass.

TOM: Where is this sight I saw?

MAR: I saw him comply with his dug before he sucked it.

PET: The cup at her lips I saw, a hit, a palpable hit!

JUL: I saw each one by itself, one accusing, one defending,
    one separating these two.

JAC: I saw them wrapped in each other's arms.

KAR: I saw a man confused with the armor he wore. A ghostly
    hand pulls it off, the other holds it tight.

JAC: I saw a young man trying to know old flesh.

JUL: I saw a diseased wit in his head.

TOM: I saw nothing neither way.

KAR: I saw all the ghosts are baffled by the joint between
    spirit and flesh.

DEN: Seven graves I saw.

TOM: I saw the great slime kings gathered there for vengeance.

JUL: They were incensed I saw.

PET: I saw the dead man's son break into the palace. "Give me
    my father!" he said. I saw the father behind the broken door.

TOM: I saw the King stand his ground, with no fear of his person.

KAR: I saw the rose and expectancy of the fair state.

JUL: I should have seen his pain, but I only saw my hate.

DEN: I saw the sores are not the sores of my flesh,
    they're the sores of Hamlet and they're oozing on me.

KAR: I saw a lovely woman lean over a precipice, pour
      herself into it.
JUL: I saw no lovely woman.
KAR: I saw a lovely woman.
MAR: I saw venom.
JAC: Smooth as a snake, I saw.
DEN: I saw the evil eye of a woman serve its purpose.
TOM: I saw the secret parts of fortune.
MAR: Have you eyes? Ha! Have you eyes?
JAC: I saw that grace was seated on that brow.
DEN: I saw a fat king and a lean beggar seated at a table.
JAC: I saw them eaten, divided, drunk among whispers.
MAR: I saw he become everything by becoming nothing.
PET: They thought that death was worth it, but I saw I have a
      self to recover, a queen.
DEN: I saw Gertrude locked in the prison of her heart which
      was locked in the prison of her desires.
JUL: I saw the illusion that might give an answer.
TOM: I saw a wall. My mind could not go back!
JAC: I saw myself lying in a pool of blood, being asked a question.
DEN: I saw there was no mother here.
KAR: I saw two men holding each other as if they would burst.
JAC: I saw the King's image in complete steel.
KAR: Empty? I saw it was empty. I was full.
TOM: I saw the same.
PET: I saw the unseen good old man falling.
KAR: I saw a dying woman ask nothing.
MAR: I saw the people whispering, thick and unwholesome.
JUL: I saw the guts being lugged into the neighbor room.
PET: I saw the majesty of buried Denmark.
TOM: I saw an old man dying; just that.
JAC: I saw the King consulting his wisest friends.
DEN: Through infinite space I saw the armies marching.
TOM: I saw a little patch of ground.
JUL: I saw a territory so often claimed that it had no owner.
MAR: I saw a certain convocation of politic worms.
JAC: I saw the readiness is all.
JUL: And then I saw the Murder.
KAR: I saw no murder; I didn't see a murder.
JAC: I saw a smooth body in the blossoms of sin.

JUL: Then saw you not his face?

TOM: I saw a skull with a tongue in it which could sing.

MAR: I saw a painted tyrant.

PET: Up from the cabin I saw a man, sleepless, his face
          wrapped, groping,
          I saw the forgery of a man.

DEN: I saw it didn't matter what you name me.

PET: The next day I saw a sea-fight.

TOM: I stood there, boarded, we glared. I saw nobody knew
          what to do.

DEN: I saw pride face lack of pride.

TOM: I saw Hamlet die, I saw Hamlet buried,
          I saw Hamlet returneth to dust.
          I saw the noble dust of Hamlet stopping a bung hole.

KAR: I saw the earth turned, the earth turning,
          I saw the King coming . . .

PET: I saw the maimèd rites.

DEN: I saw the mortal coil.

MAR: Alas, poor Yorick, I saw.

JAC: I saw the King's seal.

JUL: I saw the bodiless creation.

TOM: I saw the skull's three branches.

MAR: I saw a god kissing carrion.

PET: I saw the King fucking.

KAR: In apprehension I saw—

TOM: —saw truth hid in the center.

DEN: I saw a majestical roof fretted with golden fire.

JUL: In the mind's eye, I saw myself seeing.

MAR: Dirt, soil. I saw myself fascinated.

DEN: A thousand times I saw the Clown carry the Prince on his back.

PET: I saw them defy augury.

JAC: I saw betrayal.

JUL: I saw madness being reasoned and reason going mad.

TOM: I saw two crafts meeting directly in one line.

JUL: I saw two giants struggling in a grave.

TOM: I saw Cyclops' hammers fall on Mars' armor.
          I saw Priam hacked by Pyrrhus' bleeding sword.
          I saw the spokes and fellies torn from Fortune's wheel.
          I saw the round nave bowling down the hill of heaven.

DEN: As low as to the fiends I saw.

JUL: I saw the gravedigger putting on the forceps.

DEN: Let a beast be lord of beasts! I saw his crib stand
at the King's mess.

PET: I saw the bark ready and the wind up.
I saw the Prince sailing to England.

MAR: I saw a smiling damnèd villain.

JUL: I saw amazement sitting on her brow.

KAR: I saw the words fly up.

JAC: I saw a woman in a tree, drowning.

MAR: What's Hecuba to him?
I saw no answer to that question.

TOM: I saw the players arriving, playing upon their pipes.
I saw them taunting.

JUL: Sir, a whole history I saw.

DEN: I saw the heart cleft in twain.

KAR: I saw Ophelia peeking through a pinhole, at a life
that might have been seen.

PET: I saw this machine, my body.

TOM: I saw corruption mining all within.

PET: Look, I tell you! I saw nothing there.

MAR: That would be scanned, I saw.

KAR: I saw words words words.

JUL: I saw the indifferent children of the earth.

MAR: I saw the sun breeding maggots in a dead dog.

JAC: I saw the lips of a ghost swallow a man up, whole.

KAR: Two men, I saw, young men, come to court.

PET: I saw this other man, waiting, watching, a piece of him.

JAC: I saw who was there.

PET: I saw it start like a guilty thing.

JUL: I saw the coronation of the new King with a crown of thorns.

KAR: I saw a thing unfolding.

DEN: I saw a flame light up a womb.

PET,   I saw the vortex in the ear.

TOM: I saw an idle tongue, overwhelmed, skin hanging.

KAR: A thin woman's form glistening, I saw, a flickering tongue
lick the smile off a wicked queen.

PET: I saw the guilty creatures sitting at a play.

The tape has been the conceptual music for the fight. It is now over.
They part, suspended, breathing hard. The backward movement of the
narrative has not been quite in a straight line, but in a spiral folded in,
another coil, unfolding:

4) They are sitting on the ground, facing each other. Peter speaks the only way he can speak through his exhaustion, no vindictiveness in his voice, nothing sepulchral, merely stating the proposition. Tape out. A story, simply, father to son:

> PET: *I am thy father's spirit.*
> *Doomed for a certain term to walk the night,*
> *And for the day confined to fast in fires,*
> *Till the foul crimes done in my days of nature*
> *Are burnt and purged away.*

There is a hiss from the edge of the circle, fire and serpent.

> *List, list, O list!*
> *If thou did'st ever thy dear father love—*
> TOM: *O God!*

Jack, arms extended, is on the dark side of the circle, waiting, ghost of the Ghost.

> PET: *Revenge his foul and most unnatural murder.*
> TOM: *Murder?*

> (Julie echoes.)

> PET: *Murder most foul, as in the best it is,*
> *But this most foul, strange, and unnatural.*
> TOM: *Haste me to know't, that I, with wings as swift*
> *As meditation or the thoughts of love,*
> *May sweep to my revenge.*
> JAC: *Now, Hamlet, hear:*
> DEN: *The serpent that did sting thy father's life*
> *Now wears his crown.*
> PET: *O my prophetic soul!*

Jack has approached Peter and is lifting him from behind, by touch alone.

> TOM: *My uncle?*
> MAR: *Ay, that incestuous, that adulterate beast,*
> JUL: *With witchcraft of his wit,*
> DEN: *with traitorous gifts—*
> KAR: *O wicked wit and gifts,*

Julie is singing *"How should I your true-love know. . . ."* The women's lines are from the edge of the circle, as they observe the action, reflections pitched to the emotions within the space.

DEN: *that have the power*
      so to seduce!—

Peter is being drawn backwards by Jack to the edge of the circle, as if by the strange power that causes the Ghost to withdraw with alarm.

PET: *—won to his shameful lust*
      The will of my most seeming-virtuous queen.
KAR: *O Hamlet, what a falling-off was there.*

The following is like a curse, the gorge of vengeance rising, with the force of the man who swung the poleax and smote the sledded Polacks on the ice:

PET: *If thou hast nature in thee bear it not!*
      Let not the royal bed of Denmark be
      A couch for luxury and damnèd incest.
JAC: (simply) *Fare thee well at once.*
      The glowworm shows the matin to be near
      And gins to pale his uneffectual fire.
PET: *Adieu, adieu, adieu. Remember me.*

                 (Jack echoes, ghosting.)

Jack has taken Peter out of sight. Tom is alone.

TOM: *O all you host of heaven! O earth! What else?*
      And shall I couple hell? O fie! Hold, hold, my heart,
      Remember thee? Ay, thou poor ghost,
      O most pernicious woman!
      O villain, villain, smiling, damnèd villain!
      Yes, by heaven!
      It is "Adieu, adieu, remember me."
      O wonderful!

He rises and leaves the space. He sits on the line of the circle. Peter and Jack take their places also. The inside of the circle is empty.

Rest, Rest, Perturbèd Spirit

A dialogue over the abyss. The following is the pattern to play upon. There is no movement into the circle. All the actors remain sitting, though the emotions rise:

MAR: *O cursèd spite!*
JAC: *With all my love I do commend me to you.*

DEN: *With what, i' the name of God?*
TOM: *Swear!*
JUL: *O day and night, but this is wondrous strange.*
PET: *And therefore as a stranger give it welcome.*
KAR: *You have me, have you not?*
DEN: *One may smile, and smile, and be a villain.*
KAR: *Illo, ho, ho, my lord*
TOM: *Hillo, ho, ho, boy!*
JUL: *You hear this fellow in the cellarage.*
JAC: *Swear.*
TOM: *Mad for thy love?*
MAR: *Fishmonger!*
JUL: *Let her not walk i' the sun.*
JAC: *This above all . . .*
MAR: *Ay, springes to catch woodcocks.*
PET: *Rest, rest, perturbèd spirit.*
DEN: *Mad call I it.*
TOM: *Come, come.*
JAC: *To me it is a prison.*
TOM: *I have sworn't.*
DEN: *Mad north-north-west.*
JUL: *I am ill at these numbers.*
JAC: *All my smooth body.*
KAR: *You cannot play upon me!*
TOM: *except my life, except my life.*
MAR: *More matter with less art.*
KAR: *except my life.*
PET: *Then we'll shift our grounds.*
JAC: *O vengeance!*
JUL: *Tender yourself more dearly!*
DEN: *No shuffling.*
KAR: *Do you know me, my lord?*
MAR: *I know a hawk from a handsaw.*
DEN: *Words, words, words.*
TOM: *What players are these?*
JUL: *What is the matter, my lord?*
JAC: *Between who?*

The Ghost has materialized. The commandment has been issued. But all the coordinates are confused. The reality in the center has been nothing but shifting ground. The dialogue across the abyss comes back to the self. [The actors can address the lines to whomever they wish, and that may shift also, the emotional intensities varying and unexpected, although the ground rhythm is sustained. The lines are assigned, from the point of view of the actors, "in character."] The words fly up, the thoughts remain below. The spirit wants to rest but not in words words words, nor in the commandment to act, nor in the self, nor even in the relationship between selves that is the hidden agenda of the dialogue over the abyss. There is another question to be asked now, although in this skeptical world most of us are reluctant to ask it, at least directly. As we prepare for the question, the tape plays briefly:

DEN: I pointed and asked why. And I saw he's never answered.
JAC: And I saw myself as I was before,
TOM: I saw Hamlet stop, pause, and reflect.
MAR: I saw the funeral baked meats furnish forth the marriage table.
JUL: I saw that within which passeth show,

With the tape, Denise rises and moves into the empty space:

What Then? What Rests?

With her arm she fends off, with her hand she shields herself from the "possible ineffable." She is related, "seeing unseen," to Peter at the rim of the circle. Peter seems once again neutral to will and matter, but with each answer he becomes more ironic, more the seducer.

DEN: Is there a divinity that shapes our ends?

(This is a scene—abstract in inquiry, conventional in style—that at first Peter does not want to play; and maybe not at all. After a pause:)

PET: Man proposes.
DEN: Is there a divinity that shapes our ends?
PET: There's a divinity.
DEN: That shapes our ends?
PET: What makes you think the dead know more than you?
DEN: Where do the dead live?
PET: Cold ceiling. Wet floor. Four walls.

(He is rising.)

I could be bounded in a nutshell and count myself king of infinite space, were it not that I have bad dreams.

DEN: You have nothing to tell me then?
PET: No—thing.

He has crossed behind Denise, touches her shoulder softly. She still looks toward where he was, warding something off.

DEN: What's it like?
PET: I would a tale unfold whose lightest word
    Would harrow up your soul.

He has bent over her, is speaking into her ear. The dialogue with the Ghost shifts ground, shifts personae.

DEN: My lord, I have remembrances of yours
    That I have longed long to redeliver.
    I pray you now, receive them.
PET: No, not I.
    I never gave you aught.

He continues on the diagonal path as if he'd never been diverted from it. Denise remains. Still: nothing rests. To the ultimate question the figure of the Ghost gives a shadowy answer. The question of providence returns to the carnal in the sensuousness of the sequence. The smooth-bodied Ghost strokes a smooth-bodied "son." The result is a metamorphosis: metaphysics of the flesh, whose resting place is the grave (and even there?). Denise is left with nothing but herself. The unfolding goes into the black hole.

The Secret Parts of Fortune

1) Denise rises and approaches the grave. Margaret, singing and obsessively digging (an ideographic gesture with her arm), moves center, following a serpentine path. She is clearing the ground, zero. Karen, watching, reminds us that Ophelia, too, is to be buried:

KAR: Goodnight, ladies, good night. Sweet ladies, good night, good night.
MAR: A pickaxe and a spade, a spade,
    For and a shrouding sheet;
    O a pit of clay for to be made
    For such a guest is meet.
    'Tis an unweeded garden that grows to seed.

Denise, in the center, looking down, seems to be floating above the grave.

DEN: *Let me question more in particular.*
MAR: *Things rank and gross in nature possess it merely.*
DEN: *'Sblood, there is something in this more than natural, if philosophy could find it out.*

The words are the words of Hamlet, but the voice is the voice of Ophelia, in her madness before drowning. The grave and coffin established, she raises the lid. Margaret circles this action, referring to it as if in a demonstration. To those observing:

MAR: *Here lies the water—good. Here stands the woman—good.*

Julie, sliding into the space, is beneath Denise who is preparing to lie face down in the grave. She will become her own ghost, the others wanting.

DEN: *I hope all will be well. We must be patient, but I cannot choose but weep to think they would lay him i' the cold cold ground.*

She is descending toward Julie, who reaches to receive her, floating down. No answer from the male principle, there is a shift to the female. Julie doubles. If more matter with less art (though not without art), more matter, then, but now erotic, polymorphous. Margaret is delving her own body, plucking her nipples and strewing them over the grave, into which Denise is falling.

MAR: *If I drown myself wittingly it argues an act—*
TOM: (watching) *Is this the prologue?*
DEN: *I'll tent him to the quick.*
TOM: *Or the posy of a ring?*

The bodies touch, sensually, Denise and Julie. The rest of the actors are audience to the act, guilty creatures sitting at a play. So, the legalism of what follows:

MAR: *An act hath three branches: to act, to do, to perform.*
Argal, she drowned herself wittingly.

Margaret, not looking at Tom, is nevertheless aware of his disdain. Karen, watching, speaks to Tom:

KAR: *What means this, my lord?*
MAR: *Unless she drowned herself in her own defense.*

Margaret is cupping her hands at her breast and drinking: her own life, hot blood. The image out of Cranach. The action in the grave is seductive, omnivorously transformative, festive, a dinner with the worms.

2) Gradually the sequence takes on a risky and murderous atmosphere, the signal given by Jack's lines below, out of the Closet Scene. Julie and Denise are entwined, voluptuously:

> JUL: *I have words to speak in thine ear will make thee dumb.*
> KAR: *Is it the king?*
> JAC: *Have you eyes?*

Peter has watched the women with great interest and apprehension, autoerotically. He creates his own sexual atmosphere, his own sense of hazard, which is arousing to him.

> PET: *Let us not burst in ignorance, but tell*
> *Why the sepulchre*
> *Wherein we saw thee quietly interr'd*
> *Hath op'd his ponderous and marble jaws*
> *To cast thee up again.*
> JAC: *Ha! Have you eyes?*
> JUL: *Eyes without feeling,*
> DEN: *feeling without sight.*
> TOM: *It means mischief.*
> JAC: *You cannot call it love!*
> DEN: *How is it with you, lady?*
> JUL: *Alas, how is't with you,*
> *That you do bend your eye on vacancy.*

They pass back and forth between Gertrude and Hamlet, suggestions of Claudius and old Hamlet, male and female roles interpenetrating.

> KAR: *Belike this show imports the argument of the play?*

Julie is still caressing Denise.

> JUL: *'Tis a knavish piece of work; but what o' that?*
> DEN: *Let me be cruel, but not unnatural.*

They laugh and caress each other. Julie whispers into Denise's ear, bites it.

> PET: *Have you heard the argument? Is there no offense in't?*
> TOM: *No, no, they do but jest, poison in jest; no offense i' the world.*

Margaret is singing; Gravedigger's voice:

> MAR: *In youth when I did love . . .*
> JUL: *O shame, where is thy blush?*

MAR: *. . . Methought it was very sweet . . .*
TOM: *That's wormwood.*
KAR: *The lady doth protest too much, methinks.*

There is a shrillness to Karen's voice, something like panic. Margaret has risen and is studying the action, stalking, reason going mad and measuring the extent of its madness.

PET: *What do you call the play?*
TOM: *The Mousetrap.*

Peter has risen and advances toward the women, savoring the image.

JAC: *Soft, now to my mother.*
PET: *Nay, but to live*
In the rank sweat of the enseamèd bed.
Stewed in corruption, honeying and making love
Over the nasty sty—

Tom mouths the same words, rising to audibility. Whereas Peter is playful and sensually taunting, Tom's action is in the temper of the Closet Scene, but as if the Ghost never came to interrupt him. Margaret is behind him, caressing or comforting him.

DEN: *O, speak to me no more.*
These words like daggers enter in mine ears.

Julie breathes into her ear.

No more, sweet Hamlet.

Peter is kneeling, moving to join them. Denise giggles an invitation. As Tom's voice rises, Margaret starts to panic, hands to her ears. Tom is still ghosting Peter's words. He suddenly turns and seizes Margaret. She projects the "act" upon him that objectifies her ensuing madness.

PET: *A vice of kings,*
A cutpurse of the empire and the rule
That from a shelf the precious diadem stole
And put it in his pocket—

Tom lifts Margaret high astride him (ideograph of the stallion: brute blood) and fucks her with a gross savage physicality. The rape is performed upon the figure of Ophelia/Gertrude/Margaret. He drops her like sucked skin when he's through. The sequence:

MAR:	*What wilt thou do?*

Peter is close to Denise, who shies away mockingly, cradling herself in Julie's lap.

DEN: *Thou wilt not murder me?*
MAR: *Help! help! ho.*

Peter rises suddenly and stabs the air, then again, and again:

PET: *Mother! mother! mother!*
JAC: *Is it the king?*

Jack has been watching the other two actions, as competing fantasies in the mind's eye, his own emotion still in the Closet.

PET: *A king of shreds and patches—*

Margaret has been lying exhausted. She rises now, pulls away from Tom's penitent touch, a combination of revulsion and shame for both of them, the horror of violation in the innocence of her madness:

MAR: *And will 'a not come again?*
             And will 'a not come again?
             No, no, he is dead.

Peter turns back to Denise, who is intertwined with Julie. But he is playing another scene:

PET: *How now? a rat? Dead for a ducat, dead!*

Denise is still, playfully, in the other closet:

DEN: *O me, what hast thou done?*
JUL: *O, such a deed*
         As from the body of contraction plucks
         The very soul.

For the moment, it is as if Julie has become Hamlet. Margaret is moving around the edge of the playing space from corner to corner, stalking, the ghost of a madness.

MAR: *He is gone, he is gone*
             And we cast away moan
         God 'a' mercy on his soul!

Peter turns from the murder that is seductive to the seduction that murders. He is holding Denise, who feigns at getting away.

PET:　*Look here upon this picture, and on this.*
　　　Come, come, and sit you down. You shall not budge.

He is now playfully menacing, Denise more frightened.

KAR (to Tom): *Come hither, my dear Hamlet, sit by me.*

Margaret is at the edge of the space, between the audience and Karen.
Julie is staring over Peter's arm as he holds Denise:

JUL:　*Your sister's dead, Laertes.*
MAR:　*Is it not monstrous that this player here,*
　　　But in a fiction, in a dream of passion,
　　　Could force his soul so to his own conceit . . .
JUL:　*There is a willow grows aslant a brook,*
　　　That shows his hoar leaves in the glassy stream.
　　　Therewith fantastic garlands did she make
　　　Of crowflowers, nettles, daisies, and long purples,
　　　That liberal shepherds give a grosser name,
　　　But our cold maids do dead men's fingers call them.

[Here we are in the glassy stream, the metamorphoses occurring from
actor to actor, rapidly; nor are they all recorded here, the refractions of
characters and ripples of scenes in the current. Also: if there is somewhat
less explanation and more text as the scenario proceeds, that is because
later into the work the issues that required more rationalizing—the tentative linking of images from the improvisational studies—entered more
reflexively. But the disjunct multiple perspective of this sequence, and
the proliferating shifts of identities, took a lot of discussion that is not
registered in the scenario, which I wanted to leave as much as possible as
it came to the actors, so the reader can see what they worked with. Some
lines or moments can only be justified in performance, if not explained,
by the fantasy texts of the actors, their private scenarios, which merge in
the overall structure.]

PET:　*You go not till I set you up a glass*
　　　Where you may see the inmost part of you.
TOM: *Lady, shall I lie in your lap?*

He has moved to Karen.

DEN: *What shall I do?*

[The sequence involving Denise, Julie, and Peter alternates between
playfulness and menace, so much so that the actors themselves, at the

limit, are not sure where the emotion is, which moves among them threateningly. Denise, for instance, is never quite certain that Peter won't hurt her. As for the audience, the levels of reality in the acting is part of the issue, all the more because there may be several levels present at once.]

> KAR: *No, my lord.*
> JUL: *Not this, by no means, that I bid you do:*

She is nibbling Peter's fingers.

> TOM: *I mean my head in your lap.*
> KAR: *Yes, my lord.*
> JUL: *Let the bloat king tempt you again to bed.*

Julie's is the worm's-eye view, the smarminess of the grave.

> PET: *Pinch wanton on your cheek, call you his mouse,*
> TOM: *Do you think I meant country matters?*
> PET: *And let him, for a pair of reechy kisses,*
>   *Or padding in your neck with his damned fingers,*
> KAR: *I do not know, my lord, what I should think.*

Margaret, watching, as Tom and Karen are watching, is also circling the space, her emotion moving from the zero ground, the shocked vacancy, of the rape to a prefatory rage. As she moves from one point to the other, she plays through the forms and degrees of madness, Hamlet's, Ophelia's, the two fusing through a kind of manic glee, knowing. [Each of the lines in the entire sequence has been reflecting upon the others, across the space, like the flecks and flashes of character. One of the ghosts in the perverse behavior of Denise and Julie, for instance, is Claudius: from the moment Denise descended into the watery grave the funeral baked meats were also furnishing forth the marriage table.] Now, Peter seizes Denise fiercely, as if he would murder. [The sequence has gone into every nook and cranny of the Closet.]

> DEN: *Thou turn'st mine eyes into my very soul*
>   *And there I see such black and grained spots*
>   *As will not leave their tinct.*
> JUL: *O, Hamlet, you have cleft my heart in twain.*
> MAR: *What would she do*
>   *If she had the motive and the cue for passion*
>   *That I have?*

TOM: *That's a fair thought to lie between a maid's legs.*
JUL: *O you must wear your rue with a difference.*
     There's a daisy.
MAR: *Mad call I it.*
     He is gone, he is gone.
DEN: *This is the very coinage of your brain,*
     This bodiless creation ecstasy
     Is very cunning in.
PET: *Ecstasy?*
     Stay, I'll go no further.

3) Where are you when you're with the Ghost? Elsinore. Not only a prison, but grave-garden-bed-closet-womb. The metamorphosis consumes, full circle, the uroboric snake, crown worn by the serpent that did sting thy father's life. If there is no fixed principle (divinity) or principle of fixity, there is no alternative but the shifting ground. The bad dreams of the infinite nutshell hold the secret, like the play-within-the-play-within, whispered into the ear. But there is an erotic limit to the metamorphosis. In this case, Peter's orgasm, which comes out of the mutual sexuality of lovemaking and murderousness. The Ghost is still there: I'll go no further. Sex is dying.

JUL: *If your mind dislike anything, obey it.*

Julie and Denise are erect on their knees, side by side above Peter, like two sentinels. He rises and goes to the edge of the circle. Jack takes his place.

MAR: *Bloody, bawdy villain!*
     Remorseless, treacherous, lecherous, kindless villain!
     O, vengeance!

Jack, reclining, looking up at Julie and Denise:

JAC: *O God, what a wounded name,*
     Things standing thus unknown, shall live behind me!
     If thou didst ever hold me in thy heart,
     Absent thee from felicity a while,
     And in this harsh world draw thy breath in pain,
     To tell my story.

              (Denise laughs.)

JUL: *To whom do you speak this?*

JAC: *Do you see nothing there?*
JUL: *Nothing at all; yet all that is I see.*
JAC: *Nor did you nothing hear?*
JUL (coldly):   *No, nothing but ourselves.*

Which is, so far as can be seen, the living truth—though Jack's appeal
for identity, his story, seems to be cruelly erased. What has been seen, in
the cross-reflections, is a network of identities, through which the self-
ing moves, the nothing-at-all that is yet the all-that-is-to-be-seen, the
nothing-but-ourselves. The sequence thinks out, in the interplay, the
implications of the first darkling moments, the challenge of the ramparts in the source-play, the issue of who's there and the unfolding of an
answer: the self is a ghost that comes and goes in the emptying mirror.

4) Rising from the void of closet and grave, Julie now circles toward
Margaret, in her movement the grotesque embodiment of the spirit of
Vengeance, tongue flickering (like Jack's earlier in the mortal coil), an
adder fanged. [Here there comes into the continuing play-within-the-
play contrasts of "character" between Julie and Margaret, Denise and
Jack, Tom and Jack, active and passive elements of their "natures,"
which have been explored during the investigations. Tom and Karen
have been observers at the infolding play in which the two women, by
refusing to acknowledge presence, have "reduced" Jack to an absence—
what Tom, in his willfulness, fears in himself: the vain outcome of a self,
its mockery. The pure subjectivity of him, captive to the self, rages:]

TOM: *Yet I, yet I, I, am I a coward?*
   Who calls me villain? breaks my pate across?
   Plucks off my beard and blows it in my face?
   Tweaks me by the nose? gives me the lie i' the throat
   As deep as to the lungs? Who does me this?
KAR: *You are merry, my lord*
TOM: *Who, I?*
KAR: *Ay, my lord*
TOM: *What should a man do but be merry? For look you now how*
   cheerfully my mother looks, and my father died within's two
   hours.

Julie, stalking Margaret, is passing in front of him, like a deranged figure
from the Dumb Show, the poisoner, that ghostly thing that pours the
hebona in the ear. Denise is still kneeling above Jack. She is, for the moment, played out—though with Julie's flickering tongue we may recall
the earlier words Denise had whispered into Jack's ear. The tone of the

brief exchange that follows is—in contrast to Tom's explosiveness—at the quiet of readiness, the fall of the sparrow, its providence:

DEN: *The players cannot keep counsel; they'll tell all.*
JAC: *Will 'a tell us what this show meant?*
DEN: *Ay, or any show that you'll show him.*

Tom is following intently the approach of Julie to Margaret, with an emotion like that at the climax of the play-within-the-play:

TOM: *This quarry cries on havoc. O proud Death:*
    What feast is toward in thine eternal cell
    That thou so many princes at a shot
    So bloodily hast struck.
KAR: *You are as good as a chorus, my lord.*
TOM: *I could interpret between you and your love, if I could see the*
    puppets dallying.

And, indeed, Julie has grasped Margaret from behind, like a puppet. Margaret quivers in her grip, suggesting a reprise of the earlier Yorick-skull sequence with Peter. But she is whispering with a harsh sibilance into Margaret's ear, almost strangling her with the words, which Margaret repeats graspingly.

DEN: *Be not ashamed to show, he'll not shame to tell you what it means.*
JAC: *You are naught, you are naught. I'll mark the play.*

The words come chokingly out of Margaret's mouth, prompted by Julie:

MAR: *The spirit that I have seen*
    May be a devil . . .
KAR: *You are keen, my lord, you are keen.*
TOM: *It would cost you a groaning to take off my edge.*
DEN: *Still better, and worse.*
JAC: *So you must take your husbands.*
MAR: *. . . and the devil hath power*
    T'assume a pleasing shape, yea . . .
TOM: *Begin, murderer! Leave thy damnable faces and begin.*

Margaret is choking, being choked, with rage.

MAR: *Now might I do it!*
DEN: *Adieu, adieu,*
JUL: *Remember me.*

Margaret approaches Jack, rather plunging toward him. He is still lying on the ground, soft, receiving. Her body shakes with rage. Her arm is raised to stab. At last, the commandment to be fulfilled, the actual deed. The blade lowers, she hesitates, body jerking—the moment coming as a consummation, spurred on through the last indecision by Julie, out of the long mad continuity from the rape. As with Tom's stubborn knees at the outset, she tries to force the blade down. Peter, who was also played out in the metamorphosing closet, has been a spectator to the event, in which Jack had replaced him. Now:

> PET: *Lights! Lights!*

The knife is still quivering above Jack. He speaks quietly to Margaret:

> JAC: *Where is the beauteous majesty of Denmark?*
> PET: *O Lord, I have remembrances of yours*
>   *That I have longed long to redeliver.*
> DEN: *Like the hectic in my blood he rages.*

Margaret's shaking is now the shaking of the bones, like the body invaded by the leperous distilment. The Avenger becomes the Skull, the dead Fool, the Ghost.

> JUL: *Now get you to my lady's chamber, and tell her, let her paint an*
>   *inch thick,*
> MAR: *My mother,—*
> JUL: *to this favor must she come.*
> MAR: *—father and mother is man and wife, man and wife is one flesh,*
> TOM: *There shall be no more marriages!*
> DEN: *Make her laugh at that.*
> MAR: *and so, my mother*

Margaret's jiggling dance is almost obscene.

> DEN: *In the rank sweat of the enseamèd bed.*
> JUL: *Your husband's brother's wife.*

Jack is rising in a coil, as if from the water in which Ophelia drowned, this time an ascent, shuffling off the mortal coil (after Hamlet's dying lines), flesh falling away, yin, flights of angels. Singing:

> JAC: *They bore him barefaced on the bier*
>   *Hey non nony, nony, hey nony.*
> TOM: *Get thee to a nunnery, go.*

Jack coils center like a maypole, Margaret jigging around him, opposite directions. An antic disposition, like a manic seizure, fills the space:

    KAR: They say the owl was a baker's daughter.

Tom is moving on the circumference:

    TOM: God hath given you one face, and you make yourselves another.
           You jig, you amble, and you lisp. You nickname God's creatures.
           To a nunnery, go.
    JAC: You must sing 'A-down a-down, and you call him a-down-a.
           O how the wheel becomes it.
    PET: This nothing's more than matter.
    DEN: A man may fish with a worm that hath eat of a king and eat of
           the fish that hath fed of that worm.
    PET: I see a cherub who sees them.
    JAC: There's rosemary, that's for remembrance. Pray you, love, remember.
           And there is pansies, that's for thoughts.
    DEN: O, there has been much throwing around of brains.
    KAR: A document in madness,
    JUL: thoughts and remembrance fitted.

Jack is still coiling center.

    JAC: O you must wear your rue with a difference.

Out of the mania, a chorus, the cost:

    TOM: Thou wouldst not
    KAR: *thou wouldst*   *think*
    JUL: *thou wouldst not think*
    DEN: Thou wouldst not
    PET: *thou wouldst*   *think!*
    TOM: how?   *about my heart*
    KAR: how ill all's here all
    JUL: *all*
    DEN: *ill*   *about my heart.*
    PET: how ill all's here
    JAC: There's a daisy!

Margaret is crying.

    TOM: High and mighty, you shall know when I am set naked on your
        kingdom!

JAC: *And in his grave rained many a tear*
           Hey nony no, hey nony no
JUL: *That great baby you see there is not yet out of his swaddling clouts.*
DEN: *The body is with the king, but the king is not with the body.*
PET: *The doors are broke!*
KAR: *The king is a thing—*
TOM: *of nothing.*
DEN: *Bring me to him.*
JUL: *Hide fox, and all after.*

They all run center toward Jack, as in a children's game, the panic of it; then they split, scurrying in all directions, behind the audience, leaving the space empty, repeating one or another of Julie's words: *"Hide . . . fox . . . etc."* as they run off. The tape is heard, muted at first, gradually audible. Soon the actors start returning, one and by one, tentatively, to the outskirts of the playing space, skittish with each other, keeping distance, crossing, as in a dance of tentativeness, eventually reconstituting the circle, as perfect as they can make it, standing. The tape:

JAC: I saw it distilled almost to jelly with the act of fear.
KAR: I saw the ambassadors leave for Norway.
JAC: I saw the action slip to the floor like sweat.
PET: In the vast dead and middle of the night, I saw a man shiver.
DEN: I saw the vowels of the earth dreaming its root.
TOM: I saw the shifting mother ground is sour with the blood
       of her faithful.
JUL: I saw the undiscovered country.
KAR: I saw them break up their watch.
TOM: A garden, I saw, and all the uses of this world.
PET: I saw the appetites of gravity.
DEN: The fearful summons, I saw.
TOM: I heard the trumpets braying out, I saw the King
       with a goblet on high.
DEN: I saw the thing coming, coming again tonight, appear,
       that thing.
KAR: I saw the bell then beating one.
MAR: I saw a vicious mole in nature.
DEN: I saw the sullied flesh.
JUL: I saw a hallowed and a gracious time.
JAC: I saw it fading on the crowing of the cock.
TOM: I saw the imperial jointress of this warlike state.

DEN: Frailty, I saw.

TOM: I saw her marry with mine uncle.

JAC: Post with dexterity to incestuous sheets—I saw.

[About here the actors are returning to the space, as described above.]

KAR: I saw the shape before it was unshaped, before it was
pulled and twisted, two feet with blue veins like rivers.

PET: Red scar in the sky I saw, disasters in the sun.

TOM: I saw a crab going backwards.

DEN: I saw the history of the theater on my shoulders.
I saw that it was very heavy.
I saw that I could not carry it.

JAC: I saw the crime of judgment.

MAR: I saw dark water birthed, the glowing wind mind-voiced.

JAC: I saw the right ear of being, male and female.

MAR: I saw the breasted sky, I saw the cunted river.

TOM: I saw a giant egg, divided, swallowed.

PET: I saw a man eating his children.

DEN: I saw a woman eating that man.

PET: I saw the earth without form and void.

DEN: I saw something to be told for the telling of which
we all wait.

JAC: Old human life, new human life, fancied human life,
avid, I saw.

MAR: I saw footsteps in the garden.

[They are moving among each other, delicate distances, forming the
circle.]

JUL: I saw we are explainable and not explained.

PET: I saw we will leave the emptiness as emptiness.

KAR: I saw we will go on craving.

TOM: I saw it smashing against a wall!

DEN: Craving, saw.

TOM: I saw the baby babble.

KAR: I saw a form come forward, back away and spin and
foam at the mouth.
I slapped it and saw I'd become its mother.

JUL: I saw shadows.

PET: I saw my bad dreams.

DEN: But I never saw my father.

KAR: I never saw my son.
TOM: I saw only what I saw.
JUL: Mostly I saw what I wanted to see.
MAR: I saw the Queen take the precious diadem and put it
        in her pocket.
PET: I saw the seven corners of a circle.

[And they are now assembled.]

KAR: I saw blood on the floor but not where it came from.
MAR: I saw seven times two eyes glaring.
JAC: This above all, I saw.
DEN: I saw a ghost. I saw the horses of God but saw men
        ride through the sky on the backs of turtles.
JAC: I saw a spirit but not a soul.
MAR: I saw its naked chest.
        I saw I'd rather not believe in ghosts.
JUL: I saw no sense in seeing.
TOM: I saw the baby babble.
PET: In the corner I saw the mother shiver, lose the son, take
        on the father.
KAR: I saw it all empty. I was full.
JAC: Shadows, I saw.
PET: I saw the inside of the light of light.
DEN: I saw: this never happens but it always is.

The circle is restored. Silence.

More Than Matter

The following sequence is played with the actors standing in the circle,
like another dialogue over the abyss. The lines, permutating the opening
exchange, are mirror images in a concrete poem. The lines assigned are
fixed in sequence, but they may be addressed to any actor in the circle at
any emotional pitch. That part is improvisational and the emotional
convention [that is, the range and pitch of it] will vary from performance to performance. The playing is very rapid, so there's almost no
chance to think about how to respond once the opening passage from
the Closet Scene is committed:

KAR: Now, mother, what's the matter?
MAR: Hamlet, thou hast thy father much offended.
KAR: Mother, you have my father much offended.

PET: *Come, come, you answer with an idle tongue.*

KAR: *Go, go, you question with a wicked tongue.*

DEN: *Why, how now, Hamlet?*

PET: *What's the matter now?*

DEN: *Have you forgot me?*

PET: *Now, mother.*

JAC: *Why? how?*

JUL: *What's the matter?*

JAC: *Have you forgot me?*

DEN: *Hamlet!*

PET: *You have my father much offended.*

JAC: *Mother?*

DEN: *Thou hast thy father much offended.*

JUL: *Come, come.*

JAC: *With an idle tongue.*

KAR: *Go, go.*

JUL: *With a wicked tongue.*

PET: *Now, mother.*

MAR: *How now?*

TOM: *Have you forgot?*

KAR: *Offended.*

DEN: *What's the matter?*

JAC: *Matter!*

TOM: *Thou hast thy father much offended.*

JUL: *You question.*

DEN: *Forgot?*

MAR: *Have you forgot me?*

TOM: *Answer!*

JUL: *My father.*

JAC: *Mother?*

PET: *Offended.*

TOM: *What's the matter now?*

KAR: *Me, me, me.*

JUL: *Forgot?*

JAC: *You have my father much offended.*

MAR: *Hamlet?*

TOM: *Now, mother.*

JUL: *What's the matter now?*

PET: *Why?*

DEN: *Matter?*

KAR: *Have you forgot me?*

TOM: *Offended.*

JUL: *How?*

DEN: *With an idle tongue, with an idle tongue.*

PET: *Have you forgot me?*

MAR: *Come, come.*

JUL: *Question!*

JAC: *What's the matter?*

PET: *Mother!*

TOM: *Forgot me?*

KAR: *Now.*

DEN: *Answer?*

JUL: *Offended.*

PET: *My father?*

JUL: *You, you, you.*

TOM: *What's the matter now?*

KAR: *Answer, answer.*

JAC: *Mother!*

DEN: *Question!*

KAR: *Have you forgot?*

PET: *Matter now, matter now.*

DEN: *Tongue.*

JAC: *Wicked.*

DEN: *Tongue.*

MAR: *Forgot?*

JUL: *Offended!*

PET: *Father?*

TOM: *Have you forgot me?*

DEN: *Me?*

JUL: *Have you forgot?*

PET: *Come.*

JAC: *Forgot.*

KAR: *Me.*

MAR: *Come.*

TOM: *Forgot?*

PET: *Offended.*

DEN: *Have you forgot?*

TOM: *Have you forgot me?*

KAR: *Forgot.*

JUL: *Mother?*
MAR: *Offended.*
PET: *Forgot?*
JAC: *Hamlet?*
DEN: *Forgot.*

In the intensity of the disconnections that fill the space, the actors have finally broken from the circle and are backing away, out of the space and behind the audience. [In the acting process of this fugal round, its music, there has been every inflection of role, character, self, voice, persona, mask, in the generation of a collective emotion, as there has been every effort to understand, at the personal level, the nature of the offense, the material cause, what prevents the crossing into the otherness that is so desired.] As they withdraw, their voices puzzled, entreating, still longing, questioning, there are variations on the theme: *"Forgot me. Forgot. Have you forgot? Me? Forgot. Have you forgot me?"* until they are out of sight.

The Kingdom and the Power

When the playing space is empty, a last tape is heard:

JAC: I saw Claudius, King of Denmark, dead.
MAR: I saw Gertrude, Queen of Denmark, dead,
DEN: Hamlet I saw, Prince of Denmark, dead.
PET: I saw Polonius, the old counselor, dead.
JUL: I saw Laertes, son of Polonius, dead.
KAR: I saw the nymph Ophelia, dead,
TOM: I saw Horatio among the living-dead.
DEN: I saw Fortinbras, with rights of memory in this kingdom,
       king.

(1976)

7. Deep Throat

The Grail of the Voice

Some propositions, first, about our overall subject, the searching for alternatives to the aesthetics of the text; and then some remarks about recent theater history, out of personal memory and actual theater work, reflecting on the propositions or subtextually glancing off:

In over thirty-five years in the theater I have lived through the living distinction between the literature and the performance and have also been involved in performance that seems to have discarded the literature. But I want to start by saying that whatever the aesthetics, there is *no* alternative to the text. I think that is so in the final analysis or "the final finding of the ear" (Stevens), the *sounding* of a text down to the last fugitive syllable, or phoneme, when the words seem to have left the page as if there had never been any words, dematerialized in the air. I think that is so even when you are sounding without words, only to discover that you are *being-sounded,* verbatim, as if the words being denied are the words being performed, reading you out as on a computer, word for word, spectral as they are, the metaphysical "temptations, indraughts of air" around thought, as Artaud perceived in his onomatopoeic madness.

There is only, so far as memory can reach—through imaginary worlds, perceptual worlds (the world on the screen of the Balinese shadow play), or the mimetically real world (on the corporeal screen of the play-within-the-play)—thought echoing thought, sonorously, within the infrastructure of thought, even in silence, like the revolution against reason that can only be made within it, even in madness. And so it remains in the lapse of modernity, word within a word unable to speak a word, *more or less,* more or less theologically (or, the going word, phallogocentrically), even when the Word—like Artaud's "dispersion of timbres," the sonorous incantations—seems secularized, shredded, musicated, scattered, or otherwise abolished or vanished.

That was the lesson not only of Derrida's critique of Foucault on *Madness and Civilization* but of the last generation of theater practice. In the theater we have been through a period where, if the beginning wasn't the Word—the authorizing text—the body became the book and "the grain of the voice" a grail. The phrase is Roland Barthes's in his concept of *writing aloud,* like a desideratum of theater, deep-throated, diapasoned, tongued, "the patina of consonants, the voluptuousness of vowels, a whole carnal stereophony: . . . the breath, the gutturals, the fleshiness of the lips, a whole presence of the human muzzle . . . throwing, so to speak, the anonymous body of the actor into [the] ear: it granulates, it crackles, it caresses, it grates, it cuts, it comes: that is bliss." Or, untranslatably, *jouissance.* Or so it seemed.

It wasn't the first time, however, that language was exhorted to wrap itself carnally around its own phonic substance, the brute materiality of no-presence but its own self-composing force, erotic, somatic and subliminal, ecstatic and even sublime. As Hugo Ball wrote about the polyphonic performance of Dada:

> The subject of the *poème simultané* is the value of the human voice. The vocal organ represents the individual soul, as it wanders, flanked by supernatural companions. The noises represent the inarticulate, inexorable and ultimately decisive forces which constitute the background. The poem carries the message that mankind is swallowed up in a mechanistic process. In a generalized and compressed form, it represents the battle of the human voice against a world which menaces, ensnares and finally destroys it, a world whose rhythm and whose din are inescapable.

That was another country and a pre-cybernetic world. The wandering soul is a romantic legacy mourning, through the clamorous Dada manifestations, the absence of a spiritual world, toward the remembrance of which Ball eventually withdrew in relative monastic silence. One of his supernatural companions, Tristan Tzara, had foreseen some inevitable fusion of ecstasy and high tech—"the trajectory of a word, a cry thrown into the air like an acoustic disc"—but even he might have been astonished when it was picked up by satellite and transmitted everywhere, raising the decibel level. And as the silicon chips take over, we worry as the voice rises that we are merely becoming a part of the *noise*—that the rhythm is so inescapable, the means of distribution so insidious, that the battle can hardly be waged.

As for alternatives to the text, in this serial, cyclical, and solipsistic time, it also seems—when all that was formerly said is done, *voiced*, in ideographs of self-reflexive sound—that we move off the page to realize (again) that, at least for us, the oral tradition is *written* and the performer's body inscribed. Anybody who has been around actors' improvisations will know what I mean. The aleatoric spontaneity is a repertoire of cliché, in the body, in the voice, in the whole carnal stereophony, until—the defenses exhausted over long duration—there arises, sometimes, a structure of apprehension that really fleshes out a thought.

Which is to say, perhaps, what some spiritual disciplines appear to say, or Shakespeare's *Sonnets*—an authoritative text on sounding and *jouissance* (the prophetic voice of the wide world dreaming on things to come)—that however it granulates or crackles, when the *jouissance* comes it comes like love in the Idea of loving, however much in the body very much in the mind. And the phenomenology of the voice still seems in complicity with a metaphysics that teases out a thought. Which is why Shakespeare could have the longing lover of the sonnets, who thinks he is not *thought of* and wants desperately to be with the other, totally, *totaled* in thought: "But ah, thought kills me that I am not thought. . . ." As I have said elsewhere, theoretically, that may be the most compulsive passion of theater.

Lest we lose ourselves in that thought, let me return to actual theater practice. I would like to look back briefly over the past generation, when there was much experiment in "the oral mode," attached to the notion of body language, or the rites of Love's Body, with more or less polymorphous perversion.

In the beginning there was Lee Strasberg, who, as you may have heard, died the other day (the same day as another ideologue of sound, Thelonius Monk). The sound sponsored by Strasberg at the Actors Studio in the self-reflexiveness of the Method was the voice of the autonomous self: psychological, provincial, "truthful" to the origins of the self, thus not a borrowed voice; to be truthful, maybe ethnic, and at its most self-indulgent (at a loss for origins?), if not pathological, narcissistic.

The Method was an extrapolation from Stanislavski's concepts of sense and emotional memory and Public Solitude to the self-saturation of the Private Moment. The extremity of the Private Moment for the

Method actor (with Brando as the archetype) was—for maximum truth of emotion, insensibly there—the moment of an almost unspeakable, maybe illicit incitation, at the brink of transgression or taboo, like a rape that has never been confessed or breaking the incest barrier or some actual or desired self-mutilation—what in the repertoire of postmodern sexuality is being played out in S&M or B&D. In the performance art of the gallery scene we saw a conceptualized equivalent of the Private Moment in, say, the autoperformances of Vito Acconci, such as *Seedbed,* where he masturbated soundingly through an amplifier while hidden under a ramp, or decorated his penis mutely in a closet. The theater inevitably raises questions, however, because of its obsession with exposure and the memory of itself as a public form, as to how much privacy in performance can be entertained.

There were, I should say in all fairness, considerable virtues in the Method that we are now beginning to appreciate again. In the return from a nonverbal theater of role transformations or unmediated reflections of the self to plays of character and dialogue, we realize that the actors from the Studio were better equipped for developing character than those who were doing sound/movement exercises in La Mama through plotless "tasks," activities, and games. If there was too much sympathetic affection and false empathy in the Studio, there was also a technique for crossing the distance to character, *becoming the other,* a greater specificity of social behavior, more attentiveness to time and place. But time and place could be, as I have suggested, very local, ingrown, with a deficient sense of history; and the vices of the Method led in the fifties to a tedious psychologizing corresponding to the emergence of packaged therapies, and a reification of very limited forms of personal or confessional experience. "Attention must be paid," they said in *Death of a Salesman,* one of the better plays in the tradition. But when we tried to pay attention, sometimes we couldn't hear.

I mean at rehearsal *and* performance. *Speak up! We can't hear you!* was the director's refrain. I cannot tell you how many times I said that to actors during that period, or how many times, wanting to say it, I kept it under my breath. For we are talking about an ethos and, implicitly, a critique of the theater's responsibility, no longer taken for granted, to "communicate" with an audience. There were, as the director bit his tongue, all the conceptual, ethical, and aesthetic intricacies of whether the actor *should* be heard. At what distance? overheard? or—at the margins of perception—not heard at all? It was a considerable crisis in a theater still predicated on a psychology of realism, with its arguments over whether or not, at any distance, an actor should wear makeup. It was also a question of "authenticity."

To pass in and out of hearing was an equivocal response to what was then called the Identity Crisis. What was not heard would be, so far as the dramatist's words were concerned, more or less "line perfect," but it was on the way, refusing to be heard, to a more conscious rejection of the text. The actor who was self-determining by refusing more voice may have learned later—encouraged by Brecht on ideological grounds—not only to withhold the voice but, if he or she could not agree with the text, to rewrite it or to discard it altogether. To some of us that seemed a necessary conceptual advance.

There was, however, the worst of it, having much to do with principle or the Alienation effect, for which purpose Brecht also wanted the actor to speak up. I mean by the worst of it what became for a while the scratch-and-mumble T-shirt school of acting on television, in the image of Brando, who created the image in principle but who, in *Apocalypse Now*, was a parodic whisper of himself. Politically—in the period of what *Time* named the Silent Generation—it seemed that the whispers and mumbles were the objective correlative of a kind of delinquency, the refusal to speak up so as to be "committed," the quietism of the Cold War and the Age of Ike. When we came to the new conservatism of Ronald Reagan, there was talk of a return to the fifties, which might have been so were it not for the shift from an economy of abundance to an economy of scarcity and the inequities of Reaganomics. The noncommitment of that other period may have been, though, an early adumbration of a new delinquency, as if having run out of things to *say*, we say them over and over through the non-semantic poetry of the deconstructed word, tape-looped and tautological, or the repetitive sonorities of Philip Glass— the trickle-down solipsism of a libidinal economy, with supply-side electronics.

But to stay with that other period and fill in the history:

In the fifties and the early sixties there was a lot of justifiable complaint about the vocal incapacities of American actors. The truth is that very few of them had any sort of extensive vocal training, whatever the method—or any concept of the voice, no less its metaphysical dependence on the enigma of a theological presence, what Derrida writes about in "La parole soufflée," one of his essays on Artaud, who felt that from the moment of birth his voice, his birthright, was stolen away. It was a time, too, when we knew very little about *the vocal image* or theater as a structure of phonic or graphic signs; nor did we think so subtly of speech, as Artaud did, "as an active force [like the sleeping serpent of Quetzalcoatl] springing out of the destruction of appearances in order to reach the mind itself" instead of representing itself "as a completed stage of thought which is lost at the moment of its own exteriorization." Derrida writes of the consciousness that enfevered Artaud, that something is being dictated so that the signifier says something more than we mean to say, a metonymic disaster of speech in which, as Artaud says of himself, "the cyclonic breath *[souffle]* of a prompter *[souf-fleur]* who draws his breath in . . . robs me of that which he first allowed to approach me and which I believed I could say *in my own name.*" If there is an ontological theft in the background of performance, it is "a total and original loss of existence itself," thought flying up, the body remaining below, bereaved by the duplicity of escaping words, which are not our own to begin with.

The real depth of the ontological cause was not what disturbed us in the sixties, the subtle subversion of signification. The actors were not conscious of it, even when they became aware of Artaud. If the body was bereft, it was not because of *la parole soufflée*, but rather, simply, because the throat so often hurt, through plain misuse or abuse. Actors had poor voices and did not know how to take care of them—to breathe, to use the diaphragm, resonate, project, cadence the complex rhetoric of a classical speech, even if they had the stamina for it, no less think of themselves as the possible instruments of a sound poetry fusing the ideographic body with the revolutionary semiotics of the tape machine, which could disperse semantic meaning into an alphabet of signs and, presumably, divest performance of the surreptitious corruption of the phallocentric presence in the hegemony of the Word.

It was another sort of presence that distressed the actors in San Francisco in the early sixties. When we first introduced electronic music at The Actor's Workshop—I was collaborating then with Morton Subotnick, when he was just starting the Tape Music Center—the actors were intimidated by the potential magnitudes of processed sounds. How can we match that? they thought. Subotnick did a score for our production of *King Lear*, which was an experimental model of feasible integration, the actors' voices embedded in the sound, rising over it, laminated, voice embracing sound, extended, random and concrete sounds suspended in the risible air, stage-struck, like visible signs, but cutting to the brain, the storm itself appearing (through multiple speakers strategically deployed) as a dimensionless sonic space, immense, the actual stage expanded, as if the music were in all its inexhaustible and exhausting amplitude the very breathing thought of Lear—who seemed at the apogee of defiance, in every syllable of his madness, *locked* into the sound. Our actors at The Workshop eventually learned, as they said (once the risk was applauded), to sing along with Subotnick, or other composers; but the work we did with electronic sound was, in the overall American theater, a very isolated experiment.

There still is not much of it on that scale, or with anything like that complexity. I remember, too, when we went to New York, the actors at Lincoln Center, many of whom had come out of the Studio with Elia Kazan, thinking I was out of my mind when they first heard sound textures from the score Subotnick was composing for our first production there; and then the sound and fury about the music, by critics and others, when we actually used it in performance. But back in San Francisco, despite these experiments, we were still very concerned—and for good reason, it was true all over the country—about the sound-producing capacities of the actor in an unaccommodated and unamplified body.

At the end of the sixties, as the regional theaters that had struggled for survival were more or less securely established, there was a concerted attack on the problem of the voice, along with greater attention to training for the actor, sponsored first by the Ford Foundation and later by Rockefeller's. It was obviously with the intention of preparing inadequate American actors to be adequately British, but with some mediated accent (or what they called "neutral") in classical plays. If we were wary of the British model so far as it was merely rhetorical, with a questionable "inner life" (the Angries were to change that by borrowing a realistic guttiness from American acting), we nevertheless found a savior from England, a young woman named Kristin Linklater, who was surprised if delighted to find herself in that role, since she had no extensive credentials either but had been, as I recall, a student of the woman who had taught Olivier at the Old Vic.

Linklater's work was patient and effective so far as it went, but it went on the whole very slowly, proceeding from the smallest sound. There was excellent attention to centering, breathing, and relaxation of the body, but the relaxed body tautened again under stress of performance, and there was something in the process that parsed out the voice as something of an enigma. If we saw improvement, there was also—not only with the Linklater method, but with others as well—further mystification. The more voice work we did, the more mysterious, it seemed, the voice became. And there was often so much self-consciousness about the voice, such protectiveness, that as soon as anything went wrong in the psychology of the actor, it was as if there had been no training, the throat clutched, and the voice went out first of all. Indeed, so long as be-havioral psychology remains, even in classics, in the center of the stage, with the obligation to perform something other than a dispossessed or unmediated self (and even then) the voice remains a problem—no mat-ter how strong it otherwise is.

Meanwhile, however, the decibel count was also rising with the politi-cal activism of the sixties. Stridency in the streets was matched by primal screams in the workshops. It was not quite the scream of the Chinese actor outvoicing the desert wind and thereby acquiring, as Artaud imag-ined, some primordial power in the contest; but there was very elemen-tal work done with the voice as the actors learned to engage their bodies, taking greater risks. That work expanded the repertoire of performance possibilities through psychophysical exercises, some invented, some bor-rowed from other cultures, not only from the Chinese actor, but the Indian, Balinese, Japanese, and from spiritual disciplines such as Yoga. There was also the impact of Jerzy Grotowski who, seizing upon Artaud's vision of the actor signaling through the flames, advanced the concept of the holy actor, shamanistic, burning the body away and leaving visible impulses or holographic signs resonating, a *via negativa* in which the high frequency of metaphysical being is like a Tantric power diagram where every color of the emotions is the inciting register of a concurrent sound.

It was in this atmosphere that my own work on the voice developed as a further articulation of the methodology of the KRAKEN group. That work was an intense activity of mind, highly verbal, physically charged, like a kind of brain fever in the body, caught up almost acrobatically in the incessant ghosting of thought. I had over the years become familiar with almost all of the available systems of vocal training for the actor and had worked with some of the better-known teachers. I admired as-pects of these other systems but remembered from long experience in various kinds of theater the distress signals of voice in the discomfited actor who might show much improvement in the training but would regress through rehearsal and performance, despite the exercises and warm-ups. The methods also seemed to me at times needlessly slow and usually better when actors were being instructed individually, one on one, though we wanted a collective method. I wanted a way, moreover, to exercise the voice that would be at every moment inseparable from the art of acting, something of a performance itself.

What evolved cannot really be separated from the investigative pro-cedures of the group, the reflective disposition of all its exercises, of which I used to say that they are all, the innumerable variations, only *one*. The Vocal Sequence we developed was the result of considerable trial and error and also draws upon vocal ideas and exercises familiar in other forms of training. But the distinguishing feature of the work is that every exercise is an idea, a heuristic concept. It is not so much the particular element of the sequence that is distinctive but rather the *sequencing* itself, the structural dynamic of its conception, the momentum of execution, the *idea* of a performance, and the particularity with which the particulars are rehearsed, moving into performance through what we called *the teleology of an impulse*. By this we mean—even in silence or seeming stasis—the following through of any gesture, physical or vocal, at any behavioral level, recognizably mimetic or utterly abstract, as if it were ordained, *inscaped*, moving once committed toward the consummation, *beyond exhaustion*, of something generic, some indeterminate and (sub)liminal choice.

There is not, so far as I know, any vocal idea, any conceivable way of using the voice that is not suggested by the Vocal Sequence that follows below. The emphasis is on vocal *production* but with attention to articulations and within the structuring of *perception*. There is a perceptual issue posed by every increment of the sequence or the interchangeability of elements—the transposition being the act of perception itself. So when, at the beginning of the sequence, there is a movement from silence to audibility, the perceptual question involved has to do with the threshold moment when audibility is *achieved*. But then: for whom? at what distance? self-reflexively or projected? and even before that, the precise determination of the threshold moment when sound *materializes* on the lips or, with a view to the instantiating reflex of the origin of the sound, the decisive moment when, in the recessions of silence, the lips begin to move. Certain moments of the sequence have, if conceived through performance, what Artaud speaks of as a *"metaphysics-in-action"* or ontological implications, like the gathering and reduction of sound in (7), where the sound may go through a diminuendo of being until, like the spotlight of the legendary clown Emmett Kelly, gathered into absence, it disappears.

The Vocal Sequence would not have taken the form it did were it not for a whole series of Impulse Exercises developed along with the vocal work. These were meant to explore marginal and transformative states, exponential limits, in which the actors could make the exploration only by exceeding themselves. The idea of the Impulse Exercises was absorbed into the structure of the Vocal Sequence, as indicated in the version here. That version is what was written down for the actors in KRAKEN after much experiment with the disposition of the initiating elements and the sequencing of the entire structure. We have given demonstrations of the Vocal Sequence, and those who have seen it may remember it as a performance in which the elements are orchestrated with collective and solo variants, permutated, syncopated, single voices rising, antiphonal, as if the prescribed order of elements was the basic melody of the sequence, which is disrupted and dispersed by improvisation, as in a jazz ensemble, and *reconstructed* in the playing out—a playing out, however, without closure. We have also performed the Vocal Sequence within other structures of performance, as in the extraordinary ramification of the basic mirroring exercise—known in almost every acting technique—which in our work becomes an epistemological field, "mirror upon mirror mirrored . . . all the show" (Yeats). And what it shows is a *power structure* whose determining source of energy is obscure, once the mirror is in motion, not only to those observing but to those performing it as well (as it develops, the entire group), although the formal power *of* the structure is inarguable.

The sequence is taught with the elements in the order indicated, but the actors in KRAKEN have long become accustomed to modulating the sequence as if it were—after the movement from silence to introjection—a combinatory set or a palette of vocal options whose limits are indeterminable. Because our work has been so obsessively concerned with the problematic of language, the sequence is never performed without words. The text of the sequence that follows, let me emphasize, was prepared for the actors and addressed to them. It assumes their familiarity with a number of techniques or exercises named that should not, however, make for any problems in following the principles and design of this approach to the voice. Since we have also taught the Vocal Sequence in workshops, some of the introductory remarks are anticipatorily responding to certain well-known anxieties and arguments over the voice. First of all, that it should be used organically, not artificially; or the ambiguity as to which comes first, body gesture or vocal expression. Grotowski says body first, then voice, but I think that's a non sequitur, as the introduction suggests.

Vocal Sequence

This is designed as a structure for searching with the voice, searching out the possibilities of the voice. The body will be instinctively involved, organically—that is unavoidable, and the voice can originate nowhere else but in the body, propelled by it and propelling. The rapidity with which it should eventually be done and the rhythmic play of it should eliminate interferences that come from wondering which comes first, voice or body—the emphasis is on the voice as body language.

Take a verse passage or any other speech, and use the voice as the instrument of investigation; not as the outcome of another process as if it were not part of the body. Do the following in a series, repeating any part at will and, after slow motion, in any order, though you will eventually want to score it in very personal ways. Remember: the structure allows for "recovering the losses" whenever you feel the voice has overstretched itself; it can always be brought in, introjecting or silently, but also remember that the point is to *stretch* the voice, in amplitude and articulation. There is a kind of dramatic structure involved, with climactic sequences of diminishment and expansion, speed, and the expansion and contraction of space. The climaxes should be attempted, gradually building by some means of returning to a center or altering impulse, but the superobjective is to discover and exercise the range of the voice. Other elements may be added and more stringent particulars (e.g., you may only sweep the floor with fricatives; set your own challenges).

When the elements are understood, then the sequence should be performed as an Impulse Exercise, rapidly, without mental interferences, rhythmically, voice and body. It should be ideographic finally without your thinking of it, the passage you used to motivate it virtually dissolving into the composition of an impulse. In this sequence it may seem that the verbal passage is not important, though any single exercise may be a valuable exercise for studying, parsing, assimilating a text. *You are acting/performing all the time.*

1. *Speak silently,* gradually moving up to the level of audibility; a precise sense of when the words pass over your lips. Start without lip movement.

2. *Speak normally:* point of focus necessary, moving from relatively close to some distance ("stage" distance) you can reach without shouting.

3. *Slow motion:* exploring personal values of each word; exploring images behind the words; exploring the phonemic structure of the words, vowels and consonants; different varieties of slow motion, biting words or caressing with air, exploring words as if they floated in space, etc.

4. *Introjecting:* the opposite of projecting, but also—as in psychological terminology—incorporating the words; speak as if relat-

ing outward, but address speech to the inner ear, as in a subjectively played soliloquy. In this and slow motion, the act of reflection is inevitable.

5. *Project atmosphere:* assertion of distinct presence by means of voice; as when a person walks into a room, s/he brings an atmosphere (what Michael Chekov means when he speaks of the radiation of character); but the voice does it; change atmosphere.

6. *Speak from imaginary center:* moving at will; movement will naturally be incited by previous exercises and vocal gestures.

7. *Diminish and expand:* also reverse (like Emmett Kelly's spotlight, or any other image that serves—images will be invoked in every phase of the sequence, or will propel exercises that follow).

8. *Line by line ideographs:* speak line, make gesture, let gesture condition next line; also word by word.

9. *Faster and faster:* keep increasing the speed to the limit of intelligibility; slow down, then see if you can take it further, faster. Intelligibility is always the limiting condition at any point in the sequence; you may stretch beyond but should be able to make it clear by exploring the problem of articulation at any limit.

10. *Densities:* harden the air, pack it, soften the air; gravity or weightlessness; the vocal equivalent of the Space Substance exercise in movement.

11. *Expand space, contract space:* this combines imagination with power and concentration; think of the entire space as a resonator; fill it, draw it in by power of will—capacious sound, tight sound, psyche affecting pitch.

12. *Duration:* a critical section in the sequence; an idée fixe, obsessionally extended; either a prolonged massing of sound, an almost unnavigable pitch, speed or volume—but a difficult assertion of sound, sustained beyond imagining.

13. *Varying pitch:* low to high and reverse; actually pitch will vary in several of these exercises, although you may want to set as a technical requirement in practicing individual sequences the fixation of pitch. (Relate to *resonators:* head, chest; laryngeal, nasal, occipital, maxillary, and combinations.)

14. *Perform actions with voice:* cover the wall, drive in a nail, put out a match, sweep the floor, tie shoelaces, embrace someone, kiss, assault, kill, etc.

15. *Change character of voice:* voice as axe, scissors, honey (as in Walking Exercise).

16. *Experiment with vowels and consonants, syllable weighting:* this too will occur naturally in previous sections, as in slow motion.

17. *Unusual or grotesque or mimetic sounds:* natural sounds, such as bird, wind, storm, animals; roars, hisses, etc., never-heard sounds.

18. *Mouth sounds:* using lips, hollows, teeth, cheeks, tonguings, spittle; blowing, wheezing, gurgling, razzing, etc.

19. *Laughing/crying:* this is actually a diaphragmatic exercise as well; keep changing from one to the other, giggles, sobs, hoarse laughter, gasps, hiccups, spasms, etc.

20. *Wailing/keening* the wildest lamentations.

Which must be returned to *speech.* Which is to say the production of meaning and semantic continuity. If Wittgenstein cautions us about the limit that defies communication—"What we cannot speak about we must pass over in silence"—Derrida imposes an auditory responsibility: "It remains, then, for us to *speak,* to make our voices *resonate (résonner)* through the corridors in order to make up for the breakup of presence *(pour suppléer l'éclat de la présence)*"; which might also mean "in order to supplement the impact of one's presence." That impact is not established merely by the grain of the voice, if the grain of the voice is taken to mean a carnal stereophony without semantic continuity. But that does not actually seem to be what Barthes had in mind, as we can see from the essay with that title in which he compares two singers, using Julia Kristeva's distinction between the *pheno-text* and the *geno-text.*

"From the point of view of the pheno-song," which includes everything that pertains to culture, style, communication, expression, representation, the rules of song, "Fischer-Dieskau is assuredly an artist beyond reproach: everything in the (semantic and lyrical) structure is respected and yet nothing seduces, nothing sways us to *jouissance.*" It is an art that, respecting the pheno-text, "never exceeds culture: here it is the soul [with its "myth of respiration"—hence *inspiration*] which accompanies song, not the body." But Panzera, on the contrary, is no mere agency of *pneuma,* the mysticism of the "soul swelling or breaking" with the passion of the lungs. "The lung, a stupid organ (lights for cats!), swells but gets no erection; it is in the throat, place where the phonic metal hardens and is segmented, in the mask that *signifiance* explodes, bringing not the soul but *jouissance.*" What is heard in Panzera is the geno-text, through an extreme rigor of thought that regulates "the prosody of the enunciation and the phonic economy of the French language. . . ."

It is an art totally material *and* totally abstract, and while the space of the voice is an infinite one, its truth hallucinated, that art was achieved in Panzera, according to Barthes's ear, by a patina of consonants, "given the wear of a language that had been living, functioning and working for ages past" and that becomes "a springboard for the admirable vowels." It is *that* patination that fulfills *"the clarity of meaning"*—the grain of the voice in the grain of language, like the Russian cantor he describes, producing a sound from "deep down in the cavities, the muscles, the membranes, the cartilages, and from deep down in the Slavonic language, . . . the materiality of the body speaking the mother tongue. . . ." What Barthes is objecting to, of course, is known and coded emotion, immunized against pleasure (but *is* that so?), and reducing meaning to the tyranny of meaning, instead of writing the geno-text, which exists in the grain of language from which the voice draws its sustenance, whatever else the body gives.

Whatever we do with vocal production, it is the grain of the language that eludes us in this country, what made it so hard, for instance, for William Carlos Williams ever to be certain of the variable foot. Barthes worried that with the death of melody the French were "abandoning their language," if not as a normative set of values, then as the site for pleasure, the place "where language works for *nothing,* that is, in perversion. . . ." In our vocal work we think we have restored that site, that place, although it is hard to abandon a language whose grain has never yet been truly ascertained. That still remains the quest of the voice, the grail, in theater, sound poetry, or on tape.

(1982)

8. A Valediction

Chills and Fever, Mourning, and the Vanities of the Sublime

Age comes today with aneurysm on the brain, long before the physical symptoms. We make up the symptoms as we go along: I am writing this in Paris, seized by *la grippe,* and as little pulses of pain, no mere headache, strike my eardrum, my temple, I wonder whether the SAMU (ambulance) number has changed, and whether we shouldn't have a family doctor here, a consulting physician, to refer us to a cardiologist when the blood vessel bursts.

This is not something that would have occurred to me when I first came to France, toward the end of the fifties. I was lured then by the promise of *théâtre populaire,* which seemed the living consummation of a dream of youth, a market-impervious institutionalized avant-garde, merging socialism and surrealism; not chills and fever but "convulsive beauty" (Breton)—especially when the Mistral swept over the walls at Avignon, as if on cue during a performance of *Mère Courage,* whipping open the flap of the wagon, which dropped, to reveal the one-eyed man who was looking for Swiss Cheese.

If that was a perfect collaboration of art and nature, the dream itself burst in the euphoria of the sixties, with its theatricalizing propensities and participation mystique. That was pumped up in France by the Living Theater's disruption of Jean Vilar's benign leftist dominion at Avignon, then subsided all over the world into the society of consummation, the spectacle itself, of which the internationalized festival, with its requisite panoply of avant-garde performance (no longer on the fringe), is merely a subsidiary site of commodification. Brook's *Mahabharata,* sequestered expensively in a quarry at Avignon, would appear to have been the centerpiece of this expansion, "like gold to airy thinness beat," as John Donne wrote of another sort of ecstasy, in "A Valediction: Forbidding Mourning," now revealed as the repressed emotion of the postmodern scene.

The question in France today is whether socialism itself has a future or, as one of its leaders recently declared, needs to suffer a "Big Bang." What is true, meanwhile, of the French theater is that, with an enduring legacy of the avant-garde, however quiescent today, its future is pretty well assured by its panache as a cultural asset, with provision in the national budget. What remains a cause for envy is that the theater has status here even when it is rather seedy, as it is periodically at the Comédie Française. Whatever the course of socialism, one simply cannot imagine somebody at any level of the French theater bursting out in a rage like that of one of the directors of Theater X, when—shortly after abandoning my work with the KRAKEN group—I came to Milwaukee and was briefly on its Advisory Board: "I've been working in this fucking theater for twenty years," he cried, "and I don't even have a fucking medical plan. I can't go on without a medical plan!"

There is a desperation at the core of the American theater that is not merely, however, a function of age, and that has had repercussions not only in the conventional theater but also in the deepest underground.

If an aging avant-garde is a contradiction in terms, to age gracefully in our theater is mainly a non sequitur. I have written of this elsewhere and long ago, in *The Impossible Theater: A Manifesto,* but think of it again: even in the mainstream it is hard to find really mature character actors of the kind quite common in European theaters, with a commanding discipline and a sense of dignity in the profession. Our actors aging with any eminence are, if anywhere, in the movies (overlooking the ruins there), and those who find themselves growing older around Broadway or in the regional theaters are, with rare exceptions, still warding off rejection, wanting in self-esteem, mere spectral visions of old desire, or, more or less hysterical, sad, anecdotal, doing their shtick, with the further humiliation of knowing themselves burnt-out cases. There are other forms of desperation among the relatively few of those who have managed to persist somehow through a generation of experimental theater. A (very) few of the actors may have made it into the movies, and if some rare directors, like Richard Foreman and Robert Wilson, have managed to sustain their own work into another period—in Wilson's case with help from abroad—the same cannot be said for the numerous performers who have worked with them, most of whom were un-equipped to begin with to perform, as some are now trying to do, in conventional plays. Some have simply passed out of the theater scene entirely, not having had at the outset the same tenacious stake in it that, for better or worse, professional actors need. As for an artistic community itself, I have always felt—at every echelon of our theater, including the experimental—that we have collectively suffered from the absence of a replenishing matrix of discourse. Whatever the case, we simply do not have a sustained rite of passage from the avant-garde that, out of resistance and contestation, empties itself dialectically into the established theater, or takes over its directorship, as it invariably does here or in Germany, where there is at present no extraterritorial site of the avant-garde, because it exists within the state theater apparatus—where it is also entitled to a medical plan.

A medical plan for the avant-garde may also seem like a contradiction in terms, but to the degree that an avant-garde exists at all today, it seems to be thinking differently about that. Given the recent politicization of the arts—overwrought besides by the incursion of AIDS—health care is as much part of the agenda as it is with Hillary Rodham Clinton and the new president. That concurrence brings me back, however, to my own earliest affinities to the notion of an avant-garde, in which the cry of rage was, with whatever fringe benefits in the social order, something that arose from an "essential rupture," the break in being, an aneurysm at the heart, what made it possible, even obligatory, to dream like Artaud of an "essential theater," corrosive, purgative, homeopathic, impelling us once more to think of the sublime, however impossible its realization in any form that we knew. I realize, meanwhile, that the reflexes of such thought, gazing as it does at "the incandescent edges of the future," were nurtured in the theater before the dominance of a critical theory more than suspicious of the sublime.

As it turns out, I find myself, after a long period of withdrawal, back working in the theater again, somewhat reluctantly (a one-shot deal, I say), but with undiminished reflexes of this and other kinds, shared in various measures by my collaborators: the composer Morton Subotnick, the singer/performance artist Joan LaBarbara, the video artists Woody and Steina Vasulka. Their bloodlines are decidedly of the avant-garde. They have their own eminence now, of course, in the music, performance, and video establishments, and are by no means averse to medical plans. Whatever the outcome of the work, there is an attitude in all they do that I remember from other days, a rudiment, a dominant, a without-which-not that has little to do with current views of art as "social praxis" or "cultural production"; nor is it "transgressive" or "subversive" because it happens to be in the right "subject position," whether of race, class, gender—or for that matter, age.

I suspect that all of us share what are, for those on the Left, quite acceptable political views, and more or less act upon them. But among the reflexes is, if not a separation of art and politics, an unswervable sense of the distinction of art, which, at the time I wrote the manifesto, I had rarely found in the theater. That may be generational, but it is also, I think, *generative*—and no matter what anyone thinks, it is not now and never has been guaranteed by the right political opinions, one of the ironies of art still being that those who do not have them may be, as through the history of modernism, better artists than others. If that is a liability of art, it will remain so even as we widen the parameters of what we take to be art, for good reasons and bad, having to do with exclusion, though art itself will up the ante on the liabilities it assumes.

The older I get, what compels me to art is what brought me there in the first place, when other options (I was, to begin with, a chemical engineer) seemed a lot safer, with reliable benefits. Art is still what you do because you must, or because you cannot do without it. Since I had been doing without it for some time, not making theater, I have come to think of myself as a theorist, though with reflexes there still determined by the art of performance, what I have meant by "blooded thought." Whatever the impulsions of a politics—or the required activism of any historical moment—I have never quite bought the critique of formalism or of modernism, and still believe that new forms are themselves the prospects of new social content, models, method, and that a certain historical obscurity in art may be an unexpected source of energy, liberating in ways that political attitudes are not. I believe I have been as responsive to critical theory as anybody working or writing about the theater, and thus realize these ideas may seem widely out of fashion and, so it goes, politically incorrect. But what can I say? The art that moves me most, that seems to me wisest and most compelling, is itself moved by declaring, recovering, discovering in a devastation of value a sense of reality without mere rhetoric or social coding. If it is in any way avant-garde, that is because there is in what it discovers the capacity to be confounding.

Discovers for whom? For those who may come to see. If I were still working in the theater I would have, as I do in my writing, no other expectations. The means of production? Given, first of all, certain dimensions of mind: imagination, daring, audacity— *"l'audace, l'audace, et encore l'audace"*—which, with their now formulaic charges of elitism, other forms of vanity may never understand. The avant-garde is itself a lifeline. It has had a populist strain from time to time, but its essential substance is the extraordinary. Our new art may be of blade running diversity, multicultural, polysexual, cyberspatial, you name it. But it should be apparent that diversity itself will soon be a commonplace, and virtual reality the merest servomechanism of an interactive illusion, unless some exceptional imagination is brought to it, making it extraordinary.

What is it, meanwhile, that remains extraordinary about the theater? For myself, what made it impossible to begin with: in every generation, though repeating itself impossibly, the form of (its) disappearance. I have not, as I say, been doing it for a while, and may not—after the "opera" I am working on now—be doing it again; but those are the terms in which I will be thinking about it till I die. Which is, as I have written in the theoretical books derived from the theater work, like dying into the thought of theater thinking about itself. I would not expect anybody in the world but me to be really obsessed with that, except if they think twice about what they have been reading and seeing in the canonical drama—which now, of course, is ideologically suspect, and probably deluded.

(1994)

9. The Dubious Spectacle of Collective Identity

It occurred to me after accepting the invitation for this talk that I might be here under false pretenses, given the theme of "Ceremonies and Spectacles, and [particularly] the Staging of Collective Identities," which I have come to think of after many years in the theater as a rather vain enterprise. As for the scholarship that takes for granted that theater is the site of the social, or an affirmation of community, that appears to me now—though I believed it when I was younger—an academic ceremony of innocence, assuming as a reality what is, perhaps, the theater's primary illusion. Since I have written extensively about that illusion, I will not belabor it here, but want to back up somewhat behind our immediate subject, whose immediacy is an aspect of the society of the spectacle, with its superfetation of image, as well as the anthropological slant on performance that has, over the last generation, almost promiscuously widened its parameters. When we think of stagings now, they are likely to include, beyond the play that was once the thing, or even performance art, everything from politics and fashion to voodoo rites, from carnivals and festivals to sporting events and sex shops, from the mise-en-scène of the unconscious to the presentation of a self in the psychopathology of everyday life. At the same time, moreover, that international travel has made us familiar with hieratic forms like the Kathakali and the Noh, performance is coming from everywhere, out of the savannahs, from the bush, and in the worldwide circulation of commodities there was even the spectacle of the aborigines from Australia in the rural

137

heart of Manhattan, chanting and dancing in Central Park, within a be-mused ring of spectators increasing their cultural capital. In all of this the question of collective identity is somewhat up for grabs—certainly in postindustrial cultures—as it was not, presumably, in the tradition of canonical drama out of the legacy of ancient theater, where ceremony and spectacle were thought to be a function of ritual, which in its repeti-tive stagings reaffirmed or certified what we cannot quite count on now. As for the place of ritual in the origin of drama, that remains shrouded in myth.

The myth I am referring to, however, is not the myth from which it was once thought ritual derived. That myth was formulated by Sir James Frazer in *The Golden Bough,* surely one of the more seminal works in the history of modernism. As Lionel Trilling remarked in an early essay, "On the Modern Element in Modern Literature," just about the time that the story of Resurrection in its most institutional form was losing its hold on the world, the literary mind was captivated by Frazer's account of death and rebirth,[1] and those falling and rising gods who seemed to as-sure a cyclical continuity while the center was coming apart. For the Cambridge School of anthropologists, the ritual theory of myth co-incided with the ritual theory of drama. As Jane Ellen Harrison put it, and almost all theater histories preserve it, the drama had its roots in some originary rite, the *dromenon* or nuclear event ("the thing done"), or the *legomenon* or primal Word ("the thing spoken").[2] What the thing was or the Word that was in the beginning remains a mystery. There were variations on the nature of the initiating rite—tomb or funerary ceremonies, vegetation cycles, the year-god or sacrificial king and, in re-cent years, shamanism—but the theory was that the shaping principle of a ritual source eventuated in the classical form of drama and the civic institution of theater.

That was pretty much how things looked when I started working in that dubious civic institution, my view of the origins of the drama con-ditioned, through the fractures of modernity, by established ritual theo-ry. It was not so much a theory, however, as an allegory constructed by Frazer from diverse ritual manifestations that subsequent anthropolo-gists looked upon as conflicting evidence of a dismembered whole. Even before we began to suspect, as in Derrida's reading of Artaud, "that there has never been an origin,"[3] it became apparent that few scholars of the ancient world really believe that all myth—including Homeric epic and the sacred literature of the Near East—has its beginnings in ritual. Clas-sical scholars are skeptical now, too, about the common view that ritual illuminates our conceptions of Greek culture. They are even more skeptical about the ritual origins of drama, whether out of the goat song or tauriform rites or the cult of Dionysus, whose forms we can approach at best as the remembered shards of broken signs.

There are still powerfully regressive theories, like that of René Girard, with a strong desire—the more the world reveals itself as a marketplace of signs—to ascribe redemptive value to the illusions and mystifications of ritual.[4] (And I was just at a symposium on "Theaters of the Dead," in which participants were entranced by talk of spirit possession in Mozambique or in the African burial grounds discovered in the construction of a federal building a short subway ride from where we were in New York.) As he went, however, about reappraising the mythic element in the history, there was a kind of evangelical desperation in the enterprise of Girard. It had the fervor of Artaud's victim signaling through the flames. At that "fragile, fluctuating center where forms never reach,"[5] it is hardly a question of theater being derived from ritual, theater *is* ritual— and a far vertiginous cry from the Cambridge theory of the drama's origins. Despite all the archaeological research in Greece since the turn of the century, the assumptions of the Cambridge School have never been proved, nor any archetypal ritual discovered from which, as Northrop Frye once put it, "the structural and generic principles of drama may be logically, not chronologically, derived." Keyed in to the archetypal— and the symbolism of a divine-human victim as a latency in the unconscious—Frye adds: "It does not matter two pins to the literary critic whether such a ritual had any historical existence or not."[6]

Nor does it matter to this day to certain artists and theater practitioners, who at some rudimentary, nostalgic, or visionary level were confirmed in ritual desire by the "alchemical theater" of Artaud. Or even before that, if they were sufficiently literary, by the occultism of William Butler Yeats, and in various parts of the world by the ongoing tradition of symbolism. Like García Lorca, Cocteau, and T. S. Eliot, Yeats was one of the poetic dramatists of the century who sought in ritual forms an alternative to the domination of theater by realism and naturalism, the materialistic insolence of the modern, which denies the affirmation of a transcendent principle—a denial of the divine in the name of Man. For Artaud, the theater of Cruelty is born not only to separate birth from death but to erase that defiled and usurping name. The powers of spectacle do not exist, he would say, for so trivial a purpose as to describe man and what he does. Nevertheless, the history of realism has its own mysteries and—however domesticated—ceremonial tendencies; or, in the masking of ideology, processes of occultation. From Ibsen and Strindberg through O'Neill, the skepticism of the modern preserved the residues and shadow-structures of ritual forms, even as the corrosion and distrust of a historicist sensibility eroded their powers, while confronting an apparently gathered public, that fiction of an audience, with the developing absence of collective identity.

Despite the erosions, and the doubtful view of ritual origins among classical scholars, the interest in ritual persists from the legacy of early modernism into the postmodern, even in historical materialists like Walter Benjamin in his definition of the theater of Brecht. From Artaud to Grotowski to the Mabou Mines, from deconstruction to queer theory and the butch/femme aesthetic, attention to ritual occurs, however, for quite different reasons, as vision, critique, structures of irony, or—as in the notion of "performativity," with its *stylized repetition of acts"* [7]— agency and instrumentality through mask, drag, retro, or masquerade. Meanwhile, the idea of the *festival* persists not only as an image of cultural memory, but as a memory of the sixties and the utopian spectacle of its "participatory mystique." Or as Derrida sees it through Artaud and "the closure of representation," as a virtual alternative to the Western metaphysical tradition with its "phallogocentric" structure of domination and power and its vitiating principle of *mimesis*. It is that principle that Girard, aware of the critique of representation, tried to defend for salvational purposes, along with the ineliminable but generative violence of ritual desire. Speaking of which—though Girard's work has receded in recent years—I just received an announcement from Hermann Nitsch, one of the talismanic figures of Viennese Actionism in the sixties, that his Orgy Mystery Theater, which seemed to have disappeared, "will take place from the sunrise, the 3 of August to sunrise, the 9 of August 1998 at Prinzendorf castle and its surrounds," around which Nitsch showed me some years ago when he was still planning the event. The weeklong festival will include the slaughter and disembowelment of a bull and various blood-pouring actions with mythical leitmotivs of transubstantiation and communion, invoking "the rending of dionysos / the blinding of oedipus / the ritual castration / the murder of orpheus / the murder of adonis / isis and osiris," matricide, patricide, fratricide, with all "the sado-masochistic primal excess" of Girard's mimetic Double, ending with ceremonial processions on "the day of resurrection."

We may get still another view of ascension in the less mythic, more secular, but no less spectacular, body art of Stelarc, who has suspended himself over a street in New York, above the waves on the coast of Japan, and high over the Royal Theater of Copenhagen by a precisely inserted array of fishhooks through the flesh. But as there is, with his notion of "the obsolete body," a certain excruciating solipsism in such performance—as there was when Chris Burden had himself crucified on a Volkswagen or Gina Pane climbed up a ladder of knife blades—let us back up for an older view of transcendence to Eliot and Yeats, both of whom troubled over the body but valorized the Word and sought—with more or less apocalyptic violence in the vision—a recovery of cultural unity, as classical modernism did. In referring to the ritual concerns of Eliot and Yeats, we will be turning up issues that were not at all exhausted by their experiments in the theater. Dormant for some years, those issues were reactivated over the last generation in the revival of Artaud, who became a tutelary figure not only in the theater but in poststructuralist theory, which in turn—obsessed with the thought of performance in a mediated age, where capital *is* spectacle—reshaped our thinking about the theater, with its production apparatus and vices of representation, including a soporific or self-edifying audience, what Brecht had dismissed as "culinary theater." (All of these tendencies came from abroad, but had a formative impact on the American scene in the sixties and after, and I myself did the first production of Brecht's *Mother Courage* in America in 1957.)

We tend to forget that Brecht's earliest plays—*Baal* and *In the Jungle of Cities*—were, with similar disenchantment, more or less contemporary with Eliot's *The Waste Land,* largely because Eliot subsequently made himself persona non grata to the Left by declaring himself an Anglican in religion, a Royalist in politics, and a Classicist in literature. That was in 1928, the same year he wrote the "Dialogue on Dramatic Poetry," where we can see that his interest in ritual was a matter of formalism as well as religion. There was in the "Dialogue" not only an aversion to realism and its falsifying psychology, the vice of humanism, but an appreciation of artifice, the post-Symbolist desire for a pure aesthetic. There was also the desire to ground the drama in its proper speech, not prose—the language of devaluation—but verse, which Ibsen, master of prose drama, felt compelled to abandon as the spirit world receded into bourgeois appearances. But as Eliot searched for the grounds of authority in his experiments with the drama, he eventually took his cue from Ibsen and realism, returned to prose, and tried to suggest in surreptitious rhythms the older mythic and ritual forms behind the bourgeois appearances, to reveal the Word within a word unable to speak a word, swaddled in darkness, instead of ceremony a sort of tongue-tied pantomime of the play within the play.

In the "Dialogue," however, it was ritualized appearance that attracted Eliot. What he valued, for instance, in the artifice of ballet was precisely *closure,* "permanent form," whose strength "is in a tradition, a training, an askesis. . . ."[8] Which is to say, as Grotowski later did for the theater, a spiritual discipline, "a training which is like a moral training" (Eliot, 47), which was the nature of the training (during the seventies and eighties) in my own KRAKEN group. The other participants in the "Dialogue" having approved of ballet because "it is a liturgy of very wide adaptability," one of Eliot's voices, E, takes the opening for which he has been waiting, and for which they appear to be waiting today amidst the ethnic rivalries and sacramental upsurge in Eastern Europe and elsewhere: "I say that the consummation of the drama, the perfect and ideal drama, is to be found in the ceremony of the Mass. I say . . . that the drama springs from religious liturgy. . . . And the only dramatic satisfaction that I find now is in a High Mass well performed" (47). When E adds that the church ritual through the year affords a complete drama of creation, B takes issue: "the question is not, whether the Mass is dramatic, but what is the relation of the drama to the Mass? . . . Are we to say that our cravings for drama are fulfilled by the Mass?" (48).

We are more likely to say today, as Raymond Williams once did, that our cravings for drama are being fulfilled by the mass media, even when the Mass is conducted by the Pope, as it was recently in Cuba, only to be preempted—with another revelation turning the TV anchors and viewers away—by the sexual scandal around President Clinton. In any event, what we now have, in an overdose of theatricality and supersaturation of image, is what Williams described some time ago: "drama as habitual experience: more in a week, in many cases, than most human beings would previously have seen in a lifetime."[9] Or as Jean Baudrillard would put it, so much more that it becomes an obscenity, a religion of appearance, with the simulacra as sacred, the cybernetic inertia of hyperrealism.[10] This impasse of mass culture may seem as distant from the genteel debate over the dramatic properties of the Mass as the Pope himself was when he celebrated the Mass in Papua New Guinea and used pidgin English while the tribesmen, throwing up clouds of yellow and orange smoke to ward off evil spirits in the offertory process, shouted, "Mi laikum you Pop!" We may also remember, however, that as far back as the banyan trees on the cannibal isle in *Sweeney Agonistes,* there was always in Eliot—not only in the irony but in the most civil inflection—an early warning signal. He knew long in advance that in the aesthetic of fascination which now takes us everywhere, with a baggage load of signs, Walkmen glued to our ears, that "a kind of non-intentional parody hovers over everything" (Baudrillard, 150).

There is something queer in the modern sign that, reaching everywhere through the media into everything once sacred, exposing it to derisive eyes, still "dreams of the signs of the past and would well appreciate finding again, in its reference to the real, an *obligation*" (Baudrillard, 85–86). Well, maybe not too much of an obligation, a reasonable facsimile, perhaps, or simulation of necessity, so long as it feels like a new *experience*. That is what B distrusts in E. He feels that there is something salacious and excessive about this fascination with the Mass. He speaks of it as an orgiastic self-indulgence, an illicit affectivity, and—what looks like second nature in a world of simulacra—a confusion of genres as well, based on unbelief. He says of E what Eliot suspected of himself, that his "dramatic desires were satisfied by the Mass, precisely because he was not interested in the Mass, but in the drama of it. Now what I maintain is, that you have no business to care about the Mass unless you are a believer" (48).

Now what I maintain is what I have already implied, that while ritual interest has shifted from the Christian Mass to the sacred forms and figures of other cultures—from Korean shamans to Shinto priests to Kutiyattam temple dancers to gospel singers in Brooklyn to the Cristo Rey festival of the Yaqui Indians in Arizona—the issues of the "Dialogue" still remain suspended in an age of disbelief. That was apparent less than a month ago in New York, where, as I said, a major symposium was devoted to mortuary ceremonies and the ghostly attractions of Theaters of the Dead. What we are dealing with inevitably is the substance of ritual desire in an era of suspicion whose secularity seems to blush and increase exponentially with every born-again religious impulse. At the same time, our cravings for the drama seem to have weakened in proportion to its mass-mediated availability. It is certainly true that the drama as it comes out of the canonical texts has had a bad press in the past generation of experimental theater. While it has been somewhat revived in revisionist productions, a case can still be made that the most interesting performance today, to some extent in the theater but mostly elsewhere in the other arts, is still doing without it. Thus, we look to ritual again—and the ceremonial forms of other cultures—not only for ideas of community, but for missing energies, psychic liberation, desublimated sexuality, carnival spirits, structures of participation, the redemptive side of repetition, or an awakening festival that relieves us of it, and—so far as there is still an aesthetic in all this—an alternative theatricality. Or in the age of identity politics, an alternative identity too, like the mock-Amerindian Gómez-Peña encaged and exhibited with Coco Fusco, or the performance artist Orlan, who has staged the ongoing spectacle of nine cosmetic surgeries by means of which—with the surgeon and attendants dressed by famous fashion designers, Issey Miyake or Paco Rabanne—she has had her face radically transformed, with features from the Mona Lisa, Moreau's Europa, the Diana of Fontainbleau, and other mythical figures.

All of it is a legacy of the sixties, its body consciousness and unfulfilled desires, but either more sophisticated, theorized, or ironically mediated, as it was during the eighties in the quoted figurations of the new Expressionist painting, or, ripping off high and low culture alike, the most cunningly referential of the MTVs. That it can be fascinating or provocative, no question, though the ritual elements are, almost in proportion to our new ethnological curiosity, divested of anything but a pretension of the sacred. As for the ritual performers coming out of the rain forests, ramadas, and precincts of the sacred, manifesting themselves to adoring and despoiling eyes, are they not, as an endangered species, likely to lose their alluring theatricality as well? Deployed to other purposes, the ritual appearances are becoming only too familiar as they are appropriated, infallibly, into the system of representation that sustains its power by doubling over and representing itself.

There is an understandable interest in borrowing from the theatrical forms of other cultures. But there is always the chastening moment when we realize that whatever it may have been for those others, it is inevitably only appearance to us. As we pick up ritual gestures and techniques from Java, Haiti, Ghana, Bali, we enter another order of illusion in which it is hard to determine what it is that we have acquired. For what is transferable in performance across cultures has to be able to survive the breakdown of cultural autonomy. Here there is a political issue that we are sometimes only too ready to forget in the ardency of ritual desire. If the transfer is possible at all, it occurs over the ruins of the territorial and despotic, and that applies to both ends of the exchange. If the borrowing does not screen out, say, the human cost of the hieratic gesture preserved in that other world, it forgets the taboo or interdiction on which the gesture is based—and maybe even the cruelty of other cultures that may be, as in clitoral circumcision or other mutilations, somewhat more literal than what we imagined in the exciting prospect of Artaud's theater of Cruelty.

In any case, what is being transferred is never what we believe is being transferred. The performative gesture derived from another culture remains in the world of representation from which no culture appears to be exempt, although other cultures appear to have made other adjustments to appearances. These may appear more or less enviable until, indeed, we look into the human cost. What may change, as in the movement of "objective" myth into the contents of the unconscious, is the degree of *subjectivity* in the representation which, once it enters the unconscious, like Oedipus, may be infinitely ramified and extended, but never lost. In this way, ritual borrowings may be metabolized into the secular, which may not be entirely gratifying to ritual desire, attached as it is to longings for absent communion or an irradiated reality touched again by the sacred.

If we look around the world, almost everywhere we can see the capsizing of hopelessness into faith, with one or another form of religious fundamentalism. But so far as we can see, perhaps *because we are looking*, it remains a world without miracles (*X-Files* notwithstanding, or the shamans just brought in by Brasilia to save the rain forests from Amazonian fires). We know we can develop through structures of repetition forms with the apparent resonance of ritual, by which we are now beguiled in what is now called "cultural performance." But that, too, is mere appearance. Ritual structures in our time leak through the activity of perception. If that is true in the church, it is doubly so in the theater. If the eye altering alters all, it particularly alters those things that appear to cycle through the sacred, from which we are twice removed in the age of modernism by its critical vigilance and suspicion. If desire could restore ritual, it would be subverted by desire, which arouses specular consciousness with its repetitive fantasies of desire, as we see in the stagings of delusive identity in the drama of Jean Genet.

As for the repetition that is central to ritual, all those reflexive variations of the Eternal Return, modernity has left us with the dilemma of distinguishing between ritual and habit—the repetition that repeats itself insensibly, the form perhaps of realism's revenge. "Habit is a great deadener," says the tramp in *Waiting for Godot*,[11] that plaintive play of repetitions in which the "Nothing to be done" (1) is the nothing that is repeated in two acts, of which it has been said that nothing *happens*, twice. On no religious grounds whatever, it seems to recuperate a ceremoniousness that merely recurs. Of course, what merely recurs may never have been ceremonious—I was going to say like taking out the garbage. But if we really think of it, nothing—however banal or inconsequential it seems—recurs with any *consciousness* of its recurrence that is without a ritual element. Habit is after all not merely divided from the living processes of the world. Often it appears, like ritual, to be their mirror image, inverted, unreflective, as if escaping thought, and some performance art—like the merely living processes (eating, drinking, breathing) of early Fluxus events or the figures of the Tai Chi Ch'uan—has made an issue of that, as if it were just happening, with no thought of its happening at all. That is, for all the ceremony, what ritual must also be, as if there were nothing mimetic about it, the *as if* itself secreted, the body and then the blood, the blood and then the body, and everything perfectly natural in the devotional currency of its reiterated phases.

Or so it apparently seemed until the modern era, with its fine ontological line between ritual repetition and deadening habit, and something always missing in the recurrency of desire. This is the recurring subject of our drama, where mimesis is never sufficient unto itself. And as we try to negotiate that fine line, as in a rehearsal (Fr.: *répétition*)—the director saying: "Do it again!"—the question remains, as it does in the ruptured sensibility of a secular age: what does the *it* refer to? Do *what*? What *is it that we want to repeat*? We will return to that question in Artaud, for whom—as he prepared the consummate spectacle of the recovered mystery, its naked, sonorous, streaming realization—repetition was unforgivable sin.

It is a question that used to be approached through the relationship of poetry and *belief,* which receded in theater and critical discourse with the rising affirmation of *play.* During the period of games and improvisation, when the pleasures of repetitive activity seemed undeniable—to the point of boredom or *jouissance*—we were also taking seriously the possibility of doing without the drama: the text corrected, rewritten, dispersed, ravaged, or simply tossed away. The return to ritual came with the communitarian dream of the sixties, pushed to its limit by the Living Theater in the disruption of Avignon. In the participatory ethos, nobody worried much about the complicated question of credibility of belief nor, like B in Eliot's "Dialogue," the ultimate matter of ritual ends. B says in the argument with E that "if we can do without the drama, then let us not pretend that religion is drama"—or, to transpose his argument, that ritual is theater except in a very weakened form. "If we are religious," he says, "then we shall only be aware of the Mass as art, in so far as it is badly done" (48).

Art badly done was anathema to Yeats, who against all realistic evidence sustained, with every tatter in his mortal dress, an undiminished vision of that artifice of eternity where the blessed dance. Not at all a Christian, he had other ritual ends. He might have appreciated the Mass for unabashedly aesthetic reasons, since he never wavered in his desire, through the weakening of religion, to sanctify art instead. What he admired in ritual was the hieratic forms, and their affinity with dreams and trance. He agitated for a national theater and longed for "the emotion of multitude,"[12] but what seduced him was essentially solitary. What he describes in ritual is an evocative hauntedness, like incense around a High Altar, but no less precise for that, mummy truths to tell, running through the nerves like fire. As for those forms drawing on ritual, he observes how the dancer in the drawing room achieves, with no studied lighting and human means alone, an imaginative intricacy, introversion as distance, the recession of mind into a more powerful and subtle life, the intimacy of a "separating strangeness" (224). What attracted him to "the noble plays of Japan," translated by Ezra Pound, was their decorous ritual character: verse, music, incantation, "figures, images, symbols . . . too subtle for habitation"—a rich languor of association where the interest is, if achieved by human means, "not in the human form but in the rhythm to which it moves" (231), as in the Sufi whirling and petrified motion in the early stagings of Robert Wilson.

There is in Yeats an early modernist aversion to the tacky worldliness of realistic character, with its tepid humanism and psychological disguise. There is also an impatience with the objective metabolism of the world as we commonly know it, its material gravity, weighed down by history. And there is in the passage that follows a theoretical anticipation of the long-drawn static abeyances and mesmeric suggestiveness in the imagery of Wilson's theater, especially when it first appeared: "If the real world is not altogether rejected, it is but touched here and there, and into the places we have left empty we summon rhythm, balance, pattern, images that remind us of vast passions, the vagueness of past times, all the chimeras that haunt the edge of trance; and if we are painters, we shall express personal emotion through ideal form, symbolism handled by the generations, a mask from whose eyes the disembodied looks, a style that remembers many masters that it may escape contemporary suggestion" (243). With his titles invoking Einstein, Freud, and Stalin, Wilson made the contemporary suggestion even as he escaped history, evoking but a totem or token. And one may wonder in due historical time whether the real world had in these orchestrations of rhythm, pattern, and chimera been touched sufficiently here and there or, like Yeats in some of his earlier plays, too vaguely.

While Yeats persisted through a long career sustaining ritual desire, he had to abandon the illusion of what, from his reverence of myth and ritual, he had called the emotion of multitude. The truth is that the multitude had abandoned him and his plays to an elitist audience in Lady Gregory's drawing room. While still persuaded at the end of his life that a ritual theater was possible, he could not escape contemporary suggestion in the close quarters of Ireland. Nor, after the Easter Rebellion, the material grasp of history—in which, for Brecht, the theater really belonged. In his conception of the Alienation effect, Brecht drew upon ritual forms, but his "separating strangeness" was of another estranging kind, assuming to begin with "the splendid isolation" of the actor and "the splendid isolation" of the spectator. In the ceremonial aspect of the *gestus,* it was not trance or dream that he was after, and if there were ritual incantations, they were likely to be ironic, subject to historicizing or ideological control. The equivocal attitude conveyed in Brecht's essay on Chinese acting is that while the actor prepares a performance *like* ritual, he makes no ritual claims and, by various technical means, voids the symptoms of regressive, ergotropic behavior that we associate with the more trancelike, shamanistic, or ecstatic aspects of ritual performance, still alluring to scholars in the anthropological mode. Such behavior is in fact associated by Brecht with our realistic and naturalistic traditions and their ideal of a thoroughly subjective acting out of the Stanislavski Method, with its (seemingly) mystical moments of psychological truth, in which the actor presumably forgets himself in the emotion that carries him away. By contrast, Mei Lan-fang—whom Brecht saw in Moscow in 1935—is making *comparisons* and *distinctions,* symbolically shaping reality by a kind of analytic in his ideographic technique.

There is, strange as it seems, a similar analytic in the theater conceived by Artaud. Far from the "family shamanism" (Eliade's term) that characterized most ritual theater experiments in the sixties, like *Dionysus in 69,* Artaud calls for a rigorous intellectuality and "mathematical meticulousness" in the midst of trance. As Derrida remarks, it is an occult "theater of dreams, but of *cruel* dreams, that is to say, absolutely necessary and determined dreams, dreams calculated and given direction, as opposed to what Artaud believed to be the empirical disorder of spontaneous dreams." Out of the experimental empiricism of the surrealists Artaud came to believe that "the ways and figures of dreams can be mastered." It is not the randomness of the unconscious that he favors but its articulating and linguistic processes, as in recent psychoanalytical theory, though he would have rejected a psychoanalytical theater in the ordinary sense, as he had rejected the psychological theater. "It is the *law* of dreams that must be produced or reproduced" (Derrida, 242). Despite the lure of the originary mystery, Artaud refused either a secret interiority or a secret commentary. "The *subconscious,*" he says, "will not play any true role on stage." It is possible to conclude, then, that the theater of Cruelty is not intended as a theater of the unconscious. What Artaud imagines in the notion of cruelty is an intensification of *consciousness* and, in all its naked and emblooded realization, an "exposed lucidity" (qtd. by Derrida, 242).

Brecht, too, believes that the subconscious will not play any true role on stage. And in a remarkably perceptive passage of the essay on Chinese acting he points out—as Artaud does in the cultural analysis of *The Theater and Its Double*—that "it is becoming increasingly difficult for our actors to bring off the mystery of complete conversion," the sort of conversion we associate with ritual, because the unconscious of our theater has become so unsuspectingly occupied, colonized, politicized, that "their subconscious's memory is getting weaker and weaker, and it is almost impossible to extract the truth from the uncensored intuitions of any member of our class society even when [as in the case of Marlon Brando] the man is a genius."[13] As for the mystery of the theater's origins, memory also falters there. If, for the genius of Artaud, priorities are reversed and, somehow, in the uncensored intuitions of the race, theater was not born of ritual but ritual born of theater, Brecht did not worry too much about which came first. As he observes in the "Short Organum," while theater may be said to have been derived from ritual, "that is only to say that it becomes theater once the two have separated; what it brought over from the mysteries was not its former ritual function, but purely and simply the pleasure which accompanied this." That pleasure is not, however, simple, so that we can retrace through it the ritual from which it derived. It is rather a pleasure that attains its climaxes "as cohabitation does through love. . . ." If what we have in ritual is a fixity of signs that can be duplicated and repeated, what we have in theater is an open scrutiny of signs keeping its distance from ritual in the irreversible rupture of history. For Brecht, the pleasures of theater are laminated by history, "more intricate" than ritual, "richer in communication, more contradictory and more productive of results."[14]

In the essay on Chinese acting, Brecht addresses the issue central to the ritual concerns of contemporary performance: the transferability of ritual techniques. What is often overlooked in that essay is the distinction he makes between the rational appropriation of a technique and the uncritical acceptance of what often goes along with it by way of cultural oppression. "Among all the possible signs," he writes, "certain particular ones are picked out, with careful and visible consideration" (93). Among the signs he does not like in the signifying detachment of the Chinese actor is that the A-effect in his performance is achieved "by association with magic" (96). While he could admire the singular performance of Mei Lan-fang, he was put off by the hierarchical structure that preserved, in secrecy for the privileged, the "primitive technology" or "rudimentary science" out of which the performance was made. Brecht had a quick appropriative instinct for "a transportable piece of technique" (95–96) but an equally quick aversion to what it might represent. He knew with his friend Walter Benjamin that behind any cultural treasure there is inevitable human cost, which is the best-kept secret in art, the anonymity of the labor behind the admired object that does not disclose its barbarous truth. Techniques are also cultural productions. They may require in their historical emergence, as in the case of Chinese acting, a repressive social system for the aesthetic pleasure they give. Carried over through the exchange mechanisms of bourgeois culture, the use value of such techniques is in some measure always already soiled, and one would expect that perception to manifest itself in performance, to avoid an obtuse nostalgia, with more or less irony.

When he wrote dramatic criticism, Roland Barthes was alert to such irony. He was also aware of the structural impediments of achieving in our culture—through the manifest "density of our narcissism"—what he perceived, say, in his conception of the system named Japan in his *Empire of Signs,* "one altogether detached from our own." He is not, he says, gazing lovingly at an Oriental essence, the Orient being for him a matter of indifference, but rather suggesting through the practice of an unheard-of system, after a trip to the "real" Japan, "the possibility of a difference, of a mutation, of a revolution in the propriety of symbolic systems."[15] What Barthes admired in the Japanese puppet theater, the Bunraku, is the unsoiled appearance of its signifying detachment, "cold like a white onion freshly washed."[16] He sees in Bunraku performance a lesson in writing (the play of signs in the construction of meaning), but an earlier lesson came actually from Brecht, on whom he wrote three essays in the fifties—after the Berliner Ensemble came to Paris—defining a Brechtian criticism. Barthes's early book *Mythologies* is a demonstration of this criticism, but mostly not on the theater. It is a remarkable exercise on all kinds of popular forms, spectacles, commodities—from wrestling to detergents to striptease—of a critical activity directed to the deritualization of thought.

As with the myths he exposed in the earlier book, the essay on the Bunraku follows Brecht in exposing the mechanisms of concealment in our theater, "the very artifice of the process of revelation (machinery, painting, makeup, sources of light)" (173). This surreptitious ensemble of appearances constitutes a space of deceit, "spied on and relished by a hidden spectator; a theological space, that of moral failing: on the one side, under a light of which he pretends to be unaware, the actor, that is to say, gesture and speech; on the other, in the darkness, the public, that is to say, consciousness and conscience." (Had he pursued the issue further, Barthes might have gone on to say that even with lights up, thrust stages, and the illusion of participation, the fetishism and moral division persist.) By contrast, in the Bunraku "the sources of the theater are exposed in their void. What is expelled from the stage is hysteria, that is theater itself, and what is put in its place is the action necessary for the production of the spectacle—work is substituted for interiority" (173–74). And use value is presumably restored.

There is nothing particularly ritualistic in what Barthes admires in the Bunraku performance, which, as he sees it, also eliminates for the actor the alibi of the sacred. Do we forget as we watch the performance the presence of the manipulators? Barthes considers that a vain question. By neither dissimulating nor emphatically disclosing how it does what it does, the Bunraku abolishes "the metaphysical bond that the West cannot stop itself from setting up between soul and body, cause and effect, motor and machine, agent and actor" (174). Nor is there any pretense of spirituality in all this. If the manipulator is not hidden, he cannot be turned into a God. Furthermore, as opposed to the Western marionette, there are no strings attached. Without an originary thread to an invisible source, there is no metaphor, and thus no spurious linkage to an absent Fate, although one wonders if that linkage is restored, or metaphor, when my former assistant Lee Breuer becomes the manipulator, adapting the Bunraku puppet for productions of the Mabou Mines, in a new dialectic of theatricality with an anti-theater bias. If Barthes shares with Brecht an aversion to hysteria, he shares with Artaud—with whom we associate hysteria, whom we think of perhaps as the supreme hysteric of the modern era, its exemplar—a distrust of theater itself. What Artaud treasures in theater is precisely its *disappearance,* the resistance in its true nature to the pressure of the very repetition through which it appears.

There is a remarkable passage in "No More Masterpieces" where the complexity of Artaud's provocative image of theater merges with his attitude toward ritual repetition in a cathartic function at the virtual limit of thought: "The theater teaches precisely the uselessness of the action which, once done, is not to be done, and the superior use of the state unused by the action and which, *restored,* produces a purification" (*The Theater and Its Double,* 82). The word *restored* is of course peculiar to an idea of theater that wants to abolish repetition. And Derrida tries to deal with it at the end of his essay by pointing out that Artaud, whose theater was never achieved, set himself the task of the unachievable, resigning himself "to theater as repetition" but unable to "renounce theater as nonrepetition"—thus, a theater of repetition that, at some unimaginable boundary of its tautological form, does *not* repeat itself (249–50). As for the act to be forgotten so that the unused state may be restored, that is also implicit in the Brechtian *gestus,* where we are meant to see not only the uselessness of the action that, once done, is not to be done, but also the action *not* done that should be. Once again, in Brecht, there is nothing sacred about it. The sign includes an absence that, so long as it continues, marks the victim in history, while we think about a violence that will put an end to the violence that, for Artaud, is part of the order of things, a generative violence, ancient and generic, remembered but invisible—like the truth of the victim being signaled through the flames.

If the great myths are dark, it is because they are concealing as they reveal something criminal and evil at their core. However it got there, we know that the drama is obsessed with the sacrificial act or its sublimation and displacements. Artaud does not specify such an act, but he anticipates Girard in the perception of the primordial violence as both "a *sacred obligation*" and "a sort of criminal activity" (1). What I have been calling ritual desire desires this obligation and is, with more or less romanticism, tempted by such activity, as the outbreak of ritual experiment was preceded in the theater by fascination with the drama of Genet. But the drama remains another matter, abrading upon the sacred, as Genet demonically knew, in the derisively poignant return of those Allegorical Forms in the Grand Brothel of *The Balcony.* While there are residues of ritual or ritual elements in the drama, drama is by its nature a more open, risible, and fractious thing. It is doubly so in the theater, if not by virtue of its mysterious Double, then to the degree of its compulsive doubling. The representational mechanisms of the form are further confounded by the dispersive activity of perception. The theater neither sustains myth by repetition nor discloses deity like ritual. To the extent that the theater is dramatic, it is both critique and tribunal. (It is perhaps dramatic to that extent.) As far back as the *Oresteia,* it is not ritual practices that are being upheld but the oldest claims of ritual that are being mediated. I say *mediated* specifically. What is set in motion by Aeschylus in that etiological drama—which establishes not only the judicial system but the mechanisms of Western drama as they might have been imagined by myth—has passed through the long semiosis of history. Heraclitus said that justice is strife. Now it can be said that it is only mediation. The liabilities of mediation are compounded by the actual omnipresence of the *media* in our time. That not only demoralizes judgment and justice—as in the Clinton scandals and the ceaseless spectacle of the O. J. Simpson case—but seems to make, in the proliferation of image and appearance, a mere redundancy of theater.

Still, there is in the reflexive memory of theater a congenital tension with the appearances of ritual order, however alluring or consoling they may seem. Whatever it was in the beginning (and the worst we can say of it now), drama is the subversive impulse that moves the theater into an open practice that abstracts itself from ritual ends. From Euripides to Ibsen and Genet, it has turned the myths over and over until, as Marx did with Hegel, they seem to be standing on their head. What we have in the canonical drama, and in revisionist productions of the drama—as well as in the refusal or rip-off of the drama in performance art—is the reconstitution of myth by history, and a dissociation from the rigid or static practice and magical purposes of the societies in which ritual prevailed.

There was over the past generation a new incitement to ritual from what appeared to be the signals coming from Artaud. But while he seemed to make a fetish of certain hieratic forms, nowhere does he subscribe to the necessarily repressive fixity of ritual. He calls, rather, for "states of an acuteness so intense and so absolute that we sense, beyond the tremors of all music and form, the underlying menace of a chaos as decisive as it is dangerous" (51). And when he raises the question of origins, his notion of an "archetypal, primitive theater" leads "metaphysically" (50) to the materialization of an essential *drama* that implies nothing like the communal unity we associate with ritual. Sexual rupture and carnage are the ontological grounds of an "essential separation" (30–31). What he is reimagining then is "the essential principles of all drama, already *disposed and divided,* not so much to lose their character as principles, but enough to comprise, in a substantial and active fashion (i.e., resonantly), an infinite perspective of conflicts" (50). It is certainly nothing like the tribal and psychedelic manifestations of an earthly para- dise, the bull-roaring rituals that petered out in the sixties, we thought, until elements of it showed up—multi-mediated but solipsistic—in the mutilations and disenchantments of punk, the parody and taxidermy of video and body art, and the sensory overload of new expressionist forms. What Artaud had in mind, with his insistence on "a meticulous and un- remitting pulverization of every insufficiently fine, insufficiently ma- tured form until it has passed through all the filters and foundations of existing matter" (51), is far more exacting.

What arises from ritual desire in practice is a sort of pathetic trompe l'oeil of "collective dramaturgy upon the empty stage of the social" (Baudrillard, 48). Our problem with ritual remains, then, political. Nostalgia keeps eluding that issue. Whatever meaning there may be in a High Mass in Bolivia or a Hasidic Seder in Brooklyn or a pilgrimage to Mecca, there is no way of having anything like the order of ritual in a so- ciety predicated on the open competition of overproduced signs mostly divested of value. For a ritual to have efficacious authority it must also assume something as irrevocable in the order of signifiers as in the desig- nation of status, caste, practices of exchange. The clarity of the sign de- pends on the power of the law or interdiction that preserves it from abrasion or slippage. If the characteristic gesture of postmodern perfor- mance is parody, that is because—with ritual elements in the *bricolage—* we make a pretense of reveling in the slippage. We play with signs. But it is like a game of Monopoly in the supply-side economy. The currency is false, as it is, too, in the recycled illusions of performative border cross- ings, which claim to undermine the game. The ceremony we remember, as Baudrillard says, tolerates no counterfeit, "unless as black magic and sacrilege, and it is thus that any confusion of signs is punished: as grave infraction of the order of things" (84). It is also characteristic of post- modern performance, and the new theoretical discourse that surrounds it, to love in ourselves the image of infraction. What we are playing out, as the signs collapse around us, is a melodrama of subversion and trans- gression, with talk about cyborgs or bodies that matter.

But who is being subverted, transgressed—or deluded? We deride the logic of late capitalism as if there were other cultures somehow exempt from what Barthes once called "the tyranny of uncertain signs." For an uncertain time and a privileged few, perhaps there were. As with the seeming alternatives to the manic aggressiveness of modern life, we are forced to confront an unsettling truth: those alternative or nonaggressive cultures were never what they seemed to be in the *huya iniya* or the flow of the *chi* or the ceremony of *ikebena*. As Brecht observed about Chinese acting, there is the dirty secret of repression in every hallowed gesture. "If we are starting to dream again, today especially," writes Baudrillard, "of a world of sure signs, of a strong 'symbolic order,' make no mistake about it: this order has existed and it was that of a ferocious hierarchy, since transparency and cruelty for signs go together" (84). (Baudrillard may bleakly overdo his accounting of the world of simulacra, but he seems to me accurate here.) It was an implication that Artaud could never quite accommodate in his cruel passion for an alphabet of perfect signs, "the dry, naked, linear gesture all our acts could have if they sought the absolute" (66). His own quest for the absolute was better perceived in "those strange games of flying hands" of the Balinese dancers, "like insects in the green air of the evening," which communicate "an inexhaustible mental ratiocination, like a mind ceaselessly taking its bearings in the maze of its unconscious" (63). Without the hierarchical ordering of signs, what seems to remain in the maze is the nearly unbearable ferocity of that mind, discovering beyond exhaustion the certitude which escapes it.

Make no mistake about it either, ritual is fascinating. But the struggle now in performance is naively served by the fantasies of ritual desire. We live in a world of broken reciprocity. In our most radical desires we dream like Deleuze, drawing on Artaud, of a "body without organs." But our reflexes seem formed by the estrangement of an essential fracture. Whatever ritual has done to heal wounds or seal the divisions of cursive time, it is this fracture that seems ritualized in desire, the anxiety of an absence that we glut with representations. The psychopathology of everyday life is polysaturated with them, as natural as breathing, an overmastering convention, the *image* of performance as fundamental need. In this context, ritual is myth, another representation. Even when ritual appears to be purely ritual it still depends on representation, a system of exchange in which divinity can be attested to by the power of its signs. What we are dealing with today, however, is not the faintest shadow of a ritual renewal, a virtual impossibility, but rather the incorporation of ritual desire into the mechanisms of a signifying system where signs are no longer, as Eliot said, taken for wonders, nor an approximation of the real. Where signs are still taken for wonders, either tyranny prevails— and not merely the tyranny of signs—or we see the power of divinity on the video screen, where we also see the shadows of our most legible desires. If there is a collective identity there, I am not sure it is the one we want.

Divinity or desire, what we take for reality is a dominion of signs that extends now through our information systems—by satellite transmission through the green air of the evening—to Kinshasa and Bangkok and Kerala, and all those other parts of the world from which we seek the reassuring plenitude of ritual forms. Our addiction to ritual and ritualized performance has intensified just when those symbolic forms are coming out of temple and jungle and suffering the attrition of an exposure they were perhaps never meant to have. Or is it that, in all things of the world, exposure was the first intention? Thus it appears to be with the theater, never more so than today when, however it resembles ritual, it dissolves with it into the real, which—without sanction or obligation—must live by resembling itself.

(1998)

10. Fantasia and Simulacra

Subtext of a Syllabus for the Arts in America

On several occasions over the past few years I have been asked to talk about training in the arts as we approach the twenty-first century, and this essay—with instincts of affirmation and negation—is a sort of summary response to that. While it points, then, to the future, let me start with ancient history, blurred perhaps by personal memory and suffused as it is with myth:

In the middle of the journey of my life I came not to the drear wood, like Dante, but to southern California, the sun-baked canyons above Hollywood, where I had an opportunity to think about training in the arts, from the ground up. What is more, I was given the resources to do something about it. It was the sort of fantasy that I do not expect to materialize again in my lifetime, and that does for few in any lifetime. I am speaking about the inception of California Institute of the Arts, now perhaps the leading arts school in America, for whose originary design I was very much responsible. Some thought at the time that I might as well have been entering the drear wood, since Cal Arts—radical in its aesthetic and politicized by the sixties—was funded by a vast legacy of the late Walt Disney, whose soul on ice (cryogenically, so they said, awaiting resurrection) was not exactly Eldridge Cleaver's. You remember Eldridge Cleaver? If you're not part of the solution, you're part of the problem. Now that Cleaver has found God, perhaps he and Walt will make it to heaven together, but so far as I could tell then, with the Movement on the threshold of what they called the Days of Rage, there were no disguised, no less conspicuous, sympathies for either the avant-garde or the radical Left among the members of the Disney family—a rather extended family at that, which included, aside from immediate relatives, a former tight end for the Los Angeles Rams, the anonymous animators of the legendary cartoons, and the maverick inventors at WED (acronym for the name of the Father), where the magic mirrors and "people movers" of Disneyland were developed.

The family was involved in Cal Arts, ardent about its prospects. They took as a mission the fulfillment of "Walt's dream," which—even more than Disney World (then under construction) and Epcot (city of the future)—was a great "community of the arts." Since whatever Walt had imagined, it was likely to be a far cry from what we were imagining, they were taking their chances as we were taking our chances. For one thing, people affiliated with the board of Cal Arts were confidants of Richard Nixon and were later identified as members of Reagan's kitchen cabinet; and I should confess, too, that the man who actually hired me as provost there—the head of the board at the time—was H. R. Haldeman, who, shortly after we arrived, was recommended by the Disneys to head Nixon's campaign for the presidency and was later convicted in the Watergate scandal. Still, this time was the apex of the sixties, before Watergate, and we were coming off the momentum of a period of revolutionary idealism. Everything seemed doable. I had written a book that was a sort of preface to the period, *The Impossible Theater: A Manifesto,* whose thesis was essentially that the reason you want to do it is precisely because it is impossible. I will eventually get around to suggesting what, in our context, still needs doing, but I should probably say right off, since it is always impossible, that the thesis is the same. Anyhow, if we wanted to believe then that, through some quirky mutation of American history, this strange crossbreeding of right-wing money and unconventional talent might work, we were not entirely naive. With a socialist background in my own family, I also remembered that the Disney Studios had been—with all the sweetness and light they brought to popular culture—union busters in the thirties, quite as lethal as Henry Ford. Yet, as Ford said, virtually anticipating the sixties, history is bunk, and going into the seventies, *Fantasia* had become a cult film for the psychedelic counterculture, Claes Oldenburg was willing to give us his metamorphic Mickey Mouse as a logo, and in what seemed like a postmodern consummation of the American Dream, I took my gold pass to Disneyland (yes, for real), one of the emoluments of my appointment, and went off to a new town in the foothills, called Valencia, with what I kept telling myself was no illusions. Or rather, as I remarked about the impossible, with no illusions on one level and those you cannot do without.

The example of Cal Arts, given the magnitude of its initial resources, may still seem pretty far removed from the realities of the arts in certain places in America where illusions disappear quick, say at a small liberal arts college with an overbearing president and a Bible Belt aesthetics, or a state university with englutted governance and dwindling budget. Or within the School of the Arts, a music department eating up the large share of it (while wanting to be a conservatory), not to mention a theater program with an expensively mounted "well-balanced season": if you are lucky, a Shakespeare, a Chekhov, along with the usual junk. So far as the students are concerned, it is a little hard in these environments to put the arts, conceptually, into any perspective at all, no less in the prophetic heart of the wide world dreaming on things to come, to imagine them in the twenty-first century. There are those on the faculties—here we may not differ—who still have to be dragged kicking and screaming into this.

If the lodestone and liability of music are, perhaps, the canonical repertoire and the doctrine of professional competence—with some students who have been taking Suzuki lessons since infancy—one of the major problems in theater is, still, how exactly to define competence, particularly with those students for whom the canonical repertoire is the movies or who have their eye on the tube. Aside from coming to the theater belatedly, many of them come illiterate and then suffer a double whammy: training in programs that are almost congenitally anti-intellectual, they not only remain benighted but, having acquired some makeshift of professional competence, feel a little uncomfortable thinking of themselves as artists at all. (This is putting aside the ongoing reality in America of a nonprofession in which over 90 percent of the actors are unemployed, and those who are working are mostly employed ignominiously.) There are also similar tendencies in other departments, even in the belated arts, photography and film.

I have few illusions about altering either consciousness or the state of the art in such departments unless there is, in the social order and institutional processes, some cleansing action like Artaud's Plague or an unexpected apocalypse of educational reform between now and the end of the century; or—what was to have come in the nineties before the budget cuts—a beneficent rash of propitious retirements. We cannot, even then, count too much on that. With the life span longer than ever, I am

often astonished at how quickly they age, some of my younger col-
leagues, or become resistant to innovation, despite the blessings of art
that, whatever its other powers, is not infallibly a fountain of youth.

For reasons I can understand, a school might be a little wary of con-
structing a program around Artaud's aesthetic, despite the influence of
his notion of Cruelty on a good deal more than theatrical performance.
But as there is no other enlivening aesthetic that offers structural guar-
antees, there is no alternative to teaching—with all due respect to forerunners, progenitors, exemplary figures of the past—in response to the
most seminal ideas among us, as well as to what art is now doing and is
likely to do. In the almost baroque eclecticism of our pluralistic scene, it
seems, of course, to be doing everything, and since that includes, since
Andy Warhol, publicity and fashion, you are surely aware of it. Since I
have a certain aversion to prophecy, I am reluctant to catalog here, particularly after the cautionary period following Black Monday, an array
of "index futures": high-tech or neoprimitive, generic or multimedia,
object or performance, iconic or deconstructed, literalist or emblematic,
diaristic or documentary, processed information or privileged process,
visceral or digital, solipsistic or ecological, cross-cultural or specifically
ethnic, (en)gendered or androgynous, conceptually based or fetishistic,
another new abstraction or recycled figuration, neoromanticism, neo-
expressionism, born-again dada, the perpetual present of "the futurist
moment," neo-neo to infinity. . . .

It was, we now hear, the index futures that, as "portfolio insurance,"
sold the stock market short and led to what, after all the wheeling and
dealing, the neologism of "arbitrage," they are now simply calling "contraction." As the market keeps us guessing, perhaps that will happen in
art—after supply-side extravagance, another neoclassicism. Which does
not mean, however, that the market will go away, since it started with neoclassicism and the belief that the world is rational. We are now told, however, that the market is emotional, and so, of course, are artists, as if they
were made for each other. William Carlos Williams once spoke of "the
poetry of the movement of costs," and this would suggest that there is,
after all, an economy in art that we ought to think about in the curriculum. Nor would we be, as teachers, any more responsible than econo-
mists in not taking in what has happened and guessing, perhaps somewhat
better, where art, demoralized by excess, will be making its next moves.

But: *art is not economics! art is not fashion!* But nobody said it was, not
entirely, though caught up increasingly in the fashion system. Mean-

while, Hans Haacke may be working up a *tableau vivant* or visual documentary titled *Black Monday*, with meticulous research on the arbitragers; Cindy Sherman will have herself photographed as if for a remake of *The Grapes of Wrath*, remembering the Great Depression; and Kenny Scharf may have to sell his Day-Glo Cadillac, the Suprema Ultima De Luxa, to underwrite his losses. Meanwhile, too, nothing about the protean production of our time reminds us, if they ever existed, of eternal values in art. If we have the courage of a Saint Athanasius, we might, as he did with orthodoxy, uphold the sublimity of art alone against the world. True: what the individual artist does—out of whatever inexplicable gift, craft, passion, conviction, idiosyncrasy, hallucination, or monomania—*that* is something we might leave to the gods. So far as I know, however, the gods are not running an art school at the moment, nor working up a syllabus for the future in which we shall have to negotiate the fine line between art and economics, art and fashion, with its exuberant hold on aesthetics and—in the widespread seduction of indisputable talent—inarguable mastery of the *fascination-effect*.

That effect, it would seem, is of crucial importance to contemporary art, as well as to those who are heartened by the growth of the arts in mass culture. In a world in which more people appear to go to museums than to sporting events, and in which the average time before a painting is five seconds, the fascination-effect is virtually a necessity if a work of art is to get any public attention. Since the earliest days of modernism and the avant-garde, getting public attention has been not only an objective but objectified in art, as a vanity of the artist, especially as the public, which was already the merest fiction, had disappeared into the mass. This is the historical datum registered by Steve Barry in the fascinating blink of the huge megaphonic eye of his construction called Polyphemus, made for the exhibition of the technological group P.U.L.S.E. Some of the works of P.U.L.S.E. are like a fast-food version—dadainspired, and no less sophisticated—of the earlier technological experiments by the Kluver/Kaprow group E.A.T.[1]

Whereas E.A.T. coincided with the era of happenings, aimed at audience participation, the work in P.U.L.S.E. is far more critically conscious of how audience participation is itself a mark of disjuncture, like the art trips of tourism, a delusion of the social that is a form of appropriation. There is in American museums the little counting meter that a guard at the museum entrance may use to keep track of the crowds. Barry's surveillance machine is more specific than that: it identifies a particular spectator by a swerving cone regulated by a light sensor. The spectator's own blinking eye activates a film loop in which the black-and-white image of the eye is projected for five seconds; then the cone waits until another spectator comes by and repeats the process. This mimicry of perception in museums—now organized pedagogically and functioning like a track meet—may suggest that the artist should start thinking again about doing without any public attention, relieved of the burden of the fascination-effect or, as we think about the training of artists, trying to outguess the future.

Some artist-teachers have real convictions about that. With a certain contagious arrogance about past and future, some of us claim to teach not in terms of where art was or where it is going but only in the reality of what is *there.* So far as the teaching is concerned, the fascination-effect is in nothing else, and nowhere else, but "what comes from the student." Putting aside the possibility that, with more than a few students, that may be nothing much, this attitude is a nice illusion, too, and some live by it better than others. "I'm going to make a last confession," said Le Corbusier, "I live in the skin of the student." I like to believe I do too when I am teaching, but with a sort of double residence, the part that remains in history. At the same time, I would have to acknowledge that more and more students are getting under my skin because they know nothing whatever about history, not only past or conjectural future, but since they have no way to place it, the present moment as well. I certainly do not want to sound here like our former Secretary of Education William Bennett, whose sense of history is not mine, and who would return us to "fundamentals" for mostly the wrong reasons, and the wrong fundamentals at that. But often as not, among the teachers we know, living *there,* where the student *is,* is what keeps them there, while art itself is moving ideologically *elsewhere,* leaving the student behind—and often the teacher as well, denouncing ideology.

That is what used to be known as "false consciousness": ideology by delinquency, pretending it is not. For what is there is always ideology, though the wall comes tumbling down as if, once more, to signal its destined end. And some once-awaited walls are still up, as we can now see in the Marseille housing, which is the appalling outcome of the pure aesthetic of the formalist Le Corbusier, or the towering impersonality of literally high modernist glass making a canyon of Third Avenue in New York. It is there, moreover, not only in the social application of artistic theory but in the given circumstances and technologies of art making: the brushstroke, the bassoon, the synthesizer, fiberglass or fiber optics, the inclination of neon tubes, the emulsion, the montage, the invisible sutures of the filmmaker, only more openly a symptom of power in the downbeat of the conductor's baton, and with a memory of the prompter (insidious whisper of the textual god), the "teasers" and "tormentors" that, in the (theological) space of a proscenium stage, disguise a hidden authority. In this regard, ideology is the illusory ground on which, as at the vanishing point of perspective, history turns into myth.

Ancient history is suffused with myth, but so is history at the moment of its occurrence. This is all the more true, of course, in a world of instant mediation. If you have been keeping up with current tendencies in the visual arts and performance, not to mention recent theory, you know how obsessed they are with the dominion of representation, image and afterimage, a profusion of simulacra, and their cybernetic recycling into a Society of the Spectacle. It not only confounds our sense of history but, in the ceaseless network of reproduction and hypertrophy of floating signs, makes a sort of mockery of any established aesthetic with a die-hard insistence on dubious standards. It is not only that the genres were breaking down and, in the mixing of media, multiple unnamable forms and new hybrids were emerging (all this, after all, had been happening since the advent of futurism and the classical avant-garde) but that culture itself, in the political economy of signs, had much to answer for. (Given a century of rational, systematic, and technocratic slaughter—at the founding of Cal Arts, still proceeding in Vietnam—some of it was unanswerable because virtually unspeakable.) Since Benjamin's famous observation that behind any masterpiece of any period is a history of barbarism, we have been asking about standards: established by whom? where? under what circumstances? perpetuating what mythology? and, for our collective edification (forgetting those excluded), who is paying the bill? This question is not, of course, irrelevant anywhere in the world, as the dominance of the media portends the end of art, or its consumption in mass culture.

If you start thinking about training from the ground up, as I did at Cal Arts, these are elemental questions. They are not, however, usually accommodated in the curriculum, benignly plural but apolitical as it is, ideological only in the presumed innocence (or hypocrisy) of its exclusions. They are not only elemental, they are also aesthetic questions. I mean questions that determine technique and style, relations between form and content, artistic judgment as well. I mean judgments, moreover, about the most minute particulars in the making of art and the most discrete issues in the reception of art, ranging from whether you can afford to pour this can of paint on a canvas or acquire the footage for a sixteen-millimeter film or digitalize your studio for extended sound to whether or not the sound is welcome in the performing arts center or the film (after the further cost of editing) can find a distributor or the canvas is suitable for hanging on a corporate wall.

Never mind the preposterous sums that are required today to support the budgets of the Metropolitan Opera or a major symphony. To deal with that we would have to integrate the Juilliard School of Music with the Wharton School of Business. Keeping our discourse in reasonable scale, there is even the complicated problem inherent in the most recent work, or turn of fortune, of Ettore Sottsass, the irreverent Italian architect who was the guiding genius of the Memphis group (in Milan) that, out of the "advocacy design" of the sixties, was committed to accessible mass production at affordable prices. A couple of years ago in New York, however, Sottsass exhibited a new collection of furniture, huge marble and granite pieces, set off by exotic woods, mirror, glass, mosaics—what he calls "Furniture for the Ritual of Life," one giant piece of which was titled "What's the Name of Your Swiss Bank?" About this change of materials and proportions, Sottsass said: "Many years ago I hated marble as a symbol of richness and power. Now, maybe because I'm getting old or getting rid of sociological fear, I am able to see marble just as a texture, as a natural. Then it becomes very beautiful and gives you nice feelings."[2]

I must admit, I have a feeling for those feelings, not only because I am getting old, sociological fear behind me. It is rather because I had similar feelings for a while, when (in 1965) I opened the Beaumont Theater at Lincoln Center in New York, designed by Eero Saarinen in specially quarried and imported travertine, with a bar in the lobby that is almost solid bronze. This was a pretty long way from our first theater in San Francisco, in a rundown loft behind a Judo Academy that later became the vestry of the Ebenezer Baptist Church. I recall this only to allay, again, any impression I may be giving that the possibilities of art are merely a function of money. As we could tell from the Baptist choir, there is also the evangelical spirit, not to mention the visceral energies that came up from below, usually during performance, when somebody hit the mat and a voice shouted: "Banzai!" In the days of their impoverishment, good artists will find a way to do it no matter what, though "it" will surely change depending on the answers to such questions. My own theater changed those many years ago in San Francisco when the Ford Foundation first came into the arts to improve our culture, and after some debate in the company as to whether we were selling out, we decided to accept half a million dollars, the first of the operational grants ever given to regional theaters.

At a time, however, when the Japanese are on the way to owning America, the questions are even more specifically attached to the marketplace and the exchange value of the dollar. When I speak of the marketplace and exchange, I am speaking of a marketplace of signs, as Marx does of commodity fetishism. And that artists themselves are asking these questions—about art as sign and commodity—one could see at last year's Whitney Biennial or the Biennale in Venice or the New Music Festival in Philadelphia or the Documenta any year in Kassel, or just about any film festival no matter where in the world. Unless an artist is totally out of this world, you can also see it in the studios, where the covert activities of the art world, and a dialectic with the marketplace, are not only seeping into process, but virtually—like the dollar signs on Warhol's silk screens—constituting the subject of the work. This takes a slightly different course at the regional theaters, which now pretty much determine actor training, under the aegis of boards that, nonexistent when we began, look at the bottom line of the well-balanced season. They are naturally delighted to have the theaters substitute for Philadelphia and Boston in the production of new plays as tryouts for Broadway.

None of this means that the work will inevitably sustain this particular form of signifying consciousness, with its sense of art as commodity, into the twenty-first century, though it will no doubt be at the time an unresolved function of whatever we see in art. And if the deficit is cut untold billions and the market stabilized, it will still be a marketplace of signs. One of the signs will be—as our best artists struggle to ward off a sense of irrelevance or appropriation—the figure of the artist who still insists that he couldn't care less about any of these issues. This figure may be a woman, but is less likely to be, since—as we see in feminist theory and any number of feminist artists, from Yvonne Rainer to Barbara Kruger (both of whom are also theorists)—women have had a longer history of being a mere function of bourgeois exchange and are fed up with being merely empty signs.

As some of the most significant work since the period of minimalism and conceptual art has had a theoretical aspect, some of it veering into cultural critique, we have also had those around who insist that theory has nothing to do with art. There are, to be sure, all kinds of art, and artists who are not now and never will be theorists, but as Ezra Pound wrote in his book on the vorticist sculptor Gaudier-Brzeska, "It is nonsense to say that great artists do not theorize or that they do not talk about art."[3] I remember the days after the garrulousness of abstract expressionism when you would go into a studio, and it would be considered, like, bad manners, man, to say anything more than "It stones me." For some artists, that still remains the ground rule, and some art departments endorse it more or less, but that hardly dismisses the issues that will stick, theoretically, to the mythic autonomy of art, like the fat, tallow, and beeswax in the epistemology of Joseph Beuys or the pink bubble gum that Adrian Piper wore on her ambiguously black body at the Met.

Among the theoretical questions that artists are asking today are those about certain propositions of formalist art that we still tend to take for granted, none more so, perhaps, than the notion of "technique as discovery," or revelation, like a Joycean epiphany. That was the view of art that prevailed when I first became interested in poetry and started working in the theater, and it is still very much at the center of most training programs in acting, which are almost universally oblivious to the more advanced movements in the other arts. What is curious about that is the degree to which theater has become the medium through which the other arts (and other disciplines) have been redefining themselves. It had happened before, in the classical period of the avant-garde, but we saw it again in the movement from assemblage and environments to happenings and "action events," with the art object dancing off its pedestal or tumbling off the walls, to begin performing in the space of the spectator who was being asked to participate, to start performing too. In the sixties, of course, everything seemed geared to performance, with the theatricalization of everyday life. And with that development, theatricality itself became a debatable issue, as in Michael Fried's famous attack on the conversion of the object into performance, and his declaration that it is precisely theater that is the end of art.

Music is also performed, but those who might be working in a tradition defined by a range of composers such as Elliott Carter, Milton Babbitt, George Rochberg, or Charles Wuorinen are by no means especially enthusiastic about the theatricalizing tendencies arising from the Fluxus tradition, indebted to John Cage, and represented in a virtual renunciation—or deflection into space, body, objects, thought—of music as we used to know it. It was quite another sort of music we had when Nam June Paik destroyed a piano, or La Monte Young released butterflies, or in the concept pieces of Philip Corner, or—not particularly associated with Fluxus—in a meditative composition for the soles of the feet by Pauline Oliveiros, or the early optical music of John Zorn, who insisted, then, that music has never had anything to do with sound. Fried's position on art is formalist, focused earlier in his admiration of the work of Kenneth Noland, Jules Olitski, and Frank Stella, whose recent work is not oblivious at all to the performative impulse returning to the canvas with the resurrected figure, but whose Norton lectures at Harvard were a theoretical defense of formalism, with its valorized act of discovery, which cannot escape, however, the logocentric structure of representation.

This has been the desire of art since the advent of cubism, which was going to abolish perspective, where a secret power lurks at the vanishing point. In the recent critique of representation, all formalisms have been looked at askance, including cubism, and questions have been asked over the past generation about what those epiphanic discoveries covered up. These are complex theoretical issues that have shown up in praxis, with a shift of focus from the meaning discovered in art to the way meaning is *constructed,* as with collage, montage, or the combinatory sets of *bricolage,* or the development of a photograph or editing of a film. What many artists are concerned with today, moreover, are the institutional structures within which art is made, not only art-as-process, but the network of production and circulation, and the very materialities of art, not merely the old Bauhaus "materials and methods," but what gives a material texture to the grain of history, adding cost to the movement of poetry. At some basic level what every art school worries about, all the more as new technologies are on the scene: *Who gets what to work with when? and who has the power to determine that?*

At this conceptual impasse, let me back up again to my experience at Cal Arts. All the people most immediately engaged with its conception were artists, some of them avant-garde, all of them highly reputed as artists or teachers or both. They knew from long experience that these were crucial questions. They also knew that these are not exactly new questions. As I have suggested, they were, in fact, recurring questions within the traditions of the avant-garde, and they have been on the current scene, obviously, since the sixties, but without at first the ideological backup that, in theory, they have had in recent years. People in our art departments may be thinking now about training in the twenty-first century, but Disney beat them to it. That is exactly what he wanted us to do in the conception of Cal Arts. It is been nearly a quarter of a century since then, during which time we have become, if anything, more aware that the material problems I have been raising not only exist in the studios and department meetings but in the age of energy crisis at a global level as well. With the proliferation of technological resources and the inevitable competition for them in a multinational world, the questions I have been asking are more than ever unavoidable questions. For this competition also includes the struggle for control of the major signifying apparatus, the electronic media, which, by satellite transmission, not only construct meaning for the world but also colonize the unconscious, determining our fantasies and dreams, perhaps the most fundamental material of the arts.

"I like being an artist," says Robert Irwin, not about the exquisitely lit environment of one of his meditative discs, but after describing how difficult it is to explain to corporate sponsors why one of his landscape projects is not like the *Pietà*. "We really have," he says, "tremendously beautiful questions."[4] When I was still doing theater, I liked being an artist, too, though I do not know if the following question is beautiful. It could not help occurring to us, however, as we thought about Cal Arts, and as we now speculate about the future of training, it still seems to me pretty basic: Was Walt Disney an artist? And if not, what difference does it make when, in the determination of standards through the fantasy life of America, and much of the rest of the world, his power exceeds almost anything we can think of in any of the arts, outside the cinematic apparatus itself, that great American invention that, even as the dollar falls, appropriates the world.

I said fantasy life, but there are some young artists who see it another way. "We grew up with TV," says Rodney Alan Greenblat, who moved from the East Village to the Whitney Biennial with his "cartooniverse," about which he adds, "Disney makes it real."[5] Moreover, he has also provided us, according to Jean Baudrillard, "with a perfect model of all the entangled orders of simulation." He is speaking, of course, of Disneyland, whose "objective profile of America" is articulated "down to the morphology of individuals and the crowd. All its values are exalted here, in miniature and comic strip form."[6] Baudrillard has it wrong. It is not exactly miniature; Disney was smarter than that. One of the things I learned from Thornton Ladd—the architect chosen by the Disney family for the building at Cal Arts—is that the scale of Disneyland is five-eighths, because it is, thus, "sufficiently real" but makes you feel taller, "a little like John Wayne." This is not quibbling over a small matter. About the meaning of Disneyland, Baudrillard—whose ideas are having at the moment a considerable influence on the art scene in America—gives us the worst possible case: "Disneyland," he writes, "is presented as imaginary in order to make us believe that the rest is real, when in fact all of Los Angeles and the America surrounding it are no longer real, but of the order of the hyperreal and simulation" (*Simulations,* 25).

What one thinks of that will vary, depending on definition of the real, which, even as it escapes us, absorbs all the debates on mimesis, perspective, illusion, figuration, nature/culture, art/life, and the whole problem of representation itself, which has by no means subsided through the "dematerialization of the object," the various deaths of art, the emergence of art-as-performance, or, with more or less "musication," the synesthesia of merging forms—which further disrupt the genres that we could once reliably teach. For Baudrillard, reality is so thoroughly "impregnated by an aesthetic which is inseparable from its own structure" (152) that, confused by its own image, it is no longer capable of taking on the appearance of reality. That is in part a function of speed, the swift consumption of image in the fantasy machine, as if the future had, in the nonintentional parody that inhabits everything, overtaken futurism with the speed of light. At the limit of this phenomenon, "the real is not only what can be reproduced, but *that which is always already reproduced.* That is the hyperreal" (146). And that is the order of Disney's world, which in presenting itself as imaginary, preserves the reality principle by concealing the fact that the real is no longer real.

How you size up "Disney" and what he represents is, beyond the momentary impact of anyone's ideas, a critical issue in the arts, and surely in a conception of training, since he obviously occupies, like it or not, a large space in the alienated void of our students' heads. And not only our own students: that is why it was quite possible, to what once might have been universal disbelief, for the Chirac government in France to have arranged for a new Disneyland not far from Paris, mythical home of the avant-garde, which has long been mad for the cartooniverse of American film. Meanwhile, the Wonderful World of Disney is itself being reconceived by artists brought into its service by the new chairman of the company, Michael D. Eisner, an executive far from the avuncular image of brother Roy, who ran the family enterprise after Walt's death. All invention used to come from the "imagineers" of WED, but with radical change in the corporate structure there came a new hierarchy of imagination in the fantasy kingdoms. Now there are world-class architects— Frank Gehry, Robert Venturi, Arata Isozaki, Charles Gwathmey, Elizabeth Plater-Zyberk, and Michael Graves—at the drawing boards for new projects. The one conspicuous continuity with the older Disney tradition is that all were sworn to secrecy. But the model of Graves's design for the Dolphin Hotel at Epcot was eventually made public, along with a theoretical discourse around the question of whether the architecture would be "Disneyized." With Floridian colors, banana-leaf walls, an exotic new ecology, and a tourist-friendly postmodern bestiary, the hotel is designed to be part of a giant convention complex, like a small city, financed by Metropolitan Life Insurance and the Aoki Corporation, real estate speculators and developers from Japan, where the most advanced art is shown in department stores.

"You might not even notice the Disney influence on the hotels," said Eisner, "they are so Graves-like."[7] Speaking of the visible language that conceals invisible power! or in the culture warp of the postmodern, simply affirms that there is no reason to hide it anymore. Not only are some artists today, major artists, doing art that seems to document the theory of simulation, but particular young artists, like Greenblat, inspired by fantasy parks, are making objects like pseudomachines with a sort of Goofy technology and junk-food pastiche—the apparent premise in the process being that the Magical Kingdom is the equivalent of the real. What is more, there is nothing satiric about it, as there might be in the cartoonish figures of Red Grooms, and certainly nothing as threatening as there might be in the kandy-kolored tangerine-flaked polyurethane delirium of a fantasy park by Judy Pfaff, who was Greenblat's teacher in sculpture at the School of Visual Arts.

The point is that a lot of equivalents of the real are coming from sources that are light-years from what used to pass as culture, as in the new art of Noise, postpunk Industrial Music, or the funkier images that are still on the scene of Chicago art. Sometimes it is genial, and sometimes it is not. And I have simply been using Disney as perhaps the most dominant paradigm of what, to adapt a Nietzschean phrase, amounts to the "devaluation of value," certainly the kind of value by which we once made judgments in art, from which we could then make options about a curriculum. Much of this was on the agenda when we were thinking about Cal Arts. But even if he were not the direct source of our money, what came under the sign of Disney was something we could hardly ignore. If you cannot ignore it, that does not mean you have to like it, but whatever you do in your personal work, this much has become increasingly self-evident: you cannot develop a concept of training in a program hermetically sealed from popular culture or, like guardians of the ring hoard, protect some formalist truth of art that is, in the aberration of its own imaginary, also concealing the fact that the real is no longer real.

That also raises the possibility that, in a certain respect, art is no longer real. We have had any number of litanies about the death of art, though they usually arise beyond the periphery of homogenized pleasures, as modernism tries to absorb into its superbly failing structures the repeated outrage and depredations of history. It may seem in its extremity like a withdrawal from history, but as Adorno remarked in his *Philosophy of Modern Music:* "Art today, insofar as it is at all deserving of substantiality, reflects without concession everything that society prefers to forget, bringing it clearly thereby into conscious focus. From this relevant source, modern art designs irrelevance—offering nothing more to society."[8]

This is not the place to do a critique of Adorno's effort to reconstitute the dispossession of art as a transgressive or subversive force, aiding enlightenment "only by relating the clarity of the world"—of which in its commodified form he doesn't think much—"consciously to its own darkness" (*Modern Music,* 15). What he suggests, however, in the dialectical opposition of Schoenberg and Stravinsky is what has become increasingly apparent in all the arts through the history of modernism, that whatever else art is, it is also an interior critique that has eventuated in the postmodern de-definition of art. That has been further complicated in all the arts since the classical period of the avant-garde—dada performance or Russolo's futurist noise or Duchamp's conundrums of perception—which radically shift the ground of meaning to the spectator or listener or, in the overflow of art to life, the participant. You can measure out according to your own perceptions the degree of residual definition in any event, but the artist who pretends to ignore the critique, or is insufficiently aware of it, is simply outside the discourse of art that now, for better or worse, makes the art that even changes our view of history.

Only one observation about Adorno: what he wrote about modern music after his exile from Germany was suffused with the experience of a history that had almost invalidated art. No wonder, then, he could ask the sort of question that we tend to overlook in our programs because it would suggest the insubstantial grounding of what usually passes for a curriculum. For example: "How is a total world to be structured in which mere questions of counterpoint give rise to unresolvable conflicts? How disordered is life today at its roots if its shuddering and rigidity are reflected in a field no longer affected by empirical necessity, a field in which human beings hope to find a sanctuary from the pressure of horrifying norms, but which fulfills its promise to them only by denying to them what they expect of it" (xiii).

I quote this while recognizing again that art takes many forms, and people do it for diverse reasons. And I am certainly not urging that we forget the recreational powers of art, no less the joy, and even ecstasy, that may attend its consummation—both for those who do it and those who experience it when it is done. The focus here, however, is not leisure painting or amateur theatricals, both of which I sometimes envy for their unpretentious pleasures, perhaps because I have been victimized by the greatest art I know, which invariably troubles my thought. (Despite all I have said about cultural change, this may identify me, in the very phrasing, with another generation.) The art that determines our habits of mind and informs our work—and for which, somewhere in the world, people are still willing to give their lives, and that, no matter where they live, is somehow, against all de-definition, unalterably defined by that idea—is, simply, the art *in which we live*. Postmodernism has been impatient with anything that looks like a romantic idealization of art, but it is an idea that living artists of different generations—Solzhenitsyn or Salman Rushdie, Martha Graham or Pina Bausch, Jasper Johns or Marina Abramović surely understand, and it will hardly have been exhausted by the twenty-first century.

To review: having brought up, aside from Adorno's impossible question, the unsettling concept of ideology, I may have added, for some artists, insult to injury by talking in a space of subjectivity that is theoretical as well. I trust I have done so, out of long experience, with an eye to praxis, but the theoretical is, some would say, the present state of the art, which—in the self-reflexivity of the postmodern—may seem like an infinite regress through the myth of history itself. That may very well be, however, as we think back over the century, the modernist nightmare from which we are still trying to awaken. As for the particular history through which I regressed at the start, that might have been an occasion for nostalgia, but given our futuristic subject, it seemed to me a pretext for reflection, the subtext of a syllabus. And if I return again to the figure of Disney and my experience of Cal Arts, that is because it still seems to me decidedly emblematic of the anomalous situation of the arts in a postmodern world, with immiscible elements working side by side, as in the recycled kitsch of Robert Longo or the B-movie personae of Cindy Sherman or the *Tonal Plexus* of Glenn Branca or the video operas of Robert Ashley or the *United States* of Laurie Anderson. Or for that matter, not merely working side by side, but with "a radical *separation of the elements*,"9 as in the choreography of Merce Cunningham or the

Ontological-Hysteric Theater of Richard Foreman or the painting of David Salle or the text by Kathy Acker that Foreman staged and for which Salle provided a backdrop.

Actually, the phrase about radical separation of the elements was not from Cunningham or from Cage, or any of these artists, but from a seminal essay on the modern theater by Bertolt Brecht, whose theory of alienation is not only the conceptual ground of Foreman, and others like David Bowie, but virtually imbedded by now in postmodern thought and practice. Within the ethos of the postmodern, it can be said that you cannot begin to think of art *except as alienated*; that is, defamiliarized, estranged, encoded by history. Brecht was laying out at the time the politics of *Mahagonny* and the concept of an epic opera, refusing in its process the Wagnerian illusion of the organic unity of a work. By the time we come to the abrasive sonorities of Branca, mixing up the harmonic series with hard-core punk, we seem to have a revisionist version of the Wagnerian illusion requiring the invention of new instruments and a personal system of notation. The infinite varieties of such systems Cage tried to reduce to a manageable sample in his book *Notation,* from ideographs and symbols to Cy Twombly–like inscriptions to mandalas and maps and numbers that look like the price list on a menu. Putting aside the claims of sheer volume in Branca's music, the aesthetics of amplification, it is no surprise to learn that he thinks of himself as a formalist whose compositional method derives from a natural process. "I have a lot to say," he reminds us, "about the technical aspects of music," and he does. "Sometimes people will ask me about the acoustical phenomena, and I have thought a lot about that. I have started working with a system of music which is not taught in the schools, which there's no real frame of reference for, necessarily, and I'm not even totally sure of what I'm doing myself."[10]

While there were various people at Cal Arts who—powerfully trained in conventional forms—were quite sure of what they were doing, it was a place which did, indeed, provide a frame of reference for the process of Branca and various experiments in the arts that were a good deal stranger. As a matter of principle, first principle, there was an ethos that supported those who were not at all sure what they were doing themselves. I was one of them. What was true for the students was true for the faculty, the ones who were supposed to know. I was not only the provost of the institute but dean of the School of Theater, yet out there on the San Andreas Fault I was going in my own work through a radical change of direction, down where it hurt, like a geological shock. I will come back to that in a moment. What was also obvious, however, is that for the younger artists there we were close to where the action was. After all, it was out of the Disney tradition that the animators came who developed the visual mythos of Spielberg and Lucas; and there we were on the freeway heading to the Sunset Strip, Muscle Beach, Universal Studios, and the worldwide dominion of the fantasy-making machine itself.

Many of the artists there—faculty and students: John Baldessari and David Salle, Morton Subotnick and Charlemagne Palestine, Judy Chicago and Matt Mullican, Mamako Yoneyama and Bill Irwin; Nam June Paik, Allan Kaprow, Barbara Smith—were wild about or bemused by the iconography of Disney and the Hopalong Cassidy movies made in those canyons. I am dropping those names not merely to certify what a grand place it was, but rather to suggest again the polymorphous (and polyglot) diversity of what we have to deal with as we move toward the next century. What we can foresee, as the hybrid forms proliferate and cultures cross, is a superabundance of images and sound circulating throughout the world. There is a certain exhilaration in that, the dazzling speed of reproduction of which the futurists hardly dreamed. At the same time, however, we can be pretty much assured, whatever young artists do, that the cultural apparatus and system of reproduction, controlled by Disney and MCA, with Microsoft moving in, will have saturated the image repertoire, occupying the unconscious like a kind of second nature, determining the character of what they do.

I am not going to try to judge it, because even in Valencia I felt both intensely engaged and, with a sort of Brechtian doubleness, also a little removed. This is, without question, a generational problem. But the implication is that we can hardly think about the arts, except in the most recidivist way, without now taking for granted the intersection, or conflation, of high art and low art, elitist culture and popular culture, as well as the subcultures that are, to this day, not quite part of the American Dream. Still they force themselves upon us like graffiti on the freeways or the subways or, in the appropriation by the market of the return of the repressed, the autistic line and ghoulish figures of Jean-Michel Basquiat, whose grandparents on his mother's side were from Puerto Rico and whose father was from Haiti, and who grew up in Brooklyn himself, scrawling concrete poetry on the sidewalks, though—having grown up in Brooklyn myself—I saw his work last at the Templon Gallery in Paris. Which, if it started as regression, is quite a digression. As for the reality of digression, it is—as we move toward the twenty-first century—a modus operandi or major strategy of postmodern forms, as well as a pedagogical problem for the schools: both the nature of the student body, who will be studying *what* leading *where,* and how we are going to keep up with the diversity of it all.

Before I go any further, you may be wondering why, given what I have said, I am not still at Cal Arts. Let me simply say that not long after it did get off the ground—more or less according to blueprint—I left it in just the sort of political controversy, with the Disney family, that we might have expected. That part, so far as I am concerned, can be bypassed here, a good story for another time. The better part of what I remember is that, while I was there, it was day by day the most volatile and rewarding experience in education, at any level or of any kind, that I ever hope to know, for virtually everybody involved. That was because during the time I was there (I cannot speak for it now), it was—like the Bauhaus or Black Mountain—not only a school but very much what Disney wanted, a community of the arts, in which students and teachers trained together, performed together, constructed "environments" together, and even somehow managed—where the particular work was not of a communal nature—to leave each other alone.

Another emolument of my arrangement there was the chance to forget what I had been doing for nearly twenty years in the professional theater and, in middle age, to think out the issue of training by starting all over again. By pretending to know nothing, I knew very little. The elemental questions surfaced that are in correlative ways now being asked in the other arts and, in the adoption of performance as a heuristic principle, in other disciplines as well: linguistics, psychoanalysis, ethnology, literary studies, philosophy, and history. Foucault has called this performative aspect of the human sciences a *theatrum philosophicum,* but the questions are elemental. They begin at the point where, in the initiatory gesture of art, theory meets praxis, or, in the art of acting, these questions are confronted: *act how? where? why? what for? for whom? under what circumstances?* and—even after the anti-ideological revolutions in Eastern Europe—on what ideological grounds? With these questions in mind, I locked myself behind studio doors with young actors who were, without yet knowing it, asking similar questions, and after a year and a half emerged with the KRAKEN group.

That group, like other groups of the seventies, is no longer in existence, not only because, as in our case, the money was running out. That was a time of collectivity, and this on the whole is not. Such groups varied in methods and quality, to be sure, but while they were on the scene, they provided strategic models of learning that were, in our work, predicated on the structures of modernist art itself. Just briefly: if one thinks of certain prototypes of modernism—from Joyce's *Finnegan's Wake* to Schwitters's *Merz,* from Picasso's "hoard of destructions" to Eisenstein's montage—it is possible to see that they were (whatever else they were) configurations of knowledge and pedagogical structures dealing, among other things, with the sheer proliferation of knowledge in the accumulations of history. They were keys to a curriculum, as were the spiritual disciplines we studied, from the martial arts to Saint Ignatius, whose exercises resemble nothing so much, theology aside, as the Stanislavski Method. They not only consolidated information and gave us new forms but, though artists' methods differ, a new sense of process, how to go about getting it done. And the same was true of certain prototypical works that moved toward the postmodern, say, in the line of investigation from futurist noise to Cage's silence. In our work we learned so much less from the established methods of theater than we did from the automatic writing of the surrealists or the alchemy of Artaud or, though it seemed to have nothing to do with performance, the annotations for the *Large Glass* in the *Green Box* of Duchamp.

What we learned from these examples was communicable as knowledge and method. After we left Cal Arts, we were in residence at various colleges and universities, doing workshops, teaching classes, and in two places at least—a distinguished liberal arts college in the Midwest, with carefully chosen students, and an average suburban university in the East, with open admission from the inner city—the nature of this work entirely changed the programs not only in the theater but in the other arts as well. There was no particular magic in our method (impelled as it was by a technique of "ghosting"),[11] though some suspected us of madness when we first appeared on the scene. As for the resistances to what we did, they came from the usual quarters: not only the burnt-out cases on the theater faculty or painters still suspicious of Jackson Pollock or the good-hearted folk at the kiln (Ken Price, Robert Arneson, and such ceramicists forgive me!) helping the kids to toss pots, but from quite accomplished performers who hate new music with a depthless rage, and with a long investment in the institution of the symphony orchestra. What that usually means in a university is that the students in music, to keep up standards, need costly private lessons that drain the overall budget, while it remains a national scandal, along with the rising rate of illiteracy, that multitudes of students can graduate without ever learning music—this most universal of the arts!—by making music at all.

The adoption of rock music by young people in the sixties was in part a response to that. They wanted a music that they wrote and made themselves—never mind at first the obvious rhythms or simplistic beat—instead of having old people make it and play it for them. The situation is needless. Anybody who knows something of found music or the methods of Cornelius Cardew or Pauline Oliveiros or the work done with made-up instruments or the more natural instructional properties of the gamelan, where you learn at first by performing and can perform from the day you begin, realizes that there are other ways into music than the one that keeps most of us out, and this is all the more true now with the cheap availability of electronic synthesizers. In a theater program the issue is sometimes quite the opposite, the feeling—with the dominance of psychological realism—that just about anybody can do it by merely playing oneself. It is true that just anybody can do it, but not merely that way, and if we thought a good deal more about it, we could build in the *humanities,* particularly at the undergraduate level, an entire program around that, so that a student who thought of himself or herself as an actor would be far more comprehensively educated than by the current pathetic return to distribution requirements. And I mean educated not only as actors or in the theater but in other modes of thought.

What I am talking about would not happen, by the way, simply by doing plays (usually a waste of time), but by construing acting technique, as every one of the masters did, from Zeami to Stanislavski to Grotowski, as something like a way of life. As anybody who really has studied Stanislavski knows, his method involved precisely the kind of de-conditioning or unlearning one finds in any great technique. Actors do not know how to walk, he would say, and then he would teach them to walk so that when they walked in a play they would appear to walk naturally. But there was far more to it than technique. His chapter on ethics, for instance: don't come into the theater with mud on your feet! The problem for us was, however, even in acting, that the available techniques with various ethical systems—from Décroux's mime and Dalcroze's eurythmics to Kathakali and the Tai Chi Ch'uan—were also proliferating around us, along with all kinds of performative ideas in the other arts. And the question then is what do you study? why? Among all the attractive but difficult technologies of acting, how would you make a choice?

This is a question that becomes urgent at every conceivable level in all the arts as we proceed toward the twenty-first century, where technologies even in the plainer sense abound, along with different antecedents and contexts in which art is likely to be made: from pigment to laser beams, from a kiln to a cloud chamber, from Terry Riley's solitary and incessant middle C to the polyphonies of a gamelan, photographs to holographs, from a kazoo or piccolo or Laurie Anderson's vocoder to the water bells of Harry Partch or computer banks at Boulez's IRCAM; from the unaccommodated body of the actor with his/her autonomic system and emotional memories to one with the athletic grace of a Lynn Swann (once wide receiver for Pittsburgh) as trained by Twyla Tharp; and a prospect yet to come, the performer out there in a space suit at zero gravity on the moon. Quite simply, the choices are myriad as to what one may choose to do, with what materials, or, since the days of concept art, without any materials or methods except philosophy, linguistics, and a text stenciled on a wall.

This was the atmosphere of thought in which my own work was developing with the KRAKEN group. Beyond the issue of technologies, the question for us was one that confronts any program that really thinks itself over: how to decide among all the possible options of instruction what should have priority? on what principle? Our principle was constrained by the collective enterprise, the psychic investment in a group, but it was the one we had enunciated at Cal Arts for the individual artist, for whom there are also constraints, but so far as possible of his or her own making. There is nothing new to the principle, it is simply this: you learn best and most fluently what you feel impelled to learn for whatever you want to do. You learn it because you need to learn it, and I am not only talking about technique, no more than Duchamp was when he seemed to abandon it for chess and something like pure thought. A program should be set up to encourage an appropriate resourcefulness within its means. Students will always cooperate regarding the availability of particular technologies if the overall enterprise is open and inquisitive; they do not usually expect linear accelerators, for instance, two miles long underground. They have every right to expect that research materials, responsive guidance, and certain kinds of technical support will be accessible. Beyond that, *ideas*.

And I do not only mean ideas about art. T. S. Eliot once said of Henry James that he had a mind so fine it was unviolated by ideas. You haven't the faintest idea what Eliot was saying if you think he meant that James did not have any ideas, or a wide range of learning. Remember, too, that we are teaching art in the context of a university, whose major purpose in life, I still take it, is not to get people jobs or to gratify parents but the pursuit of learning, for people who like to read and think and believe that while these activities can be hazardous in other ways—as with

Nietzsche's wild and dangerous territory of the mind—they are not necessarily corrupting either in life or art. Some of us remember the time
when the arts were looked at rather disdainfully by other academic disciplines, as if they had no legitimate right to be in the curriculum (that bias
may still prevail, for the most part, in European universities). To this day,
against my own allegiance, I sometimes think they are right. I worry
about our legitimacy when, unlike the sciences, we do not know how to
relate the most advanced research in our fields to what we teach at the
lower levels. I see no reason why the arts on a campus should not be at
least as audacious and experimental as high-energy physics or marine bi-
ology or fractal theory in math. One would like a school of the arts to be
as charged with possibility as a radiation laboratory, which is not to say
that art is science, only that it should not be less (and I say that as one
who has a first degree in science).

I will bring this to an end now with something like a last will and testament. What I have been saying, if you have followed the subtext, applies not only to art but to literary study and other disciplines in the
human sciences as well. Critical theory today is suspicious of the imagination. On ideological grounds. It is spoken of, along with the idea of
genius, as a "transcendental signifier," the name of an authority and
power that obscures the fact that it is human beings, not some higher
(metaphysical) agency that constitutes the meaning whose name is history. I am, as should be apparent, sympathetic to this critique, but I have
been in the arts too long and, ideology be damned, swear by the imagination, which is what, for me, brushes history against the grain. As for
genius, that is a troublesome idea, but as Hamlet knew a hawk from a
handsaw when the wind is right, I know genius when I see it. That we
do not see it very much, anywhere, is one of the reasons we have to think
about training, since genius pretty much thinks for itself.

Meanwhile, the world bursts, techniques change, forms are transplanted, like hearts. Some will continue to do, generically, what they
have always done well, following the true slope of their own passion, as
Gide said the artist should do—and will teach (despite all denial) in the
image of their own desire. But as the ozone layer changes and icebergs
break from the pole, atmospherically and geologically, as it were, the arts
are undergoing a metamorphosis too. It is not necessarily always promising, but even with the utmost imagination we live in no other world.
Much of it is exciting, and as we move into the twenty-first century, we
need to transmit that to our students, to whom all prospects should
seem to be open, the sense of a threshold that is privileged—imagine!

once in a hundred years!—since the barriers will be lowered soon enough, as the Wall will go up again, displaced.

Whatever art they start from, there are certain things they should certainly know about what has happened in the arts, since where they started from may or may not be significantly there. In recent years we have moved past kinetic sculpture that parodies mechanisms to plastic events that look like theater in an age of desiring machines, while images on film behave like music or flow graphically through design, which not long ago thought of itself as systems theory and now more and more as high art. Behind every art as we once knew it there is the dance of an unnamed form we have yet to perceive. Whatever conventional things are done, the special character of a responsive training would come from the radiant center where forms cross, however they differentiate, even specialize themselves again, as they surely will. What I find particularly exhilarating now, however—what justifies the arts in a university more than ever—is that the forms that are now crossing are not only the forms of art.

(1994)

11. With Your Permission

Educating the American Theater

I must confess to some uneasiness about the subject here today, for I am beginning to feel like the Ancient Mariner with his baleful eye telling the same story. Nor is it any consolation to think that it is not merely my story, nor even quite the same, since when history repeats itself, it may, tragic to begin with, repeat itself as farce. That, you may recall, was the way Marx put it in *The Eighteenth Brumaire,* as he described how revolutions occur in theatrical dress, within the nightmare of history from which we are still trying to awaken. What Marx did not exactly say is that if the heightened energy and volatility of farce may—like melodrama at a certain impasse of history—seem liberating, it is in the theater's hierarchy of illusory forms perhaps the most discouraging. In the recycling process of postmodern forms where, along with the kitsch, parody is prosperity, there is a certain affection for farce. But while I am attentive to these forms, and have learned much from the Marx Brothers and Laurel and Hardy, there may be in my temperament and pedagogical inclinations an unpurged quotient of modernist pathos, or too much acquaintance with Beckett. It's funny, and then it's not funny. As Didi said, "AP-PALLED!" But then I cannot quite blame it on Beckett, for I am also one of those who thinks that that most appalling play of all, *King Lear,* is a metaphysical farce. Bear with me, then, and a certain circuitous reminiscence, and I will see if I can manage some variations on a theme with which I have been long engaged: the question of theater education and the professional American theater.

Many years ago, when I was—for as brief a time as I could eventually make it—a graduate student in a theater department, I was particularly moved by certain anecdotes in the theater histories, which were repeated by my teachers in the two-semester course on the Development of Dramatic Art. Aside from the anecdotes, to which I will return in a moment, the course did not have much to say for itself, since it was mostly chronology, more or less encyclopedic, but without much sense of history— I mean, not the faintest concept of history—no more than Freedley and Reeves or the standard theater histories that students have been reading since. I hardly knew this at the time because the notion of history as an idea was about as remote to my mind as a black hole or the principle of superconductivity that is making the silicon chips obsolete. Had anybody said "historicize," I would have said the Romans invented the *aulaeum* and, like Allardyce Nicoll in *The Development of the Theater,* pretty much left it at that, without asking by what accretion of history or astonishing shift of perception or phenomenological earthquake that strange phenomenon had occurred, the curtain, which was not there before, but when it appeared, *why?* there and not-there, in all its subsequent permutations: parted, rising, draped, disappearing into the wings, or hoisted into the flies—or now, when not used at all, leaving its imprint on the stage. Whatever the origins of acting, even more obscure, once you start thinking about it the questions proliferate, and its various techniques—in their permutations, sometimes crossing cultures—need to be historicized as well. When, much later, I left the mainstream theater and more or less started from the ground up, the questions were unavoidable, and I have asked them recurrently since: *act how? where? why? under what circumstances? to what end?* and, historically speaking, this method or that method, *on what ideological grounds?*

The merest presence of an actor is not only an existential fact, but of considerable ideological consequence, though the history books merely tell us, as I remember, that Aeschylus introduced the second actor and Sophocles the third, neither of whom (apparently) were women, and we all joined in the chorus about the Festival of Dionysus as an exemplary image of community, though it had been initiated by the tyrant Pisastratus as a function of foreign policy, and Euripides soon came on the scene to examine the horrific premises of that festival in *The Bacchae* and to tell the world at large, in *The Trojan Women,* that this eminently civilized polis, which had just sacked the island of Melos, as we napalmed the jungles of Vietnam, was pretty barbarous after all. As I believe I learned in the course on Dramatic Art, Euripides merely won second prize for that, though there was not much discussion of the fact that the Athenian Empire, with its chorus and actors and citizens (but not its slaves and women) dancing in the exodus, collapsed soon after. These were not the sort of things, however, that were going through my mind in the Green Room, or when, to keep the labor force supplied in a mammoth auditorium, I was pushing flats behind the stage. Let me abbreviate the first semblance of an ideological struggle by saying that I didn't do that very long.

It was after I left the theater department that I began to learn—from Marx, Nietzsche, Freud, and the canonical drama itself, from Ibsen, Strindberg, Büchner, Kleist—that whether it is linear, cyclical, a vortex, a set of concentric rings or a Chinese puzzle box, a retrospective hypothesis or, as they say in deconstruction, an originary breach, history is the thing that hurts. And what really hurt at the time I am talking about is the realization that they didn't really believe, my teachers, those anecdotes from the history books that I had been taking to heart.

But then I was quite naive. I had come into the theater program with a degree in chemical engineering. I had not even seen a play until I had written one when I was nearly twenty, and it was an outright thrill to enter Memorial Auditorium at Stanford University and go backstage for the first time. I gaped at the pinrail, gazed at the flies. The dust around the single bulb on the forestage was, though I had only recently read *Hamlet,* a mote in the mind's eye. This was obviously long before I began to realize that the stage itself was, as Foucault might later say, the mere replica of a specular world given over to surveillance, the panopticon itself, the repetitive space of the primal scene or oedipal locus of the family romance. What they called theory of theater in those days—before Brecht, before Artaud, those incurable pedagogues—did not even vaguely suggest that back there in the wings was the silent shadow of a phallocratic power, and that the curtain itself, not to mention the teasers and tormentors, whose very names give themselves away, was merely a cover-up. The first time I ever acted at Stanford was in a bit part in *Cyrano,* where down on the forestage they had a prompter's box, but how could I ever know—before Watergate or Derrida's essay on Artaud, "*La parole soufflée*"—the insidiousness of its whisper and its affinity with Deep Throat? The words flew up, the thoughts remained below, down there in the subconscious, which, as I later read in Brecht, is not without considerable instruction subject to guidance, in a society whose educational system is, with its organs of mass communication, part of an apparatus that absorbs "whatever it needs in order to reproduce itself."[1]

Perhaps, for the time being, that was just as well. I proceeded in the theater, to use Nietzsche's term in *The Birth of Tragedy*, with something like
"true naiveté."

No wonder I could really believe, as perhaps some of your students
do, that all you had to do to create a great theater was to sit over a table
and talk nonstop for eighteen hours, as two men did in Moscow, at a
place called the Slavic Bazaar. I also bought the story about the gas man
who started a theater in a sort of loft, which revolutionized the stage,
only to discover many years later—history catching up with me—that it
must have been an illusion, like revolution itself, as the gas man discovered when he played the Bishop in a fantasy rigged by Genet.

But, as I say, I was gullible. And the theater department at Stanford,
which still thought Chekhov was avant-garde, and never once mentioned the name of Brecht (though he had been in California for some
time, right down the coast in Hollywood) would no more have produced Genet than it would have permitted on its stage the suppurating
sores and "perverse possibilities of the mind" in Artaud's Plague, though
The Theater and Its Double is not only "an idea of culture-in-action, of
culture growing within us like a new organ, a sort of second breath,"[2]
but the prospect of a curriculum that, like his true theater, has yet to be
realized, though Grotowski gave it, before he turned to more secret rites,
a good try. As I later felt about Brecht and Artaud, I thought that
Stanislavski and Nemirovich-Danchenko, over the table at the Slavic
Bazaar, and Antoine the gas man all had the right idea. I thought the anecdotes about them gave us exemplary models of how to start a theater
for which, out of passion and necessity and a desire to save the world,
you would have to develop a craft, and you would have to do it—as
Artaud said of the alchemical theater in the best definition of rehearsal
that I have ever read or heard—with a "rigorous intellectuality, . . . a
meticulous and unremitting pulverization of every insufficiently fine,
insufficiently matured form, since it follows from the very principle of
alchemy not to let the spirit take its leap until it has passed through all
the filters and foundations of existing matter, and to redouble this labor
at the incandescent edges of the future" (51).

I see this labor as consonant with the "terrible and never-ending
labor" of which Brecht speaks in the last section of the "Short Organum"
when having raised the complex issue of the appropriate representations
for a scientific age, and the technique for achieving them, he says that
"our representations must take second place to what is represented,
men's life together in society; and the pleasure felt in their perfection

must be converted into the higher pleasure when the rules emerging from this life in society are treated as imperfect and provisional" (205). And this includes the rules of theater, as Stanislavski's pupil and rival Meyerhold understood when he wrote that his Theater of the Straight Line "needs a new school of acting, which must not be a school where new techniques are taught, but rather one which will arise just once to give birth to a free theater and then die." Meyerhold, unfortunately, died himself for denouncing after the Revolution the theater that refused to die, its boring sameness, but he was confident that the Theater of the Straight Line would "grow from a single school as one plant grows from one seed. As each succeeding plant needs a new seed to be sown, so a new theater must grow every time from a new school."[3] I am well aware now that we are discussing these issues within an educational system also conducive to boring sameness, entrenched department structures and impacted tenure, but unless such notions are something more than the folklore of theater, we will, indeed, remain part of the cultural apparatus that is, as Brecht said, merely reproducing itself, even more efficiently today in the culture of information of a cybernetic age, never mind the superconductors, by satellite transmission and the speed of microchips.

Meyerhold, Artaud, Brecht: they later became part of the fantasies out of which I thought a theater could be made, fantasies that were constructed out of the high modernist critique of an alienated world, nothing indeed more alienated, and alien, in the United States than the theater profession itself. It is after all—with the world now made out of the movies—a quite minor, belated, or secondary form in a culture in which culture itself was belated and secondary, and as we could see in the eleven weeks of the Iran/Contra hearings, with its performances for the American people and the reviews in opinion polls, still is. But when I was taking the course in the Development of Dramatic Art I was very impressed with the eloquence with which Stanislavski and Meyerhold—who taught Eisenstein and collaborated with Malevich—thought of the theater as a cultural enterprise and that actors had to be in, through, by means of, and beyond their technique, cultured. Forgive the word. I can almost understand why when some people use the word *cultured*, Hermann Goering—like some members of the futurist avant-garde—wanted to pull out a gun. It is something like the word *standards*, which, more often than not, people who don't have any talk about all the time.

Back at the time I have been referring to, I had no standards at all, and so far as the curriculum was concerned, no way of ascertaining them. Nor had it occurred to me that what, in the Development of Dramatic Art, I accepted as a kind of gospel was not even going to be a question on the comprehensive exams, no less a guide to action in the professional theater nor the basis of a training program in the university. Those anecdotes about the formation of the Moscow Art Theater or the Théâtre Libre, they were merely charming interludes in the history books, like the story of Eleanora Duse who—speaking of history that hurts—was betrayed by her lover, D'Annunzio, and could apparently make people cry if she read from a telephone book. They smiled and smiled, my teachers, when you took it more seriously than that, as if indeed Duse's behavior—an art that, from all accounts, was apparently without rhetoric—was merely a divine gift and history not a promise but some sort of dead end. The same thing happened when, say, somebody like Beckett came on the scene, and they thought he was a mere passing fancy—"fashionable" was the word—or some avant-garde aberration, though he is still showing us, more or less, how to create the outside possibility of a new promise on the premise of a dead end. He now has a Nobel Prize, and we all love Beckett, of course, but I am sure they are smiling today over something else, probably not a playwright but maybe a piece of performance art or some hybrid of an unnamable form coming into the theater like recombinant DNA.

Or worse, perhaps, they are not only taking it seriously but smiling because they like it, and what the hell, since we live in a theatricalized period where, as Andy Warhol said, everybody can be a star for fifteen minutes and, in the profusion of image, art is fashion and you don't have to train for it anymore, for if you cannot live it, you can buy it and who needs experimental theater anyhow: with the commodification of the spectacle even the most unregenerate squares can be way out. Where things have a certain avant-garde respectability, as with the New Wave at BAM, it is hard to imagine most of the younger people, at least, in theater programs throwing up much resistance, as they did in the old days, the Old Style, as Winnie says up to her diddies in the ground, not if they get around, as they probably do, with everybody traveling everywhere and everybody seeing everything and, if you cannot go there and see it, even the remotest ritual performers coming out of the bush, like the Australian aborigines doing their thing in Central Park. But it is not yet clear what sort of theater culture is going to accommodate all this; nor is it clear—after Lee Breuer and Robert Wilson or Pina Bausch, no less the combination of Richard Foreman, Kathy Acker, and David Salle—what the new style of training should really be.

But returning to the Old Style, where we might get a grip on things—

what, really, are we to make of an afflatus like this in the age of Star Wars, simulacra, and the diplomacy of Ollie North?: "International conferences do not consider the world questions before them so closely as we considered the foundation of our future enterprise, the questions of pure art, our artistic ideals, scenic ethics, technique, the plans of organization, our future repertoire, and our mutual relations."[4] Thus Stanislavski, on the enfabled meeting with Nemirovich-Danchenko. As they parceled out responsibilities and debated training, Stanislavski would not easily yield authority over acting and directing; but there also arose the question of literature, and he felt Nemirovich-Danchenko's superiority at once. "The literary veto belongs to Nemirovich-Danchenko, the artistic veto to Stanislavski" (*My Life*, 218), Stanislavski recorded in the minutes of the occasion. One tries to imagine a similar relation between the artistic directors of our regional theaters and the new breed of play readers we call dramaturgs, even if the literary superiority is unquestionable.

But we are talking of training, of course, and what has this to do with training, when you train you train actors? So, what about the actors? Well, first of all, according to Stanislavski in the chapter on ethics in *Building a Character,* they should not come into the theater with mud on their feet. Then, as Tortsov exclaims angrily in *An Actor Prepares,* "An actor cannot be crippled! He has to have all his organs!" Not a blank eye and immobile face, a dull voice, speech without inflection, wooden arms, or slouching gait. "Let us hope our actors will devote as much care to their creative equipment as a violinist does to his beloved Stradivarius or Amati."[5] But long before he came to such refinement or the ablutions and protocols of a perfected technique, Stanislavski had to argue out with Nemirovich-Danchenko, over the table at the Slavic Bazaar, the question of the kind of actor worthy of the technique. These are not exactly student actors of whom they are talking, but various models of what student actors become:

> "Take actor A," we would test each other. "Do you consider him talented?"
> "To a high degree."
> "Will you take him into the troupe?"
> "No."
> "Why?"
> "Because he has adapted himself to his career, his talents to the demands of the public, his character to the caprices of the manager, and all of himself to theatrical cheapness. A man who is so poisoned cannot be cured."

"And what do you say about actress B?"

"She is a good actress, but not for us."

"Why?"

"She does not love art, but herself in art."

"And actress C?"

"She won't do. She is incurably given to hokum."

"What about actor D?"

"We should bear him in mind."

"Why?"

"He has ideals for which he is fighting. He is not at peace with present conditions.

"He is a man of ideas."

"I am of the same opinion. With your permission I shall enter his name in the list of candidates."

(My Life, 217–18)

None of what I am saying is meant as a particular case for the Stanislavski Method, but no matter what the method, I happen to be, with your permission, of the same opinion.

(1987)

12. The Pipe Dreams of O'Neill in the Age of Deconstruction

Despite the implication in my title, this is neither a theoretical approach to O'Neill nor an exercise in deconstruction. For that would seem to be a vain enterprise, a little pretentious or redundant for the drama of O'Neill, whose "blindness of insight"—the malady diagnosed or exposed by deconstruction—is as palpable in his work as the painful experience from which it is made. The vulnerability of O'Neill is that he was, to begin with, so utterly exposed and, at the end, almost unbearably so. In his last plays, the revelations were so obsessive in their eloquent inadequacy that they almost required no insight. The confessions are so unceasing, the drama so transparent, and the experience so painful, you would have to be blind to miss it. There was, we might say, nothing left to deconstruct.

Or so much to deconstruct that it almost seems hopeless, as in *The Iceman Cometh*. The back room of Harry Hope's saloon is a derelict cosmos made of illusions too absurd to be looked at, too necessary to take away. The characters, each in his own way, seek peace. But the final illusion is that there is any peace, either in detachment, confession, drink, drugs, or illusion itself, the most desperate of which we see in the hustling high spirits of the fast-talking Hickey, the illusion of no illusions.

In this regard, O'Neill seems to bring us to a critical impasse in modern drama, already anticipated by *The Wild Duck* of Ibsen. It is an impasse that seemed to arise inevitably from the irony in its structure, which was based upon *exposure:* now you see it now you don't, and the more you see the less you see. It is as if there were a self-reflexive vengeance in the drive toward truth that returns us to Oedipus, whose vision was so appalling he literalized the blindness of insight by gouging out his eyes. If Bertolt Brecht preferred, in his theory of Alienation, to turn the theater away from the paralyzing fatality in this truth—which impedes social action—the most compulsive instinct of O'Neill was to compound its irony. And thus we have his equivocal feelings about the "pipe dreams" of his characters, ruthlessly exposed and compassionately sustained, as if the truth that has to be faced—and not only in Harry Hope's saloon—is that there is no alternative. Which is why—most conspicuously in *The Iceman Cometh* but all through the drama of O'Neill—we have an excruciating sense of life having to be lived under the sign of illusion, when the drift of modern thought has been, with its ethos of suspicion and corrosive skepticism, to demystify illusion.

O'Neill, like Ibsen, has done his share of peeling away the layers of the illusion, that is, false value, half-lies, outright deceit, and the beneficent practices of myth itself, the apparent naturalization of truth—what Roland Barthes calls ideology, Marx's phantoms of the brain. There is the sequence in Ibsen's *Peer Gynt* where his runaway hero, a sort of Don Quixote of free enterprise, ever seeking truth, peels away the layers of a symbolic onion to its empty center. So in O'Neill, when it came right down to the final mystification, what he found there was nothing but a phantasm, that blank of empty being, a cipher at the center, the mask of nothingness in the dominion of illusion. If not a phantasm, then a fog, that swirling mist of being that obliterates the real, as it does for Edmund in *Long Day's Journey into Night,* removing him for an illusory moment from the grievance of history, the material sources of pain in a world of mere appearance. But if the fog moves out of history it is into a double bind. If, as Edmund says of the fog, truth is untrue there "and life can hide from itself," even that refuge is a momentary dream. And in the seeming dissolution of pain, which is for O'Neill a virtual definition of history, there is the ceaseless question of *unmeaning* or, what may be worse, a painful indeterminacy—brought on by the epiphanic recurrence of a meaning that is lost: "For a second," cries Edmund, "there is meaning! then the hand lets the veil fall and you are alone, lost in the fog again, and you stumble toward nowhere for no good reason."

That was never, for O'Neill, sufficient reason. He has no answer to this absurdist vision except compassion, an unyielding, anachronistic, romantic faith in art, and toward the end of his life, until the peace of oblivion, the secret and uncertain beatitude of a transcendent love. The dedication of *Long Day's Journey into Night* to his wife, Carlotta Monterey, is supremely moving. But their dependency was, to say the least, very strange (as José Quintero confirmed in a recent memoir); and despite the ardency of the dedication—or the dramatic power of "this play of old sorrow, written in tears and blood"—to speak of such transcendence, and really to believe it, was if not beyond O'Neill's capacity, a sort of regressive act of will on an altar of wish fulfillment, though it may be that *speaking* itself is part of the problem.

For, as various critics have observed, pointing to what seems to be a self-assessment of O'Neill himself in one of the final speeches of Edmund, he had everything as a dramatist except the linguistic gift: "The *makings* of a poet. No, I'm afraid I'm like the guy who is always panhandling for a smoke. He hasn't even got the makings. He's only got the habit. I couldn't touch what I tried to tell you just now. I just stammered. That's the best I'll ever do. I mean, if I live. Well, it will be a faithful realism at least. Stammering is the native eloquence of us fog people." O'Neill wrote this before any of us had heard of Jacques Derrida or Paul de Man, but now that deconstruction is more or less established on the American scene, the figure of Edmund who is a figure of O'Neill is, in a sense, the figure of deconstruction, which is after all a discourse on our collective stammering, the slippage of the signifiers, the inadequacy of any eloquence to a definitive truth, or origin of truth, as if language itself were the cover-up, what in our desire for the expression of meaning keeps us from meaning.

We are once again at the impasse: what we have discovered through the history of modern drama is—as Derrida said of the blind rewards of structuralism—"the possibility of concealing meaning through the very act of uncovering it." In O'Neill, it seems, the meaning being concealed in its exposure is that there was never any meaning to be concealed. With the possible exception of *Ah! Wilderness*—a sort of fairy tale of remembered promise—there is in the memory of O'Neill the trace of a desirable meaning that was never there to begin with, since life is from the beginning compounded of error and illusion. The pathology of O'Neill is in the intersection of this Nietzschean sense of the primacy of illusion with American history, its congenital optimism and self-deception, whose "supply-side theory" (to use the phrase that describes the illusory economics of our actor-president) was nothing but a tale of possessors dispossessed.

That is the name he gave to the garrulous, brooding, full-confessional (double) cycle of plays that, in his later years, constituted both an account of American history and, for O'Neill, a spiritual autobiography. Dispossession, however, was the substance of his earliest work, along with various forms of vain or demented idealism that accounted for the deep measure of remembered pain in the pipe dreams of the later plays, the illusions adhered to by his characters when—everything exposed, unmasked, hanging out (as we say)—they would seem to be beyond illusion.

With limited time for the magnitude of what O'Neill eventually wrote, let me return to one of the earlier plays, *The Hairy Ape*. One might approach it in terms of "the melodramatic imagination," but it is also possible to see the play, in an age of deconstruction, as one of those allegories that—as Walter Benjamin said of the drama of the German baroque—seem to arise from a kind of spiritual fever that transforms all language "into the extravagant images of delirium." As in the dramaturgy of the unconscious—with its melodramatic images of delirium—such a play is likely to have the disjunct, emblematic, ideographic properties of a puppet show or a pantomime. Or for that matter, in a period of the New Expressionism, the bold and fragmentary figures of the older Expressionism, to which of course *The Hairy Ape* was indebted, as it might be indebted today, in its production, to various techniques of Asian drama, including the melodramatic images of Japanese films and plays. It may in fact be—now that we have studied the articulated excesses of Far Eastern forms, from the Kathakali to Noh and Bunraku—that we may have, in America, a more appropriate methodology for staging a "naive" play like *The Hairy Ape* or the other plays of O'Neill, more or less experimental and long languishing, like the choral *Lazarus Laughed*.

It was after all our own Western (European) traditions of naïveté and excess that had influenced O'Neill when he composed *The Hairy Ape*. He had already studied the dramas of Strindberg and Wedekind when, in 1922, he read George Kaiser's *From Morn to Midnight*, now a classic of German Expressionism, of which he said that *The Hairy Ape* is a "direct descendant." More important than the question of influence or resemblance is the large aspiration—and the critical dimension—of the apparent naïveté. O'Neill says in his preface that he was trying to create "a symbol of man, who has lost his old harmony with nature, the harmony which he used to have as animal and has not yet acquired in a spiritual way. Thus, not being able to find it on earth nor in heaven, he's in the middle, trying to make peace, taking," as Yank says in the play, the "woist punches from bot' of 'em." "Yank can't go forward," writes

O'Neill, "and so he tried to go back. . . . The struggle used to be with the gods, but it is now with himself, his own past, his attempt to belong."

The play is a critique of capitalism, and Yank is a member of the dispossessed proletariat. But while O'Neill even wrote a play, *Marco Millions,* with an incipient Marxism, *The Hairy Ape* is something more than an assault on bourgeois reality or a social critique in a leftist mode. It is an image of man divorced from origin, which is to say the sources of being that gave meaning, order, authenticity to his experience. In a way, moreover, that O'Neill may not have anticipated, it is also a critique of the last resort of primitivism that persists through the modernist tradition as a desperate alternative to its demythification of Western culture. From Gauguin and Rimbaud to the extremities of the counterculture in the dissidence of the sixties—and even now among the indeterminacies of the postmodern, its anti-oedipal bias—there has been an insistent desire to get back to aboriginal roots, the uncanny, a regressive otherness, the primeval source: a libidinal economy without a Federal Reserve. The liability is still, however, something lethal in the other, an uncanny violence or "the uncontrollable mystery on the bestial floor" (Yeats) or "the beast in the jungle" (Henry James) or—without the self-reflexive artfulness of the modern masters of other forms—O'Neill's gorilla, who in that grotesque return to origins makes a mockery of evolution. The gorilla, who mirrors Yank with no illusions, kills him without compunction, and the problem remains: in the great conflicts between self and other, image and reality, being and becoming, where *do* we belong? what polity? what social order? what dispensation? now that—as Nietzsche thought—origin itself is revealed not as godhead but no more than illusion. Or—as they say in the deconstruction derived from Nietzsche—now that the logocentric tradition, the basis of Western metaphysics, is ungrounded, uncentered, destabilized, and the whole vertiginous structure of appearance is about to collapse.

The techniques of the play are those made familiar by German Expressionism: nothing subtle in analysis, rather staccato scenes reflecting the nightmarish distortions of Yank's mind in the nightmarish metropolis of modern life. As the ship is a floating inferno, Fifth Avenue becomes the mimetic scene of mechanized behavior, its pedestrians like robots, amidst the astronomical prices of conspicuous consumption. The theme of belonging that is so dominant in this play recurs in the work of O'Neill, as it does in all the major dramas of the American theater, from the characters in Odets who see their lives written on dollar bills (whether they have them or whether they don't), to Blanche DuBois and

Willie Loman, who are either at the mercy of strangers or have no roots in the ground. "I will always be a stranger," wrote O'Neill, "who never feels at home . . . , who can never belong." In *The Hairy Ape*, Yank does belong to the camaraderie of the stokehold, the sweaty banter and good-natured abuse, the choral uproar of his mates, but this we see quickly is a place of maximum energy and illusory security, whose own traditions are not what they were. Thus, Paddy's lament over the good old days: "We belong to his, you're saying. Yerra then that Almighty God have pity on us? *(His voice runs into the wail of a keen . . .)* Oh, to be back in the days of my youth, ochone! Oh, there was fine beautiful ships in them days—men that was sons of the sea as if 'twas the mother that bore them. . . . Oh, to be scudding south again wid the power of the Trade Wind driving her on steady through the nights and the days! Full sail on her! . . . Then you'd see her driving through the gray night, her sails stretching aloft all silver and white, not a sound on the deck, the lot of us dreaming dreams, till you'd believe 'twas no real ship at all you was on but a ghost ship like the *Flying Dutchman* they say does be roaming the seas forevermore widout touching a port."

As we move forward on the Trade Winds, however, into the historical irreality of a world of trade, the dreamscape itself transforms for the disinvested visionaries of O'Neill, from Yank and the Emperor Jones to Con Melody and Edmund, the stymied, stillborn, or aborted poets of the later work. In the lamentations of Paddy, the image of the ship driving dreamily through the gray night, there is a premonition of the desire for oblivion in Edmund, who remembers a similar transcendence at sea, and in the lot of them dreaming dreams on the ghostly *Flying Dutchman* there is a long foreshadowing of the eventual ghostly stasis, down in the hold again, not of the ship, but of Harry Hope's saloon.

Unlike the estranged loners of the later plays, Con Melody or Edmund, there is a unity of dispossession in the pipe dreams of the bums, like an inversion of the time when, as Paddy recalls, men belonged to ships and the ship "was a part of the sea, . . . and the sea joined all together and made it one." Now, however, they are drowning in their dreams, as Yank was enveloped in the black smoke from the funnels, the throb of the engines and the bloody furnace that had, for O'Neill, become a symbol of industrialized society, with men "caged in by steel from a sight of the sky like bloody apes in the Zoo." In an aberration of belonging, Yank sees himself as the genius of the machine, "de ting in coal dat makes it boin. . . . I'm smoke and express trains and steamers and factory whistles; I'm de ting in gold dat makes money! . . . I'm steel—steel—steel." He is in short the somewhat demented myth of un-bridled individualism now confronted by forces, within and without, too subtly brutal or complexly dehumanizing for sheer will to overcome. (I should say, parenthetically, that as America becomes increasingly a cybernetic culture with service industries and new Japanese management techniques, this vision of oppression has not entirely been displaced into Third World countries going through the process of industrialization.)

There are, as in *The Emperor Jones,* the psychic forces that the new Freudian psychology was to free from the hard rock of Puritan convention, desire under the elms, the terrors of the unassimilated Id. Again, O'Neill's economic analysis leaves much to be desired, since it is by no means systematic or, even dramaturgically, as acute, say, as Brecht's. But O'Neill did see that the new industrial forces, the intricate system of bourgeois exchange, projected onto the uncanny power of money—after all, an empty signifier—could not simply be equated with the elementary personification of a Robber Baron, as in vulgar Marxism. In the exaggerated figures of *The Hairy Ape* there was, rather, a sense of an economy of death, monopolistic forces as absent power grown as indecipherable as the structure of Kafka's Castle.

In this regard, the loveless and neurasthenic Mildred Douglas, though the daughter of a financier, is not so much an image of power but of power's *hysteria* (in modern drama's tradition of assigning this burden to women), another victim of its overbearing absence. Yet her tour of the stokehold confronts Yank with what he had never been conscious of before, a figure of privileged otherness, driving him from the protective companionship of the hold.

Despite Yank's defiance of Paddy and sense of belonging, the outburst against Paddy is already paranoid. Without even the "character armor" of realistic drama, Yank is immediately vulnerable. As for Mildred and her aunt, they are also abstractions, contrasted in the next scene with the beautiful vivid life of the sea: *"two incongruous, artificial figures, inert and disharmonious. . . , the younger looking as if the vitality of her stock had been sapped before she was conceived, so that she is the expression not of its life energy but merely of the artificialities that energy had won for itself in the spending."* Even her aunt calls her, in the acid repartee between them, a natural-born ghoul. For the emblematic character of allegory, this seems perfectly suitable, but since the perceptual habit of an American audience is determined by psychological realism, the language—as usual with O'Neill—may seem to overstate a case that the action will quite formidably make: "I'm a waste product," Mildred says, "in the Bessemer process [for making steel]—like the millions." Hers is a life not only inscribed on dollar bills but, like the nature of money itself, the mere *sign* of power that is *empty* in itself. When she descends to the hold, it is as the frightened vestal of surplus value. When she encounters there the monstrous mechanical rhythms of the stokers, it is for her, at the psychological level, like walking into the realm of pure libido.

In that context, but only there, Yank *is* fittest to survive—the end product of the Darwinian process of natural selection. The encounter between the two is preverbal, and the drama is mainly in the stage directions. Mildred, appalled by the brutish chanting Yank, listens paralyzed, *"her whole personality crushed, beaten in, collapsed, by the terrific impact of this unknown, abysmal brutality, naked and shameless."* (If the play were produced today, it would obviously need a certain historicization in the Brechtian sense, while recognizing that the choral action has something in common with the biomechanical methods of the Russian director Meyerhold, who had a considerable influence on Brecht, and Eisenstein, both of whom were attracted to similar techniques in the ritual dramas of China and Japan, which entered the mainstream in America through theater experiment with physical disciplines in the sixties, and the attempt to develop a "body language," which came back to Japan in other forms.) Behind Mildred's reaction to Yank is, to be sure, the repressed and desiccated woman of the Puritan tradition. On his part, Yank is stripped of all dignity by the pure terror of her petrified stare, which he breaks by throwing his shovel.

If we were to analyze the Action according to the Stanislavski method of naming the "objective infinite," that is, the stating of a dramatic action in the form of a verb, it would be: "to prove that he is not an ape." Like some expressionist inversion of *Beauty and the Beast,* the Action is not only melodramatic, it is parabolic, like a fairy tale. And like the grimmer fairy tales, it does not—as in the Golden Book/Disney versions—have a happy ending. For when Yank does go to Fifth Avenue, grassless and cordoned by skyscrapers, like the Ginza or Shinjuko today, fantastic prices on the objects in the windows, he cannot get the identical-looking frock-coated marionettes who have just come from church to recognize him, or accede to the fact that he is there. For them he does not exist, and in all their assembly-line sameness they seem even too vaporous for retaliation.

As Strindberg's Captain said in *The Dance of Death,* "How insipid life is now! One used to fight; now one only shakes one's fists." When Yank will not settle for that, attacking the 1920s' equivalent of a corporate type, he is advised to go to the Wobblies (International Workers of the World) for salvation—and the rest of the play constitutes a movement from one panacea to another for the alienation that proves incurable except by death. If Mildred, like money, is a pure empty signifier, "Allegory," as Benjamin says of the earlier German drama, "goes away empty-handed."

One of O'Neill's profoundest contributions, however, to American drama was to give it some of the moral/spiritual dimension we associate with those great allegorists of our own tradition: Melville, Hawthorne, and Poe. For better or worse (and O'Neill remains a begrudged presence among American intellectuals put off by the ponderousness of his writing), he brought to the stage an ontological anxiety that was, before him, largely missing in our theater, as well as a sense of the Absurd that we were to come to know better, after World War II, through existential literature. While in 1924 he already saw the forces at work that would become the focus of the proletarian writers of the next generation, he was not susceptible to ideological causes nor much drawn to social action. Which is not to say he did not have a social conscience. (The psychic dispossession of some of his characters—for instance, blacks and whores—is clearly shown as the outcome of real material deprivation.) He lacks the tough, nauseated, stylistically precise despair of postwar European drama, but he does convey—without the subtle textures of ambiguity in a Beckett or a Pinter—a sense of serious, almost irreversible psychic damage to our culture. It is the sort of damage you may be facing today, with the rapid pace of industrialization in Japan, and the wholesale appropriation of a younger generation by illusions made in America and, even with the weaker dollar, the colonization of the unconscious by the American fantasy machine.

While the social and political implications are material and prophetic, the tragic vision of O'Neill is drawn to the metaphysical, and to causes in the end that are almost unspeakable. If they can still be dramatized, they remain beyond solution. If he knew, like Freud, that he would have to live in the modern world in uncertainty and doubt, he also thought much, like Freud, about the future of illusion. That is not to say he was merely passive before historical events, blaming circumstances on the human condition. He speaks of *The Hairy Ape* as propaganda, but if there is a mission to it, that is on behalf of a restoration of man's harmony with the natural in himself. If he fails to see, as we do today in the context of deconstruction, that the "natural" itself is suspect, a function of ideology, he was way in advance of the critique that led to our anxiety about ideology itself, which all through the century seems to have failed us. When Yank turns up at the IWW on the waterfront, he finds he does not belong with the workers either. He sees the unions themselves, as we may do today, as appropriated and repressive agencies of bourgeois power. When he wants to blow up the factories, he is bounced by the Wobblies as a spy or agent provocateur, sent down by the Burns or Pinkerton police. Too literally radical for the workers, they also call him a brainless ape.

On the street he derides the union solution, along with other agencies of social improvement: "Feedin yer face—sinkers and coffee—dat don't touch it. It's the way down—at de bottom. You can't grab it, and you can't stop it. It moves, and everything moves." What it is that is moving is unformulable, unnamable, and certainly unstatable in social terms. Yank is a little obscure about this intuition, but the final scene at the Zoo brings us to that dark corner of human experience where life becomes a tale told by an idiot, full of sound and fury, signifying nothing—the brainless gibber behind all the forms of reason and modes of action. That has by now entered the canon as among the major fictions of the twentieth century, no less ominous for its fictional status. To draw upon the vision of another seaman, Joseph Conrad, it is a modernist image at the heart of darkness, "in the destructive element, immersed." O'Neill knows that the tragic hero has come to his nadir or low tide in Yank, for what he has created is an anti-hero whose behavior is like that of a cyborg, mechanized itself, but however factitious or emblematic, residually human.

So he calls the play "A Comedy of Ancient and Modern Life." It is the notion of comedy that modern drama has inherited from the abyss, with demonic laughter—the idiot grin of catastrophe, the giggle of the gallows, the comedy of dread. And that is something that, in the later, more realistic plays, is neither drowned in drink, which is the dead end of illusion, nor—in the delirious confessions of Long Day's Journey into Night—dissipated in the fog. It is a comedy we see much later in, say, Beckett or Genet, whose devastating laughter arises from the smashing of the pipe dreams that return, and return again, because like the very substance of illusion, that thing without a substance, they are impelled by desire and need against the need for deconstruction.

(1988)

13. Readymade Desire

Out of his frightened heart, Tennessee Williams once wrote "that the only somebody worth being is the solitary and unseen you that existed from your first breath and which is the sum of your actions and so is constantly in a state of becoming under your own violation. . . ." This was three years after the opening of *The Glass Menagerie* in Chicago and four days before the New York opening of *A Streetcar Named Desire*. By that time, the solitary in Williams had been violated by the little vanities and deceits and equivocal pleasures of dubious reputation, which caused him to say as well: "Many people are not willing to believe that a playwright is interested in anything but popular success."[1] One of the more scathing unbelievers about this particular playwright was Mary McCarthy, who wrote in her notorious put-down, titled "A Streetcar Called Success," that "Mr. Williams' lies, like Blanche's, are so old and shopworn that the very truth upon which he rests them becomes garish and ugly, just as the Kowalskis' apartment becomes the more squalid for Blanche's attempts at decoration."[2] I want to come back to these charges in a moment, but at the time she made them it was not very likely that McCarthy had seen very much of Williams's drama, except perhaps for *The Glass Menagerie*, which even among his detractors usually escapes disdain. It was not very probable, in any event, that she knew anything of his earliest work.

That work is still unknown and unpublished. One does not normally think of a little theater in St. Louis with a name like the Mummers as being political, but the plays by Williams that were produced there in the thirties were specifically so—to which, if scholars cannot, the FBI can apparently attest. Williams was later to study with Brecht's friend Erwin Piscator at the New School in New York, but there were Brechtian inclinations from the beginning. They persisted, we know, into his "memory play" about the Wingfield family, where legends and titles were to be back-projected in order to give "structural value" to scenes that might seem "fragmentary rather than architectural."[3] It is still hard to know what was being signaled, what incipient violation or subsequent depth of capitulation, when the alienating "screen device" disappeared in the transparent gauze of the Broadway production and—as Williams said in explaining why the device was cut—the auratic power of Laurette Taylor's performance. Williams thought enough of the idea to want it in the published manuscript, but actually, even if the legends and titles had been used, they would have occurred in the form of magic-lantern slides, an effect of mood as well as meaning that may have been dominated anyhow, as in *Streetcar,* by the chiaroscuro of lighting and music. Augmented thus, the magic lantern would have lent a certain romantic atmosphere to any effects of alienation, "emotion, nostalgia, which is the first condition of the play" (*Menagerie,* 133), a condition that, to the point of hallucination in *Streetcar,* seemed a considerable distance from the politics and techniques of Brecht.

If we thought of Williams then as an evocative writer with the susceptible delicacy of his glass figurines, he eventually seemed to become, as he might have said of Blanche DuBois but actually said of himself, "a definition of hysteria."[4] It may seem an appropriate justice that the early plays were forgotten, but as we rethink the later work on the jaundiced ground of the postmodern condition, as cultural productions or social texts, it is probably good to remember that the first things produced were overtly left-wing dramas about union busting, a prison strike, and a flophouse for what we would call street people today. One of the plays, *Candles to the Sun,* had not only a premonitory touch of the poet but, in the character of Birmingham Red, a conspicuous touch of Marxism. And in a period whose dominant playwright was Clifford Odets, the opening performance ended, according to a review in the *St. Louis Post-Dispatch,* like the legendary *Waiting for Lefty,* with the audience joining the actors in singing "Solidarity Forever."

About a week before the production of *Streetcar* on Broadway, *Life* magazine had a photographic feature on the House Un-American Activities Committee hearings,[5] but by then Williams seemed immersed in "the broken world" of the epigraph to the play, as if the voice that was no more than "an instant in the wind" had no political content, and "each desperate choice"[6] now made was, far from being collective, increasingly solipsistic. Nor was gay pride ever sufficient in Williams to entirely overcome self-contempt, no less to arouse a sexual politics in a participatory mode. Yet the homosexuality of Williams was hardly a trade secret, and there are those who have believed—putting aside the stereotypic, if not homophobic, revelations about Blanche's young husband—that if he "covered the waterfront" in his personal life (which he told David Frost in 1970),[7] the homosexuality suffused the conception of *Streetcar* in more or less ambivalent, surreptitious, or overheated ways, most especially, so far as the production confirmed it, in the sullen charm and narcissism of Brando's performance as Stanley. Whatever the gender constructions, they were not likely to be thought of in political terms, as they may very well be now; if not in the theater, surely in theory, with Williams seen (if still in the closet then) as an undercover agent of eventual critique.

He later made statements about all good art being revolutionary, but so far as most of us knew in the late forties his ideological past was not as vulnerable to the other McCarthyism as that of the director of his play, Elia Kazan, who later named names before the committee, or that other most promising playwright of this period, Arthur Miller, who refused. Despite the gestures at "social background" in *The Glass Menagerie*—"the huge middle class matriculating in a school for the blind," Guernica in Spain, labor disturbances at home, "the fiery Braille alphabet of a dissolving economy" (145)—the social conscience of Williams seemed to have dissolved into the psychosexual Braille and sometimes fiery (or purple) passages of the drama of lyricized loners.

As for the critical conscience of Mary McCarthy, she wrote of *Streetcar* in *The Partisan Review*, whose own Marxism was shaken and diminishing in the New York intellectuals' anti-Stalinist wars. Given the state of our theater at the time, where not only Williams's radical plays but Brecht himself was virtually unknown, ideas of any kind were at a premium, and one might have welcomed an ideological debate. But sadder by far than McCarthy's assault on Williams was that the deflection or sublimation of his politics appeared to have little to do with the withering retrospective of her most plenary contempt: "His work reeks of literary ambition as the apartment reeks of cheap perfume; it is impossible to witness Williams' plays without being aware of the pervading smell of careerism" (134).

What beguiles me now, aside from the raw gratuitous virulence of the judgment, is the anachronism of its piety on the postmodern scene, where it is hard to imagine anyone, either artist or critic, getting so worked up over the sweet smell of success. Or mortified by it either, as Williams apparently was, with no Southern Comfort for the residual puritanism, "sweet, so sweet! . . . terribly, terribly sweet" (*Streetcar*, 382)— as if the emotional perturbations and fragile beauty of Blanche, *"which must avoid a strong light"* (245), had been exposed to the glare of publicity and, even before Marilyn or Jackie or Liz, silk-screened by Andy Warhol. After all, according to the cultural logic of late capitalism, where it is more or less taken for granted that the arts are merging with fashion, even subversion and transgression have become equivocal functions of success, and in the libidinal flow of commodified exchange it is possible to think of the streetcar named Desire as a sort of Duchampian readymade, like the urinal named Fountain or—depending on "the epidermic play of perversity,"[8] the lubricity of performance—the Deleuzian desiring machine.

This may have little to do with Williams's intentions, nor is it a preface to a schizoanalysis of a neurasthenic play, which, in passing from the political unconscious of its author to the hysteria of its heroine, seems to have acquired a hyperrealism that, in its simulation of the truth of desire—passing by way of the Cemeteries to the Elysian Fields—is dangerously on the edge of kitsch, like the song Blanche quite improbably sings, a paper-doll testament to the loss of the real ("Not sold—*lost, lost!*" [273]) in what we have come to think of as an "economy of death." That economy, with its sadomasochistic array of specular seductions, is just about literalized by Blanche, with the "Blue Piano" growing louder behind her, in her manic obsessive defense of the loss of Belle Reve, as if she were herself, iteratively, the body of the dream: "I, I, I took the blows in my face and my body! The long parade to the graveyard! . . . You didn't dream, but I saw! *Saw! Saw!* And now you sit there telling me with your eyes that I let the place go. How in hell do you think all that sickness and dying was paid for?" (262).

So far as intentions are concerned at this late date in the dominion of deconstruction, we may, I trust, pass over them in peace without any damage to the manifest content that has, in scholarship and performance, been only too much rehearsed. As for the latencies in the text, so far as they are psychological, they are perhaps better left to the actors, who will—unless the production is radically revisionist or brazenly parodistic, like the gender-bending version by Bloolips and Split Britches retitled *Belle Reprieve*—give us variations on the characters not unlike the precipitations of color and slippages of figure, or reversals of light and shadow, on the cultural icons emulsified, rephotographed, engraved, and blurringly replicated by Warhol himself, who also serigraphed a "Silver Marlon."

For all that, it will continue to be, with whatever blurred contours of a possibly bleeding psyche, a familiar surface. With Brando in particular as the referent for Stanley, in an almost preemptive performance now memorialized on film (the form that, as the theater cannot, reproduces desire in a "body without organs"), the fact is that the play itself, with its self-consciously sensuous dramaturgy, is an icon of popular culture, drawn to begin with from popular culture. This is true even when the source appears to be high art, as in the stage direction alluding to *a picture of Van Gogh's of a billiard-parlor at night.*" If the kitchen then suggests *"that sort of lurid nocturnal brilliance, the raw colors of childhood's spectrum"* (286), that is the spectrum broadly and regressively inhabited by all the denizens of the Quarter and the elements of the play. Williams constructed it of already charged and precoded materials, from the classical nineteenth-century hysteric as aging southern belle to the poker night and its master stud to the French Quarter itself, with its boozy rhythms and local color, which—like the *"infatuated fluency of brown fingers"* on the keys—invests the scene with *"a kind of lyricism [that] gracefully attenuates the atmosphere of decay"* (243).

If an elitist like Mary McCarthy could spurn this "raffish charm" a generation ago, it is unlikely that a sophisticated critic with a modicum of cultural theory would be much put off today by the lurid effects of a drama with a seductive dose of kitsch. Since the drama of Williams was the paradigm of much of what we see on television, it is no wonder that *Streetcar* might be perceived today as generously endowed with soap operatic qualities, including the enticements of a voyeuristic style. If the figures of the play seem to have come, then, from the marketplace of signs, it is as if Williams had realized before the intensified consciousness of the mediascape of the postmodern that it is only as readymades that they can function mythologically. As for the elements of the drama that, from the day I first saw it, always seemed factitious, like the vaguely Faulknerian concoction of the "epic fornications" of Belle Reve or the inscription of Mrs. Browning's sonnet on Mitch's cigarette case, they exist somewhere between the provenance of dreams and the fantasizing of history.

Speaking of which, there is always the adventitious circumstance in which history affirms the degree to which it requires fantasy, as it did in the city that is the setting of the play. About a week before the opening, there was a cover story in *Time* on the New Orleans mayor Chep Morrison, who was described as Blanche might have described her savior Shep Huntleigh, as a "symbol of the bright new day which has come to the city of charming ruins."[9] Morrison seemed to embody at the time the postwar energy in all the nation's cities. (As the play was about to open, they were debating welfare reform in New York, so that they could put employable people back to work; the army was making final indictments at Nuremberg; Molotov and General Marshall were feuding over the German treaty; and the first phases of the Cold War were creating jobs at home.) We may look back at that now with a certain nostalgia, as we dwell with increasing dismay upon the brutalizing reality of what seems at times irreversible decay, which has polluted our cities and filled the streets with those who can hardly depend, like Blanche, upon the kindness of strangers.

If in this perspective we insist on doing the play by interiorizing its characters, there are some aspects of the drama that might be reconsidered psychologically, like the period in which Blanche, on the edge of desperation, was going it alone, with nothing really to help her but the wiliness of dispossession. By whatever lies and deceits, and whatever illusory pathos at the end, Blanche has by no means been without a sense of reality that came with a certain tough-mindedness from the experience of decay. The narrative of that experience may be, at need, revised to fit the occasion, as it is under the scrutiny of Stanley, who plots her departure (and punishment) so that in another kind of fantasy he can, once more, get those little colored lights going. (Stanley's own narrative is a little tenuous in the play, like his being a traveling salesman for the machine tools plant in which Mitch makes precision parts.) When they have their first encounter over Stanley's urgency about the Napoleonic code, she sends for a lemon Coke "with plenty of chipped ice in it" and abruptly cools the repartee between them: "All right now, Mr. Kowalski, let us proceed without any more double talk" (280). That it is not quite an equal match should not deter the actor from refusing to invest her performance entirely in the conspicuous symptoms of panicked excess or the *"uncertain manner . . . that suggests a moth"* (245). It is not that Blanche can no longer see the truth but that, with all the fictions upon which her reality has been constructed—those she inherited and those she contrived herself as the inheritance fell apart—she can no longer do much about it, to the point of hallucination.

Meanwhile, as we rehearse the fantasies on which the play is predicated, it may turn out that those of Blanche are, as we see women today after the Clarence Thomas hearings, to be weighed against those of Stella or, for that matter, the neighbor Eunice, who after all appeared on the scene before the battered-wife syndrome gained public attention. When she runs down the stairs crying out for somebody to call the police, a conventional audience is on the whole, including the women, still likely to laugh. We may or may not laugh when Stanley abuses Stella and calls her back with animal cries, but it is she who returns us to the illusions understood by Ibsen and O'Neill, and focused most recently through Anita Hill, who was not only abused by the men who questioned her but disbelieved by a majority of women whose own lives, perhaps, depend not so much on the kindness of strangers but on fidelity to the phallic order of things (however diminished in other contexts), or investment in the family with some helpless dependency on the authority of their husbands. Stella sobs at the end "with inhuman abandon" (419), but as she prepared for Blanche to be taken away, we have a version of the woman whose future depends, for whatever reason, on readymade desire, on *not* seeing the truth: "I couldn't believe her story—and go on living with Stanley" (405). Eunice advises her, for better or worse, never to believe it. "Life has to go on. No matter what happens, you've got to keep on going" (406).

The lines are old and shopworn, and the very truth on which they rest becomes ugly and squalid, the state of becoming that is, inevitably, its own violation. Surely she knows better, but what would most lives be if they ever depended on that?

(1993)

14. Water under the Bridge

From *Tango Palace* to *Mud*

I liked the other title better, *There! You Died,* but Irene wanted to change it because, as she wrote me before we met, others had found it confusing. She actually wrote "incomprehensible," which I couldn't understand at all, though they apparently thought it meant "there (not here) and that something went wrong with the punctuation." I still prefer the other title because of its exclamatory point, which—it still seems pretty clear—deploys the adverbial there to stress what happened here, whether it happened or not, though even if it didn't, sooner or later it will. "Are you out of your mind? You're going to die. Are you dying? Do you feel awful?"[1] If not, you probably should. Despite the odds on that, and the impeccable punctuation, the title was changed to *Tango Palace* after we did the play, in 1963, at The Actor's Workshop of San Francisco.

Since that is water under the bridge, as Isidore might say, tossing one of his cards, I should probably let it pass, but reading the text after many years, I am struck, once more, by Leopold's remark, "I know there is a way out because there have been moments when I've been away from here" (*Tango,* 143). Where those moments were is not exactly clear, for like Gertrude Stein's Oakland, across the bridge from San Francisco, there is no there there, and when he walks through the door at the end, determined as he's ever been, the implication is that wherever he thinks he's going it's nowhere else but here. One is tempted to say, of course, that in the capricious vicinity of Isidore's shrine that is neither here nor there, which might have occurred to Leopold when he first emerged from a sack, as from a uterine dream, to the strains of "A Sleepy Lagoon." It may be a tempest in one of the teapots among the properties on stage, but with Isidore as a pudgy Ariel about to become a malignant Prospero—pedagogue, wizard, master of the revels—"this music crept by me upon the waters" (*Tempest*, 1.2.394) back to the metaphysics around the grammar of *There! You Died*. For, enchanting as the song may be, it is merely the derisive accompaniment to the parody of a birth. "Look what the stork has brought me," says the enraptured Isidore (*Tango*, 129), who might even be thrilled at the thought that we die into this world, though the prospect was, I am sure, always already there, written on one of his cards.

Needless to say, he dismisses the voice coming from elsewhere that Leopold claims to hear, and as for the inscription tattooed on Leopold's chest—"This is man. Heaven or bust."—he considers it in "terrible taste" (133). With the logos out of the picture and teleology itself a bust, collapsing the bridge from here to there, Isidore himself is ready to fill the breach, declaring himself (in falsetto) the one and only voice: "It's me . . . me . . . It's me . . . and only me" (135). Unfortunately for Leopold, all that this establishes—as Isidore cheerfully admits—is that he is way down at the bottom, while Isidore is at the top, with the space around them infinite, "enclosed as it may be, because there is not a third person. And if the space around us is infinite, so is, necessarily, the space between us" (138). Which is not exactly a void but more like an extension or echo chamber of the narcissist's lagoon. "The memory of / the moments of love / will haunt us forever. . . ," but the spatial dynamics are tricky, as to where (or when) that was, so no sense dwelling on the water into which, like the Greek's imponderable river, you can't step twice. But wait: to whom does that *you* refer? for there must surely be a card saying, "Never say you can't." Or, in another language, "*Dime con quién andas y te diré quién eres . . . (Card)* Spanish proverb meaning . . . You know what it means" (135). What it means is that, if it can even be imagined, Isidore might attempt it, as if what was really in the cards were, for all their scattered redundancy, a Word Perfect program to the Eternal Return.

"Memorize them and you'll be where you were *(Card)*. Be where you are. Then and now" (133), transferring to the plane of the temporal the problematics of "there (not here)." As it is, even before he returns as an angel to end the play beginning again, Isidore seems to determine events that are going to happen twice: once in thought, then sooner or later done, though the inevitable seems to occur as if, being remembered, it were merely improvised (which may be, *pace* Heidigger, what we mean by being itself). A typical scenario, or case in point: "I'm supposed to sit there imagining a field of orange blossoms and then you're going to pour a bucket of water on my head" (143). Which is precisely what Leopold does—is it water from under the bridge?—when Isidore can't erase the boundless orange grove that, prompted to imagine an elsewhere, he invented to forget. Never mind that old conundrum of stepping into the river twice: in those "thousands and thousands of acres" (145) with their infinite mess of rotting oranges, how one steps at all is a matter for chaos theory, as it is on a smaller scale when Isidore is teaching Leopold the Argentine tango and reminds him that dancing "is the art whereby the feelings of the mind are expressed by measured steps. . . ." Here the problem would seem to be that, whatever the feelings are, the habits of Isidore's mind incline to the immeasurable, though with a certain fastidiousness in his profligacy, there is always a lesson in that.

The entire play is pedagogical, but Isidore's demonstration is a sort of catechism in "the poetry of motion," by which, moving from here to there, "One. . . two . . . three . . . dip," you can easily lose your step, as indeed they dip and do, in a rather semiological way: not here, *there!* not there, *here!* When I think of Isidore now, he seems to be, *avant la lettre,* an avatar of what, since Saussure's revival in Barthes, we have been fussing about for years, "One. . . two . . . three . . . rotate" (130), the metonymic play or circuitous prattle of the slippery signifier itself. A little retard in the tango, but what else is Isidore? "Does the text have human form, is it a figure, an anagram of the body? Yes," says Barthes, "but of our erotic body."[2] With Isidore, however, it is the erotic body itself that seems to have found its form, androgynous, polymorphous, overcome with itself, or so profusely what it is that the anagram *is* a body, displaying in human flesh something like the "text of bliss" (*Pleasure,* 14)? To which the cards are, then, a copious annotation.

"I read on, I skip, I look up, I dip in again" (12), which, though it may sound like him, is not Isidore doing the dipping, for that is more like skinny-dipping, and Isidore is "stout" (*Tango,* 129), if nothing but his babble, the figure of plenitude. What Barthes was describing in that series is the desultoriness of reading. Such intermittencies, however, have "nothing to do with the deep laceration the text of bliss inflicts upon language," nor—in the *"brio"* of Isidore, manic obsessive as it is, his *"will to bliss"* (*Pleasure,* 13)—upon the baffled Leopold. What is captivating in the cruelty, as in the fervor of children's games, is not "the winnowing out of truths, but the layering of significance"—the excitement coming, however, as "the hole, the gap, is created and carries off the subject of the game" (*Pleasure,* 12). "Look, everything is moving," says Isidore, when Leopold is about to thrust. "But I am steady as a rock." But if the rules of the game require it, even rocks have holes, like the moon is a piece of cheese. *"(Leopold lifts the sword slowly, points it to Isidore's heart, and pushes it into his body.)"* There! you died. "Say you're sorry and my wound will heal" (*Tango,* 161). For which the rules do not quite provide, neither an apology nor the healing, as the game comes round again.

Actually, in a previous letter, asking what I thought, Irene said she was feeling "more and more" that either *The Machine* or *The Wise Parrot,* two still earlier titles, were preferable to *There! You Died.* She did not say anything about the parrot, though there is parroting in the play (and a toy parrot too), but in the same letter in which she explained what troubled her about the title, she said that in her "original conception of the play, Isidore was not a man, but an IBM machine who communicated with Leopold by means of printed cards, lights, and sounds. The IBM machine was, to put it in very simple terms, the master mind of society." While that idea was displaced in the actual writing of the play, she went on to say that "if an IBM machine were a man, he would be like Isidore. This would, I imagine, be helpful to the actor." As Isidore's charm is quite infectious, even on the page, I was not so sure about that at the time we were doing the play. But as I am writing this now, shortly after Deep Blue, in winning the match with Kasparov, actually laid claim to being the master mind, it is not altogether far-fetched to believe it will become like Isidore. That there is in the machine, along with a certain mystery, "a very human sense of danger,"[3] as Kasparov has indicated, may not be quite enough. But who can tell what's in the cards? It may be that, in the accretion of human qualities upon artificial intelligence, it will be impulsive, fantastic, bizarre, and in the erotics of digital process, polymorphous perverse, with Isidore's almost demonic gift for exploiting the sense of danger. But then there is another prospect that comes up in the letter, which may be already within the scope of the redoubtable Deep Blue: it arises from a somewhat conflicted statement of what, for Irene, was "a main theme" or "a message perhaps," or what at the time she "wanted to say": "Be able, be willing to be alone. Be able to relinquish all."

Maybe with additional human qualities that will be a problem for the machine, but at the moment, surely, it is still a problem for us, and for all his virtuosity, maybe more for Isidore. As it turns out, while he seems to know "what it is to be alone. It's horribly . . . lonely" (*Tango*, 160), it is not entirely certain that he is able, in the finality only imagined, to really relinquish all, unless relinquishing means possessing, as it appears to do with his death. He can instruct Leopold in the necessity of giving up what he wants, but Isidore himself is, dressed for vogueing, "throwing shade,"[4] a virtual figure of desire. With that word almost exhausted by the "discourse of desire" (or subsequent theorizations, such as the notion of "performativity"), his lust for living, the *brio*, almost requires another name. In Barthes's terms (anticipating some of that discourse), Isidore refuses the textual mandate to arrive at bliss by "subtraction," or to accept the consummate loss that is the "zero of the signified" (*Pleasure*, 41): in short, with absence as more than metaphor, the mortal fact of having vanished. "Vanished? I have never vanished" (*Tango*, 143).

Now the same might be said for the Devil, who, in defining her theme around Isidore, Irene's letter said he is, which then elides into the statement, "Solitude is God. Destroying the devil is not enough, because it always lives. One must be capable of destroying it and also of living with it." Who is doing what to whom is, among the slippery signifiers (in and out of the play), well worth thinking about, and as she approached the dilemma of the title, she seemed to be doing that: "Perhaps I am getting a little carried away, but I just thought that this play is an homage to destruction. Not destruction for itself, but because of the renovation that follows." No wonder, at the time, I inclined to *There! You Died:* with the homage culminating in a rather kitschy aphanisis, it seemed conceived by Isidore, the triumph of his stagecraft. It was not entirely clear, however, what the renovation was, unless it was the enlivening prospect of dying over again.

As for the other titles, *The Machine* or *The Wise Parrot*, not only do I prefer *Tango Palace* to either of the them, but now that I think it over, almost thirty-five years later, it probably best conveys the quality I had in mind when someone asked, back in San Francisco, what I was rehearsing at the time. I said a new play by a woman born in Cuba who had lived in France and was, at least in her dramaturgy, a sort of exotic Beckett. (I might have described it as "magical realism," if that omnibus term for anything Latin had been current at the time.) The feeling of the exotic abated as, in the homage to destruction, the tango lost its footing, dipping down and out, and the house of cards collapsed eventually into *Mud*. There are significant differences, obviously, but what Fornes still shares with Beckett, aside from a sense of "the muck" (his term for *How It Is*), is the knowledge that play is deadly, really a dirty game. There is a certain paraplegic momentum in Beckett, and the autistic spectacle of dismembered bodies, at which, perhaps, we laugh too readily now. That was not yet the reaction to Beckett at the time we discovered Fornes; nor could we deal with the political impasse ("Nothing to be done")[5] as the ideological inadequacy that, compounded by nostalgia, came with the end of modernism. When it was not merely nervous, what made the laughter so painful is that, visceral, inarguable, it could only be ontological, what he called the *risus purus* (the laugh laughing at the laugh), out of the abyss defined by Pozzo as giving birth astride of a grave.

It is by no means to diminish the cultural politics of Fornes, or the gender and ethnic concerns of the later plays, to suggest that they proceed from a similar datum: even if not explainable, as in *Fefu and Her Friends,* something lethal at the heart of things. This is no mere cultural construct, nor is it to be encompassed, psychosexually, by an "epistemology of the closet."[6] (Fornes actually wrote, relative to the physical appearance of the characters: "Whether this is a play about two homosexuals who are giving each other a hard time or a play about entirely different matters, depends greatly on the aspect and behaviour of the actors.") As for the quality of play in *Tango Palace,* some of it is very funny, as when Isidore first trips Leopold, exclaiming, "There! You died"; but when push comes to shove, as after the mock bullfight—when Leopold is impaled, then kissed by Isidore—what is laughable is "putrid with death" (161) and up to its neck in rot.

Or so we may gather from Leopold's assessment of Isidore, which is also, in utter revulsion, a judgment upon himself. It follows upon Isidore's story of the man who, because he lost his beloved rat, virtually worshiped its picture until, as if "summoning his own death," he picked up his axe to smash it, only to find the rat, trapped in the wires behind it, dead of starvation there. "The dead rat turned his head to face the man and said *(as if imitating a ghost)* 'If you had not been satisfied with my picture you could have had me. You chicken-hearted bastard,' and then disintegrated into dust" (153). It is this parable that leads to the moral about relinquishing all, but Leopold, frightened by whatever it implies about him, is impelled to a diagnosis of what, for all his mesmerizing affection, is the malice in Isidore. So far as there is an issue of authenticity that asks to be understood, there is really little to choose between the picture and the rat: "I understand one thing," says Leopold. "There is something that moves you. There is something that makes you tender and loving, only one thing: nastiness . . . and meanness and abuse"

(154). As for the immanence of the muck, Leopold himself appears to be the dead-level expert on that, his whole being given up to crawling, like the creature of Beckett's *How It Is,* in the dirt that comes from everywhere, the universal filth:

> And it comes to us from within us. It comes out through each pore. Then we wash it away, we flush it away, we drown it, we bury it, we incinerate it, and then we perfume ourselves. We put odors in our toilets, medicinal odors, terrible odors, but all these odors seem sweet next to our own. What I want, sir, is to live with that loathsome mess near me, not to flush it away. (157)

Isidore mocks him, of course, but this is the one time he seems to be taking instruction—in the nightmarish scene where, after his propaedeutic on beetles (versatile and invasive, and also the most fertile of insects), they perform a ritual dance wearing beetle masks. "To make the dirt come out through the mouth," Leopold says, crawling in the dance, "you have to make your holes very tight, and let the dirt rot inside you. Then it will come out through any opening" (158).

As a contribution to the ethos of play, the intensity of self-contempt was a considerable qualification in the sixties, when games were all the rage in the forms of alternative theater, and polymorphous perversity was, as defined in *Love's Body,* often self-edifying as the stuff of celebration. There is, if the actors are up to it, a bizarre hilarity even in the morbidity of these scenes. Nor have I meant to minimize, in my emphasis on the dying, the quotient of vivid living that goes into imagining that. Which is, to say the least, hard to miss in Isidore. His teachings may not exactly add up to the model of a model curriculum, but it is an anticipatory paradigm for the pedagogy in later plays, and not merely for the process but its mortifying substance as well. Like some of her characters, Fornes seems blessed with a passion for knowledge, which has not abated over the years in which she has been doing her own teaching. Her work has moved in various directions, from the brain damage of *The Danube* to the Dantesque transcendence of *Abingdon Square,* but whatever the subjects she is writing about, some very valuable part of her drama is still down there in the muck, where somehow the love of learning may energize desperation.

So it is most specifically with the indefatigable Mae in *Mud.* With Lloyd bloated, puky, rotten, dying "like a pig in the mud," so that not even the flies will go near, she is determined "to die in a hospital. In white sheets. You hear? . . . I'm going to die clean."[7] That is going to be accomplished by her going to school and learning things, and while she is only "intermediate" (21), not at all advanced, the more advanced the text the better, as with the inscrutable medical terms. The text may need more study, but what does seem apparent, as she listens with *an air of serenity*" to Henry reading aloud, is her pleasure in the text and, even when it is read at high speed, her ability to get the point: "perineal pain, irritative voiding, aching of the perineum, sexual impotency, painful ejaculation, and intermittent disureah, or bloody ejaculation." Here the issue of gender is focused in a "chronic bacterial infection" of the masculine prostate gland (21–22), but the rottenness spreads through the play, with Mae struggling against it, like an existential condition.

When Henry asks her why, since there is no binding blood relation, she is so attached to Lloyd, and why she doesn't do something about it, she says: "There's nothing I can do and there is nothing Lloyd can do. He's always been here, since he was little" (28). Here is a "wooden room, which sits on an earth promontory," whose earth is "red and soft" and, though without greenery, "so is the earth around it." The wood, by contrast, "has the color and texture of bone that has dried in the sun. It is ashen and cold" (15). With a "vast blue sky" behind the promontory, one has a sense—despite the brutal immediacy of behavior, itself frozen like a still photograph at the end of each scene—of something not merely alienated, historicized, but unaccountably remote. Thus it is with Mae's story of her father's bringing Lloyd to keep her company. There is something primordial about it, like the base opposite—in memory encrusted by mud—of Miranda imagining Ferdinand through the dark backward and abysm of time: "I don't know what we are. We are related but I don't know what to call it. We are not brother and sister. We are like animals who grew up together and mate" (28). Henry's coming is another matter, first enlightening, then crippling. If the space between Isidore and Leopold is infinite, because there are only two, the situation in *Mud* is impacted by successive degradations in the unsuccessful life of three. When the whole thing becomes intolerable—with both men exploiting her, cheating and lying, soiling even the muck, constituting an offense, not only to each other, but to high heaven if it were really there, or to the last dwindling promise of a "decent life" here (38)—Mae herself is almost murderous and resolves to break away. But it is more than the drama's plot that makes it seem too late.

Is it that the learning curve is a problem? "I feel grace in my heart," says Mae, when she hears Henry recite grace. And while she can give as good as she gets, in the tawdry agons with Lloyd, part of her life has been lived in a kind of active forgetting. "I feel fresh inside as if a breeze had just gone inside my heart." But "what were these words?" she asks, because she finds it hard to remember. "I have no memory," she says, and (whoever he happens to be) her teacher seconds that. "Not enough to past the test. But I rejoice with the knowledge that I get" (26). Her desire is extremely moving, and her capacity to love or cry with joy, but in the accretion of reality around her, its grievous tedium, the ironing, the protoplasmic irritation, it is as if there is something else she has forgotten: something is very sick, something is rotting away, somebody is going to die. Unfortunately, even when her reading improves—as with the inspired passage about the starfish that "keep[s] the water clean"—it does not protect her from that, as if she failed the test. The memory of / the moments of love / will haunt us forever . . . , but what the "starfish's eye cannot see" (27) is that, clean as the waters are, the sleepy lagoon is also inhabited by bloodsuckers and hermit crabs—which, as the discourse sometimes forgets, but Fornes certainly does not, are also moved by desire.

(1999)

15. Fervently Impossible

The Group Idea and Its Legacy

While I am gratified to be the keynote speaker on this occasion in honor of Harold Clurman, I do not pretend to be an authority on the workings of the Group Theater. Most of what I know of it, beyond myth and rumor, comes from the writing of Harold Clurman. Having written two books, however, about the theaters I have directed, I am well aware that my most conscientious honesty did not necessarily get it all, and that even people who loved me—maybe especially those who loved me (I like to think I was much loved)—had a somewhat different take on what I thought I got right. There are various people on the program today who know about the Group as I do not, or who might think of its legacy in other ways. I am not going to enumerate the groups, or practitioners, who were influenced by the Group—some of them are here to speak for themselves. What I want to do, instead, is to make some distinctions about the Group *Idea*—I am not sure how affirmative—by way of reflections on Harold Clurman's view of it. As for the distinctions I make about its legacy, they will be modulated by my own experience, which occurred in another time, or since I was in the theater a long time, in rather distinct ways in quite different times. The last work I did, with the experimental group KRAKEN, overlapped with various groups that, as part of another history, might have remembered the Group, but with more or less departure from, if not indifference to, *its* Idea.

I would like to begin with a piece of dialogue, which is a sort of affective memory of what became for me, in the making of (a) theater, the plain fact of an obsessive theme. It also remains the recurring burden of what, having left the theater, I have been theorizing since. That theory has been much concerned, in an age of demystification—some call it now deconstruction—with the future of illusion. That illusion has a future is, aside from confirming Freud, the subtext of the dialogue, which is under no illusions except the one that counts:

"'It's a very hard job,' he warned. 'It's an impossible one,' I answered." That is not an excerpt from my book *The Impossible Theater: A Manifesto*, written in rage and promise, with revolution on its mind, at the outset of the sixties. It is, rather, an exchange between Harold Clurman and his father, who said in the midst of the thirties, as the Group was inscribing itself in history, that it was nevertheless doomed to failure. He said it, apparently, in the customarily implacable, relentlessly impersonal way that with more or less oedipal passion must have driven Harold up the wall. I can see him now, voice rising, about to pump his fists . . . but maybe not with his father. Earlier in *The Fervent Years*, there is the quotation of another dialogue, which Harold himself had written in 1929, the year of the Great Crash:

> The Layman. If you will omit the evangelical tone, you may talk to me about the theater.
> The Theater Man. Fanaticism is not only inevitable with us; it is almost indispensable.

Indispensable as it was, one senses a wavering in the evangelical tone—maybe even within the company—by the time of the exchange with the father, which is recorded objectively in the book as part of what was, between them, an "almost perpetual" philosophical debate. "Who was right," Harold asks, "my father or I?" The elder Clurman was quite aware of the Group's determination and achievements, and its honorific semblance of material success—one of its plays, *Men in White*, had just won a Pulitzer Prize—but he was pointing to the anomalous ground of its mission in an "impatient, money-minded world," and the inevitable erosion of any "collective ideal" in an individualistic society further atomized by competition.

There was, moreover, for an always susceptible group of actors, the allure of the main chance, if the chance was big enough. If for various reasons, Franchot Tone took it (sending in conscience emergency checks from Hollywood), most of the Group resisted, while others never got the chance, which is still, in our professional theater, the common fate of actors. For the Franchot Tones of our day, in the few groups that survived the sixties, where the group idea flourished, the problem has been dealt with by a certain permissive itinerancy, the actor going and occasionally coming, as with the Steppenwolf in Chicago, or even appearing on the video screen, as in the current production of the Wooster Group in New York—making a conceptual virtue of the dynamics of atomization. Or perhaps, with the desire for unity, we should think of it as a dialectic. Either way, it is a not unimportant part of the legacy of the Group, while its analysis remains, for those of us who have tried to create and sustain a company, one of the acutely familiar aspects of the story, as rehearsed so vividly by Harold in his still-inspiring book. Video was not available then, but under duress the Group Theater did make certain allowances (for leaves, on salaries), and a similar policy might have been unavoidable if, with growing reputations among the actors and the massively remunerative, overpowering seductions of film, it had managed to survive through World War II and beyond the McCarthy period.

I will return to that period shortly, and the rather suspended animation of the Eisenhower era when, while defining my own idea of a theater, I first read *The Fervent Years*. But let us stay for a moment with the sixties, a period (or periodization) so fervently full of itself as to make us forget sometimes that much of it happened in the seventies. One would think that the theaters that developed then, out of the communitarian idealism of the time, and its "participatory mystique," were lineal descendants of the Group. And it is very likely that, as the only memorable antecedent in the American theater, it did serve as an unavoidable historical referent, if not exactly the ideological model, for some of those groups. If some of the younger groups in a youth culture seemed to have no historical memory, virtually all of them developed on radically different premises from the Group Theater, with another principle of authority or dispersed authority or denying authority (or the pretense of denial), and with considerable disdain for the tradition of acting that, as taught by Lee Strasberg at The Actors Studio, was still, with whatever modifications, associated with the Group. There was in all this an antihumanist critique that—with certain mixed feelings, to be sure—could look upon the acting even of a Marlon Brando or a Kim Stanley or a Geraldine Page as if it were the apotheosis of individualism turned utterly solipsist; or like the Silver Marlon silk-screened by Andy Warhol, before his dollar signs, the sold-out iconic reflection of late bourgeois capitalism. Which was only confirmed, of course, by the Studio's accommodation of Marilyn Monroe, whose body language was not quite that of Grotowski and the "alternative theater" groups.

I will not discuss the array of alternative techniques, from the transformations of the Open Theater (a variation on Stanislavski's late method of physical actions) to the psychophysical exercises of Grotowski, with various borrowings from Yoga, Kathakali, Chinese opera, and the martial arts. There were, with these resources—plus circus, acrobatics, org(h)astic soundings, games and ritual too—some remarkable things done by a few of the groups, while at the same time dismantling the text or doing without any text, thus liberating the actor who was merely a submissive subject of the old repressive dramaturgy and its institutional structure. Some actors, refusing the name of actor, thereby became *performers,* sometimes acquiring in the process, ostensibly, shamanic powers. This was, as I have suggested, an ideological matter that has somewhat abated in the theater, or been displaced, for it has actually been taken up by theorists who have valorized the idea of performance or, since the bravura of Roland Barthes, even think of themselves as performers. With a rhetoric of transgression that might have been borrowed from the Living Theater—which, indeed, had a considerable influence on the continental thought recycled here *as* deconstruction—they continue to assail the hegemony of bourgeois drama, and the oedipal family romance, in the ceaseless vigilance of desiring subjects in the antihumanist critique.

Here, theater and theory join again, as in the ancient etymological connection. For in the trickle-down economy of cultural production, this critique has entered into performance art and the theatrical practice of feminists, blacks, Hispanics, gays, and other marginal groups, like the LAPD in Los Angeles, which bear little resemblance whatever to the one assembled (wholly white in the pictures, and looking middle class) first at Brookfield Center, then at Dover Furnace or Green Mansions, those summer retreats at which Harold and his codirectors, Strasberg and Cheryl Crawford, fought with each other, consolidated their methods, and rehearsed the productions that were not going to lofts, garages, basements, the streets, but—with whatever ambivalence—back to Broadway and into the mainstream of American theater. I do not say that critically, because there are complex issues at stake, having to do ultimately with our conception of American culture, increasingly multicultural, in which the mainstream, politically, feeling itself slighted, or forgotten, is itself a major issue, calling now, too, for affirmative action.

There is still a tendency to think of the Group Theater, because of the radical animus of the thirties and the agit-prop legend of *Waiting for Lefty* (done somewhat marginally to the Group), as a theater that emerged from social necessity out of predominantly political motives. There were certainly leftist inclinations among members of the company, who eventually initiated debates about the choice of plays, directorial authority, and with more or less ardor for an ideological slant, internal and surrounding economic and political issues. If that raised consciousness along socialist lines, it is not exactly how the Group started. Harold writes of the first working summer at Brookfield Center, in 1931, that—though they were considering production of a Soviet play—there was actually very little political discussion. "Of radicalism," he says, "there wasn't a spark." Of the Soviet play: it "was not at all suited to our needs" but would provide more sizable roles for those with bit parts in *The House of Connolly*, the first play staged by the Group. Then he asks what we might have asked had we been there; that is, *why*, for all his talk "about the need of facing our times and of finding affirmative answers to the moral and social problems of our day, politics received so little of our attention. One answer," he suggests, "may be that my education and inclinations had been chiefly aesthetic."

With whatever social passion or desire for affirmation, those inclinations never changed. Harold had, in his formative years, lived in Paris and studied at the Sorbonne, where he had done a thesis on French drama from the fin de siècle until the advent of modernism, whose aesthetic values he shared through the late book on Ibsen. And if he was not at all insensitive to the urgencies of the Depression, thereby feeling some common cause with the worker, he was essentially a New Deal liberal in the bourgeois enlightenment tradition who—against the grain of critical theory today—upheld the privileged particularity of the artist's vision.

In that regard, whatever the Group Idea, Harold Clurman was—dare I say it?—elitist. And his father may have been speaking better than he knew, or maybe he did know better, that in the society of individualism that threatened the collective ideal, the son was capable of writing, as he did at the end of *The Fervent Years,* that the artist "sacrificed his birthright" if he gave up that particular vision. Only by preserving "his own special sight—the more individual the better—could he best serve whatever causes he had come to believe in. The artist to be of value in any capacity must always proceed from what is—from what he is in the first instance—rather than from what he believes he should be." He might have been, nevertheless, if he were still among us today, a little more judicious about the masculine pronoun, but would, I think, still proceed to make a case against (even using the word) any kind of "correctness," not only political, that is, the conforming of the artist's vision to a "preconceived pattern," or even to a worthy cause. As soon as the artist, he wrote, "begins to exert his will in relation to what he sees, as soon as he allows any value beyond his actual sight to shape his creation, a distortion will set in that will end by betraying even those he hopes to help. When the artist is sincere—true to his own observations and impulse—even his mistakes may be useful; when the artist obeys considerations foreign to his own truth, however worthy his motive, he will fail even in terms of that motive."

It should be apparent, if you have been reading cultural critique over the past generation—whether as theorized in *October* or mediatized in *Artforum* or subcultured in *High Performance* or anthropologized in *The Drama Review*—or simply been following the politicization of the arts themselves, that everything about the passage above would be anathema to those on the antiaesthetic left, formed by the neo-Marxist/feminist turn of poststructuralism and the new agenda of what, in our graduate schools, they now call cultural studies. What might remain, however, a saving grace is what Harold describes, in speaking of himself and Strasberg as "the two most truly labyrinthine characters" in the Group, as his foundational belief. It is that belief that suffuses what he is in the first instance. More or less evangelical, he was convinced about "the interdependence of people, the need for a common faith and co-operative action," and that conviction was spurred on by an irrepressible optimism that he situates in the humanist tradition of Emerson, Thoreau, and Whitman—though it seemed to be rooted as well, as I knew him, in some indomitably fundamental personal buoyancy of being.

"To be truer collectivists," he concludes, as if still answering his father, "we must be more deeply individual." But his individuality is such that, as he thinks of the "human vibration of people" in even the most ordinary kinds of theater, he clamors "for greater occasions, for closer embrace, for a more rooted togetherness." This occurred early on, before his liaison with Strasberg, and so far as Clurman was responsible for it, that clamor, grown more vociferous, *became* the Group Idea. As we might expect, the Idea was always threatened by the individuality of some of the most gifted people in the Group, even as it developed the gifts of some, like Clifford Odets, whose peculiar, obscure individuality longed, too, for a closer embrace, and embraced it with vehement faith in the *rightness* of the Group, even as he felt cut off, "excluded, special," and eventually went to Hollywood, exercising thus—at Stella Adler's involuntary suggestion, prompted by Harold's preaching—another rightness: the "right to sin."

Despite the postlapsarian pathos of Odets, what seemed perfectly normal then, but is a paradox from our postmodern perspective—after the vicissitudes of the sixties, and its disenchantments—is that such a complex of individuals could not only commit themselves to a collective ideal, but took for granted that, with whatever subtleties of the actor's craft or incursion of private moments, the playwright's vision *must* be served. Not only was the author not dead—which death has since been declared by Barthes and Foucault—but finding new plays and playwrights seemed, for Harold Clurman, something like a moral obligation. As indicated earlier about the dismantled (or revisionist) text, that was something else again in the sixties, when the playwright—sought out and dutifully served by the Group—gave way to "collective creation" or, with the almost totalitarian display of authority in the work of Robert Wilson or Richard Foreman, a Theater of Images. Which often preferred—to the dismay, no doubt, of a teacher like Stella Adler—untrained actors or performers.

I do not mean to be misleading. As implied earlier, too, there could also be, as grounding for collective creation, the most rigorous regimen of training, as in my own KRAKEN group. If that work (the last I did in the theater, over a period of eleven years) was highly charged in the body, there was also—in a generally antiverbal, nonverbal, or spastically verbal period—a relentless engagement with language that, if improvisationally developed by the group, eventually materialized in an intricate text. About the text or its absence, or a sometimes minimalist, sometimes parodic presence, groups varied; but the nature of the training, or its absence, did raise another issue that had to do with the substance and quality of the acting. In much of the work of the period, whenever the actor, by whatever name, approached anything like character—even as a residue of the deconstructed text or, playing games, over a transformative spectrum of "roles"—it often left much to be desired (and not in the sense of the desiring subject). While the "psychological acting" that was a legacy of the Group was—in *The Village Voice* or *The Soho News,* or the performer bias of *The Drama Review*—getting a bad press, various of those who were then receiving Obie awards, and receive them to this day, could hardly have managed to develop their reputations if, like the actors of the Group Theater, they had tried to do it on Broadway. That the Group Theater did what it did on Broadway was, of course, a very large part of its problem.

As for the father's prophecy, made in 1935, when the Group was on the threshold of its major accomplishments, Harold writes simply and immediately after the little dialogue: "The Group did fail in 1941." One of the ubiquitous credos of our theater—Harold invoked it with considerable eloquence, as I did too in my time—is about "the right to fail," but though that right hardly exists in certain echelons of our theater, I am afraid it will never be litigated by the American Civil Liberties Union. When toward the end of *The Fervent Years,* Harold wanted to summon up an emblem of the desire of the thirties, he thought of the boy in Odets's *Awake and Sing* who doesn't want life printed on dollar bills. Lifestyles have changed since the thirties and the sixties, but as we are living in the age of the bottom line, the theater is still haunted by the sweet smell of success, not only in the boardrooms of our "non-profit resident theaters," but even in the off-off remnants of our alternative theater. That smell remains, of course, pervasive on Broadway, which was, unfortunately, the material horizon of the Group's enterprise, the fiscal shadow that always threatened to make a facsimile of its idealism.

On Broadway, the Group was constrained, like any independent producer, to operate from show to show, at the mercy of the reviewers and the market. No announcement of its closure was ever made, but in summing up the reasons for its failure, Harold wrote: "The fundamental economic instability from which the Group suffered, its piecemeal, bread-line existence, accounts for its hectic inner life and explains more about its real deficiencies than any analysis of the personal traits of its individual members. . . . None of the Group people themselves, though individually aware of their money problems, ever quite realized how this pressure shaped their opinions and feelings." (Far off-Broadway, the dynamics had changed somewhat, and the expectations, but I was some time ago, as an advisor to a quite admirable experimental group that had managed to endure for many years, at an emergency meeting—about money, of course—in which one of the directors suddenly burst out, "This is the end, the end! no way, I can't go on without a fucking medical plan!" It was not quite the end, and fragilely, somehow, that group persists, anxiety aging without a medical plan. Nor is it likely that Bill and Hillary Clinton will come soon enough to the rescue.) One might add, despite what seemed the exceptional nature of the Group's plays, that even the repertoire was shaped by the same pressure, working at the elastic limit of what was possible on Broadway.

If the compromises that the Group was forced to make for ten years (compromise, too, may be a form of courage) were no longer possible for Harold Clurman, he did not feel, when the Group ceased to function in 1941, that it was really played out. A theater group like any organism may have a limited longevity, but discouraging as things may have been, the financial pressure enervating, Harold still did not accede to the analysis of his father, or not entirely. It was not the Group that relinquished itself to an atomized reality, in an accession of self-interest, diffusion, or mere resignation. "It suffered from neither defeatism nor slothfulness. It had not lost its inspiration," he wrote, and what follows is, perhaps, the most percipient passage of his book. "The Group could not sustain itself as such because it was isolated. The Group Theater was a failure because, as no individual can exist alone, *no group can exist alone.* For a group to live a healthy life and mature to a full consummation of its potentiality, it must be sustained by other groups—not only of moneyed men or civic support, but by equally conscious groups in the press, in the audience, and generally in large and stable segments of society. When this fails to happen, regardless of its spirit or capacities, it will wither just as an organ that is not nourished by the blood's circulation through the body."

If they did not have the moneyed men or large-scale civic support, the groups of the sixties did have an alternative press, a countercultural audience, campus gigs, miscellaneous grants, and the proliferating sustenance of other groups. But with the demise of the communitarian ethos of the period, most of the groups disappeared anyhow, and what Harold said may appear to be, in a powerfully destabilizing society further diffused by the media, an open philosophical question. The issue may be arguable, but after more than forty years since first reading that passage, I still treasure the eloquence, and the large measure of truth that may, nevertheless, like any truth, eventually fail us—as the Group failed.

Yet, ten years later, at the other end of the country, which acts like a centrifuge on the ideal of collectivity, it remained the exemplary model of what it means to be a theater if—as with our regional or resident theaters today, which did not exist at the time—it has pretensions to anything like a public scale, and not entirely in the countercultural sense. (Those pretensions, true, may be in even more jeopardy now, when the idea of a public has disappeared into the video screen, along with the concept of the social, which was, according to recent cultural theory [Baudrillard], nothing but fantasy to begin with, adrift today in the "society of the spectacle" [Debord], a mere simulacrum of itself. If these ideas have taken hold, as they have, in the visual arts, there is something about the theater that resists them, about which I have written at length—while exploring the theater's major illusion, the tenacious fiction of community itself—in a recent book called *The Audience*.) With the Group as a model in a wasteland of theater, The Actor's Workshop became, over the course of fifteen years, an institutional presence in San Francisco, though it began as nothing more than a workshop for actors in a loft over a judo academy with (now mythic) rat shit under the stairs, as if it were, foundationally, the admonitory emblem against any pretension. As for a public, it was the remotest mote in the mind's eye when, in 1951, Jules Irving and I were planning The Workshop, which was eventually seen, too, as an exemplary, if idiosyncratic, model of what was then called regional theater, as *The Impossible Theater* was, surely, the most polemical statement in our history on behalf of *decentralization*. Its ambition was to reverse the old notion of Tributary Theater (tributary to and paying tribute), inherited from the twenties, thereby tipping the axis of power away from Broadway—on the premise of impossibility that was, I said, a kind of Manifest Destiny, as if an egregious delinquency of culture were to be rectified, finally, in the continental tilt. If the opening chapters were, as I intended, a devastating critique of the reigning hypocrisies in the American theater, the larger part of the book was, like *The Fervent Years,* a detailed analysis of the work done by our theater over its first ten years.

I remarked that, as a model, The Workshop was idiosyncratic. If that can be characterized by some of the young directors who were, with whatever dissidence, encouraged there (Ronnie Davis, Lee Breuer, André Gregory, the late Ken Dewey), it was mainly because of what evolved from the originary actor-oriented workshop activity: an avant-garde repertoire of now canonical dramatists (then relatively or entirely unknown) with a dialectical view of all productions, one reflecting on another (no such *King Lear* without that *Endgame*), and a commitment, like the Group, to the development of a company, even if it kept us not only in nonprofit residency, but below the poverty line, always on the edge of bankruptcy. Institutionally, in its operative procedures, The Workshop was like the Group, a benign despotism (Jules and I made the decisions, as the Group's directors did) with democratic propensities and with an almost familial attentiveness to the needs of the people involved, distributing thus what money we had. There were eventually—in several theaters playing simultaneously—about 150 people attached to The Workshop, at various levels of remuneration or, often voluntarily, none at all. Fortunately, until the Ford Foundation came along, we had no board—and even then it was a rubber-stamp board to receive the money that kept us bankrupt at digitally higher levels.

We are sometimes given the impression that, as opposed to such theaters today, there was something protestant or revolutionary about the early regional theaters, but in the most critical ways that was generally not true at all. If not quite revolutionary, The Workshop did become controversial, and as that image of it extended beyond San Francisco, it attracted in the sixties gifted younger people with a talent for dissent. As we became more politically engaged and aesthetically unpredictable—now Brechtian, now Beckettian, then Genetic, existential, absurd, decisively un-American in the immanence of the Cold War—we were even charged with being obscene, and this was before the emergence of nudity and the Free Speech Movement at Berkeley across the Bay, with which, when it came ("Fuck You!"), there were affiliations. (There was also, as Jules and I discovered to our dismay, at a time when you could be busted for possession of marijuana, a thriving drug scene at our shop in the Mission District, mainlining LSD.) The production of *Waiting for Godot* that was memorialized at San Quentin was taken—with the civil rights movement developing, at first, around the idea of passive resistance—as the aesthetic form of a possible politics. And when we later did *Endgame,* it was ritually attended, over and over, by younger people in the Movement, even as others wondered why The Workshop betrayed a leftist politics (we had done Brecht, Miller, O'Casey in a sequence) with such bleak and disconsolate, essentially hopeless plays—what they would surely speak of as (the word was not current) "disempowering" today, though I have made the claim that *Waiting for Godot* was probably, all told, the most affective political drama of the fifties.

In various ways, then, The Workshop was more embattled than the Alley Theater in Houston or the Arena in Washington, D.C., or the Seattle Repertory Theater, which developed at the same time. Survival required courage, and they were tenacious in their own way. The directors no doubt knew and even referred to the Group, but without the same fervent commitment to the Group Idea, not to mention the ideological disposition emerging at The Workshop from the plays we chose to do—all of which made the Ford Foundation uncomfortable when, somewhat reluctantly, it *had* to include us in the first grants that, as they

said, "pump primed" these theaters—separated by thousand of miles—
as the inaugural sites of what are now several hundred resident theaters.

But I do not want to rehearse again what I have written about in *The
Impossible Theater,* though given all the controversy it occasioned (furi-
ous in New York; in San Francisco, one reviewer compared it to *Mein
Kampf*), it is no wonder that a certain rage persists against it to this day.
There is material in the book about The Workshop's affinities with the
Group, but I want to end by referring to something else I wrote that also
conveys the legacy of the Group Idea. It was written when, after eight
years of ceaseless work, I had persuaded Jules to let me accept a personal
grant from the first arts program of the Ford Foundation—people
do not remember when there were no such things, no Ford, no NEA, no
nothing—and let me go to Europe. I went because I was desperate. Outside of the accomplishment of the Group—whose work, after all, I had
never seen (I had grown up not in the Bronx, like the boy in *Awake and
Sing,* but in Brownsville in Brooklyn, and never went to the theater)—
there seemed to be nothing on the landscape, retrospectively or at the
moment, with which I felt a conceptual or aesthetic connection. While I
made a good-faith effort to see everything I could in New York, and
elsewhere, and the road shows coming to the Geary and Curran in San
Francisco, meanwhile reading everything I could get my hands on (not
much at the time), there seemed nothing of any consequence to be
learned in this country.

I had recently directed the first production of Brecht's *Mother Courage*
in the United States, and just before I left had staged simultaneously
Sean O'Casey's *Cock-a-Doodle Dandy* and, if not quite the earliest, one
of the earliest productions of Beckett's *Endgame.* With the help of
Michel Saint-Denis, Copeau's nephew—founder of the Compagnie des
Quinze, also invested in the idea of a group—I met most of the major
figures of the theater in France, Germany, and England, where Michel
had also started the Old Vic Theater School while in exile with de
Gaulle. I spent considerable time with Beckett and, through him, Roger
Blin in Paris, met Jean Vilar and Roger Planchon in the halcyon days of
théâtre populaire, and—because of the production of *Mother Courage*—
was invited to the Berliner Ensemble by Helene Weigel. I was in Berlin
when I wrote a letter to The Workshop company, a copy of which was
seen by Alan Schneider (I didn't know him then), which he sent on, urging that it be published, to Robert Corrigan, who was the founding editor of the (then) *Tulane Drama Review.* Corrigan wrote, asking permission (we hadn't met then either), and did publish the letter.

That was over thirty years ago (in the autumn 1960 issue). It is quite a long letter, with commentary on much of the work I had seen abroad, putting our own work in San Francisco in that long-distance perspective. To suggest what kind of affirmation was necessary then, let me read a couple of passages. The first follows on some favorable remarks about the work of Planchon and Joan Littlewood, and with somewhat elliptical reference to an unfortunate decision that Jules and I had made before I went. It was the sort of compromise we wished as we made it that we had not made, and that we soon enough regretted, as it brought on fairly loud reproaches within the company. I am sure you will notice, past the rationalized group dynamics, the evangelical tone:

> You have all suffered, I gather, one of the nastier consequences of our misalliances. Let be. Nothing ventured, nothing gained. . . . I don't want to wriggle out of my responsibility by reminding us that each theater has to discover its own course. Though Planchon may have started with two boards and a passion, and Littlewood with zealous amateurs and left-wing opinions, neither of them—and I am minimizing nothing—have had so formidable a job as ours. They were both working in countries with theatrical traditions better defined and cultures more consolidated, with less to offer in the way of diversion. . . . The great achievements of The Workshop are these: to have persisted through unwillingness to believe in it, outside and, more harmfully, inside; to have wrenched diversity by the scruff of the neck and made it into a reasonable facsimile of unity; to have made it possible to be guilty about compromise and, as a result, to compromise less.
>
> There is debilitating guilt and efficient guilt; the first can cripple your power to act at all, and there have been times when we have had to fight it down; the second, which presses past all your rationalizations makes it necessary to change your ways. [Amongst the ways we had to change was that from San Francisco to New York, to which periodically, despite all ingenuities of persuasion, we would lose one or another actor.] The saddest part of my experience with The Workshop has been to see some of our better people still judging their own merit by their distance from Broadway, or worse, from the Geary and Curran—impairing their powers accordingly, never quite believing that *their* gifts and *their* intelligence can make what The Workshop will become, a great theater.
>
> This is not presumptuous, it is Manifest Destiny, despite part-time

actors, defecting actors, Equity minimums, envy, backbiting, or the natural skepticism that will greet all I have just said. There are no perfect theaters: there are gripes about casting in Theater Workshop, Littlewood having shifted leads from one play to another when the second came to the West End; there are uncooperative people everywhere—in Avignon, Vilar himself had to take over the part of Oberon because another actor refused to play it, and Vilar was awful; . . . and the Berliner Ensemble is shaken by political discord and in danger, now that Brecht is dead, of becoming academic. This is not to say that theaters shouldn't try to be perfect. If I must choose, and I come to this more and more, I'll side with Artaud and the saint who upheld orthodoxy against the world. Coming down to earth, I have seen nothing in those theaters to which we might be compared that we cannot accomplish. We have the institution, the means, the city, the cultural drift, the historical occasion, and sufficient ability to begin with, so long as it has the foresight to make itself available. We need the undeflected courage and tenacity of purpose that we have not always had together, or having, have let slip in the press of affairs.

Someone will say this is the old idealism again. But let me remind you that idealism (if that be the word) is hard—rocks impregnable are not so stout—and that we've gone through a whole series of developments that few of us believed possible eight years ago.

I read from this letter because, among the many responses, two in particular thrilled me at the time. I hadn't met them either, but one was from Bobby Lewis and the other from Harold Clurman—and both indicated that they had heard nothing like it since the disappearance of the Group. All of what I had written may have been the merest illusion, presumption built upon impossibility. But that endorsement, when I was still rather young, not sure of my own future, made the impossible seem only a matter of time.

The Workshop failed too, I should add, but not in San Francisco. It failed when I was invited to replace Elia Kazan and Robert Whitehead at the Repertory Theater of Lincoln Center in New York, at first refusing, and then—seemingly against my principles, and my polemic about decentralization—decided, with Jules Irving, to move a large part of the company across the country. Speaking of presumptions, pretensions, or hubris (I assure you, it wasn't naïveté—I knew, as they said, that the knives were out), when we came to the Beaumont Theater, I said, and said it publicly, that we were still three thousand miles off Broadway. Of course, we weren't, and you may remember the rest. Stories and ironies come round, and I have written of them before. But as you can see, even that woeful experience—impossible, to be sure—was not altogether separate from the legacy of the Group.

(1995)

16. Noise, Musication, Beethoven, and Solid Sound

New Music and Theater

At a time when I could hardly read a note of music, I had the double good fortune to be working in the theater with various composers who were, then, among the more innovative in the country. I can still hardly read a note of music, but that is partly their fault because at the time they did not care very much about musical notation—at least not in any conventional sense, though some of what they innovated has since become conventional and, if some of that was scored, some not, among the issues at stake were, who could read it? or want to repeat it? and why keep track of it anyhow? since noise was everywhere and music was free, there for anyone who would trouble to listen.

Among sounds, music as a particular aesthetic production is quite another thing, based on a structural distinction between noise and signal, or specifically designated signals that, among all the noises we don't want to hear, take on the aspect of an acoustical code. When we have the impression that it is music we are hearing and not noise, we are filtering out an ideological bias, since there is no such thing as music uninscribed with noise. In the history of noise, what we think of as music is actually a relatively recent invention, which very quickly became the audible register of the manufacture of society and, in its reversed evolution as background noise—the cloaca of repetition—an immaterial pleasure fetishized as a commodity. That is why it was possible for François Mitterrand's advisor Jacques Attali to say in his book *Noise: The Political Economy of Music*, "wherever there is music, there is money." Unfortunately, the money is not always the musician's, and that was certainly the case with the musicians I worked with, some of whom were engaged with more or less reluctance in that desperate enterprise of destroying music as a commodity, while trying to re-create it through a transposition of the senses or as a spatial proposition or, if not in the circuitry of the primitive synthesizers, in the unprivileged sounds of everyday life.

Yet if music could be found, it seemed now and then that it was meant to be lost or, if produced synthetically and raveled in tape, eventually thrown away. Or at some ontological level of the redundancy of the noise, music was to begin with what could neither be lost nor found, since it was, as Nietzsche thought, something like the beginning itself, the whispered metabolism and pulse beat of the world, the replica of "original Oneness, its pain and contradiction," but like Dionysus himself, god of the theater, not identifiable because essentially imageless, the vertiginous empty shadow of the world as appearance. This is the place where, like the prayers in *Measure for Measure,* music and theater cross. In the period of symbolist drama, they used to speak of theater and poetry, and indeed all the arts, as attaining the condition of music. Whatever the battles within music itself, among musicians, those in the other arts still tend to evoke music when, in an access of unspeakability, they are purifying themselves. The drama may tend toward the lyric and the lyric toward the drama, as T. S. Eliot once said, but when an art is detoxifying and transcending itself—and doesn't want anybody to talk about it—it thinks of itself as "musicated," to use Diderot's word appropriated by recent theorists like Julia Kristeva for the language that escapes itself in a pure semiotic, beyond language, below meaning.

Music remained the valorized model of the inarticulable even when it became dissonant or consumed in mass production so that, as Adorno observed, "certain anthropological shiftings in standardized society [now] extend deeply into the structure of musical hearing." Whatever it is we hear, we can no longer pretend that this once intangible or ineffable art "was even in its pure and uncompromising form excluded from an all-dominating materialization." Which is to say that while the intangible or ineffable is part of its mythos, music too is not only stained by ideology, but stunned, damaged, and silenced by the concussions of history. And so it is in this exquisite threnody from a sometimes cacophonous, now talismanic play that, when it came on the theatrical scene, seemed very strange indeed, as if it had its ear to the most delicately dreadful noise in the anthropological shiftings or, at the declivity of exhaustion, the deep structure of our musical hearing:

> You're right, we're inexhaustible.
> It's so we won't think.
> We have that excuse.
> It's so we won't hear.
> We have our reasons.
> All the dead voices.
> They make a noise like wings.
> Like leaves.
> Like sand.
> Like leaves.
> *Silence.*
> They all speak at once.
> Each one to itself.
> *Silence.*
> Rather they whisper.
> They rustle.
> *Silence.*
> What do they say?
> They talk about their lives.
> To have lived is not enough for them.
> They have to talk about it.
> To be dead is not enough for them.
> It is not sufficient.
> *Silence.*
> They make a noise like feathers.
> Like leaves.
> Like ashes.
> Like leaves.
> *Long silence.*
> Say something!
> I'm trying.
> *Long silence.*
> Say anything at all!

But what is there to say? (The play is, of course, *Waiting for Godot.*) And
if what is really being listened to in this piece of chamber music is, as I
think, not merely the heartbeat of the audience, but maybe, restless,
their asses on their seats—they whisper, they rustle, unspeakably bored,

as they usually are when anything is new, in music, in theater—what is there to say? To be dead is not enough for them, it is not sufficient. Nor is being the center of performance, as they are in a sense in this sequence, and as the futurists thought they should be, by seduction or provocation, when they proclaimed the Art of Noise.

"Today," wrote Luigi Russolo in his seminal manifesto, "musical art, complicating itself still more, searches for the amalgamation of sounds more dissonant, strange, and harsh to the ear." Asking as they did for more "ample acoustic emotions," the futurists were thrilled by the advent of the machine, from the clamor of heavy metal to the whiz of a dentist's drill, which—along with the "natural" sounds of an urban landscape: the trot of a horse on the pavement, the grumble of air in a pipe, the diminished fifths of laughter and augmentation of crowds—they thought would help them to conquer the infinite variety of "noise-sounds" and outdo anything imagined in Beethoven's *Eroica* or the *Pastorale.* At the same time, their synthetic events, processions, abstract scenography, and Theater of Surprise anticipated just about all the modes of new performance, as well as dramatic experiments ranging from the extravagances of the Theater of the Absurd to the abbreviated image of Beckett's *Breath:* lights up faintly on a pile of rubbish, recorded breath (inspiration), faint cry, recorded breath (respiration), faint cry, lights down.

"Our multiplied sensibility," Russolo predicted, "after being conquered by Futurist eyes, will finally have Futurist ears." Audacity, he adds, is the criterion, positing its own rights and responsibilities. But now that we have manifold and subtle cybernetic capacities for the generation of sound of which the futurists, with their clumsy *intonarumori,* never dreamed, the question remains, what is there to say? And if we did know it and wanted to say it, out of audacity or responsibility, how in all the cacophony of our standardized society is it ever to get through the noise unless said over and over, endlessly repeated, perhaps, like the attenuated autism in the operas of Robert Wilson, thinned out by repetition in the music of Philip Glass—which, as a matter of principle perhaps, doesn't have much to say.

As the sounds keep circling, however, like the Sufi whirler, arousing—along with the dreamlike spectacle of inexhaustible signs—strange and exotic acoustic emotions, there is the suggestion that the anxiety about saying something (a legacy of the Western Logos) will be relieved or dispelled by other scales, other keys, the age-old circuitous wisdom of other cultures. That was something, by the way, which was looked upon with a certain jaundice by the most nihilistic of avant-garde movements, as it searched with facility and cunning and the self-deflating music of its theatricalizing absurdity, "ohoho, bang bang," for "the central essence" of the outside possibility of a future that had anything to do with art. "DADA remains within the framework of European weaknesses," wrote Tristan Tzara in *Monsieur Antipyrine's Manifesto,* "it's still shit, but from now on we want to shit in different colours so as to adorn the zoo of art with all the flags of all the consulates." So in the Americanization of our multinational world, it is, no doubt, a commendable intention to look for promise in other cultures, but as we think of the inevitably and unchangeably marginalized relations of new music and theater in the expanding economy of a marketplace of signs, we do so within the framework of American weaknesses. And I am not sure we can ever adequately respond to the poignant question that Adorno posed, after he came to this country, in his *Philosophy of Music:* "How is a total world to be structured in which mere questions of counterpoint give rise to unresolvable conflicts?"

Having circled to this impasse, let me return to where I started. At the time when I began thinking seriously of music in the theater, mere questions of counterpoint were, to me at least, very much a mystery, and all the more so because the composers I was working with gave the impression that they couldn't care less. Yet that could be seen, if not as evasion, then as a sort of defensive strategy, and the question that Adorno asked remained a kind of unstated counterpoint, or subtext, to the enterprise of destabilizing our conceptions of music, which corresponded in this period to the plays we were doing and how we thought about them, from the decentered universe of Beckett to the decentered universe of *King Lear* where the question was anticipated, cutting to the brain, as the reality of the (modernist) storm undid the music of the spheres. I have described elsewhere how we approached the condition of music in *Lear,* and I will say something more, in a more conceptual way, about the issue of evanescence or the vanishing point of perception where, as the music disappears, there is something of a reversal, and it attains the condition of theater.

At the time I am speaking of, however, moving into the sixties, everything seemed to be in the condition of theater: politics, education, fashion, therapy, life itself as performance in a superfetation of image reproducing itself as image with such venereal intensity, and by satellite transmission, that it has since come to be known as the Society of the Spectacle, wired however for increasing noise, Walkmen on the ears, a boom box in every bush. For Jean Baudrillard, this spectacle has led not only to a wiping out of the real in the production of the hyperreal, but to the wiping out of theater as well, to the end at least of "the theater of representation," leaving "the space of signs, their conflict, their silence, only the black box of the code, the molecular emitter of signals," the new music by which "we have been irradiated, crossed by answers/ questions like signifying radiations, tested continuously by our own program inscribed in the cells." But if we were not yet then in what Baudrillard has called the Age of Simulacra, caught up digitally in the metaphysic of the code, indeterminacy was already with us, and not only in the music of John Cage.

Before Cage performed in our theater with a radio piece disturbing to established ears (as I recall, there were fourteen radios on different stations), we were already interested in Bertolt Brecht, who detested the way music was being used in the theater when he started and who wrote in the 1920s of the need for a music and a theater responsive to a disintegrating world, a world of pure phenomena, with the atom breaking up and forming itself anew. By the 1960s, of course, the dissonances of the high tinny ironic orchestrations of the theater music he encouraged, with Hanns Eisler and Kurt Weill, hardly seemed so unnerving, and the mordancy of Mack the Knife—which had the distinction of being played over and over in the Nazi museum of decadent art—had been charmed onto the hit parade by Bobby Darrin and Louis Armstrong. But in a stereophonic world, music moves on several tracks. And in the animus of the eye that almost deafened the ear, music itself became, in the higher decibel count, what Prospero said of theater as he seemed to abandon its powers: an insubstantial pageant fading, leaving not an analogue or metaphor behind. This was not only true of rock concerts, those mass extravaganzas or spectacles of sound, but of other music as well, for there were those who had begun to realize that "even a conventional piece played by a conventional symphony orchestra" is, in the activity of perception, essentially a piece of theater: "the horn player, for example," as Cage once observed, "from time to time empties the spit out of his horn. And this frequently engages my attention more than melodies, harmonies, etc."

Cage's is not a specifically historical attention, but for a Marxist like Brecht the spit is part of the materiality of music, what in fact makes it historical and requires a double attention, like the words that pass from mouth to mouth, stained and flavored by the salivary glands, in the dialogical continuity or polyglossia of history as conceived by Bakhtin. The stratified particulars and peripheral detail that may be, in the making of music, seen as theater, extend beyond the behavior of the performers to certain material conditions that determine the music and, on any given occasion, might as well have been written down or marked in the score. If, for example, the Henry Cowell piece that I heard recently at the New Music Festival in Philadelphia seemed a little quick in tempo, that was not only because it was the premiere of a neglected work, new to conductor and musicians, but also because it had to be concluded before five o'clock since the Historical Museum on the harbor, where it was being performed, is unionized. At such a festival, with an emphasis on experiment, you would have liked to hear it over, give it a double attention, alienate or estrange it (as admonished by Brecht), to find out among other things whether it was worth hearing over. Well, where music is, there is money. More on materiality in a moment. Actually, at the time Cage said the spit in the horn engaged his attention more than melodies or harmonies, we were in a period when an actor's warm-up exercises, psychophysical medleys of sound and movement, were more like music than enactment, and the sonorous sweat of those warm-up exercises was more likely to engage my attention than character, plot, etc. In that ideographic period, moreover, some of us were making theater as Pound wrote of the image, in the shape of the musical phrase, if not quite as Nietzsche dreamed it, in the spirit of music itself.

In any case, the one substantial, unequivocal piece I have from that period is a musical object, an elegant upright Hazelton Brothers piano that had belonged to Morton Subotnick, who—after studying with Darius Milhaud and Leon Kirchner—founded the Tape Music Center in San Francisco and was musical director of my theater there, and then later in New York. Subotnick and I collaborated for many years, and when I afterward went to Los Angeles as one of the founders of Cal Arts, he joined me there to work out a conception of that institution (though it was coming to the end of the sixties) as a complete sound environment or Total Theater, with gamelans in the open air, happenings in the foothills, and a consciousness of performance, scored on the Richter scale, in every pulse beat or tremor of the San Andreas Fault. Dick Higgins and Allan Kaprow were also there, conceiving Fluxus compositions by trans-Atlantic telephone, very conscious of the rumblings in the continental tilt. There was actually a severe earthquake while we were there (somewhat stronger than the recent ones), and the rolling murmur of the tectonic plates took on—as if from Wagnerian depths or the prodigal undulations of Artaud's vision of the Balinese theater, with flights of elytra and sudden cries—the resplendent aspect of a universal mise-en-scène.

It was back in San Francisco, however, that Subotnick gave me the piano, after composing a woodwind quintet for the Dorian ensemble. *Gave me* is a euphemism. He didn't give it to me, I salvaged it, took it away from him. For as the quintet was designed, in the spirit of the time, to destroy all woodwind music, Subotnick—a superb clarinetist—packed away his instrument and was threatening to destroy the piano, which piece of musical vandalism I aborted, though it was not long after that Nam June Paik (who also joined us at Cal Arts) performed a similar piece in what was becoming an established tradition. This was the period in San Francisco when Pauline Oliveiros, who composed a work (as I remember) for lawn sprinkler, accordion, and garden hose, was playing the accordion in our productions, which also had music scored for air-conditioner vents, soffits, and auto parts. Some time before the arrival of silicon chips, Donald Buchla showed up with a sort of Tinkertoy wizardry in electronics that, in experiments with Subotnick and Ramon Sender, came up with the synthesizer that competed with Moog. As the sounds came out of the circuits, they were amplified on the stage, eventually quadraphonic, blowing the minds of the actors, who thought they could not compete. In fact, unless electronic music remains relatively tame, familiar, Star Trek spacey, platitudinous—as its use in the theater usually is—this conflict remains a problem, especially for any play in which there is also a substantial text.

Subotnick, who subsequently composed the first electronic score directly for a recording, *Silver Apples of the Moon,* began to experiment in our productions with the materiality of space, increasing a visual sense of the magnitude of the stage by laminations of sound, or articulating space with incisions of sound or with particles that seemed arrested, suspended, now here, now there, so that the actors could actually reach for the sounds as if they were airborne objects. While this correlated then with my own desire for an all-dominating materialization of scenic scope (what some in our company thought my own delusions of grandeur, and what I did call grandly "risking the baroque"), there were also minimalist tendencies in the air.

Terry Riley was in the vicinity at the time, obsessional with middle C, and La Monte Young was there as well, though I am not sure whether it was before or after that he notated a similar piece of monomusic with a straight line drawn on a sheet of paper, which might have been a pilot project for the one that Walter de la Maria drew some years later through the desert, where he also set up a composition for lightning rods. I do not recall if La Monte Young's line was ever performed, or if it had already been achieved by being there, but I do recall that the director of the noontime concerts of contemporary music at UC-Berkeley refused to let him do either *Composition 1960 #2*, which consists of building a fire in front of the audience, or *Composition 1960 #5*, in which a butterfly (or a number of butterflies) would be released into the auditorium. Unlike Peter Brook's more didactic use of a butterfly in a later theater piece, *US*, there is no fixed duration for this event, simply provision for the butterfly to fly outside, the composition ending when it does. This was, it will no doubt be remembered, a period in which music was being transposed not merely from this key to that but with more or less synesthesia from eye to ear, and in which somebody could write just about anything on a piece of paper and say, "Listen." The impulse that led John Cage to think of musical composition as a form of attention eventually shifted attention away from sound, or through the observation of silence to music as theater. And this is a tradition that did not go away with the sixties.

"Music had never anything to do with sound," wrote John Zorn some years later, in a manifesto for his Theater of Musical Optics, where in the simple presentation of discrete objects on a grid—for an audience of eight in an eight-foot square room painted black, the objects viewed through a magnifying device—he performed a serial composition of "solid sounds." In his *Experiments in Polyphony and Harmony*, where the music was still visual, having eliminated sound, Zorn was moving toward the elimination of time as well. Composers in the tradition of Cage liked the notion of somebody listening to something he or she is ordinarily supposed to look at, and speaking of synesthesia, some of them transferred the musical experience not only from ear to eye but to the even more primitive senses. Pauline Oliveiros had not yet composed her communitarian meditations for the soles of the feet, but La Monte Young said: "Once I tried lots of mustard on a raw turnip. I liked it better than any Beethoven I ever heard."

Despite my affinities for these musical tastes, I didn't. The Beethoven I liked I almost never heard in a concert hall, or even on record. I tried to get at that later by studying music with Leonard Stein, curator of the Schoenberg Collection now, who was also with us at Cal Arts. We read Beethoven scores together as a kind of pure graphism or ideogram, a spatial abstraction at the vanishing point of thought, which somehow corresponded to my own habits of mind, though I still couldn't read a note.

What did occur to me then is what Roland Barthes observed in an essay written about this time: "The truth is perhaps that Beethoven's music has in it something *inaudible* . . . something for which hearing is not the exact locality," and this brings us to another Beethoven than the demiurgic composer who requires a deified interpreter, which music inherited from the idea of Romantic genius. "It is not possible," Barthes adds, "that a musician be deaf by pure contingency or poignant destiny (they are the same thing). Beethoven's deafness designates the lack wherein resides all signification; it appeals to a music that is not abstract or inward, but that is endowed, if one may put it like this, with a tangible intelligibility, with the intelligible as tangible." That is what we would like to believe it is (for it isn't always) in the space of theater that is not only tangible but carnal, "a whole carnal stereophony," in fact, which is what Barthes says elsewhere of the shift of value to the signifier, the corporeal act of signification itself, "the pulsional incidents, the language lined with flesh," the breath, the spittle, the muzzle, the tongue, "the anonymous body of the actor" brought into the ear.

It is as if Barthes sees this happening to Beethoven in the composition of his music. Such a category of intelligibility is what is truly revolutionary and not, he suggests, thinkable in terms of the older aesthetics. Nor can the work that complies with it "be received on the basis of pure sensuality, which is always cultural" and not what he means by carnal. Nor is he talking about an intelligible order of mere rhetorical or thematic development, but rather that without which "neither the modern text nor contemporary music can be accepted." He is, to be sure, talking of texts and music that are likely to be, in some fashion, disjunct, fragmented, semiotically dispersed, which is also how he sees the music of Beethoven. What Barthes is getting at in displacing conventional hearing or performance of Beethoven's music is what he calls *writing* or, in the full corporeal pleasure of the text, *writing aloud.* I still prefer to call it *performance,* although quite another kind of performance than that which is simply dutiful to some prescribed reading of a text. In the theater we speak of revisionist performance, which is resisted and debated like revisionist history. The grounds for such revision were most powerfully laid out in the theater in the theory and practice of Bertolt Brecht, whose opera (with Kurt Weill) *The Rise and Fall of the City of Mahagonny* pays, as he says, "conscious tribute to the senselessness of operatic form," as he calls for "a radical separation of the elements" which, in his conception of *gestic* music, would have to be put together another way. What that entails in performance is the making of history, which is something other than musication, what much new music now rejects.

Even in the new Romanticism, there are elements of quotation, recycling, pastiche, kitsch, parody, and ironic distance—techniques of
historicization—that suggest there is no way of avoiding the idea of
music as a signifying process, material, coded, constrained by a world
that doesn't know any longer what to make of counterpoint. At the same
time, it hardly knows what to make, in the recycling process itself, of the
sheer proliferation of sound that, in the runaway system of reproduction, with maximum amplification, seems to remake the world in the
image of futurist noise. Actually, this problem was defined by Tristan
Tzara when, along with the "great destructive, negative work of dada,"
futurism was still on the scene: "The representation of noise sometimes
really, objectively becomes noise . . . ," of which the myriad musics of
the world, popular music and classical music, secular music and sacred
music—on records, cassettes, and compact disks—are a by no means
negligible part. Here it is that music, which often denies that it is re-
ducible to meaning, almost loses its meaning entirely. In any case,
amidst the unresolvable conflicts, including noise pollution, music has
had to refuse itself the alibi of the ineffable, an immaterial innocence,
and this may be the most material way in which it has grown closer to
theater, the most time-serving of forms, which never had it.

As regards the issue of meaning, it was Adorno who remarked that "if
we listen to Beethoven and do not hear anything of the revolutionary
bourgeoisie—not the echo of its slogans, but rather the need to realize
them, the cry for that totality in which reason and freedom are to have
their warrant—we understand Beethoven no better than does one who
cannot follow the purely musical content of his pieces." If not a contradiction, Adorno complicates this view of Beethoven (as Fredric Jameson
points out in his foreword to Attali's *Noise*) by recognizing that "he is at
the same time the prototype of a music that has escaped from its social
tutelage and is aesthetically fully autonomous, a servant no longer."
Aside from the poststructuralist problematic of an autonomous music,
this raises at the ideological level another recurrent question. As with rethinking the significance of futurist noise, disaffiliating it from fascism,
it is the quite complicated question of the political meaning of formal
innovation itself, the degree to which disjuncture, for instance, is not
only a kind of content but a lure to "an unknown praxis," which is how
Barthes describes the process of deconstructing Beethoven and (re)writ-
ing him aloud.

Subotnick, too, unlike La Monte Young, preferred Beethoven to raw
turnips. Although he was experimenting with play, games, chance, with

audience choice among musical options, and with the disintegration of sound textures that were, at first, carefully wrought but then seemed like pure phenomena, one can hear still the legacy of Beethoven, the Romantic Beethoven, throbbing with gigantic strength in the pulse of *The Wild Bull*, generated on the Buchla synthesizer. While he was doing his most substantial work at the time with electronically generated sound, the two of us tried to think through the relation of music and theater in a context that was pretty much dominated—even with our repertoire of avant-garde plays—by the formal constraints of the theater, its architecture, its stage, its actors, directors, designers, intensive labor and division of labor, its Cartesian habits of mind, and the old Oedipal inheritance of representation; in short, the entire apparatus that, as Brecht once said, "resists all conversion to other purposes" and "theaters it all down." (I should say that in this context Subotnick did produce at least two of the greatest scores for theater that I have heard in nearly forty years of working in it.)

These habits of mind persist, and the inheritance is there to haunt even what are thought to be nontheatrical modes of performance, what we call performance art, once there is a move back from its matrix of conceptualism and minimalist abstraction to what performance artists now speak of as *better* performance. Which is to say, more skillful presentation, improved scenic effects, more and better acting, and the correlatives in the theater of melody and harmony, that is, in the return to narrative, character, and plot. And this is true as well of certain kinds of new performance that fuse or deploy music and theater; say, the disarming artlessness in the virtuosity of Laurie Anderson or, after *Automatic Writing* (of words becoming nonsemantic sounds) and the laid-back stream of consciousness of *Private Parts,* the latest work of Robert Ashley. We also see it now in Robert Wilson. As his operas are constructed around classical texts, the words are not merely litany, non sequiturs, or gibberish, but are given more importance and legibility. This corresponds to a turn from the mesmeric whirling of the aphasic Christopher Knowles, and the mute suspension of the deaf man's glance, to the garrulous Beckettian actor David Worrilow, and to other more professional performers who will not be wholly satisfied with merely crossing the stage—duration, say, a half-hour—in the long slow petrification of solid sound in the orchestration of a visual score. (This has certain affinities with the meditative suspension of the actor/dancer in the Japanese Noh drama, which blends music and theater in consummate form; but such motion is usually limited, and even then with more variation, to the actor's entrance on the *hashigakara*, where he seems in virtual silence, contoured by the visible music, to bring his *space* along with him. But try to get one of the Japanese National Treasures, which is what they call these actors, to give up the rest of the scenario and merely leave it at that.)

Over the past generation, we have been much absorbed—not only in the arts, but in all disciplines—with the truth of the body and body language, and sometimes with the implication that while we have our mental hang-ups, the body does not lie. But one of the truths of performance (not only in the American framework, with its weaknesses, but in whatever culture) is that the corporeal body—the belly, the voice, the muzzle, the gut, the windpipe that emits or the lips that retain the sound—brings its institutionalization with it, and that is what we are seeing in new performance, with or without music, as the body of the performer repossesses the stage from abstraction, whether in the shape of a musical score, notated, or any variant of a theater of objects (like, say, Richard Foreman's) from which the psychology of the actor was dispossessed, as it was in early futurism and in various movements since.

And then there is another problem that has to do with definitions of music, as well as what is new, to the degree that music has become autonomous since Beethoven and, as a result, even in the fusion, an unavoidable distinction from theater sticks in the mind. The problem I am thinking of, even with solid sound, is the *quality* of the sound, astonishment, novelty, and the historical intelligence it brings to a world of pure phenomena, the atoms breaking up and the spit emptied from the horn. Is it the same old spit, or shit? even with a cultural transfusion, and the flags flying from every consulate? Or is it really something new? I do not mean to minimize the versatility, the wit, the shifted gears in the level of entertainment, or the elements of cultural critique in, say again, the work of Laurie Anderson. Nevertheless, when one thinks of the powers of music and the ontological dimensions of theater, of the theater's emergence in time from the spirit of music—Nietzsche's replica of original Oneness, its pain and contradiction—which shadows time as (dis)appearance, and when one remembers too that history is the thing that hurts, it is hard to attribute much magnitude of mind even to so ambitious a project as *United States,* which reflects the framework of American weakness, the fundamental split that persists in music and in theater both: that is, the anti-intellectualism that pervades our desire to reconcile high art with popular culture or, forgetting art, to attribute much intelligence to our culture.

And this is true even as the work reflects upon the mechanisms of its meaning, communicating in the activity of entertainment the material grounds of its production. To identify the structural conditions that threaten it in no way dissipates the choices that sustain it: the collaboration with the apparatus of cultural production and the assent to a form of "community" that is, for all the sly charm of the engendered subject, by no means a "subversive," "transgressive," or "oppositional practice"— those terms that are virtually musicated through the wishful thinking of recent theory. At the same time there are those who, in the redundancy of such thought—which hardly makes a dent in the surrounding noise—want to believe that the movement of music in unheard-of directions will lead not only to a symbolically constructed collectivity but to "the post-theoretical form" of a sensualized cultural politics. I'm not quite sure what those unheard-of directions are, but it sounds like what we thought music would do in the most exhilarating days of rock before the counterculture subsided and, in the feedback cycle of reproduction, its psychopolitical agenda was sublimated into theory. That's not, however, the only reason why the most unheard-of new music will remain marginal in our theater, which was after all belated in our culture and remains, all told, a secondary form in a culture dominated by the cinematic apparatus, which commodifies the spectacle, including music, in the omnivorous power of the fantasy-making machine.

So, as we think of the relations of new music and theater, it does not seem fundamental that there is a derangement of the senses or confusion of genres, for there was always such confusion, generic and archaic, but more or less forgotten; nor that we can with state-of-the-art technology mix all the media; nor produce a new music that sounds like a raga in an extravagant spectacle with the appeal of old opera; nor that all the world's musics are rising from the savannahs or coming out of the bush (the aborigines actually performing in Central Park!); nor that we have proliferating means of amplification and distribution extending now to outer space, spreading the decibel count; nor—like the tribal performances of "family shamanism" (Eliade's term) of the sixties—that we are able to make an essentially shallow or misconceived piece of theater seem exciting and profound not by picking up the pulse beat of the world, but by the lamination of emptiness with acid rock or Heavy Metal or the banal insistence of raw percussion.

All of these things have happened or are still happening, and the prospects are what they always were, though harder to guarantee in mass culture: a matter of perceptual intelligence and conceptual power. Aside from making music and theater for simple pleasure (by no means to be demeaned), the deeper relation of music and theater still resides in understanding the peculiar and maybe even perverse relation of pleasure and pain, as well as the different magnitudes of art from which, with more virulence in the modern era, we have acquired a sense of nature as nothing but the fact of its repeated fragmentation. Call it dissonance if you will, or *decomposition.*

If one absorbs this fact into social analysis, one may conclude, as Adorno did, that "art today, insofar as it is at all deserving of substantiality, reflects without concessions everything that society prefers to forget, bringing it clearly thereby into conscious focus. From this relevant source, modern art designs irrelevance—offering nothing to society," except perhaps its own obscurity or "definitive negation." Whether or not one assents to this somber modernist view with its uncompromising critique of commodified music, one may hear in that critique the fear that if theater was born from the spirit of music, music itself will, in the Society of the Spectacle (our major commodity now, wholesale image, the mockery of Total Theater), disappear into the noise.

But one last word on disappearance, evanescence, to which I said I would return, having complicated in this the problem of notation—not, I hope, to excuse my failing on that score. There is a sense in which music is the art of memory precisely because it disappears, an art that it shares with theater, as if slippage were a saving grace. It is as if, in these two temporal forms, the transience were a sort of transference, temporality a form of amnesia, which in the operations of the unconscious, as Freud so acutely discerned, is the deepest form of memory. Of course notation itself is also a form of slippage, as Boulez has pointed out, between *"smooth [lisse] or amorphous time"* and *"pulsating, or striated* time," which may act upon each other by a kind of osmosis, "thus following a biological process"—not to mention the sort of time where involuntary memory is stored, the process in abeyance, the space of forgetting itself.

It is this forgetful space that causes Beckett to speak in his precocious essay on Proust of "the poisonous ingenuity of Time in the science of affliction," the thievish progress or Time cancer itself that not only erodes the human subject but can "only be apprehended as a retrospective hypothesis" that, in a moment out of time, a phrase of music might evoke, only to have it slip away again, as music does in the nonextensive seduction of its consummation. Thus Beckett speaks, musically, as he does in the impeccably scored compositions of his plays, of the way in which all of this works upon expectation, memory, habit, and perception. "The individual," he says, "is the seat of a constant process of decantation from the vessel containing the fluid of future time, sluggish, pale and monochrome, to the vessel containing the fluid of past time, agitated and multi-colored by the phenomena of its hours." I have spoken of various connections between new music and theater, but it is in this process of decantation that all music most profoundly connects with theater, where we have the additional problem, very distressing to Beckett:

> The observer infects the observed with his own mobility. Moreover, when it is a case of human intercourse, we are faced by the problem of an object whose mobility is not merely a function of the subject's, but independent and personal: two separate and immanent dynamisms related by no system of synchronization. So that whatever the object, our thirst for possession is, by definition, insatiable.

He spoke of the observer rather than the listener, but what Beckett says of perception in general also applies to music, which is inevitably distorted by that impure subject, the listener—listening, as Wallace Stevens said in a poem, to the nothing that is not there, and the nothing that is. I may have never learned to read a note of music, but after many years in the theater, thinking of its relation to music, I think that is the problem of counterpoint, which I think I understand: not merely the succession of notes in their textured opposition, *punctus contra punctum,* but the rip, the tear, in the musical fabric itself, the warp and woof of perception. In any case, there is nothing new in the theater that does not address it, since the issue is nothing less than the absence in/of the audience, the nothing that is not there, and the nothing that is.

(1988)

17. Flat-Out Vision

She closed her eyes, and Felix, who had been looking into them intently because of their mysterious and shocking blue, found himself seeing them still faintly clear and harmless behind the lids—the long unqualified range in the iris of wild beasts who have not tamed the focus down to meet the human eye.

Djuna Barnes, *Nightwood*

Tokay grapes are like photographs, Mr. Ekdal, they need sunshine. Isn't that so?

Henrik Ibsen, *The Wild Duck*

We don't see what we look at.
Alexander Rodchenko, "The Paths of Modern Photography"

My own first reflexes, when thinking of photography, are somehow not a remembrance of pictures but in the unqualified range of the iris a regressive association through the tactility of the form: fingers on a glossy surface, grained, a stringent odor at the eyes. That phototropic sensation might have come from some old forgotten experience of a darkroom, but I suspect it was, like the daguerreotype itself, nurtured in the theater, where I have spent much of my life as a director, sitting in the dark, I mean really in the dark, struck by the wild and furtive odor, when the sunshine hits the grapes, of the thing forbiddingly seen, in a landscape of specularity that is, all told, a field of dispersed speech. This has been extended through the camera obscura into that rhetoric of the image that is, according to Barthes, a message without a code, or like the mutely alluring syntax of the stains upon the ground (tar like blood? behind that man, a shadow?) in Rodchenko's picture with the somewhat duplicitous name: *Assembling for a Demonstration* (1928)—a flat-out vision in an estranging frame. If we don't *see* what we look at there, it is not only because of the unpurged persistence of "old points of view," as Rodchenko thought, what he called "'shooting from the belly button'— with the camera hanging on one's stomach";[1] rather, it is because the thing to be seen is in its copious imaging, like the theater's god itself, or its ghosts, essentially *imageless,* invisible, though the stomach is a decisive factor, as we shall momently see.

Meanwhile, the synesthesia in these thoughts corresponds to what Lacan describes—in answering the question, "What is the gaze?"—as the function of *"seeingness,"* from which the I emerges as eye in the radiant "flesh of the world, the original point of vision,"[2] as it does with the smell of defilement, the hunt, the feast, in the most ancient drama we know. If this is myth and not history, it is of some historical significance that Ibsen preserved it, late in the nineteenth century, in the subliminal wilderness of *The Wild Duck,* the recessive hunting ground of his devastating realism, where there is the compulsion "to find that imperceptible point at which, in the immediacy of the long past moment, the future so persuasively inserts itself that, looking back, we may rediscover it." That is actually what Benjamin says, in his "Short History of Photography," about the optical unconscious, "a different nature that speaks to the camera from the one which addresses the eye."[3] The double exposures of Ibsen's play, and its time-lapse dramaturgy, occur with photography in the foreground, already commodified, as the emblematic image of the illusions of history, whether in the retouched portrait of the family romance or the culinary theater of the bourgeois parlor, where the Fat Guest says, savoring his Tokay, "it's an excellent thing for the digestion to sit and look at pictures."[4]

This is a virtual setup, of course, for the later critique by Brecht of theater, of photography, which has subsequently grounded further critique, including the question raised by Benjamin about "the aesthetics of *photography as an art*" ("Short History," 22). But before we return to that, it may be chastening to remember, or particularly difficult for some of us to digest, that the realism of Ibsen—driven, like Marx, toward a *"ruthless criticism of everything existing"*[5]—is about nothing more devastating than the vanities of critique, as if the future of illusion were the illusions of demystification. I take that liability as the anxious datum of any pretense of deconstruction, as well as the limiting prospect of any "oppositional practice," inhabited by the structures it would oppose, as photography still seems to be inhabited by painting (an avatar of theater) despite the mechanical reproduction that, repetitively, punctures the auratic and brings an end to art; or the beginning of the end that has been our history, repeating that beginning, almost from the time that photography began. That is, I suppose, what we mean by modernism.

As for the looking at pictures, I won't review the history that brings us to the indigestion, which may be, in our fast-food version of the "gastronomy of the eye," the symptomatic condition of the postmodern scene, where the *flâneur* memorialized by Benjamin is caught up in the visual orgy deplored by Baudrillard. This tactile vertigo of the image can be exhausting and was so, apparently, long before Baudrillard, as in *The Waves* of Virginia Woolf, where in the receding voices of an undertow of consciousness, there is longing for release from a surfeit of pictures, image upon image producing a torpor, and the desire to find something *unvisual* beneath. But in the lugubrious perspective of Baudrillard, release from the vertigo can hardly be imagined, for the superfetation of image is a function of the obscene, which "is no longer the hidden, filthy mien of that which can be seen," but its paralyzed frenzy, "the abjection of the visible"[6] a sinkhole of fascination in which—with America controlling the fantasy machine, the viral contamination of image satellized through the world—the real is nullified and there is nothing to see.

Whether things are all that null in the void we'll put in abeyance, but at the still-breeding end of the real, the question before us, perhaps, is whether seeing—the most impatient activity of the senses, ever avid for more to see—has been irreparably damaged in our visual economy, the proliferous spectacle in which, to say the least, there is now without respite too much to see. If seeing was once the most dangerous of the senses, punished in myth for overweening desire, looking at the forbidden, the subject of taboo, it has now become a sort of endangered species. "We must revolutionize our visual reasoning," said Rodchenko, after he reduced painting to its primary colors, said it is all over, and turned to photography and photomontage. But in the atmosphere of recent discourse, the other side of seeing too much, or having too much to see, is that one is almost induced by the critique of the specular—the hegemony of surveillance, its secret archives—to conduct one's life with lowered

eyes. (Or in the now obsessive rhetorics of the body, to reverse the hierarchy of the senses, as if the essential truths were certified by touch or,
without the taint of logocentrism, metaphysics came in through the
pores.) For we think of sight as a categorical faculty, analytic, obstrusive,
discriminative, even exclusive, encroaching on otherness with an appropriative gaze, as if the scopophilic drive itself were engendered in the unconscious as an ideological fault and the dialectic of enlightenment
spawned in Plato as a mere bourgeois hoax.

Neurobiologists tell us, however, that the dominion of vision actually
began with a single light-detecting spot like the aperture of a camera in
the body of an animal three million years ago. That spot may be, with a
certain "protoplasmic irritation" (in a speculation by Freud, the reluctant source of life) the site of the incipience of *time* as well, drawn into
history by the sun. That was—in its huge imagining of the unremem-
bered, hinged on the granting of sight, with fire, to subhuman creatures
underground—the heliotropic substance of the Promethean myth, the
still-flaming divinity of which haunts our visual technologies, and which,
despite all deconstruction, is still sovereign on the mediascape. That's
why we can still argue whether or not the photograph is "an emanation
of the referent" that was indubitably there, as Barthes insists in *Camera
Lucida,* invoking the phenomenology of Sartre and the memory of his
mother (in the photograph he withholds: "just an image, but a just
image")[7] against his semiological past. This emanation comes not from a
mere historical construction but, he says, "a real body," whose radiations
"will touch me like the delayed rays of a star. A sort of umbilical cord
links the body of the photographed thing to my gaze: light, the impal-
pable, is here a carnal medium, a skin I share with anyone who was photographed" (81).

One may not want to go so far as to revive the "layers of ghostlike
images" or "leaflike skins" that, in the paranoid theory of Balzac reported by Nadar, would be "removed from the body and transferred to the
photograph" each time someone had his picture taken, every successive
exposure entailing "the unavoidable loss of subsequent ghostly layers,
that is, the very essence of life."[8] Yet in the concept of the photographic
trace there linger variants of this notion, a photochemical transfer of the
real resembling fingerprints or palm prints, the tracks of birds on beaches, or, with intimations of spirit-photography, "death masks, cast shadows, the Shroud of Turin,"[9] or the stains upon the stancher, the hand-
kerchief or Veronica that, in the camera obscura of Beckett's *Endgame,*
with its attrition of ghostly layers, inscribes the face of the blinded

Hamm. And if in this memorial plenum of imprints there is still anxiety about what is being left *out,* and *why,* what also remains at issue, unresolved, is whether photography's essence is to ratify what it represents, if not claiming it as recoverable—that imperceptible point at which, in the immediacy of the long past moment, the future seemed persuasive—attesting that it *was.* Whatever it was, it came to us in a dazzle of light, and it is this "solar phenomenon," eventually acceded to by Alphonse de Lamartine, who had called photography "a plagiarism of nature,"[10] that still shadows our finest photographs in something like a foundation myth. It may strike us now, however, as the shadow of a shadow, and there are some memorable photographs that seem to attest to that, if not, as in the lamentations of *Endgame,* to the waning of the light.

There is a picture by Brassaï, in the *Paris de nuit* series—there are others of spectacular light at the opera or splayed in a brilliant haze over the Place de la Concorde—of the railroad tracks at Saint-Lazare taken from the Pont de l'Europe. The tracks curve dimly from the foreground, with several trains at the *quais,* a monitoring trestle overhead, and a wash of light on the tracks from the banded glare in the concourse and the headlights of the trains. It is a picture that seems to require scanning, for there is nothing conspicuous to compel attention, except perhaps for the leaning ray from an indeterminate source. But then, back of this angled ray, recessed in the frame, there is a row of nubby bulbs leading to another glare, and high above, as if it were the enlarged memory of that spot on the brain, looking for a moment like the moon, a clock, its handles barely perceptible, but an immanence in the scene, presiding not over the movement of traffic, half forgotten here, but over the spectral fact, the negative itself, which is to say the dark obscure. There is, as a variation on this theme, a photograph by Minor White that seems, in its most startling element, the inverse of Brassaï's. Over a frozen field, with the spikes of a gathered crop, the granaries behind, there is way up in the frame, about the size of Brassaï's clock, not the image of an eclipse but an adventitious black sun. It was caused, according to White, by a temperature so cold that when the picture was taken the camera's shutter froze, and in the severe overexposure certain tones were reversed. "I accept the symbolism with joy," White wrote. And then with the vanity of imagination whose power yields nothing but its complicity to the operations of chance: "The sun is not fiery after all, but a dead planet. We on earth give it its light."[11] Every now and then we may see a photograph whose startling contingency is such that it seems justified in getting its science—in this case, astronomy—wrong. I am reminded of William

Butler Yeats who, when informed that the sun doesn't rise, simply said that it should.

Rising or setting, it is in terms of the solar phenomenon, its economy of exchange, that we may think of the history of photography as an analogue of our cultural history. Or—not only because the camera disrupts the envisaged tissue of our cultural codes—as the fate of representation that is the representation of our fate. I was very conscious of this recently in Japan, land of the rising sun, at the Tokyo Metropolitan Museum of Photography, which had just bought up an astonishing collection of the earliest work, much of which was hard to see in the vigilantly low kilowatts of the exhibition: daguerreotypes, including Chavaut's *Portrait d'un mort,* death in the photograph doubled over, that vision, light unto light protected from the light in the miniature of a coffin, its velvet reliquary box; salted paper prints, including the famous autoportrait of Hippolyte Bayard (1840), the photographer who, because unrecognized like Daguerre and Niepce for his pioneering effort, performed (for the extended period of the exposure) his own death; calotypes and calotype negatives, suggesting the double hauntedness of photography in the hauntedness of its object. It was, in the remembered suspension of light, a spectacle of disappearance.

Which is why Barthes, speaking of entering, with the photograph, into *"flat Death,"* associates photography with the theater, the economy of death whose substance is disappearance: now you see it now you don't, the photograph raising the question in its apparent permanence of whether you see it at all, "it all, it all" as the figure says in Beckett's *Footfalls,* for "it is a denatured theater where death cannot 'be contemplated,' reflected and interiorized" (*Camera Lucida,* 90). However lifelike, then, the photograph may be, however activated its surface, it is the energetics of its flatness that makes it a kind of primitive theater or *tableau vivant,* "a figuration of the motionless and made-up face beneath which we see the dead" (32). This is a theater, however, in which there remains the abyss between actors and audience, like that between the living and the dead, which was, in Benjamin's imagining of an epic theater, filled in with the orchestra pit, and its indelible traces of a sacred origin. The earlier Barthes was Brechtian too, remaining so through much of his career, and the ontology of photography in *Camera Lucida* is quite specifically conscious of the illusory status of a sacred origin, which required us to seek in the modern world a new image of "an asymbolic Death, outside of religion, outside of ritual" (92). Yet if he claims that putting aside the social and economic context permits us, provisionally, to think of photography *more* discretely, not less, that's because the click of a camera literalizes, for him, the division between this life and a "total, undialectical Death" (92)—the representation of which is, as the first and last vanity of the dispensation of light, the fate of representation. We may have ideological sentiments in the matter, but on the difference between Benjamin's vision of a tribunal rising from the abyss and Barthes's vision of a severed space, an edge, shutter closed, between the living and the dead—these two forms of theater, and what they imply for action and demand of actors—history itself has thrown a variable light, from culture to culture, and particularly recent history. As for the course of our cultural history seen in terms of the history of photography, there the darkness drops again, as in the nightmare vision of Yeats's poem, where images came out of the *Spiritus Mundi* with all the wonder of their appearance on a photographic plate. The question, of course, was how to keep them there, and, as Ibsen saw in the constructed wilderness behind the photographic studio, where the miracle was to occur, as in the darkroom itself, there was the reality of the image that will not take.

Thus, even before Fox Talbot's calotypes—the photogenic but unstable botanical specimens and light-gathered lace—there were Thomas Wedgwood's frustrating experiments, around 1800, with the imprinting of leaves, the wings of insects, and images of paintings on glass. The problem with these early "sun prints," or photograms, was how to preserve them before they turned black. Wedgwood had to keep them in the dark, virtually unseeable, snatching a peek in tremulous candlelight, because the unexposed silver salts were insoluble in water, and without discovering how to dissolve them, it was impossible to fix the fugitive image. This task, to *fix the image,* marks the laborious history of early photography, as of early modernism, sometimes to the point of fanaticism, the crux of the problem being, as with the history of culture, *how to ward off the action of light before it goes too far.* The distressing thing is that it seems to have gone too far even after the quick fix, as if the hypo released hysteria, a cataract of the eye.

"History is hysterical," writes Barthes, of the history inseparable from the photographic image, "it is constituted only if we consider it, only if we look at it—and in order to look at it, we must be excluded from it. As a living soul," he declares, working up thus a little hysteria of his own, "I am the very contrary of History, I am what belies it, destroys it for the sake of my own history (impossible for me to believe in 'witnesses' . . .)" (65). But as he examines the rip, the tear, the wound, the breach, the *punctum* in the personal array of photographs, in what might be regarded as the self-mesmerized domain of a capricious eye, ahistorical, arbitrary, purely affective, the hysteria seems contagious. (Barthes, we know, was perfectly capable of reading the photograph as a cultural production or a specimen of mythology.) And even when we return to what he calls the *studium,* the reading that passes through knowledge and culture, none of us is excluded, for there seems to be a *punctum* in reality as well, between private and public, the two kinds of history, and there are times when, fixed and fascinating as they are, monocular, quicker, chemically occulted, the hallucinatory profusion of photographs around us seems to be an immense defense mechanism of culture itself, a last-ditch defense, trying to drain the light before another sort of breach, when the ozone layer widens and, after an imprint of the "intense inane," it all turns black, a photogram of apocalypse—the one master narrative of the modern that we can hardly do without.

Which is why mourning, or the repression of mourning, has been, when we think it over—as a photographically oriented art history has started to do—the constitutional emotion behind the politics of the postmodern, with Benjamin's panoramatic vision of the baroque as its material setting: a place of ruins and corpses, funerary, bereaved, the seeds of history spilled upon the ground.[12] I am reminded of the stains of Rodchenko's picture, assembled for a demonstration, like the Soviet youths in formation at the top of the street, demonstrating nothing after all but the making of a picture. Without eschatology, as Benjamin said, only allegory in sight, but as in the photomontage of John Baldessari today, a "blasted allegory," where even the captions are collapsed into the combinatory sets, with meaning as a prospect, but always impeccably severed from any semblance of truth. These are not at all, however, the Brechtian captions whose antecedents were, in the ruined landscape of the baroque, the emblematic inscriptions around the tombs. Nor is the mood of Baldessari's work, the wit and irony of its teasing opacity, anything like what suffuses Benjamin's study of the *Trauerspiel,* no less the emotion that rises from the surface of Rodchenko's photograph if, the revolution already failing him then, we happen to look at it now.

Could we really contain that within a caption? and what kind of caption would it be? The problem of the caption posed by Brecht was brought up by Benjamin in the "Short History," that of attaching an instructive reading to a photograph of the Krupp works, since without a construction put upon it, the indifferent camera "yields almost nothing about these institutions" (24), where, with reality slipping into the merely functional, reification takes over. It is at this point, Benjamin writes, that "the caption must step in, thereby creating a photography which literarizes the relationships of life," directing attention to the scene of action like, presumably, the photographs of Atget (25). That the photographs of Atget seem to lead, as Benjamin implies, to the scene of a crime does not seem to me invariably true, but even when they do (impossible for me to believe in witnesses), what crime are we supposed to see? "Is it not the task of the photographer—descendant of the augurs and haruspices—to uncover guilt and name the guilty in his pictures?" (25). This is the mystical side of Benjamin mixed with his social conscience. We can also see in his feeling for prophecy and divination that, while he rejected the mystical-scientistic nexus in photography, he was always fascinated by the prospect of the aura, its rematerialization, even when as in Atget the object seemed to be liberated from it.

As a practitioner of the art of light, Atget is surely in the tradition of the augurs and haruspices, like Fox Talbot himself speaking of photography as the pencil of nature. But if he was not quite in the tradition of the spirit-photography described by Huysmans in *Against the Grain*, or that of Buguet, who was called upon after the Franco-Prussian War to photograph the first ghosts, which he did—by overexposures superimposed upon images of the living dead who would thus return—he did photograph himself as mirrored in the entrance of a café, and among the ten thousand pictures in the archive there are numerous multiple exposures and superimpositions that suggest either playing with visual identities or experiments in spatial geometries or the resources of light itself or the self-reflexivity of the photograph rehearsing how it was made. However we read all this, and the enormous body of Atget's work—whether as mostly utilitarian, documentation for artists, or, with various ventures into the mysteries of form, the slow emergence of a master with the most scrupulous certitude of craft, or, as Rosalind Krauss does, the visual accumulation that is, to begin with, in the service of the archive itself, "*subjects,* . . . functions of the catalogue, to which Atget himself is *subject*"[13]—one certitude we do not have, because of his reticence, has to do with how he stood on any questions that bear upon politics, aesthetics, the relation between them, or photography as a discursive space.

It is hard to believe that a man so observant was totally unaffected by the innovative artists, Braque, Utrillo, that he also served. But so far as his own technique is any testimony, and the processing of his prints, they suggest that he was very much of the nineteenth century, and there is reason for Beaumont Newhall saying of Atget in his history that "it is often hard to believe that he did most of his work after 1900" (195). Even if one distrusts Newhall's contribution to the ideology of the aesthetic in photography, and the canonical in his history, there is more than sufficient evidence that Atget shared those nineteenth-century habits of mind that, as with other photographers, still moved between science and its other, whatever that was; and it could be more or less spiritistic. Thus, a photograph might have both the qualities of an effigy or fetish, while the registration of an object, the activity of the trace, might still convey its material status in an actual world. The trace itself might be understood, as in countless photographs of Atget, as a manifestation of meaning, though I would hesitate to say with any confidence that I knew what that meaning is. There is the possibility that, at the scene of the crime, he may have, in a precipitation of consciousness, uncovered guilt, as in the store window on the Avenue des Gobelins,[14] with its grinning mannequins (male) in stiff colors, all of them with a price, so caught up, however, in reflections of buildings, tree, and the window's fabric that the photograph was thought to be a mistake; or the pictures of brothel life commissioned by the artist André Dignimont, one outdoor scene so astutely composed that the sloping cobbles and angled walls lead to the self-possessed woman, oddly perched on the porch (she seems not exactly to be sitting or standing) with a shadow flowing from her black skirt into the rectangular blackness of the corridor (*Modern Times*, 107). The minimalist geometry of that black plane may be telling a story, as of something blocked or off limits, but it is still hard for me to imagine Atget *naming* the guilty in his pictures.

Or if he should approach something like that, not anymore, surely, than two pictures actually taken at the Krupp Cast-Steel Factory, by anonymous photographers, one in 1900, the other in 1911, and shown at an exhibition at MoMA in 1989.[15] It may be that being shown at MoMA is, any way you look at it, the wrong construction to put upon a photograph, even the most demystifying by Atget, about whom Benjamin conjectures that, as a former actor "repelled by his profession, [he] tore off his mask and then sought to strip reality of its camouflage" ("Short History," 20). There is nothing so melodramatic in either of the anonymous photographs, which seem part of the history of utilitarian reports on factories, machinery, industrial processes, and while they lack the "pristine intensity" of the imaged materiality in Atget's pictures—the quality attributed by Benjamin to the photographs in Breton's *Nadja*—

it seems to me that they more specifically uncover guilt, if you are looking for it, than the more impassive revelations you will find in Atget; and though maybe intended as nothing but documentation, without any captions.

The first picture is of a worker rolling the steel tire of a locomotive wheel. The man, wearing a cap, is stripped to the waist, with what looks like the waistband of his trousers flipped down, slouched below the belly's flesh. The leading edge of the tire and the man's back foot are cut off at the frame, like (if you will forgive the conjecture) the projected logic of advancing capitalism, though the muteness of effortless muscle might bring it down on either side of the unstable equation, *then,* of exploitation/productivity in an irreversibly industrial world. The second photograph is, in a retrospective look, potentially more ominous. There is another man in a cap, his somewhat grimy jacket buttoned, and a grimly mustached face, at the lower end of the frame dominated by a turbine tube. He is holding a ruler vertically to measure the diameter of the tube, of which he is—disconsolate? embarrassed? indifferent? bored?—less than half the size. Possibly because the photographer told him to, he is turned half away from the camera, looking somewhere beyond the frame, perhaps at a supervisor also giving instructions. Already diminished by the massive tube, it is as if he were belittled additionally by the photographic occasion, a "technique of diminution" (Benjamin), and so far as I can read his expression, his sense of inconsequence is not at all disguised. But, then, of course, he does not speak.

Could this muteness be a preface to action, calling for a caption? And given the guesswork in my readings, any readings, what might a caption do? That would depend, of course, on where the photographs might be shown again, when, and for whom. That would have been true at least since the Brechtian distrust of the unaided camera and the unarmed eye, but we are especially vigilant now about the social formations in which photography occurs, having become aware of the emergence of an economy in which it functions everywhere as the instrumental means of a system of surveillance and documentation. And within this dispensation of thought, the measure of photography as practice, artwork perhaps, but always suspiciously art, would be the degree to which the work itself contained an analysis, along the lines of Martha Rosler or Hans Haacke, of the institutional frame: gallery, museum, systems of distribution, the curatorial elite, and the long investment, paying off in the rising prices for photography, of the idea of photography as art. We are quite a long way now from what Nadar could say about photography in

1856, putting aside what was required for a portrait, no less the portrait of *his* mother (or wife), which Barthes—comparing it to the Winter Garden photograph of his mother—called one of the loveliest ever made: psychological acuity, a combination of directness and empathy, communion with the subject, the sitter, all of which we might consider humanistic garbage now. "Photography is a marvellous discovery," said Nadar, "a science that has attracted the greatest intellects, an art that excites the most astute minds—and one that can be practiced by any imbecile. . . . Photographic theory can be taught in an hour, the basic technique in a day. But what cannot be taught is the feeling for light" (qtd. by Newhall, 66).

It was light that once gave meaning to photography, and I want to return to that; but if it is true, as current theory would have it, that photography has no meaning outside of the specific relations of production in its historical context, one thing is clear about our present context: any caption that I might imagine for the Krupp factory photograph would contribute no more, nor less, to the class struggle, the ostensible motive of a caption, than the critical discourse and photographic practice, some of it in museums, that is presumably aligned with it. Abigail Solomon-Godeau has written of "critical practices not specifically calibrated to resist recuperation as aesthetic commodities," that they "almost immediately succumb to this process."[16] One can hardly think of a practice of any consequence, Rosler's, Haacke's, Brecht's itself, that does not succumb anyhow, just as eliminating the hard-and-fast distinction between art and activism does not prevent, even for some activists, the "apparent collapse of any hard-and-fast distinction between art and advertising" ("Living with Contradictions," 73). In this collapse of art, advertising, activism, the enigma, I suppose, is Andy Warhol, who also collapses the distinction between art, photography, and performance.

Since I have reflected on photography as a form of theater, in the drift of theory determined by Brecht, what follows is not exactly an aside, though I am conscious of a certain wariness about theorizing from experience: having directed some of the earliest productions of Brecht's plays in the United States, including the American premiere of *Mother Courage*—attentive to the class struggle (San Francisco, at the time, was a rabid labor town, with a Communist newspaper besides), scrupulous about historicization, estrangement, the emblematic coding of events, the caption—I am still not at all convinced that the double articulation of a narrative has any more ideological potency than the autonomous image in the indirections of thought, depending on the intelligence that went into the image and who, in the activity of perception, is doing the thinking. (It is very likely to be, as with Brecht's own productions at the Berliner Ensemble in East Berlin, an audience of bourgeois intelligentsia, to puzzle with him over why all the captions in the world or other alienating devices could not keep Mother Courage from eliciting sympathy, misleading emotion, and undoing what he wanted us to understand.) The fact of the matter is that the most efficacious political production of that period in San Francisco—a matter of timing and attunement to the exigencies of the time, yet almost a matter of chance—was the rather bewildering action, then, or want of it, in Beckett's *Waiting for Godot,* which corresponded, in the plaintive image of its negative capability, the waiting, the passivity, the sit-downs, to the early stages of the civil rights movement, as well as to the waiting, the slave-master consciousness, at San Quentin Prison, where our performance of *Godot* became legendary, and a model for alternative forms of theater, in prisons, factories, Indian reservations, the ghettos, the streets, wherever. Beckett, by the way, told me shortly after our production that he had always thought of political solutions as going from one insane asylum to another; this did not prevent him from working, during the occupation by the Nazis, in the French resistance.

"[One] feels the need," says Hal Foster, "all the more urgently for a historically redemptive, socially resistant cultural practice."[17] One may feel the need but practice quite differently than anticipated by those who share it, and some who do not share it, the need, may turn out to be more redemptive, socially resistant—over a period of time, historically—than those who might articulate their resistance, maybe eloquently, movingly, but rarely so, as always in art, most of them predictable, outguessable, always already heard. At the same time, the argument for a self-conscious, intentional oppositional practice has again been put in question by chance, in the political uproar around the works of Andrés Serrano and Robert Mapplethorpe. Serrano, by his own testimony, was a somewhat reclusive artist whose earliest pieces reworked Christian iconography in stylized tableaux, the images growing more rather than less abstract as he approached various social and religious taboos, using a variety of body fluids: breast milk, menstrual blood, semen, and the piss that caused a scandal, when he immersed a crucifix in it. He remains fascinated with religious iconography, though transplanted now to a more specifically political terrain: his photographs of the Klan and the homeless. The style was never quite political before, and there is nothing inarguably oppositional in his practice now. The Klan pictures—and the rapport he had to establish with the Klansmen to get them—are equivocal; and who is not sympathetic to the homeless, whom he similarly ennobled, *as images,* after paying them to pose, though we are surely more conflicted when we encounter the Klansman in full regalia and the same style. Actually, Serrano's current style—which I saw at the Galerie Templon in Paris, something like being shown by Leo Castelli in New York—is not radically different from the indirection and ambiguity of his earlier work, the technique cool, conceptual, symbols outside the mainstream (like symbolism itself), charged with his own emotions as a former Catholic who does not mind, even today, being called a Christian.[18]

What made Serrano's *Piss Christ* oppositional, then, was the award from a government agency that occasioned the controversy; not anything designed as oppositional practice, but an adventitious attack by the fundamentalist Right, which he is trying to understand better now in the formal if not formalist portraits of the Klansmen. As for Mapplethorpe, here we have various ironies, given the ideological animus of the critique of modernism. I am hardly the only one to think his photographs were not in any way oppositional, whatever his sexual practices. They were adept, rather, in drawing upon the formal resources of modernist photography, but as if filling in the prescription with a more powerful medicine, S&M, B&D, without any criticism whatever in the photographic space of the artistic regimen or its institutional structures that he was more or less ripping off. In this regard, one may want to contrast the photographs of Mapplethorpe with certain pictures by the fashion photographers Richard Avedon or Irving Penn, both of whom extend the resources at their disposal or, critically, even severely, narrow them down, as Penn did quite literally in the portraits where celebrities (Noel Coward, the young Joe Louis) are wedged into a corner, as if the imperiousness of the modernist artist were being literalized in the visual text (Coward playing it to the hilt; in the case of Joe Louis, a standoff, since he was there, ready to go, a menace in the corner). All of this is to say, again, as Brecht did to Lukács, that formal innovation may be dissident content in the mind as content alone is unlikely to be, at least for very long. As for the controversy over Mapplethorpe's most repellent content, the hard stuff itself, need I comment on the hypocrisy that eventuates when, in the necessities of a legal defense, those who have bought all the platitudes about modernism and formalism assure us that content, as such, has no existence in a work of art except as form. How, indeed, are you going to caption that?

Which is not say that captioning cannot be honest and complex, with a suggestiveness in its own right, as it is in Rosler or Baldessari, although it is a toss-up as far as I am concerned as to which of the two is more effective politically. With both of them, of course, we are dealing for the most part with either deliberately banal or appropriated photography, as on the photomontaged billboards of Barbara Kruger, which for all her intelligence, and a commendable politics, are obviously not in the same ballpark with John Heartfield—impact muted in any event by the dispersions of our history and, however specifically calibrated her resistance, the counter-appropriation of the institutions that commission her. I moved into this discussion of the caption through Benjamin's designation of Atget, the actor who tore off his disguise, as a figure of oppositional practice, but it should be obvious that whatever politics we have in the photographic work of the postmodern, little of it has the quality of feeling, the tonality, the texture, that confronts us in Atget, who almost reverses the loss of aura by drawing the banality from a boot, a doorknob, a lamp shade, a leaf, making them iridescent, not unlike Pound's petals on a wet black bough; or when the reflections deepen and glisten, warmed in the browning of overexposures, the datum of that image, not the crowd, which is "the social basis for the decay of the aura,"[19] but "the apparition of these faces in the crowd," as Pound wrote: direct treatment of the object, even when mirrored, reduced to essentials; in short, that concentrate of an image, fixed, an intellectual and emotional complex in an instant of time.

If that should make the photographs of Atget in any way a model of revolutionary practice—as Allan Sekula suggests at the end of a finely researched essay on the juridical use of archives of images of the body[20]—it is not merely because of the detective work or spying in the telling detail, but because of the *precise ambiguity* of the detail, its *profane illumination*—like the materiality of light, to which we give light—"a materialistic, anthropological inspiration," which was precisely the quality discerned in Atget by the surrealists, about whom Benjamin, in his remarkable essay on surrealism (titled "The Last Snapshot of the European Intellectuals"), used that term with that definition.[21] The surrealists also responded, no doubt, to intimations of "convulsive beauty" in the capacious reflections surrounding the details, as in another store window on the Avenue des Gobelins (*Modern Times,*

137–38), with the curled (beckoning?) fingers of the mannequins (this time female, also with a price); or leading up to the details, the classical statues like dolls in the distance, in the lonely curvature of the pond at St. Cloud,[22] trees, clouds, topiary lyrically mirrored, a chrysalis of time, as if mourning the passing of the formal existence of that culture whose barbarities paid for it—which hardly seems to me, overcast as it may be, an incrimination of the exploitative indulgence of civic beauty by institutionalized state power, represented perhaps by the exquisite presence, in some of the many views, of the Petit Trianon.

Such beauty is always liable, of course, as it reflects itself in art—and while there are many boring prints of Atget, I insist that this is art—liable to what has become the much theorized crime or vice of representation: "stylistic transcendence." This is, we know, the incessant charge brought against modernist art and its desire in a world divested of the sacred for what might also be described as profane illumination, epiphanic in its materialism or "shot through with chips of Messianic time," as in Benjamin's "Theses on the Philosophy of History," the shock, the blast, the arrest, crystallized into a *monad*, "the sign of a Messianic cessation of happening, or, put differently, a revolutionary chance in the fight for the oppressed past" (*Illuminations*, 264–65). This chance would seem to come from that "secret heliotropism" of which "a historical materialist must be aware" (257), the past seized only as image, flashing up in an instant, more or less intoxicating in its accomplishment of form. Thus it is, it seems to me (without the Messianism perhaps, although what are we to make of the obsessional patience in the archive?) in the prints of Atget, with their early morning light, made through long exposure, on aristotype paper toned with gold chloride, as if to affirm the photograph's autonomy, whether the image was a historic monument, a ragpicker with his cart, the inside of a palace or a bourgeois home. Or like his predecessors who struggled with preserving the image, the encrypted trace of natural things, spectral twigs or fallen leaves, the seeds of history scattered on the ground, as on the elegiac landscape of the baroque.

As for those with a heavy investment today in mechanical reproduction as the instrumental means, indeed, the basic principle for undoing formalism and its vice of transcendence, with photography as the ground of an oppositional aesthetic, they have not always been able to absorb from Benjamin's study of the *Trauerspiel*, along with the ethos of montage, its tone of lamentations. Nor have they picked up from its modernist inclination to disjuncture and obscurity that it may be closer to the T. S. Eliot of *The Waste Land,* and its heap of broken images, than to the plays of Brecht, unless it be the early Brecht, creator of Baal, that imageless image of the Canaanite god. Born of the great sky above, Baal exists in his successive deteriorations, like the light first trapped on a sensitized plate. The intractable referent of the photograph, what it cannot get rid of, suffuses our sense of both, the referent and the photograph, as Barthes says, with an "amorous or funereal immobility, at the very heart of the moving world," which is like a description of Baal, who is also "glued together, limb by limb, like the condemned man and the corpse in certain tortures, or even like those fish . . . which navigate in convoy, as though united by an eternal coitus." Yet, in aspiring to be a sign, this fatality of the photograph gets in the way: "photographs are signs which don't *take,* which *turn,* as milk does." Baal is a sign that doesn't take, which turns, and in turning smells to high heaven, abode of his mother and mother's milk. We may be reminded of the wild and furtive odor in the beginning, in the theater's landscape of dispersed speech, and the conflation of theater and the diorama and painting and photography (and ideology as well) through the camera obscura, so that "whatever it grants to vision and whatever its manner, a photograph is always invisible, it is not it that we see" (*Camera Lucida,* 6). The scenes of *Baal* occur with the rapidity of photographic exposures, each of them with a caption that he escapes, while his swelling and stinking body—that pale lump of fat that makes a man think, like the fat in the fetishes of Joseph Beuys—seems in its mortifications like an imprinted residue of the radiant flesh of the world, original point of vision, flat-out vision, susceptible at every moment not to the logocentrism but to the maternal womb, vast and hugely marvelous, in the vicissitudes of light.

This dubious imprint was foreshadowed in the "ungainly luminous deteriorations" of the early photograph—a phrase I take from the "shuttered" night of Barnes's *Nightwood*[23]—and the issues focused in those deteriorations have become today, as with Brecht's turn to a more rationalizable drama, profoundly ideological. That the solar phenomenon remains confounding we can also see in the negative theology of poststructuralist thought, but most particularly in Derrida's essay on Levinas, which tries to make distinctions about violence and metaphysics within the orders of light, its commandment, conceding at the outset that "it is difficult to maintain a philosophical discourse against light." So, too, "the nudity of the face of the other—the epiphany of a certain non-light before which all violence is to be quieted and disarmed—will still have to be exposed to a certain enlightenment."[24] If this "certain" seems a little uncertain, or begrudging, that may be attributed, by those who have been critical of poststructuralist thought, to an incorrigible ahistoricism.

Yet, as we historicize the matter in a visual culture whose history moves before us in the blink of an eye, we find ourselves faulting vision, the mandate of light in the spot on the brain, the ethic in the optic, the specular drive, precisely when it finds itself baffled by overdrive: eyesight fading from too much sight, and with it the difficult-to-attain, costly powers of discrimination, that is, the capacity in seeing to distinguish this from that, which remains the basis of any moral measure we have, and without which a politics is only a question of power. I say this with full knowledge of the possibility of vision's excess, the voracity of the eye that is, in the critique of modernism, the ubiquitous issue I have described. I also realize that I have conflated in passing various meanings of the word *vision,* eliding the difference at times between what's in here and what's out there, although I have wanted to project in all this not only the ideological but the visionary basis of simple sight, its capacity for *distinction,* which may sometimes occur—as it does, I think, in the greatest art—*by eliding the difference,* and in the process bringing to simple sight the resources of the imaginary. As for the ability to sort things out in the microphysics of power, that remains without vision a mere vanity of thought, or—not that *this* not this *that,* click, click, like a parody of distinction—the metonymic longing of semiotic desire.

I alluded before to the new rhetorics of the body, and a reversal of the order of things in the hierarchy of the senses, all of which are in their way, as Marx called them, "direct theoreticians"—none of them getting their way, theoretically, without incursions of the other senses, which are intersected at every moment, as Marx also said, by the entire history of the world. It may be that the theory of the eye—the evil eye, the envenomed eye, the eye whose erection constitutes the gaze—has been caught up from time to time in the wrong part of that history. But there is also the eye of conscience, the eye that parses, cuts, gets to the heart of the matter, and the eye that keeps an eye, as Shakespeare knew, on the liabilities of the other senses. We may hear around corners without knowing who is there, and if touch has been sentimentally restored as the privileged sense of intimacy, it is also the tactile measure of an unnegotiable distance of which, in the microphysics of affections, the intimacy is the index of what we will never cross.

As we reach, then, an impasse in the quest of eyes—amidst the media into which all our senses have passed, and now seem prosthetically to surpass our senses—it is the photograph that still retains the pathos of this distance, as if its surface were a screen, the flat truth of the dimension between seeing and not-seeing, where the thing to be seen remains the still-compelling shadow of what we have seen before. In my view, or viewfinder, there are those who can see and those who can't. And while I am prepared to believe that what they see or choose to see may occur within a system of representation that tends to reproduce its power, there are also those who see so profoundly deep or so thick and fast—with such flat-out vision, in short—that it seems at times that the codes are merely catching up, while the signifying practices are in their self-conscious transgressions suffering in comparison a semiotic arrest. Not that this, not this that, another version, *this,* like the tireless facet-planes of Cézanne, studied by the artists of the Photo-Secession after the scandal of the Armory Show.

"We have to learn how to see," said Stieglitz, who stayed in the shadows, but masterminded the show. And then maybe with a sense that his *Flatiron Building,* photographed ten years before, was a little too misty for flat-out vision, repeated as if referring to himself, "We all have to learn to use our eyes. . . ."[25] I know Stieglitz's reputation, that he could be imperious, that he also masterminded the perhaps dubious terms for photography as an art, but I suspect he also understood, like the superlative modernist he was, that in urging us to see, there was no guarantee that—even in his *Equivalents,* of inner and outer, the (in)capacities of all the senses—we would ever see at all.

(1995)

18. The Absolved Riddle

Sovereign Pleasure and the Baroque Subject in the Tragicomedies of John Fletcher

The riddle of the Duchess in *Women Pleas'd* has to do with the Freudian question: What does woman want? That is the question whose subject is the answer to which, as Freud might have guessed without saying, there is no question, which is why the riddle has to be not answered but— as Fletcher has the Duchess say, not once (or intentionally) but prophetically twice—*absolved* (2.5.112–13),[1] as if it never should have been asked. Her daughter's lover Silvio labors and travels through untold cities, consulting "Diviners, Dreamers, Schoolemen, deep Magitians," all of whom—like the current discourse on the pleasures of the feminine text— "give severall meanings" (4.1.3–4), as we might expect from the oracular hermeneutics of an absolutist age. For it is an age that constructs an arcane stability against contingency in a "chaos of consultation," as Jonathan Goldberg observes of the ideological mystifications of King James.[2]

But here is the answer brought back by Silvio, the absolution of the riddle in this curious play:

> In good or ill
> They desire, to have their will;
> Yet when they have it, they abuse it,
> For they know not how to use it.
>
> (*Women Pleas'd* 5.1.138–41)

Yet the daughter Belvidere apparently does. No longer disguised as the Hag who guides him through his trials and writes the answer out for

Silvio, she confronts him with another question: Does he want in her the fidelity of age or the vanities of a young brightness? The sticking point is not, however, in this medieval chestnut of a lover's conundrum, but in the subject that appears to materialize in the certitude that escapes it, as it does in *The Loyal Subject*. We are very conscious in that play, as in the other tragicomedies, of being in "a declining age of doing spirits" (1.3.14), decommissioned and entropic, where passion seems a theatrical decoy and the rhetoric of desire "consumes," as Alinda says of the lascivious Duke, "all honour, credit, faith" (4.3.132). What subverts the loyal subject in the psychic economy of Fletcher's plays is the increased dependence of an aging honor and faith on credit, which is both credibility and solvency in a world whose mystifications have come to include the dissolution of use-value in the arcanities of money and the overriding riddle of the insolvency of words. Thus Silvio, young and honorable as he seems, is already so exhausted by desire through interpretative deferral, so demoralized by the shifting signifiers of the woman's appearance, the absolving duplicity of the beloved, that he defers to her "Soveraigne will" (*Women Pleas'd* 5.3.74). Nor is she alone in exercising sovereignty in the choice of a mate. The mother emulates the daughter's example in choosing the Duke of Siena, Belvidere's disappointed suitor, for herself. "I have got the mastry too," she says (5.3.100). But the trouble is that the sovereign will, even if exercised by a woman, is not exactly a woman's mastery.

The case of Belvidere makes explicit what seems to be true of all the women in the tragicomedies of Fletcher even if, like Celia in *The Humorous Lieutenant,* they seem to deviate from subservience to a masculine power. "Now, *Rhodope,* How do you finde my daughter?" asks the Duchess about Belvidere in *Women Pleas'd.* "Madam, I finde her now what you would have her, / What the State wishes her" (3.1.1–2). Which is what, with mutating illusions of dissidence, she more or less wishes for herself. The woman's pleasure seems to consist of getting the man she desires by first deploying, then disavowing the old wanton changingness of woman—"All consuming, nothing getting" (5.3.65)—for the assurance of a wife. "No more Spells now, nor further shapes to alter me, / I am thy *Belvidere* indeed" (5.3.77–78), she says to Silvio at the end of the play. The whole thing by then seems to be something of an elaborate joke, and Silvio—the "laughing sport at this mad marriage" (5.3.85)—is willing to be laughed at, for the moment, so long as he has her securely, with the same "husband's freedome" (5.3.101) granted to Siena by the Duchess. The women seem to be running the show, but the working out of marital fortunes occurs within the libidinal economy of the old phallic structure into which the laughter subsides. "Whilst they rule with vertue," says Lopez—described in the dramatis personae as a "sordid Usurer"—"Ile give 'em, skin and all." "Wee'l scratch it off else," says his wife, Isabella (5.3.105–6), playing along with the joke that is eventually on her, though the play does not acknowledge it.

Lopez's "false key" (3.4.197) to the riddle was first to distrust and then to force himself upon her. But through the craft of Isabella, he is cured of a barbarous jealousy and, so it seems, of the sordidness as well. That does not entail, however, divesting himself of his money, which is—at the same exorbitant interest, one assumes—also what the State wishes. "Money he sayes he wants," says Burris of the Duke, who complains about nothing but money (*Loyal Subject* 2.1.18) that he needs to pay his soldiers. "But wher's the money?" says the Duke, "how now?" (2.1.59). In a totalitarian state, devoted to maintaining the pleasures of power, there is never enough money, though the King's real and stamped face, as Donne writes in "The Canonization," his currency and value, are inscribed on his coins. Meanwhile, it appears that the only significant figure in *Women Pleas'd* excluded from the pleasures of sovereign will is the person without any sovereigns, the servant Penurio—garrulously ravenous beyond gluttony—who, having helped his mistress dupe his master, wants to conglutinate carnally with her while fantasizing himself as a lobster, a pleasure she tells him to sleep off. "Remember," he says, as if banished from the Bower of Bliss as conceived by Bosch, "you refuse me arm'd in Lobster" (5.2.26), whose liability seems to be, with all its promise of a succulent *jouissance,* having no skin to scratch off. In any case, the appearance of woman's dominance is only skin-deep, as she marries into the structure from which her sovereign pleasure derives. When a woman really dominates, she turns out to be a man who is a fantasy of a woman in the displacements of desire idealized in the form. Thus, in *The Loyal Subject,* when Alinda is transformed into young Archas— whose disguise is never explained until the last act—the Duke asks Olimpia who has loved him-as-her, "Didst thou never wish *Olimpia, /* It might be thus?" To which she replies, "A thousand times" (5.6.86–87).

Given the magnitude of that wish, no wonder the fulfillments of Fletcherian tragicomedy resemble the distortions of a dream, what John Aubrey said of the collaboration with Beaumont, "a wonderful consimility of phansey. . . ."[3] The repressive cost of such "phansey" is another matter, as we think through the arbitrariness, the ruptured changes of heart, the breaks in the plane of representation, the excess of means on behalf of apparent meanings that distend the dramaturgy of pleasure and power. If the image of social control reflected in Fletcher's plays were to be taken, moreover, as the ideology of the plays, a reduction of all the several meanings to a restatement of order in dramatized or melo-dramatized form, there is another question to be absolved. That question is why, if restraint of libido were desired, we should have a drama that—with *The Faithful Shepherdess* as the paradigm—enacts hyperbolic desire before its chastening suppression. Dr. Johnson retrospectively advised Milton to keep his immateriality out of sight, seducing the reader to drop it from his thought. Thus we might ask of Fletcher: Why not simply conceal it, not show it? As Pyniero says to Panura, who labors her vulnerability as she leads him to the private vault connecting the Temple to the Palace, "If thou dost feare me, / Why dost thou put me in minde?" (*Island Princess* 5.4.52–53). It is another version of the question endemic to theater with its erotics of power, which even when secularized connects the Temple to the Palace and which, emerging from the dark vault, is—with more or less arbitrariness in the theatricality—an institution of constraint. But not before it has been seductive, panurgic as Panura in the vault, or Amarillis in the sacred grove.

"Of all greene wounds I know the remedies," says Clorin in *The Faithful Shepherdess* (1.1.33), practiced in the secret use of herbs to dispel passion, curb art, and tame madness, as if poet, lunatic, and lover were all obscene, which the theater always is, indecently seen, at its deceitful and illusory core. If there is a sure "power / In that great name of virgin" (1.1.124–25), it is in its resistance to representation or "vain illusion," theatricality itself, which is in turn drawn to the "private hidden power," like that ur-figure of the comic theater, that obscene "rough thing," the Satyr, who adores the "virgin flower uncropt" (1.1.113), the sexual object unsexed, delivered from lust and otherness at once, suggesting the pure perversion of a pleasure without sense, allusive and narcissistic, without pretense or identity, plighted to the edge of a grave and the secret virtue of death. Power seems to thrive, teasing and enticing, on this interplay of exposure and interdiction with its deep structural relation to something beyond the pleasure principle in the mortifying sexual wish. What we see in *The Faithful Shepherdess*—a baroque canonization of libidinal energy—is how power in the form of the Law constitutes desire, arousing desire by its prohibition, desire desiring the repression of "that wished thing / We all are borne for" (1.3.92–93).

"Pleasure and power do not," then, "cancel or turn back against one another," as Foucault says in *The History of Sexuality*, "they seek out, overlap, and reinforce one another. They are linked together by complex mechanisms and devices of excitation and incitement."[4] It is these mechanisms of excitation and incitement that are cultivated in the Palace of *The Loyal Subject*—"the place is pleasure, / Preserv'd to that use" (3.6.3–4). And we see them in the staging at the opening of *The Humorous Lieutenant*, when the Usher is preparing the scene for those "that come here to see the Show" (1.1.11), which is to be, after all, a show of power that reveals and conceals itself as "the tricke of Court" (1.1.8) where an audience, *given audience,* the tautological subject of power, is lured into its widening compass by the appearance of sexual pleasure: "Round, round," says the Usher in the initiating charm,

> . . . perfume it round, quick, look ye diligently
> The state be right: are these the richest Cushions?
> Fie, fie, who waits i' th' wardrobe?
>
> (*Humorous Lieutenant* 1.1.1–3)

Whoever it is that waits, censor and/or participants, attending upon the image of power, is caught up in "these circular incitements" that have, as Foucault says, "traced around bodies and sexes, not boundaries not to be crossed, but *perpetual spirals of power and pleasure*" (*History,* 45).

If the frontiers are not closed, it is the boundaries, and the binaries, which heighten the excitation as the spirals—like the overlaid inscriptions on Freud's mystic writing pad—widen into oxymorons of desire and repression, sex and dying, chastity and sexuality. In the effusion of his response to Amoret's agreement to meet him in the grove, where "chaste flames" of devotion, "chaste embraces," a "chaste kiss," and "chaste desires" will free them from the vices of "dying flesh and dull morality," Perigot elaborates in the opposite direction of their "chaste hopes," chaste upon chaste aspirations to a "long wished delight" (*Faithful Shepherdess* 1.2.93–125), the image of that dead-end plaguey otherness and "the hot polluted name" (1.2.130) to which he would be consigned if he should cease to be a faithful admirer of her virginity. The revulsion of feeling bodes no good in its excess, though Perigot is able to resist the temptation of Amarillis, who enters immediately upon Amoret's exit, and, with at most a perfunctory blush of displacement, as in the substitution of a dream, offers herself to him with all the hot polluted fervor of unrepression.

Within the moral conventions of Fletcher's theater, desire need not be so shameless to be reproved. Any instance of unauthorized love, if still chaste, uncontracted, may be an excess that is condemned, even by those like Silvio who must suffer for it:

> By Heaven it was my love, my violence.
> My life must answer it: I broke in to her,
> Tempted the Law, solicitted unjustly.
>
> (*Women Pleas'd* 2.5.37–39)

It is this juridical limit to the conception of love that persists through Fletcher's drama, where power is attached with bonds of piety to the idea of sovereignty, but only in her changingness to the sovereignty of woman. In *The Humorous Lieutenant,* the gown sent by Antigonus to Celia sits, as Menippus reports, "so apted to her; / And she is so great a Mistris of disposure" (3.4.16–17), as to indicate she will not be, when accosted by the King, disposed to be the mere subject of his desire. "She has two-edged eyes," says Antigonus as she approaches, "by heaven, they kill o' both sides" (3.4.23). It is an idea of woman as the duplicitous, altering, and therefore disloyal subject of desire that has not, we know, been bypassed by time, which is why Freud advanced the tentative question that has agitated the recent discourse that is trying to imagine a form of love that does not tempt the Law because it seeks no authorization from what, in its descent from the Logos, is nothing but a name.

What's in a name but the power of the subject to become, as in the drama of Fletcher, *rhetoric,* which, in the metonymic convolvulus of the baroque, occults the source of its status as subject, the power of naming. The loyal subject Archas (the name suggests the Derridean *arche-trace*) evokes this curious power with its originary Word. He embodies those principles of integrity or inviolable being that are sustained by the accuracy of a name, an accuracy of abundance, with no slippage of the signifier around the plenitude of the thing. There is an anomaly, however, in the loyal subject's trying to maintain this fullness of being, palpitant with integrity, in a domain of power that accommodates within its magisterial and well-stratified system those figures who are "full of businesse" (*Humorous Lieutenant* 2.3.59) in "a world of businesse" where names are "by interpretation . . . meere nothings" (*Loyal Subject* 4.2.3–4). Along with Lopez the usurer who, despite his filthy lucre, knows how to please a woman, there is Leucippe the procuress, who knows how to please a horny King. She is a sort of CIA as well, a mistress of surveillance, not only with two-edged but "a thousand eyes" (*Humorous Lieutenant* 2.3.100), and "they say she keeps an office of Concealements" (2.1.45). If there is a binarism in the body politic that, as value, separates virtue from sexuality, the loyal subject from the abject, there is a network of partial objects through a developing world of trade in which Leucippe bottoms out like Mrs. Peachum in Brecht. For Leucippe, maidenheads are merchandise or surplus value, circulating with interest, as trade. But then we learn, when somebody asks about his age, that King Antigonus himself is part of the trickle-down economy, "an old man, and full of businesse" (3.2.103), on the supply side of the chastity valorized in *The Faithful Shepherdess.*

So far as the loyal subject has entered this structure of exchange, unifying sexuality and money, the hidden treasure that Archas himself had sworn to keep concealed, the subject is subverted, reified, and subjected in the other way. He/It has become a vulnerable body in a power field whose major objective is to effectively control all independent energies and integrate the individual (the shift is from integrity to integers) within the social order, even the rebellious ones like Theodor, who capitulates and begs for mercy, but only to keep the Name of the Father. It is no accident that Archas, who loses dominion over the true body of his being in order to uphold the system of power, has been tortured. It is the lashed and humiliated Archas, emblematic source of truth, who serves as the still-loyal subject who enunciates truth, justifying the taboo that both defines the limits of dissent and demands subservience. It is only possible, however, to dramatize this dilemma at the critical juncture in history when the subject becomes the object of its own knowledge, *then* represses it, still upholding—as is not true later—the notion of a sovereign or founding subject, an originary truth, even as that truth is being shaken subjectively to its foundations. So Clorin, whose purity is predicated on an absence, a masculine image of truth, a creature without history, whose only definition is the cold embrace of holy earth. It is hard to know what to make of the "still loved ashes" (*Faithful Shepherdess* 1.1.6) of this missing paragon, as it is hard to know what to make of the old Duke who is dead in *The Loyal Subject,* where the new Duke was not, to begin with, able to bring the troops to order.

From the point of view of power, it may make sense that the Duke's father stored up treasure against the day when he might need it, considering his weakness or improvidence. But seen as an aspect of an emergent money economy—as opposed to the archaic economy within which the loyal follower of Archas, the Ancient, sells his brooms—the hiding of the money has about it the anal stink of classical economics, currency hoarding; and we have learned from Freud, as from Jonathan Swift, that the calculated prudence of the Protestant era, the ideal type of *Homo economicus,* is an anal character. Thus it is possible to see the young Duke's profligacy as a reflex against repression that perverts itself and to which, when reformed, even the Ancient—who prefers not to sell his body or his labor—eventually has to accede, since there is no possibility of a *political* economy without it. What we have in Archas is the effort to characterize this repressive order in the form of its most self-edifying fantasy of honor. But the conception of the loyal subject and this dispossessed honor is about as close as Fletcher gets to the more tortured baroque of the Counter Reformation that we see in the obsessional devotions of the characters of Calderón, who now reminds us of Kafka. It is important to see, however, that the power of the new Duke is guaranteed not by the concealed meaning of the Sacred, but by the hidden treasure that Archas is forced to reveal. The revealed truth is no longer the truth of the spirit, which upholds honor, but of the baser matter abstracted into money, which derides it, as Iago derides us when he tells us to put it in our purse. The apparent triumph of spirit in these rather schizoid plays occurs not only, as in *The Faithful Shepherdess,* on the edge of the grave but—what accounts for an incipient laughter in the most reverent moments—on the absurd edge of a dissociation of sensibility moving toward the dissolution of the subject in a new epistemological field whose real power is an invisible currency.

"No stale stuffe for your money marts," says Celia (3.2.59), but she too, resuming her true name as the daughter of a King, is restored to the exchange mechanism that encourages repression in the Name of the Law. What we see overall in the plays of Fletcher is what is realized by the drama after the Restoration, and that is an economy of pleasure in which sex, matching wits, is the measuring rod, a principle of intelligibility, a critical limit giving the impression that it is the source of pleasure when in actuality it is pleasure's Law, justifying regulation and social control. In recent years, we have had our bouts of "desublimated sexuality" (Marcuse), but the regulating agencies persist, though in more subtle, tempered, or insidious forms, still without acknowledging that at the root of sexuality (as distinguished from sex) is—as Foucault has argued and feminist theory believes—"a positive economy of the body and of pleasure."[5]

This more positive economy, which remains a utopian desire, appears as an alluring prospect only for certain spasmodic moments in the order of power mirrored in Fletcher's plays, which erect an armed citadel around virtue, as in *Women Pleas'd,* in order to secure it, the power of virtue and the virtue of power. It is an imperial order more extravagantly articulated in the masques of Jonson and Jones, and in the King's *Basilikon Doron* where, in the style of the gods, we are made privy, it seems, to the secrets of power, though—in the eyes of the royal spectator who sees without being seen or is seen as he wants to be—there remains a sustaining mystery that subsumes the lover's desire. What occurs to the humorous Lieutenant when he drinks the potion is the prodigiously absurd form of what is in actuality the tribute being paid to power, even when power seems coarse, self-indulgent, or obscene, or when the tribute itself is mocked, as in the Lieutenant's liturgies of devotion:

> He talks now of the King, no other language,
> And with the King, as he imagines hourly,
> Courts the King, drinks to the King, dies for the King,
> Buyes all the pictures of the King, wears the Kings colors.
> (*Humorous Lieutenant* 4.4.153–56)

Whatever the rhetoric of resistance, no other language but the King (who has not yet been beheaded in our language). Despite his loose desires that, "like the glow-wormes light, the Apes so wonder'd at" (4.5.31), the King sustains the mystery of his mystical body as the all-seeing "light and life of creatures, / Angell-ey'd King" (4.4.164–65), who is seen finally as he wishes to be, like James in his pageants and royal arcana.[6] The legitimacy of this riddling presence that knows how to remove itself, the Law that justifies its power, is a show of force; and one is struck by the frequency of that word or its cognates of violence in the rhetoric of Fletcher's drama. "By force he was taken," says Quisara of her brother the King in that strange scene where she challenges the suitors' passion; and "he that shall enjoy me, / Shall fetch him backe by force, or never know me" (*Island Princess* 1.3.187–88), as if the aboriginal condition of love, its ontological premise, were force. "I say, by force, and suddenly. / He lies there till he rots else" (1.3.194–95).

When the *show* of force fails, as it does for Antigonus in *The Humorous Lieutenant,* power has to be made actual. For a moment in that play, the action seems to suggest that even this will fail. It is as if the absolutism of the Jacobean Court is abrogated by Celia's resistance when, thinking she has drunk the potion, the King would seduce her. She sees him as a satiric figure, "Curl'd and perfum'd," an ineffectual Image of power, at best a "deare December" (4.5.22–24). She will love, honor, even admire him as sovereign, but as he summons up his power to persecute her, she reviles him for the perversion of his titles and emblem, the "glorious Lamp / Set on top of all, to light all perfectly" (4.5.52–53).

When he threatens to force her—"I have it in my will," he says (4.5.59)—she responds that the will of the absolute monarch is itself a regressive fantasy:

> Your will's a poore one;
> And though it be a Kings will, a despised one,
> Weaker than Infants leggs, your will's in swaddling clouts. . . .
> (*Humorous Lieutenant* 4.5.60–62)

There is in Celia's speech a subversion of the royal word, James's own rhetoric of absolute mastery, as Antigonus insists on prerogatives over the body of her love as if it were a matter of State, which, in the Court of James as in the poems of Donne, it was. Whatever woman wants, Celia suggests that as disenfranchised subject she has her own arcane resources and capacities of absence, her own secret powers. With the King ready to attack, she calls up what Belvidere renounced when the riddle was absolved, the altering nature of woman that, in the royal eye altering, presumably alters all:

> A thousand waies my will has found to check ye;
> A thousand doores to scape ye: I dare die sir;
> As suddenly I dare die, as you can offer. . . .
> (*Humorous Lieutenant* 4.5.63–65)

But it is only in this ultimate denial, the self-denial of her body, that she can thwart the sovereign will, which, however perverse it may appear, remains a Christian will, as indomitably as it does for Armusia in *The Island Princess*. Armusia sees any other worship as a wild shambles of strange gods and will have his devotion unpolluted if the plague should rage about him and the whole State storms (4.5.116–22).

There is no such storm, however, in the plays of Fletcher. Nor is there anything like an Artaudian plague, no real questioning of these strange premises of a wild devotion, though when Ruy Dias and the Portuguese bombard the island to rescue Armusia, there is an outburst of a sort of surrealism in the transparency of the baroque, what Quisara has referred to as the "pure mirrors" (5.2.119) of desire: "It is like to prove a blessed age for Glasiers," says the townsman; "I met a hand, and a Letter in't in great haste, and by and by a single leg running after it, as if the Arme had forgot part of his arrant; heads flie like foot-balls every where" (5.3.19–21). But what is being opposed in this chaos is not the established order of things, and the Letter in the hand is hastening to reaffirm the letter of the Law. Whatever the tempting of the Law in the Name of the Law, the recurring motif of Fletcherian drama, it means to fortify the royal will, against which not even the craftiest woman—not Celia, with a world of offerings to her excellence; not Quisara, a heathen with absolutist inclinations of her own—has any other court of last resort. As Walter Benjamin has remarked about the German *Trauerspiel* that, with more of mourning and melancholia, absolves the riddle of power as in Fletcher's tragicomedies: "Not even the most dreadful corruption of the person of the prince—and that is the baroque aspect of the whole business—can really disturb the norm of sovereignty."[7] The other gods are paper tigers.

As for the Christian martyr like Armusia or the faithful shepherdess or the chaste princess, the impregnability of such characters is not so much what Lopez called a "rule of vertue," presumably on Christian principles, a moral strength profoundly shaken, tested, and reintegrated, but rather, as Benjamin says of the martyred heroes of the *Trauerspiel,* something like virtue as "the natural aspect of the course of history, essential in its permanence" (88), a history without progression, however energetic or magnificent, like Almanzor's fiery steed after the Restoration: "Not moving forward, yet, with every bound, / Pressing, and seeming still to quit his ground" (*Conquest of Granada* 1.1.71–72).[8] There is something pressing in Fletcher that is more restless, and that may account for the disjunctures that are sudden and ungrounded. Whatever the perturbations of desire, it is a restlessness that goes nowhere historically, as if he understood that in historical life there is no such thing as virtue, but only in the distorted mirror of a history folded back upon itself, as in the baroque mythicization of the Court, or in his version of the pastoral, presided over by the Virgin of the Grove, where history spills its seed onanistically on the ground.

"Baroque drama knows," writes Benjamin, "no other historical activity than the corrupt energy of schemers. In none of the countless rebels who confront a monarch is there any trace of revolutionary conviction" (88). Thus, the resistance of Celia to the advances of Antigonus: the thousand doors of escaping will lead back to the throne of power as, in the context of heaven's disapproval, she returns to the rhetoric of honor and conscience, as if woman were also an empty signifier. Such is the reflected power of the Absolute that it even operates in the arbitrary excitations of the dramaturgy to restore an appropriate virtue to the pure mirrors, the illusory stasis of history. When the rapist King suddenly repents and reforms, like the fulfillment of another thousand wishes, Celia kneels in obedient service since—without more help from history—the subject's will can only go so far.

"Dye all but my desires," Celia had said as she entered the play poorly dressed. "Even those to death are sicke too" (1.1.45–46)—and they must, I suspect, remain somewhat sick at play's end, even as the humorous Lieutenant does in the Epilogue. He is "not cur'd yet throughlie," for "the glory of this place" (1.1.43–45) preserved for pleasure—the Court, the theater—is still a function of desire formed and directed, not by the woman or the actor but by another sovereign will. It is a sovereignty that is distributed through the dramatic text whose claims to credibility are pressing, forced, in a kind of martial law that—however attenuated by history—still disturbs our peace.

So far as Antigonus represents this power in the absolution of the plot, what is masked by the methods of Fletcherian tragicomedy—its spontaneity of avoidance in a fantasy of politics that is grounded in fantasy—is not impotence, far from that, but rather the usury of force, civil and personal force, a metaphysics of force diverted into a code of honor, not yet outlived, where even what appears to be true love is solemnified by the sustained resonance of the rites of war. "Come," says Antigonus at the end, that business in abeyance, "beat all the Drums up, / And all the noble instruments of war: / Let 'em fill the Kingdome with their sounds" upon which "the brazen arch of heaven" seems constructed (5.5.56–59), rather than suspended from above in the Great Chain of Being.

As the sounds of the noble instruments have hardly diminished in history, so this brazen arch of heaven is not exactly—in the conversion of the subject of desire into the consummation of love—the "strong toil of grace" of Shakespeare's Cleopatra (*Antony and Cleopatra* 5.2.351), where one feels the vital force of the pleasure even in the final labor of death. But then grace is not quite, in the drama of the baroque, the grace Lucio says it is, "despite of all controversy," in *Measure for Measure* (1.2.24). For we also feel in the ambiguous equities of that equivocal play—the rhetoric riddling, pressing—that the controversy is thickening in history, the mystique of the baroque caught up in the empirical, toiling, putting money in its purse. The increasing worldliness of the Jacobean court, its Realpolitik, was predicated on the illusion of a divine ordinance, but the artfulness of that ordinance, with its shared language of the eternal, is but a holding action against the imminence of decay, like the overstretched metaphors of the Metaphysicals.

Refusing metaphors, as if Hobbes were playing the role, the mad lover Memnon—wanting love without mediation, no riddles—exclaims, "No questions: / . . . I doe love you, infinitely: / Why doe you smile? Am I ridiculous?" (*Mad Lover* 1.2.67–69)—literally offering his heart to Calis, a heartless name. But if we laugh, what are we laughing at? *Is* he ridiculous? That seems to be the consensus of the "Court chameleons" in the play, as it is of the scholarship on the play, which is disturbed by the seeming fissure in the character but sees it as a foolish lapse of dignity. There is a peculiar irony when we tend, even at this historical distance, to identify with the Court and laugh the disturbing rupture away. For what should we expect, really, of "a Generall Generall," the pure abstraction of unmediated desire, its absolute subject, "A soule conceiv'd a Souldier" (1.1.13–14) before whom whole armies quaked and castles fell that seemed impregnable, the glorious conqueror of "countries that like the wind knew no command / But savage wildnesse" (1.1.27–28)? If the King himself could not, in a kind of ecstasy of anticipation, wait to embrace Memnon, no wonder that he expects as much of a mere woman.

They told him he was everything in the way of war. When he returns to Court like Tamburlaine with "a drum in's mouth" (1.1.85), a *miles gloriosos* beating his own triumph, he insists upon saying too that he brought "That lazie end you wish for, Peace, so fully, / That no more name of war is" (1.1.52–53). By any other name that may be his error, but what modesty is mandatory for one who has laughed at "Balls of consuming Wildfire, / That lickt up men like lightning . . . / And tost'em back againe like childrens trifles" (1.1.66–68)? Nobody denies that "the maidenheads of thousand lives" (1.1.60) hung upon his merit and valor. That he insists peremptorily upon one, what is so funny about that? Didn't the King himself say that "Valiant and wise are twins" (1.1.44)? When we laugh, then, at Memnon is it not some jealous reduction in the way of the world that looks upon his grandiloquence as vaunting, or would it be more acceptable, as with Othello, if there were more magic in his words? Or are we to think of his grappling with destruction—"No dalliance but with death" (1.1.63)—as child's play, now that the danger is over, no danger remaining for the social order except the displaced magnitude of desire nurtured by force in war and expecting no contest in peace?

To have made what appears a comic spectacle of Memnon may be the inaugural conceit of Fletcher's play, but it is a conceit that also needs to be absolved. Were it to be performed today, one might wince at the prospect of the unexamined folly of playing the first part of it for unchallenged laughs before going on to what is considered the more serious and credible business of the rest of the play. If Memnon is made foolish, as he appears to be, the question is *why*? And what is the wobbling vantage point, looked at askance, of those who think him so? Whatever Fletcher's intentions, the theatricality is not innocent, merely worked up for a passing fancy or gratuitous effect. There is a syntax of disjunct emotions in the character that makes it seem to those who do not parse it further that the plot becomes more probable the more it leaves his declaration of love behind. Out of what structure of expectancy and illusion does that impression arise?

> CALIS.   Leave the words, Sir,
>   And leap into the meaning.
> MEMNON.   Then againe:
>   I tell you I doe love ye.
> CALIS.   Why?
> MEMNON.   No questions:
>   Pray no more questions.
>
> (*Mad Lover* 1.2.65–68)

What we have in the madness of Memnon is madness refusing to reason. Whether comic or melodramatic, it is a distortion that postulates first in hyperbole—the signifier that says too much—and then in the leaping simplicity of "A loving heart, / A truly loving heart" (1.2.88–89)—the signified that cannot be spoken—excessive or embarrassing claims upon meaning that, at some degree zero of signification, makes a kind of perfect sense: "Was I so foolish?" he asks, not leaving the matter at an epistemology of the heart. "I have braines / That beate above your reaches: Shee's a Princesse, / That's all: I have killed a King, that's greater" (1.1.218–20), as Milton will be telling us very soon, when the structure of power that makes us laugh *does* go through a radical change. But as the short-lived change is insufficient in a new imperium of change, does not Memnon speak for something damaged in our hearts when he foresees an afterlife to be lived in a common language where "love is everlasting, ever young" (2.1.10)? As for the death required for the fulfillment of that everlasting desire—the insane project of the mad lover—"In dreams we doe it" (2.1.14).

And we would do it better if we approached the plays of Fletcher—once so popular and now ignored—as if they were dreams with their emotive imagination and binary oppositions, gratifying desire at almost any dramaturgical cost. To look upon them as dreams is not, as is sometimes done, to make an excuse for the faults of structure or unmotivated behavior, but to understand the cost of a structure of *unmotivatedness*, to read the arbitrariness or the fault as an index of the libidinal economy out of which such dramas arise, what needs to be thought through as in the *interpretation* of a dream. What we have in the plays is a kind of Jacobean bricolage or heterogeneous corpus of unarticulated parts, a repertoire of intense emotions achieved, sometimes absurdly, without any essential continuity or metaphysical ground and, as in dreams, with strange deformations of the family romance. In *The Loyal Subject,* for instance, there are the bizarre condensations of that sequence when the beautiful maiden Alinda—not yet acknowledged either to characters or audience as Archas's son Archas—is first responded to with ardor by Olimpia and then, in his appeal to his father, likened to his *mother* (1.5.77). Not to complicate the whirligig of gender in this psychic dislocation by remembering the boy actor, s/he even gives her/his father a favor as he goes off to save her/him from the invading Tartars. "Come home," s/he says to the father, "the son of honour, and Ile serve ye" (1.5.89). What intensifies the dream formation is the absence of transitions, a kind of detemporalization, as when the line is followed by a sequence without interval in which Archas has already beaten the Tartars, the wish fulfilled, no sooner thought than done.

As for the binary oppositions congenital to the plays—charity/lust, honor/materialism, loyalty/corruption—one is not so much interpreting the plays in naming them as designating what needs to be interpreted.[9] The binaries are the structures, as in the manichean figures of a dream, whereby we get at the repressed subject of which the categories are the symptoms: the endorsement of a dividing power whose claimed absoluteness is the question that keeps the loyal subject always at a loss. What is striking in Fletcher's plays is how the representative image of force and power aging in the service feels, regressively, some vacancy of power, an unaccountable split in the continuity of authority out of which arises a sense of illusory permanence inseparable from a primary narcissism. "I am the same, the same man, living, dying," says Archas, "the same mind to 'em both, I poize thus equall" (4.5.92–93). But such poise is the shaky equation of another wish that, for any living creature, is only to be realized in dreams, not in the social order that pretends to be a sacrament when it is only a royal illusion. It is, moreover, theatricalized to the point in reality where, as reflected by Fletcher in the theater, the growing sense of illusion torments, as it does in tragic drama, but without the sustaining recourse of the old sacred and synthesizing power. The satiric element that cuts off the pain also leaves it at times unassimilated, dramatically unusable, as when it sees the mystical body of truth as a relic tortured by its own fictions, like Archas, or given to extremities of behavior, like Memnon, which seem monstrous or absurd. (I am ignoring at this juncture characters like Antigonus or Lopez, and the satire that accrues to the more reprehensible monstrosities that, arbitrarily rectified, are restored to dominance and power.) If there is the same mind to them both, mad lover and loyal subject, it is the mind of the baroque dying into its dreams.

That would appear to be the natural consequence of having been born into a delusion. For the loyalty of the loyal subject is not so much to a higher truth but to an occulted Symbolic mirrored in the Imaginary, as when Memnon stares, frozen in passion, at the scornful fixity of Calis. There may be a perfected image of truth in the mind's eye, but what we see in that seemingly ludicrous moment is the solidity of its mirage, all the more enchanting when it is figured as a woman. The relation of the loyal subject to an actual world is, even when apparently absolved, profoundly disturbing and alienating, especially when we are tempted to laugh, which is an admission of the untenability of an accredited subject in the waste of doing spirits of a declining age. As we may feel in Beckett's *Endgame*—that last declension of the declination—it is funny, then it is no longer funny. And what we have in the strange grammar of emotion in Fletcher's tragicomedies—with their deranged absolutes of absurd desire, the subject insisting on a vanishing truth—is not avoidance of tragic pain, but the ironic dissolution of its unavoidable sensations that are skillfully evaded but, in the gap of absence, painfully aroused. As for the laughter, there is something rather hopeless about it (something still disturbing in the comedies of the Restoration), "all the hope left" being, as the Physician says when they are tricking the humorous Lieutenant back again to war, to work upon his weakness "and make him raise his passion above his paine" (*Humorous Lieutenant* 3.5.90, 92).

The trick goes against his wishes, and, as I have indicated, he is sensible enough at the end, in the no-man's-land of the Epilogue, to know he is not cured. But the formula of the Physician is the reverse model of what we see elsewhere in Fletcher: the delusive quality of emotion in the baroque subject, obsessive, incurable, insensible, who persists in excess on the edge of satire, pain reified into passion, but not sufficiently corroded by the satiric, though change is coming, to summon up the passion to change its Law.

(1985/86)

19. "Set Me Where You Stand"

Revising the Abyss

Just about the time that the sixties were achieving identity as the sixties, Maynard Mack gave three lectures for the Department of English at Berkeley in which he anticipated, with admirable learning and a particular animus (to which I will later return), the current critique of revisionism. The critique, of course, was only to be expected, after a generation in which the receding dissidence of the sixties, sublimated, recycled, and reified in theory, was the dominant force in our scholarship. That it came with a new historicism and confessions of complicity, identity politics and a rhetoric of transgression, bodies that matter and gender bending (reminding us, in a rather gleeful propaedeutic on the epistemology of the closet, that not only Ophelia, but even Gertrude was a boy!) must have been for the scholar who had illumined the world of *Hamlet,* if something more than fantasy, surely passing strange.[1] It was just passing onto the scene, however, when the lectures were published, in 1965, as *King Lear in Our Time.*[2] Reviewing the stage history, and bringing it up to date, the book confirmed the learning that was, from Professor Mack, also to be expected, though it might soon be taken to task for the limitations of the history and his faith in the autonomous text, from its time to our time, essential meanings intact, or as Stephen Greenblatt put it about the work of art, "a pure flame that lies at the source of our speculations."[3] Not only did Mack ignore, in the apparatus of cultural production, an echo chamber of maybe unsettling, concomitant texts, but along with the unruly symbiosis between the social and the poetic, the sometimes incontinent, site-specific fact that neither "the Globe on the Banksyde" nor "Whitehall vppon Sainct Stephen's night," where the play was performed for the King (nor the Stationer's Register, which noted that occasion and entitled the text to be printed), was impartial political territory; nor, for that matter, was the lecture hall at Berkeley, before or after the visitations of Michel Foucault.

It may have been too early for any of the new historicists, now established there, to have been at the lectures, taking issue with Mack, but at a time when the dubious crossing of disciplines may be overreaching itself, causing revisionist history to be confronted with rules of evidence, his learning may have the virtue of not claiming too much for itself, or not as much for itself as it does for the wisdom of Shakespeare. I realize as I say it, putting my finger in the flame, that "Shakespeare" has become an institution, which in assuming superior value discredits the other word, by now in cultural studies archaic or obsolete. No matter: for what occurs in *Lear,* even wisdom is insufficient. And so it was when Samuel Johnson, shocked by the death of Cordelia, said he was not sure he could endure reading of it again, or the last scenes of the play, until he had a chance to revise them as an editor.[4] That remark, I must confess, was more disturbing to Mack than it has ever been to me, since there is probably no more credible response to those scenes—if not "the promised end," the "image of that horror"[5]—than being unable to bear it. That Dr. Johnson would bear it by rewriting it may be the sort of revisionism that any sort of historicist might find somewhat hard to take, though such practice was later justified in the materialist theater of Brecht, who, even in the debates with Lukács (where he defended Joycean formalism as a better brand of socialist realism) and long before Fredric Jameson, insisted that we historicize.

But what makes history or unmakes it, and the modes of legitimation, were not really Mack's concern as he wrote at the end of his book "about all that the earth has known," since we came crying hither, "of disease, famine, earthquake, war," the extent of it unexplainable, by history or metahistory, or the book of Revelation. In this regard, what we have in the text of *Lear* is a virtual register or palimpsest of existential fact. As Mack sees it, and reads it, the issue is one of endurance, with maybe a residual sense of transcendence from a deflated metaphysics. "We face the ending of this play," he says, "as we face our world, with whatever support we customarily derive from systems of belief or unbelief" (*KL,* 116). While a drama so overwhelming "never tells us what to think" (117), we can pretty well guess the system from which Mack derives support, defined through every abomination and conceivable suffering by tragic vision itself, which, as Brecht developed his system with its alienation-effect, was intolerable, criminal, insupportable—and with the entire structure of theater needed something more than revising. "Shakespeare's great solitary figures," he wrote in the "Short Organum," "bearing on their breast the star of their fate, carry through with irresistible force their futile and deadly outbursts, they prepare their own downfall; life, not death, becomes obscene as they collapse; the catastrophe is beyond criticism. Human sacrifices all around! Barbaric delights! We know that the barbarians have their art. Let us create another."[6]

This outburst can still be felt in Walter Benjamin's remark, now auratic in critical theory, that the monuments of culture are part of the history of barbarism, and it is a view that has persisted, with a little more waffling perhaps, up through deconstruction into the new historicism. It happens to be a view that is, in no uncertain terms, at the heart of the storm in *Lear*, though it presumably occurs at a time, imagined as prehistoric, when the monuments hardly existed. Where they do exist, revisionist thought has not quite sorted out why in the long unbroken record of barbarism some monuments, like *Lear*, are so much better than others, or why—moving from texts to mortar and stone, and at the risk of a discredited aesthetic—there is no Stalinist architecture in, say, a city like Florence. That there happens to be pollution, rotting the monuments now, doesn't quite mean it can all be explained through the logic of advanced capitalism, which has become in critical discourse, as we deal with all the "fluidities and contradictions" of a still-barbarous world (the phrase is Mack's about the world of *Lear*), a sort of all-purpose solvent that looks like the human condition. To believe that it may for the historical moment be very close to that—in the sense that the capitalist order, with various worldwide adaptations, is the reality in which we will live for any foreseeable future—is not altogether absurd. But of the liability of a logic that is named the human condition, reflecting a fault of nature, Mack seems to be aware, as he tries to think out the relation between "circumstantial reality" and "a history generic to all human beings" (*KL*, 78), which may be the stuff of dreams, but not, unfortunately, the history we might wish.

As for the history to be wished, that was/is specifically on the agenda of cultural materialism, which "registers its commitment to the transformation of a social order which exploits people on grounds of race, gender, and class," and it assumes that it cannot be done with a literary criticism that attempts "to mystify its perspective as the natural, obvious or right interpretation of an allegedly textual fact."[7] That comes from a collection of essays titled *Political Shakespeare,* and even those sharing the politics shadowing that of Shakespeare, as he sanctions or severs the Great Chain of Being, must concede that it is just about standard operating conviction in literary studies today. The ethos of cultural materialism, while tempered by Raymond Williams, is still very much Brechtian (as it was in the case of *Screen,* which spawned film theory in Britain) in its refusal to accept history as natural or inevitable, as if, given what it was, it had to be. Life, said Brecht of the theater, had to be shown as alterable, while the theater could not survive a paralytic view of history, which was not then, and is not now, unsusceptible to change. But even in assent, there may be troubling doubts. I am not referring to the "radical doubts" of Shakespeare's drama—provoked, contained, "strained to the breaking point" in *Lear*—to which we can pay homage because, as Greenblatt says, "they no longer threaten us."[8] If subversion is not for us either, as he somewhat plaintively adds, there is still the view of history that it doesn't have to be, though the way we read it, revise it, and what we think we are doing about it, are also subject to doubt; not to mention those who think subversion is still for us. As Kenneth Burke used to say, maybe so maybe not. Some things are alterable, some not, and certainly not for the time being. And the question always to be asked of any commitment is to what extent, really, is it whistling in the wind? As somebody who once wrote a book starting with the sentence, "The purpose of this book is to talk up a revolution," and who wanted to bring about change so much that I ended the paragraph by saying that when "confronted with the despicable behavior of people in the American theater, I feel like the lunatic Lear on the heath, wanting to 'kill, kill, kill, kill, kill, kill!' "[9] it seems not unreasonable to ask that question.

Meanwhile, the degree to which mystification really occurred in displaced forms of criticism has been disputed, and some scholars of my generation who have been more than receptive to revisionist thought do not quite recognize themselves, or their teachers, in the omnibus description of an "idealist literary criticism," as if with "disembodied objectivity" as our very mode of being the spirit of Kant reigned over us all. As one thinks of the spectrum of New Critics from Eliot and Pound (who revised the entire curriculum to what is now being attacked) to Blackmur and Burke (salvaged by Frank Lentricchia) to the quite singular figure of Yvor Winters (who disagreed with them all, as I disagreed with him when I asked him to supervise my dissertation), one wonders whether even the subtlest among them was ever so adept as to make a perspective seem natural and obvious, with certified interpretation of alleged textual facts.[10] Even the notion of an autonomous text was no guarantee of that, though what should be obvious is that some allegations are, even among critics with the same bias, more substantial or convincing than others. And so it is with materialist readings, which like those of any critical dispensation begin to repeat themselves. If paradox and ambiguity are out, something has to happen to the fluidities and contradictions. And what seems to have happened in the wake of Foucault is that they have become a matrix of revelations about the insidious workings of power or—in the cryptic cellarage of negotiation and exchange, where nothing is transparent—elliptical signs of its subversion; in either case, predictably folded into the service of the ideological commitment, and when they don't fit, excluded.

There are some who are quite contentious or very acerbic about that, but as any critical dispensation is at best a partial truth, I want to move on to other kinds of revisionism of a more subjective kind. But first, since Mack was correcting history with a commitment of his own, let me return to the particular animus that I mentioned at the start. If I made a point of it there, it was not merely to place the lectures, given the setting in Berkeley, in a volatile scene of dissent, nor to use it as an ideological datum for current debates over revisionist history. The reason, frankly, was more personal than that. Nothing in the book or its acknowledgments suggests any awareness of the political atmosphere around the lectures, or the scholarship arising from it, but as Mack developed an argument around abuses of the text in theatrical history— before proceeding to what is "actable and knowable" in "what Shakespeare actually wrote" (*KL,* 40–41)—it turned out that I was the immediate cause and focus of his critique.

The charge was actually severe, if not exactly negligence, probably worse than revisionism: "the question that inevitably arises in the mind after studying either of these recent treatments of *King Lear . . .* is Robert Frost's question: what to make of a diminished thing?" (40). The diminishment in question was my staging of the play, which was presented at The Actor's Workshop of San Francisco in 1961; my codefendant was Peter Brook, whose own staging was done about a year later in London. If I received somewhat more attention than Brook, that was because I had published an article about the San Francisco production that Mack read with what seemed to me then, and still does, more than sufficient respect to cushion the reprobation.[11] It might be cushioned

somewhat more, and maybe the question dropped, by my calling attention to the fact—others have raised an eyebrow, but I don't really think
it is relevant—that he had not seen the production, although he had
heard reports (possibly from mutual friends across the bridge in Berkeley). What appeared to trouble him almost as much as what I had done
to Shakespeare's text was a directorial intelligence that had somehow
gone to waste. And that was a judgment he would hold to regardless of
what anybody thought of what happened in the theater or, then as in
the seventeenth century, any audience verdict that the performance was
successful (which, by the way, has never been for me any decisive criterion of the quality of a production, no less what we made of a text, which
was in my later work far more disruptive, and something else entirely.)[12]
Whatever he said of me, he was not nearly as kind, as he made his way
through history, about some of the actors or directors who had, with
more or less renown, attempted the redoubtable job of producing *King
Lear*, beginning with the infamous redaction by Nahum Tate, who in
1681 dealt with anything daunting by rewriting it almost entirely.

What Mack was really concerned with, as he assessed what I had
done, is the condition that made it possible, what he considers a form of
hubris, and what some are still contesting: the dangerous eminence of
the director in our theater.[13] That also has its history, though the presumptions seemed to be exacerbated as we moved into the sixties, before
the director too seemed dispossessed by the mystique of participation,
putting the text (if there was a text) at the mercy of group process and
the rising hegemony of the "performer." With the incursion upon theater of energies from the other arts (happenings, action events, rituals,
environments) or the appropriation of theatricality by the other arts
(leading in minimalism and conceptualism to the dematerialization of
the art-object), the idea of the performer (and then performance art) was
dissociated from the traditional actor, who was marked and disempow-
ered by an unbecoming subservience to the plotted schematics of character in the canonical text. As we started rehearsals of *King Lear*, we were
on some sort of wobbling pivot amidst these changes and transitions,
though still with a sense of reverence about the canonical text, and with
actors of somewhat different methods in a large, continuous, and fairly
coherent company (unusual in this country, even today), my authority
as director pretty much intact. As to what I actually did in the production, and what Mack construed it to be, it might be useful to approach
it through further reflection on actors and acting, directing, and the vicissitudes of practice, as that intersects with theory in relation to revi-

sionism, with another brief look in passing at the Renaissance stage. I might add that the way I think about it has long been affected by the work that was done on *Lear,* receding now in memory over the space of many years, as a matter of history itself, all the circumstances around it, no less what happened on stage, this night, that night, not easy to reconstruct. Whatever it is that makes history, I will be addressing what makes theater, with the liability that what I am saying is also revision.

Whatever misgivings one might have, there is surely justification for basing new interpretations of Shakespearean drama on the political character of the theater and the intercourse of social classes from the Liberties around it (the suburbs of lepers, the homeless, the whores) to the immediate vicinity of the stage, including the collaborative activity or potential performative anarchy that went into making the play. If such interpretations, revising the privileged readings of prior criticism, tend to privilege the text not merely as it was appropriated, as in the case of *Richard II* (regarding the Essex plot), but in certain kinds of appropriations—keeping tragedy in particular attached to politics, seeing through the aesthetic to threatened authority—these are not to be thought of, according to Jonathan Dollimore, as "a perversion of true literary reception, they were its reception."[14] Maybe so maybe not. But this view of the matter stops short of what concerns me here, and what the whole history of drama has been warning us about, nowhere more alarmingly than in Shakespeare's plays. The warning amounts to this: however it came into being (*before* it became an institution), *theater is not to be trusted,* no less with a sacred or an authorized text. If you work long enough in the theater, you know that as a matter of course, almost by instinct ("a great matter," said Falstaff [*1 Henry,* 4 2.4.299], who incarnates the idea), though theater is also a cover-up with various kinds of denial. You do not have to wait for performance, or a critique of the oedipal drama, you can see it in any rehearsal, including those with directors and actors who used to claim that the performance was a rehearsal, closure always deferred, and that anything resembling enactment was unmediated, inimitable, in a surface full of intensities beyond representation. They might have been reading Derrida, though it is just as likely that he, like other French theorists—Lyotard certainly, Cixous, Kristeva, Deleuze—was turned on by the Living Theater when, in one of the legendary insurrections of the spectacle of '68, it disrupted the festival at Avignon, shrine of Jean Vilar, leading to soul-searching postmortems by intellectuals on the Left.

The actors who were performers who were political activists were openly and clamorously so, but they may have been, through the "polymorphous perversity" of the sixties, models for scholarship too, as it rethought "the shape-shifting of actors" on the Elizabethan stage. It's as if, in a curious inversion of history, the performers of the sixties were prototypes or forerunners of those players who, in taking advantage of "the supposedly 'safe' space of the stage,"[15] disrupted binary thinking and initiated crisis. For while gender switches and cross-dressing had long been apparent, as conventional aspects of the play-within-the-play, it was not until after the sixties that we seemed to discover how radical it all was, as the Renaissance actors threatened, in more surreptitious or equivocal ways, "to reveal the artificial and arbitrary nature of social being,"[16] with its unstable or mutable categories that we are still deconstructing today. But there is more to be said of the shape-shifting, and Shakespeare has certainly said it. So far as that points to "the crisis of category," it is not merely, as Marjorie Garber insists, attributable to transvestitism (*VI*, 17), and while it may challenge "vested interests" related to dress, it exists when we are going naked on "the great stage of fools" (*Lear* 4.6.180), which is why to begin with, or so it seems to Lear, "the first time we smell the air / We waul and cry" (4.6.176–77).

You do not have to dress up in drag to shift categories. Think of somebody you loved or knew as well yourself, who in the instant seems to be someone else, or think, really, of how little you knew yourself. Or in the blush of self-knowledge, think of the thousand deceits practiced upon yourself, of which you more than anyone—whatever else you don't know—are really well aware. If there is a crisis of category, it also exists within, like that "which passeth show" (*Hamlet* 1.2.85), though sometimes there is the appearance, right before your eyes, of what you never dreamed. Or like a "prologue to the omen coming on" (1.1.123), perhaps you did. (Do we remember lines like that simply because they are canonized?) "What, has this thing appeared again tonight?" (1.1.21). If it does there is a problem, but any actor can tell you that if it doesn't it's even worse, for there's no performance without it, or really not much of a play. It should be obvious I'm not really talking of the character of the Ghost (and what on earth is that?) but of something that inspirits any character, or whatever it is that becomes of it when, as in some revisionist productions, character is dismembered, disseminated, passed from actor to actor, or virtually banished from the stage. More importantly, for our own "darker purpose" (shifting back to *Lear* 1.1.36), what all this ghosting comes to is what the new historicists tend to elide, and that is an ontological factor (condition or/and consequence?) in the idea of theater itself, reflecting as you see it the duplicity of seeing, which is always inadequately thought of when thought of as social construction.

Wherever the theater came from, in the dark backward and abysm of time, the best to be done by construction was somehow to try and contain it, as Plato understood, knowing that it would fail; or Nietzsche, for whom in *The Birth of Tragedy* it had not failed enough. That the problem could be devastating we have seen in the drama itself, not only the plays of Shakespeare, but in the dramaturgy of shifting shapes from *The Bacchae* of Euripides to *The Balcony* of Genet, both of which are conducting an inquest into the origins of theater itself. This is revisionism with a vengeance, as if the cover-up were historicism. As we move from the god of theater at the festival which bears his(?) name to the Funeral Studio in the Grand Brothel where all the scenarios end in death, we are being asked to remember, in all its transfigured horror or ideological ameliorations—including the smugness of the demystifiers, like the Envoy in *The Balcony*—what the institution is really about. The same with the plays of Beckett, who really thought it appalling, which is precisely what Didi said, "AP-PALLED," nor did he revise his opinion when he looked at the maw of the audience, sitting there in the dark, and called it a "charnel-house!"[17]

I know the discourse on origins as either deceit or illusion, and its notion that beginnings are always already begun. But any time you start a rehearsal, and the shape-shifting seems to occur, it is as if you are back in an ancient clearing where (the) theater seems to emerge *from whatever it is it is not,* though the moment of emergence may occur with such shape-shifting subtlety that you can think it were already there, or as we say about one kind of powerful acting, coming from who knows where, maybe the actor least of all. And then, a little more than kin, there is also the other kind, "who do not do the thing they most do show, / Who, moving others, are themselves as stone" (Sonnet 94, ll. 2–3), bringing the effect of estrangement to the very pitch of appearance. The finest of all manuals of acting, as I've said to acting teachers, is Shakespeare's *Sonnets,* from which we once made a theater piece called *Crooked Eclipses,*[18] working through the ceaseless permutations of the impasse of appearance: "What is your substance, whereof are you made, / That millions of strange shadows on you tend?" (53, ll. 1–2). This is the sort of insoluble question that is hard pressed in critical theory, with its now congenital wariness of substance, essence, authenticity. Yet, with the metonymic shadows on the monosyllabic *tend,* asking for attendance, it has the sort of microvigilance at the heart of deconstruction, so exquisitely made, however, it escapes it into perception, while leaving behind some uncertainty about who is looking at whom.

It is by the tendency of those shadows that one may see the difference between Shakespeare's view of performance, the ear and eye required for it, and current notions of masquerade, or the more nuanced notion of performativity, defined by Judith Butler, in relation to gender particularly, as *"a stylized repetition of acts"* that are "internally discontinuous," so that "the *appearance of substance* is precisely that, a constructed identity, a performative accomplishment that the mundane social audience, including the actors themselves, come to believe and to perform in the mode of belief."[19] As for the cultural materialists or new historicists, who also reject foundational truth, the substance they are looking for is of another order entirely: instead of strange shadows, not only compelling the gaze, but parsing it in the process, strange accidents or contingencies, subject to "thick description," so you move in a blink from the wink (the two of them differentiated) into the domain of knowledge/power (monarchy, hierarchy, class relations), where no matter how you look it is an economy of exchange in which any talk about millions is talk about money.

Well and good, and often fascinating, but whatever this reveals about the institution of Shakespeare, what is falling between the cracks is what Shakespeare institutionalized, which is the limitless deceits of appearance suffusing all other thematics, what makes them all in performance subject to revision. As for the incapacity of a text, the drama, or language to stabilize appearance, Hamlet sets it down in his tables with hallucinatory precision. It's as if the visible itself were contaminated by any effort to record it, no less when it is recorded the vanity of playing it back, as if the really apparitional were the shape-shifting thing itself, embodied there in the flesh, but when you really think it over, stinking to high heaven. Which returns us in its mortality to the insupportable world of *Lear.* "Do you smell a fault?" (1.1.15), yes, but we are not quite sure how to read it. From the outset of the play, history seems to fail us, as if from the very beginning it has revised itself away, or is already the nightmare from which we are trying to awaken, so that at ground zero of value, the tabula rasa of the heath, the capacity to read at all finally comes under assault: "Read," says the King to the blind man. "What, with the case of eyes?" (4.6.141–42). Make the case as you wish, can anybody read it better?

One must have a heart of stone not to be moved by the scene between Gloucester and Lear, but if you are doing revisionist history, there is not only a problem with substance or authenticity, but with the presumption of empathy too. Or at least there was when Greenblatt was first refashioning the Renaissance. He does so at one point by moving from Spenser, Marlowe, and Machiavelli to modernization in the Middle East, where the problem was, according to the sociologist Daniel Lerner (who is read as the voice of the West), to replace the constrictive personality of rigidly structured societies with something like the mobile, adaptable sensibility of our humanistic tradition. Such a process seemed to require "the ability to insert oneself into the consciousness of another," but beneficial as it appeared to be, "an act of imaginative generosity, a sympathetic appreciation of the situation of the other,"[20] the conclusion is inevitable: empathy was the agency of bourgeois imperialism, both creative and destructive, but weighted toward the malign. Or to put the worst complexion on it, as Greenblatt actually does, "what Professor Lerner calls 'empathy,' Shakespeare calls 'Iago'" (*RSF*, 225), who not only enters consciousness, but takes it over as well. If you are committed to protecting difference, you want no part of that, but if you happen to be an actor, otherness is your vocation, and if you do not want to play Iago, you had better give it up.[21] (I have never known an actor who wouldn't, as one said, give his "eye-teeth" for the part, or maybe sell his soul; or hers, since I have also known women who wanted to play him, for reasons not as obvious as one might think.) However insidiously, by whatever name—and at whatever psychic risk—the actor of any substance will cherish the capacity to cross all difference, of race or gender or class, or categories yet unthought, animal, vegetable, mineral, since there are various kinds of theater (and innumerable acting exercises) likely to think them up.

Confronted with defensiveness about difference, or subject positions, an actor may back off, but in secret heart and sullen craft, and sometimes vociferously, will insist that there is no role in heaven or on earth, nothing living or dead, that s/he can't play if given the chance. That some revisions will take place in the process seems part of the order of things, though revisionism itself has changed the order of things, as when Olivier played Othello, who was (we suppose) originally played by a white man, which is more problematic today (no less the use of black face, or mannerisms presumably black), call it colonization if you will. There were no doubt certain virtues when Paul Robeson played Othello, or Laurence Fishburne recently on film, but is it incorrect to ask, given the provenance of the text, how many degrees of identification make a diminished thing? to use Professor Mack's comment on what we did to *Lear*. Or is it only a matter of the quality of the actor? and if so, what happened to difference? Or is it that the issue of difference itself is a shape-shifting thing? about which there is already a lot of equivocation (beyond the professional matter of providing more roles for blacks) as we face the empathic risk of interracial casting, or—as in the Mabou Mines production or Robert Wilson's in Frankfurt—a woman playing Lear, one younger, one older. And what do we do with age? as they did in the Moscow Art Theater, where a woman of sixty might have been playing Cordelia, or even Juliet? Or do we have to develop an ethic in which every gain is a loss?

About the risk of casting itself, it should be said that that is the first reduction, if the role has any dimension, simply because this body, that voice, whatever the actor's resources, is always something other than what may also be imagined (and the actors who are not cast are always telling you that). Yet it may be precisely the reduction that, like the stringency of an aesthetic, opens up other prospects that would not exist without it. With a role like Lear it is almost unimaginable (and this is traditionally said) that any actor can do it all, but as it happened, the actor who did it for us could, in another sense, do the unimaginable. Perhaps that was true to begin with, since Michael O'Sullivan was only twenty-eight years old at the time. But whatever it was he might not bring to the part, he had several things going for him: he was born ineffably old, as if he had lived three lives; he was selfish, yet loving, with almost incredible charm; and with an image of his father running at high speed down the corridor from his office and shattering a plate glass window to end his life below, he was early on intimate with madness. That there was reason to it, even cunning, he also seemed to convey, as if in embracing the developing syndrome he might even invite you in, so that even before we did it, there was something cat and mouse, which is how he played the demented Lear taunting Cordelia's soldiers sent to bring him from the heath: "Come, an you get it, you shall get it by running. Sa, sa, sa, sa!" (4.6.198–99). Young as he was, Michael was an actor with superb craft, who could move like a sylph, a boomerang, a guided missile, but when the madness took over, *in the text,* you could never quite tell what he would do, or *when,* because he saw the madness before you, or saw it where you didn't, actable, no doubt, but not knowable until he did it, improvisation in his bones, including sometime later the unexpected way—of course, we should have known it—he took his own life.

"Read thou this challenge; mark but the penning of it?" "Were all thy letters suns, I could not see" (*Lear* 4.6.137–38). There are, to be sure, methodological differences about the usages of empathy, focused in our time by the distantiation of Brecht, but proleptically adjusted in the world of *Lear* by Gloucester's painful response to the King's unrelenting insistence—"yet you see how this world goes"—"I see it feelingly" (145–47). Whatever the challenge in the text, wherever, that remains the indisputable datum of any method I know. One might say that it is the very definition, or dead-end recourse, of psychological acting, which Maynard Mack posited as my basic problem with the play, when he spoke of "a group of Method actors" (28) who were not exactly that. Yet to stay with the datum of method, which is inevitably synesthetic: even through mask and ritual it is very much the same. A Chinese actor before performance gazes upon his mask, and for three hours or more summons up its spirit as the feeling sinks in. What moves a performance is seeing it thus, even through the subtle fascination of the phantasmic *yugen* in the figurations of the Noh, which is not only an impelling power but, as felt in evanescence, the theater's consummation.

Brechtian distance may resist it, but does not invalidate that. He is put off by mystification, and the rigid, archaic societies that produced it, but was nevertheless fascinated by Chinese acting, which he worked into his conception of the alienation-effect after seeing Mei Lan-fang's company perform in Moscow.[22] Nor did he, as he explained at various times, including an essay on Chinese acting, really exclude feelings, emotions, or empathy in the interests of estrangement, or retaining for the actor the capacity to make distinctions. "The alienation-effect intervenes, not in the form of absence of emotion, but in the form of emotions which need not correspond to those of the character displayed" (*BT*, 94). But sometimes, too, they do correspond, and they seem to be very close to Brecht's emotions, as when his Galileo, defending his experiments against the princes of the Church, displays intemperately what he maybe should not. "I believe in reason,"[23] he insists, and so I did, in more than method, when I directed Brecht's play shortly after our production of *Lear*, in which reasoning not the need there is reason in madness too.

In the first sentence of his book, Mack writes: "*King Lear* is a problem" (3). He went on to define it through historical attitudes about its unplayability, but the real problem, as I see it, is that at almost any distance, on the page as on the stage, we are dealing with an experience that cuts to the brain. And if it does not do that, believe as we must in reason, we are hardly dealing with it at all. There are other ways to approach it, warding off or risking feeling, but what we called the subtext came from the "tempest in [the] mind" which from the senses takes "all feeling else / Save what beats there" (*Lear* 3.4.13–14). Where? Not merely in what Jameson might call, as a kind of subtextual agenda, "the political unconscious," but in whatever we could summon up as a credible affective equivalent to what we felt accountable *there,* as we moved from horror to horror, smelling our way to Dover, or wondering why "a dog, a horse, a rat, have life," and Cordelia "no breath at all" (5.3.306–7). Or where it really came from, as he tries to push it down, the King's "Hysterica passio" (2.4.55), and (before it came up in theory) why it was gendered feminine, not forgetting the absent mother. As we thought about all that, trying to make sense of the utterly insensible, we drew on "sense memory" and "emotional memory" (Stanislavski's terms), and anything else that would not suspend but structure disbelief, which was not "merely a matter of building a rational stream of consciousness underneath a series of rational objectives—the two move, according to Newtonian laws, in equal and opposite directions." In speaking of a subtext, we were "speaking of a *world,* with an atmosphere and a subterranean life; an environment formed by the dark gods" (*IT,* 283)—and while some of the actors were, I was not particularly Jungian, but only reading the text. It is a process that may be taken even further in the theaters of the East, where the actors seem to be moved, whatever the words they are saying (some of them arcane) by some unwritten, subliminal, or "fantasy text." That is the term we used for the extremity of a subtext, which in the eastern forms, when there actually is a text, amounts to a kind of revision (can it be a subversion?) that realizes the other, or somehow evokes it. I have seen old people in Kyoto during performance fingering the manuscript— ruminative over the parchment, or dozing into memory—as if it were written in Braille.

At the time we were doing *King Lear,* I was as conscious of the difference between eastern and western theater conventions as I was of "those who tell me," as some still do, "that Shakespeare's verse ought to speak for itself," which prompted me to write: "In my scholarship, I revere the text as much as anybody, but on stage we are dealing with suicidal rage and earth-shattering self-contempt; with a vengeance so awful it penetrates through chaos; and with the maddened clairvoyance of a pariah king" (*IT,* 286) whose sense of injustice is such that, defying representation, it seems to unhinge the universe. Whatever they did in Shakespeare's age, for whatever Right Reason or not, what I have described is surely there, and the problem still remains, at least it does for the theater: how do we think it and do it now? and can we do it without revision? and what do we mean by that? If Elizabethan homilies on order and degree are not quite up to it, neither are the Foucauldian discourses of power, though either may be useful in thinking about the play, which also pushes the limits of our realistic acting tradition, which persists as much in critical theory as it does in the theater. I have rarely (if ever) read any scholarship that, even in deconstructing character, or going back in queer theory to the boy that played the role, does not move the shape-shifting of the actors back to that tradition, with a certain amount of talk about decentering and fragmentation, or the breakdown of the ego, or the psychology now gendered, colored, ethnicized in the psychodynamics of power.

When we were doing *Lear,* the drama offered us, as now, the remembered energy of its conventions, but racked upon the wheel of "its compulsively brilliant psychology." Unless displaced by other conventions, that revives the other problem, "how to say the words" (*IT,* 286), especially the most astonishing, while letting the heavens loose, cracking nature's molds, all "germens" spilling at once (*Lear* 3.3.8). As I see them still, these are not merely history's seeds spilled upon the ground, as in Benjamin's view of allegory in the German *Trauerspiel*,[24] which has come to the rescue now in postmodern theory. We were not reading in these terms then, but given the way we thought, trying to act upon it, it's as if Heidigger's Being were no mere concept being argued away, but—in the flesh—simply annihilated. As performance has entered theory, taking possession of consciousness, the body has moved to the foreground, accrediting perception or validating truth, or turning it into illusion. So: should it be shown in the flesh? And if an actor is going to do it, the question is how much? This remains a legitimate question, though deterred by any limit or faced with any taboo, sooner or later, inevitably, we will want to see more—and the return of the repressed is always revision.

To the degree, however, that the theater itself is a function of repression, there are things in its imaginings it may not want to show. Or show in other ways, by other means, perhaps from other cultures. As Brecht said of Chinese acting, there are "transportable" techniques (*BT,* 95), and by now they are very widely used. Yet even the most revisionist productions, deploying such techniques, still meet the problem of credibility on realistic grounds, unless they are the purest parody, which is the constant liability of postmodern performance. And even then, the criteria inherited from realism may be unavoidable on a western stage, which was certainly true of Wilson's *King Lear* when I saw it in Frankfurt, despite all the brilliant stylization of which he is certainly capable. For no sooner the text was spoken, with a semblance of a plot, there was no alternative: even with furtive and fractured characters, the actors had to ante up (you could feel it in your body), though nothing in the production could really accommodate that. As for doing the play in its entirety—which some immunity of the centuries (or is it anesthesia?) now permits us to read without the age of reason's impulse to revise it away—how in the world to meet its intolerable demands? When we did *King Lear* in the sixties, techniques from other cultures were, like Brechtian alienation (or his plays), not widely known at all, though we were already searching for other conventions. There was, for instance, at the end of the trial in the hovel, the extrusion of a departure, by King and Fool and madman, into the long dilatory diagonal of a nakedly grievous exit, reversing the drawn-out entrance that Japanese actors make, on the ramp of the *hashigakari*, where each movement is a millennium that, with revolving voluminous garments, seems to create an eternal space. As Edgar sang "Child Roland to the dark tower came," there was in the recessions of madness, with a dancelike turning back, the pivoting lyric of a pilgrimage, with abstracted solicitous gestures, the *gestus* of self-delusion, to what they would rather forget, coaxing each other to fantasy and, for the infantilized moment, even exchanging shapes, before they were led by Gloucester ("a walking fire" [3.4.107]) through a ravaged backdrop, a pitiless assemblage, to the next level of misery in the mythopoeic dark.

And how do we deal with that? If *King Lear* is impossible, as older critics thought—the mad King unactable (Lamb), or the drama too huge for the stage (Bradley)—that is not for want of discerning what is actable and knowable. The more we know about some of it the less actable it becomes, though recent scholarship may be giving us reasons for forgetting, deflecting, or minimizing that. For along with what we are now told of the shape-shifting of the actors—which seems to me on the more accessible side of the opacity of appearance, what makes *Lear*, for instance, want to anatomize Regan (and not merely to verify the actor's gender)—there has been an epistemological shift in the object of knowledge itself, away from the autonomous and unforgiving text to its sociopolitical genesis, or the historical contingencies in the cultural formations behind it. Whether or not they have read any of the new historicisms—neomarxist, feminist, Foucauldian, or multicultural—directors will vary as they always did in what they choose to represent, or what, given certain actors, is beyond representation, though whatever it is in theory you are always guessing at that. Mack was right for the wrong reasons: what may be an impediment is our acting tradition, even if you have the most splendid of actors, putting aside the resurrection of those who performed at the Globe. (Here my guess is that, looked at from the perspective of *King Lear* in our time, we would be appalled at their inadequacy.) We thought about other means, but unlike the Noh drama—which was actually already a relic, largely now for tourists, like Shakespeare performed at Stratford—"there is no emblematic short-hand for developing characterizations in the Shakespearean tradition. There is no gesture for storm except the whole being of the actor, checked by the skepticism of our realistic expectations" (*IT,* 286), which even in cyberspace are not likely to change in our time.

With my KRAKEN group in the seventies, we developed techniques for rethinking dramatic texts by reconstituting them entirely, as we did with a derivation from *Hamlet* named *Elsinore.* Over the course of a year, in a series of improvisations (too complex to detail here), we worked our way through every facet and refraction of Shakespeare's text, playing sequences over and over, so there were simultaneously present multiple figurations, or "ghostings," not only of character—shadows doubles allusions quotes (a fragment, perhaps, or "A piece of him" [*Hamlet* 1.1.20])—but of themes, images, phrases, even interpretations, of which in a passing moment there might be several going at once, as if in re-membering *Hamlet* no view of it would be lost, but turned over and over, then seen from another perspective, and checked out again in the text.

Each of the actors, with no roles ever assigned, knew from memory the entire play, from which they could by reflex summon up any word or image or passage that, in the instant, somehow seemed germane. It was as if, in this process, there were no other language than *Hamlet,* from which we developed in time, as if the hermeneutic had stolen upon us, teasing us out of thought, a sort of hypertext, with an incursion of other words. What we had to say about the Ghost, the garden, the Court, the closet scene, the duel, was sifted, condensed, impacted into performance, merging or collaged with Shakespeare's text, in an orches-tration of disintegrating images, with voice-overs and playbacks, a sort of analytical diary in the shape of a concrete poem, all of it impeccably scored. If that came, out of improvisation, from the sort of "ratiocinative meditativeness" that Coleridge ascribed to *Hamlet,* making the play a subtext, or the world in which it occurs, *Elsinore* was a theorization in ideographic form. To the extent, however, that there were in all the

ghostings not only images of the "original," but intimations of remembered character, the performance was still subject, even in its strangeness, and strange it really was (in the duplicities of appearance, more like
the "strangeness" of subatomic physics), subject to the skepticism of realistic expectation, which is—with the "ethos of suspicion" turned back
upon itself—the test of theory too.

Mack's objection to the notion of a subtext was part of his critique
of what he considered the long illusory project—in theater and in criticism, from Tate and Johnson to Bradley and Empsom—of bringing
some kind of regularizing pattern to what, in *King Lear*, is bizarre, absurd, barbarous, unassimilable. As I have suggested, there was no such
intention at all, though there is such a thing, as in the storm itself, as an
order of amazement, or even, as I wrote about the music for it, "chaos
dazzled by its own coherence" (qtd. in *KL*, 35). The precision of a disorder, which Mack surely perceived in the text, seemed to puzzle him,
however, as an idea of performance, which is, to be sure, always subject
through resistance to the imitative fallacy. With reservations still persisting, he nevertheless quoted with admitted fascination my long "hypnotic
account" of how the music worked with the actors, through all the contingent hysteria, for a unison of derangement that was, as he thought,
almost balletic.

However the storm is done, it may remain an insuperable task, but so
far as we approached it, Mack is right about the subtext having provided
for the disjunct speeches and gestures of the actors "some sort of organic
and, as it were, psychosomatic continuum" (33). What he did not say
is that, given the nature of the materials, the harrowing experience, the
continuum was in danger of breaking down the closer to it we came.
Actually, he did not so much object to the idea of a subtext in the conventional sense, nor to what I had written about language as gesture,
"that there is a life to which the words give life," and as perceived there
in the words, it was to that we felt responsible. What disturbed him
once again was that something fairly sensible would "with very little
stretching" make the words expendable. "Let me say this: we lost
words." But after describing the incredible amount of detailed activity
in the sustained lunacy of the scenes on the heath, the interwoven mania
of the King, the Fool, and Tom—far from unintelligible, even more
intelligible—I remarked about the issue: "To the extent that the words
are the life of the design, we did everything we could to respect them.
Even our improvisations were not emancipated from the text" (qtd. in
KL, 33–34), but read it backwards and forwards, turned it over, tried it

again, drove into it like an augur bit, as low as to the fiend's, "the sulphurous pit; burning, scalding, stench, consumption" (*Lear* 4.6.127–28), looking for "the clearest gods" (4.6.73). If what I said was not convincing, it does seem a little ironic that Mack could not see the justification in what Shakespeare actually wrote, not only for Gloucester, but whether for Edgar or Albany (there is a textual dispute) at the summary end of it all: "Speak what we feel, not what we ought to say" (5.3.325).

Of course, the new historicists might have a jaundiced view of that, since order is still unstable, and under the martial circumstances they are still the words of power. How are they to be said? and whoever it is that speaks, can we take him at his word? Speaking for myself, I prefer to read them, at least partially, as Mack would read them, that is, assuming for the historical moment that they are, let us say, relatively sincere. If we need an analogy for that of the kind used by the new historicism, think of Nelson Mandela and F. W. de Klerk as they went in South Africa through its transition of power. If it were Mandela who spoke, I suppose that most of us would believe him more, but regardless of what followed after, if it were de Klerk, my sense would be that he is, at the historical moment, relatively sincere. But putting aside the jaundice, suppose we believe the words? and in any subsequent performance—of *King Lear* or other plays—even act upon them? The problem then, like seeing it feelingly, is that it somewhat imperils the text. And what if I don't feel it? should I say the words at all? a common problem with Method actors seeking a personal truth, or who, at the limit of subjectivity (as James Dean or Brando did) think acting is a sham. Following on the sixties, there were also the sort of actors who, from an ideological perspective, might think the text a sham, or in redefining subjectivity would strike a certain passage or refuse to say the words. We will soon be coming to that, but I want to stay with the words that, whether or not you can take them, may be impossibly right.

As we saw with Samuel Johnson, but for other reasons yet, an important motive in revisionism is what we want to forget, just as much of what we hear in the theater we somehow manage to screen out, or at least, when it is as devastating as it is in *Lear*, the life that gives life to the words. This is also true of the possibility that all the world's a stage, which is all right to say in the theater (or as a romantic joke) so long as it passes away, like the insubstantial pageant itself. Are we supposed to take that seriously? where? and to what extent? In the utterly mediated "society of

the spectacle" (Debord) or the superfetation of image in the age of simulacra (Baudrillard) the ironies are manifold, but what should be apparent in what I've been saying is that, with all the work on Shakespeare's
theater, revising our view of Shakespearean drama, we seem to be forgetting what, in its relation to theater, the drama already knows: that something is slipping away in the friction between them—theater betraying
the drama, the drama suspicious of theater—and not only when it is
performed near the bear gardens, brothels, and leprosariums, or for that
matter, in Whitehall before the King. In any case, but especially in the
case of eyes (now a discourse of the gaze), we need to think it over when
using Shakespeare's theater as the key to Shakespeare's drama, whether
we are studying it in the classroom or thinking of doing the play. What
the new historicists describe as especially germane to the theater of
Shakespeare's age appears to be so, but even more so are the ceaseless agi-
tations of appearance, what beats there, where? anywhere you look, on
stage, off stage, precisely because you look, something more than a dialectic of appearance and disappearance. No wonder you have to revise.

In the theater we call it rehearsal, doing it over and over until we get
it right, and then the director says, "Do it again!" But you don't merely
want to repeat it because that would only be the Same, and that's not
"it," we'd better do it again. The problem is the referent, we are never
quite sure what it is, though it is right there in the text, like "The murmuring surge / That on th'unnumb'red idle pebble chafes" . . . brain
turning on the abyss, you either have to look away, or hear it with "deficient sight" (*Lear* 4.6.20–23). I've often thought that the problem of
textuality is summed up in those lines, with the uninterpretable immensity of that murmur in the surge nevertheless as particular as the un-
numbered pebble being chafed. "Set me where you stand," says the un-
knowing father to his still-anonymous son (4.6.25). *But where exactly is
that?* When we did it, I remembered a sequence from Beckett when
Hamm, after his counterclockwise navigation to the hollow of the chimney in the chamber in which they exist, orders Clov to push his wheel-
chair back to the center. And when Clov, begrudgingly in the vicinity,
gives it a little push, Hamm demands with ferocity that it be "in the
center!"[25] What impressed me when we did it was the manic exactitude,
which filtered down to the staging before the "suicide" in *Lear,* not here,
not there, but "Set me where you stand," the blinded father exactly in
the footsteps of the dispossessed son.

Is that what Shakespeare had in mind? Maybe so maybe not. I only
know what he wrote, though I've seen other productions of *Lear,* in

which I'm sure they studied the text, and thought he wrote something else. In short, the problem of revisionism is unavoidable *in* the theater, as it was for me in various mutations, long before it became an issue in our graduate schools.

Returning to basics, a simple case in point, before we come to the end: when I first started directing, back before the fifties, we used to insist that the actor be *line perfect* (that's the way we said it), on the assumption that the playwright's words, the text, had priority or authority over everything else in performance: acting, directing, lighting, stage design, whatever. Those were the days when we still used a prompter, that insidious figure in the brain of Artaud who would be baffled or banished in the theater of cruelty, or exiled in repetition to the brain of Derrida. As he rehearsed, in two empathic essays, the obsessive momentum of Artaud's thought, schizzy, alchemical, amniotic, my simple case was complicated with a sort of infinite text, "a verbal fabric, a logos which is *said* in the beginning,"[26] stealing the speech away *(la parole soufflée)* from another infinite text, a text that is a body, but a body without organs, "an existence that refuses to signify, or . . . a language without a trace."[27] What was, of course, peculiar about this language—which somehow left a trace on what we did with *King Lear*—is that its very disappearance seemed to be "the complete, sonorous, streaming naked realization" of the Eleusinian Mysteries, as Artaud himself declared, in a vertiginous takeoff from Plato into "the incandescent edges of the future."[28]

We were some light-years away from that when the prompter's main job, aside from keeping the actor who blanked unembarrassed in performance, was to keep a record during rehearsal of any violations of the text: a word left out, a phrase reversed, or never mind a line that is dropped, God forbid! a line inserted. The actor was given a list of lapses or delinquencies after a run-through, and it was his/her responsibility, no questions asked, to look at the text and *get it right* (again the way we said it). By 1957, however, we had done the first production of *Mother Courage* in this country, and while at first we were cool about it, devout in the A-effect, the questions began to be asked when, high on more than estrangement, the actors took Brecht to heart: why these words, not those? and why say it in any case? maybe we can do without them, or leaving nothing sacred, rewrite the bloody text. Before feminism came on the scene, there were women in rehearsal (most specifically my former wife) throwing the script away and crying out in critique, "I won't say those fucking lines!" Or in one improvisation, instead of saying nothing, Cordelia started to talk, and talk, and talk, repossessing speech until the King was forced to stop her, or left it to the director, who was playing a double game, having encouraged precisely what might undermine the playwright's and, if only for the moment, even his authority.

These were not, I should say, all narcissistic irruptions, and there was a point in rethinking *Galileo* when we turned Brecht's methods back upon him, as he had done himself in drastically rewriting the end of the play, incriminating Galileo, as a surrogate for modern scientists, after the bomb was dropped on Hiroshima. We were, after all, doing the play in San Francisco many years after he wrote it, and some years after the revision, at the height of the Cold War, when they talked of "The Balance of Terror," which was the title of a chapter in *The Impossible Theater* (all the chapters had titles from the rhetoric of the Cold War). "The Balance of Terror" began with reference to an array of articles I had talked about at the first rehearsal of *Galileo,* all but one from the previous day's newspaper, on a range of current issues: the "immense" probability of life elsewhere in the universe; the proliferation of nuclear weapons in a strategy of annihilation ("kill and overkill"); Red China's invasion of India, launched the previous day; the Ecumenical Council's debate on liturgy reforms, including the use of modern languages instead of the traditional Latin (which Galileo in the play, back in the Renaissance, writes about ironically to his spiritual advisor); and then, of most immediate urgency, President Kennedy's speech—reported the day of that first rehearsal—in which he announced a quarantine of Cuba and the decision to board all ships bearing Soviet missiles to that island (see *IT,* 87–88). If, during the course of the work on *Galileo,* some of the actors took issue with Brecht, affecting the text, what engaged them was also being debated in public.

All of the issues, public and private, questions of politics and questions of subjectivity, had the immediate virtue of forcing us to examine in contestation, whether we changed them or kept them, why the words were there in the first place, how inevitable they really were, and what might be lost or gained by any substitution. The peculiar thing is— though this may be unfathomable to scholars other than Mack—that such apparently invasive procedures may very well be, as they elsewhere say of the body, in the interests of the text (which, if it cannot quite speak for itself, might want by any means to make itself understood).

While this became in my later work a fully articulated methodology, in which the procedure became the work, dispossessing the text entirely, becoming another thing, maybe closer to the thing itself, we never went so far in our treatment of *King Lear.* What the actors spoke, as I have said, is what Shakespeare actually wrote, and the text was done in its entirety, so far as that has been established. That there was for all our deference a contestation with the text was not at all the case in the theater when the actors—who might have been amused by notion of an oedipal drama, but horrified by the death of the author—were still being dutifully line perfect, with mainly the sort of questions that were once, at the time of the New Criticism, debated as the Intentional Fallacy (a fallacy, ironically enough, now being attributed to the new historicists).[29]

These would seem to be the kind of actors, some of them very good, that Maynard Mack would want, but the mandate of line perfection went through radical changes over the years in which Brecht and Artaud were tutelary figures in the theater, as they also were in theory, which we have seen in Derrida. More than Saussurian, the early Barthes was Brechtian, and even later on, in the solipsistic *Barthes by Barthes,* he feels reproached by Brecht, for being insufficiently political, unengaged, or "as if he were the historical witness of a contradiction: that of a *sensitive, avid, and silent* political subject. . . ."[30] As for Foucault, his "theatrum philosophicum" came, by way of the "phantasmaphysics" of Deleuze, its "epidermic play of perversity,"[31] from the un(en)gendered, imageless, organless body of Artaud, which also had an effect on the reading-as-writing-as-performance inherited from Barthes, eroticizing the text, "the language lined with flesh . . . , throwing, so to speak, the anonymous body of the actor into [the] ear: it granulates, it crackles, it caresses, it cuts, it comes: that is bliss."[32] There was, we recall, much talk of pleasure, which certainly altered readings, and if it turned out that the *jouissance* was too gamy and too much, not everybody up to it, performance did become a way of "doing" theory, as well as a heuristic idea across the disciplines. And where subverting identity takes over from subverting texts, performance is sometimes confused with performativity.

If all this accounts in considerable measure for the anxiety over revisionism, my view of the matter is that the liability would be there, and was there, in the most conventional theater, as it is, even desirably, in simply reading a book. Despite his cranky defense of the canon, that is still pretty much the position of Harold Bloom, who is, in his Freudian/Gnostic version of Emersonian transcendentalism, both downright pragmatic—what's this poem good for? and what can it do for me?—

and the strictest of all revisionists. "We read to usurp, just as the poet writes to usurp. Usurp what? A place, a stance, a fullness, an illusion of identification or possession; something we can call our own or even ourselves."[33] Does this mean you can read any way you wish? Certainly you can, though if I were to have consulted Lacan in the matter, he would have assured me—unlike Bloom, who thinks there are failures of courage—that you can read no other way, that even for the most scrupulous scholar seeking meaning in a text, interpretation is desire, unless stopped by ideology, simply unappeasable, desire producing desire, which erases the hermeneutic with Deleuze's desiring-machine. It is a machine that works only when it breaks down, "and by continually breaking down,"[34] like the aphasic momentum of Beckett, given to repetition, forever revising itself, like Hamm in *Endgame,* the mirror stage of his blindness, a truncated Hamlet behaving like Lear looking, but over and over, down the sockets of Gloucester's eyes, as if no end to revising the abyss.

If there is still, today, a rhetoric of desire, it is not quite breaking down in the same way: a little shorter perhaps on deferral (as understood through *différance*), and with enough ideological stoppage to put another spin—as Lacan himself receded, history coming forth—on the problem of revisionism. As for all this compulsive revisionism, among the things to which Mack objected, in my production and Peter Brook's, was a certain Beckettian presence—with ever diminishing returns in a flux of decomposition—although that was compounded in my case by something more Genetic (not in the sense of the Intentional Fallacy). And indeed, I had staged *Endgame* in 1959 and Genet's *The Balcony* in 1961, just as we were starting to work on the conception of *Lear.* Whatever it turned out to be, if you had seen it and the other productions, you would have seen the affinities, and the same reality principle, "A Subtext Based on Nothing," which was the title of the article Mack had read. The diminishment in question was in a sense a kind of accretion, the nothing coming of nothing, producing from one excruciating, perverse, mind-blowing event to another, like the movement through a needle's eye or the warped gravity of a black hole, the psychic thrust and emotional velocity that brought us to the cliffs of Dover, where you had to see with deficient sight (beyond the magnitude of the stage) the "crows and choughs that wing the midway air," showing "so scarce as beetles"; or hanging halfway down, "the one that gathers sampire—dreadful trade," who seems at that distance "no bigger than his head"; or the fishermen upon the beach that look like mice; or (is it in the residuum of phallocratic imagination? or some rockabye remembrance of the phallic mother?) "yond tall anchoring bark, / Diminished to her cock; her cock, a buoy [pun?] / Almost too painful for sight" (*Lear* 4.6.13–20).

All of this came, of course, from the incommensurability between Cordelia's little nothing and the King's volcanic response, leading to the diminution that dwarfs almost any other imaginable drama—so much so that every great actor (whatever size or shape, "Ay, every inch a king" [4.7.106]) has wanted to perform the role ("I will do such things" [2.4.275])—while directors like Brook are convinced that no reading, only performance, can bring its sprawling, unmooring, dazzling themes together. As it happens, I don't share that view at all. In the years I have spent in the theater (nearly forty) I directed a lot of plays, but have always had a tendency to believe that a staging in the mind (like that by Edgar on the cliffs of Dover) can exceed by far anything realizable on stage, which is why I tell my students—contrary to established pedagogy in dramatic literature—that, no, it is not necessary to go to the theater to really see the play; that, in fact, seeing a performance there, even if it is brilliantly acted, especially if it is brilliantly acted (however you determine that), often gets in the way of imagining it for yourself, though to do so with *Lear*—as in the stagings of Hamm in the camera obscura behind black specs—will if you see it cut to the brain.

As for my own stagings, as a reader, as a director, I know for sure that I have had things in mind, acute, far-reaching, maybe overreaching too, that still seem to me right there in the text, justifiable, waiting to be seen, that in production, with the finest of actors (and I have worked with many of them), have never made their way to the stage; yet other things I hadn't imagined, also justifiable when you look at the text, have somehow showed up there. "Look again, look again, / search everywhere," chant the Furies in the *Oresteia*,[35] of which we also made a theater work, *Seeds of Atreus*, drawing on, drawing out, what over the millennia still eludes us there, as if the impetus of the Furies were describing—with every method at your disposal, every conceivable way of looking—the necessity of interpretation since the beginning of western drama, leading to a trial at which there are different interpretations, and to resolve the impossible more than a little revisionist history. And so it is with the immensity of *Lear*, of which I can imagine another production, moving once again through the calculus of appearance in the tempest of the mind to the leap of deficient sight that, over the murmuring surge ("Ear, ear for the sea-surge, murmur of old men's voices:" wrote a poet with insufficient Greek, revising "poor old Homer, blind, blind"),[36] will somehow manage to hear it.

   Will all the words be spoken? Maybe so maybe not. Meanwhile, there is always the possibility that all the words will be there, read, studied, and the history behind them revised, but if the drama is going to be performed in any sense we understand, on stage, off stage, in a graduate seminar or in the privacy of the mind, unless we see it feelingly, there may be nothing there. Needless to say, that is not the nothing that comes of nothing, which is not at the promised end the most diminished thing.

(1998)

20. Limits of Performance

The Insane Root

A few prefatory remarks, theoretical, personal, before we get to the root, or at least the root of the title. What I want to reflect upon eventually are the limits of performance, to the degree that approaching those limits seems to resemble an obsessional neurosis, in theater as in sports or any activity exceeding itself, its very discipline not only demanding but threatening, perilous, self-punishing in extremis—as it may be in psychoanalysis, where the accretions of the subject's symptoms may push things to the limit. It is there, as Lacan remarks in his thesis on aggressivity as *"intended aggression,"* that "the analytic experience allows us to feel the pressure of intention," while the symptoms—hesitations, evasions, parapraxes, the improvised or calculated deceits, sullen breakings off, remorse, returns, excesses of renewed commitment, and then again the vacillations, the turning off or against, "recriminations, reproaches, phantasmic fears, emotional reactions of anger, attempts at intimidation"[1]— might constitute a repertoire familiar in the course of rehearsal, especially to the director, whose own pressures of intention may be arduous to the point of cruelty. I like to believe that Freud was right, however, when he observed "that the instinct for knowledge can actually take the place of sadism in the mechanism of obsessional neurosis. Indeed it is at bottom a sublimated off-shoot of the instinct for mastery exalted into something intellectual, and its repudiation in the form of doubt plays a large part in the picture of obsessional neurosis."[2]

It is the instinct for knowledge to which I'll also return, and to theater as heuristic, interrogative, a function of thought. But when I first began working with actors, the American theater was profoundly thoughtless; about the repudiation of the intellectual, next to no doubt at all, which accounted in part for my own obsessions—all of this registered in *The Impossible Theater: A Manifesto,* which I wrote in the early sixties,[3] anticipating the dissidence about to break out. Before that happened, however, psychological realism possessed the stage, and while there were multiple versions of it—not quite as polyvalent as performance is today (or, in "performativity," the bodies that presumably matter)[4]—the Method was dominant, with its subtexts and "emotional memory" and, as a legacy from Stanislavski, ratified by Freud, the activating assumption of an "inner life." Since then, with equivocal views of authenticity during the countercultural sixties, performance has passed through a period in which notions of interiority—like the Freudian unconscious itself or, as Lacan would have it, "the level of symbolic overdetermination that we call the subject's unconscious" (14)—have been something more than suspect. As depth acceded to surface in an age of the antiaesthetic, a developing jaundice about the inner life had its correlative of suspicion in the outer world of appearance, which, if not always what it appears to be, or only a shadow of it, was fetishized in the oedipal drama because of the shadow's shadow. To be sure, a renewed historical materialism would soon be monitoring that, with the zeal of demystification; and after the emergence of deconstruction, exposing everywhere you looked the sediments of metaphysics, it seemed as if there were nothing but nostalgia assuring the future of illusion.

But then, to all appearances, things seemed at the end of the real, if not perpetuating illusion, "proving theater by anti-theater."[5] Or so it was if we hearkened to Baudrillard, who described the immanence of visual culture as an obscenity of images, but warned those still vigilant over the deceits of representation that "it is dangerous to unmask images, since they dissimulate the fact that there is nothing behind them" (9). Which is another way of describing the vanity of psychoanalysis. Whatever it is that appears in the mise-en-scène of the unconscious can be produced, says Baudrillard, like "any other symptom in classical medicine," or as "dreams already are" (6), with the metaphysical sediments in the scenography of regression. As for the interpretation of dreams, that has been seriously threatened by "the liquidation of all referentials" (4) and, in the revolving causality of a vertiginous scene, the "dead and circular replies to a dead and circular interrogation" (17).

So much, then, for what Christopher Bollas calls "a kind of *counter-*

transference dreaming" or "unconscious communications"[6] in the site of the talking cure. At the dialogical impasse of "the negative transference . . . , the initial knot of the analytic drama" (Lacan, "Aggressivity," 14), psychoanalysis itself is a factitious performance, of which Baudrillard asks, what can it do "with the reduplication of the discourse of the unconscious in a discourse of simulation that can never be unmasked, since it isn't false either?" (6–7). It might very well be, as we passed through the Lacanian mirror into the precession of simulacra, that the ancient idea was consummated and that, finally, all the world *is* a stage, but who would have thought that as Prospero's insubstantial pageant faded, leaving not a wrack behind, it would be a stage on which "illusion is no longer possible, because the real is no longer possible" (38)? As Baudrillard sees it, the pageant no longer moves through an ontology of disappearance, nor—as all of human knowledge is miniaturized and mediatized, tipped into the hyperreal—with assent to that other talismanic proposition about the Theater of the World, the tenuous notion that life is a dream.

Yet sometimes, stubbornly or involuntarily, we incline to think it is. If dreams are wish fulfillment, so are, it also seems, the waking correlatives of dreams, or facsimiles, like accident or coincidence, which occur at times as if we wished them into being, as Solness seems to do with the appearance of Hilda Wangel in Ibsen's *The Master Builder,* a drama which seems to occur out of some weird and unfathomable debt at some limit of exceeding itself. "This all must have been in my thought," Solness says to Hilda, through the mirage of a mutual gaze. "I must have willed it. Wished it. Desired it. And so—doesn't that make sense?"[7] Maybe so, maybe not. Lacan might have described the scene as a "transaudition of the unconscious by the unconscious."[8]

What I am saying was occasioned, however, by a letter I received not long ago, just as I was reading again, for a seminar, *The Interpretation of Dreams.* It was written by a former student who became the production manager of my KRAKEN group, a nerve-racking job to which he brought, though he looked like an adolescent, extraordinary poise and sensitivity. Mature as he was even then, I still think of him as a young man, as I mostly think of myself as younger than I am, though as the body that knows the difference insists on what it is—neither cultural construct nor "incorporated space,"[9] some effect of the signifier on the subject—I make a point of accepting, in the inarguable debit of age, the down-to-earth performative being that, since the gravedigger put on the forceps, in the Beckettian view of birth (unalleviated by Bion or Jung), is a lot less long for this world.

The letter began with—and was apparently prompted by—a dream about my dying, and refusing to delay the end. It seemed remarkable in that it arrived while I was thinking particularly of those dreams in which Freud is concerned with his professional life and achievement, linked immediately after to absurd dreams about dead fathers. "Nor is it by any means a matter of chance," Freud writes, "that our first examples of absurdity in dreams relate to a dead father" (*S.E.* 5: 435). Now, why did I want such a letter? I suppose it was because I had been questioning myself recently about why—after nearly forty years of it, the last stretch of which was the richest, most conceptually audacious work I had ever done—I am not still doing theater. When that work ceased on the supposition that we might begin again, I started a book called *Take Up the Bodies: Theater at the Vanishing Point,* the vanishing point also marking the fact that at the dying end of financial reasons, I would not let it resume, though it was painful to leave it at that. Perhaps there was a lingering desire for assurance about the validity of that work, to which the letter—coming, as it said, out of the possibility of a midlife crisis, his present turmoil reaching back to mine—made the warmest testament; in short, the dream of my dying and refusing to delay the end, given the nature of the work, its manic obsession with disappearance ("doesn't that make sense?"), was somehow a confirmation.

What the work of KRAKEN also confirmed, at least as I remember it (or want to remember it) is that the theater, carnal, tactile, occurring in space and time, is nevertheless at ground zero a function of thought—which, according to Freud, is also true of dream, inhabiting as it does an autoscopical space in a diffusion of time. "We appear not to *think* but to *experience*," he writes in *The Interpretation of Dreams*; "that is to say, we attach complete belief to the hallucinations. Not until we wake up does the critical comment arise that we have not experienced anything but have merely been thinking in a peculiar way, or in other words dreaming" (*S.E.* 4: 50). In his essay on "Two Principles of Mental Functioning," Freud speaks of thinking, which permitted the psychic apparatus to tolerate increasing stimulus without premature discharge, as "essentially an experimental form of acting" (*S.E.* 12: 221). It is probable, he adds, that thinking was unconscious in the beginning, while the unconscious itself, as Freud conceives it, is our oldest mental faculty. Which is how, over the years, I have come to think of theater, particularly of its incipience: the precipitation of theater from whatever it is it is not, as if mere thought ("but thinking makes it so" [*Hamlet* 2.2.246–47]) had brought it into being. There are also the times when something happens in rehearsal, so stunningly what it is that you wonder where it came from, whether by method or madness, for it seems to be other than theater, out of some pressure of intention before it was even thought, which is—as with the ghosting in *Hamlet,* which gave us a method in KRAKEN[10]—precisely what keeps us thinking. This occurs with the liability that, at the filamenting nerve-ends of thought, where intention warps under pressure, there may be a loss of control—the experimental form of acting, *thinking,* no less impelled by that.

But let me move the issue to another level, working to the extremities or limits of performance, by changing the scene entirely, more or less bracketing the psychoanalysis (or letting that be implicit) but not the aggressivity, nor—as if the mirror stage were mirrored to the size of a football field—the images of "castration, mutilation, dismemberment, dislocation, evisceration, devouring, bursting open of the body, in short, the *imagos*" grouped together by Lacan "under the apparently structural term of *imagos of the fragmented body*" ("Aggressivity," 11).

"When you think about it, it is a strange thing that we do," said the New York Giants linebacker Jessie Armstead a couple of years ago, when the NFL was, as it still is, going through a reassessment of degrees of violence in the game, crack-back blocks, leg whips, face masks twisted, kicks in the groin, thumbs in the nostrils, fingers bent and bitten, or other vulnerable parts, gouged eyes, head butts, or after a smashing tackle, gratuitous elbows in the massive piling on. Not every player, coached to perform "like a bunch of crazed dogs," as Lawrence Taylor once put it, can do so with the marauding grace of his lethal instincts, but there is among the league's statistics a ferocious inventory of serious damage, surreptitious or flagrant, intended and unintended, from repeated quarterback concussions to shredded tendons, snapped clavicles, ripped ligaments in the line. "During a game we want to kill each other," Armstead remarked. "Then we're told to shake hands and drive home safely. Then a week later we try to kill each other again." This is not to mention the subtler brutalities of psychological dominance that may erupt, too, in physical violence, or the physical violence that goes the other way, as when, before Bill Parcells brought them together as teammates, the Bears linebacker Bryan Cox, stunned and upended by the Jets' 300-pound tackle Jumbo Elliott went down punching him in the ribs. As they grappled then on the ground, the simple question was this, posed by Elliott with his hands on Cox's throat: "Do you know who's in control of this situation?"[11]

It would seem that acting in the theater is a somewhat tamer game, but at the extremities of performance—where, when you think about it, a strange thing is being done, and in certain modes of performance, outside the precincts of theater (e.g., body art, from Viennese actionism to Chris Burden's crucifixion to Orlan's cosmetic surgeries), even stranger yet—the same question may be asked: "Do you know who's in control of this situation?" And indeed, if the performance does not rise to the level of that question—as it must, too, in the knot, the negative transference—it is not likely to be very much of a performance. Which is to say that, if we are really talking of limits, it must include the kind of performance that occurs in dubious peril just this side of a loss of control—not only strange but wondrous when the peril is only a seeming. If this is not quite the case with a wide receiver who, going up for the ball, risks being sliced in midair, it may be so with the actor who in a kind of hallucination, like the blinded Gloucester in *King Lear*, jumps from the cliffs of Dover— the "crows and choughs [winging] the midway air" (4.6.13)—or in conceiving a role like Macbeth, rehearses the impossible as if, as Banquo puts it after the witches vanish, having "eaten on the insane root" (*Macbeth* 1.3.84).

I may have been eating on that root many years ago, back in the early sixties, when I wrote—with a determined psychic violence and potential loss of control, feeling "like the lunatic Lear on the heath, wanting to 'kill, kill, kill, kill, kill!' "—the first paragraphs of *The Impossible Theater,* in which I said that "if politics is the art of the possible, theater is the art of the impossible. 'Seeming, seeming' is what it's made of," as if there were no future but the future of illusion, as Nietzsche believed and Freud had to concede, given the ineliminability of civilization's discontents. What I had in mind, more immediately, was the instrumentality of illusion and the demands on intelligence at the perceptual limits of the form. But given at the time, amidst the insanities of the Cold War, the woeful condition of our theater—institutionally, aesthetically, in every conceivable way, from the consensual humiliations of actors to the vacuity of most productions to the absence of continuity making for teamwork in performance—I added "that among the meanings of the word *impossible* I have in mind is the one you get when you say it raging with your teeth clenched."[12] I will not rehearse what has happened to the theater since, except to say that, as always, the impossible takes a little time, while the insanities persist, some of them undreamed of during the Cold War.

But let us stay at the limit of performance where doing the impossible, or nearly so, remains a constant dream, though what I have in mind at the moment is, if insanely rooted, also up in the air, and, as it turns out, if not without illusion, somewhere beyond seeming—as if performance were occurring somehow in phantasmic figures on the other side of the dream. For it is even higher up in the air than the body artist Stelarc, who thinks the body obsolete, and on that forbidding premise did a series of events—beautiful at a distance, at sites around the world: over the waves in Japan, above a street on the Lower East Side of Manhattan, and way above the Royal Theater in Stockholm—in which his body was suspended by fishhooks through the flesh. This transpired, no doubt, in "the dimension of a vital dehiscence" that might have sent the spectator, who happened to be on the scene, into an "organic disarray" ("Aggressivity," 21). For Stelarc, however, "the stretched skin" was a kind of "gravitational landscape," in which he was setting up "a biofeedback situation" to compensate for the incapacities of the worn-out body, which can longer process the information it is required to take in. The hooks might have seemed nightmarish, conjuring up, as in Freud's description of mutilations in the unconscious, "dead carcasses and all that," but for Stelarc, who wished people would get over the "emotional obsession with hooks," they were merely incidental to the sculptured analytic of his suspended body.[13] Difficult as that was to take close up (you would even wince looking at the pictures), the event I want to turn to was really out of sight, and somewhere beyond the kinds of performance that, now and then still persisting, grew out of "the participation mystique" of the sixties, where anyone could perform, even the audience, regardless of talent or training, or any criteria of "accomplishment"—to use the meaning of the word Noh in the most classical Japanese theater, its ideographic slow motion resembling a dream, but in a performance that is generically *(per-form)* an act of perfection.

Speaking of which, then: some years ago, with astonishing will and impeccable control, the equilibrist Philippe Petit walked a line way, way up between the twin towers of the World Trade Center in New York, doubly endangered by the awesome drafts between them, outdoing in that imperiled image even the slam-dunk exploits of an insuperable Air Jordan, as if, indeed, the dreamer were the body of the dream, but at some literalized empyrean of the unconscious. With a superb athleticism and the highest theatricality, it is as if it were negotiating in that crossing the ultimate logic of late capitalism, and I have invoked it before as the limit condition of the most consummate performance, where the imagination's audacity, impelled by the finest discipline, could not survive without it. If this clandestine event—the rope was stretched in the middle of the night, and the performance occurred with virtually no audience but the stars—is also the apotheosis of solo performance, it lifts to its meridian the notion of "public solitude," the condition sought for the actor, out of the inner life, by the Stanislavski Method, with that solitude, paradoxically, as the emptying out of distraction into a fully reflective consciousness, being the responsive basis or datum of the ensemble effect. At the same time, it is also the perfected image of Brechtian Alienation, "the self-observing distance of a body so adept it hardly seemed carnal, no less commodified, more like an ideograph of the mind aloft at its extremity."[14]

In this regard, it suggests those figures crossing an abyss, "like Ideas in Plato's cave," in the van den Leyden painting admired by Artaud in his essay on "Metaphysics and the Mise en Scène," because it suggests "what the theater should be, if it knew how to speak the language that belongs to it."[15] It is a language, of course, which must be for Artaud material, tactile, "affecting the brain directly, like a physical agent" (35), yet as a "poetry of the senses" (37) nothing less than transcendent, though what he is describing, it seems, is the pictographic language in the dramaturgy of the unconscious. So with his notion of the actor, like a victim "burnt at the stake, signaling through the flames" (13), at that limit of performance never quite realized, nor maybe realizable, not by Artaud himself, nor by those of us, stirred by his enraptured vision, who were not quite up to that suicidal idea, but who tried to remember in all the psychophysical exercises of a generation ago—pushing the narcissistic body beyond limits to some sensation of a *déchirement*, the originary splitting contained by thought—that actors in the West had forgotten how to scream. He did not mean the indulgent noise that characterized some performance in the sixties but rather, in the "essential theater," what released the body that matters from logocentric repression into its "complete, sonorous, streaming naked realization," which is also, as in the dreamscape of the Eleusinian mysteries, a "transfusion of matter by mind" (52). Unachievable as it may be, Artaud's conception of a theater of Cruelty—mystical, alchemical, where all the "perverse possibilities of the mind" (30) are localized and exalted, opening up the "gigantic abscess" (31) of repression and deceit—nevertheless ups the ante on the crucial question of control, which in the more familiar regions of theater is part of the psychopathology of the rehearsal process that must shake off, in time, "the asphyxiating inertia of matter which invades even the clearest testimony of the senses" (32). It is as if in the deepest sense, as in the protocols of the death wish beyond the pleasure principle, the organism does not want to act, or with the illusion of commitment—as to a predictable plot or image—acts by a kind of default.

As for the Nietzschean "true illusion," which requires from the actor, according to Artaud, an inescapable commitment to "the truthful precipitates of dreams, in which his taste for crime, his erotic obsessions, his savagery, his chimeras, his utopian sense of life and matter, even his cannibalism, pour out, on a level not counterfeit and illusory, but interior" (92). As there are conventional forms of theater that hardly dream this way, and theories of theater that, from Brechtian alienation to the queerer deconstruction, distrust the energy of an "interior," or think of it as a fiction, there are evasive practices of rehearsal that try to defer it or ward it off, as there must be with working it up in practice on a football field, or for that matter, in the associational process of the analytical session. But when push comes to shove, that is where the action is, and the best of actors know it, to the point of obsessive compulsion that can make a rehearsal endless, and thrilling to the degree that it is always on the edge. Or to return to the image after Macbeth's encounter with the witches, close to the insane root, where it is sometimes impossible to ascertain who exactly is in control or, as we trammel up the consequence, "smother'd in surmise, and nothing is / But what is not" (1.3.141–42), not who, but *what*.

Of course, to begin with, like the coach with firing power, head tricks, and playbook or, more subtly, the analyst introjecting the patient's idiom—presumably a "shadow ego" (Bollas, 39) but, in the countertransference, something more than that—the director may be in control; or in the commodified theater of Broadway, the producer who puts up the money; or moving from stage to screen, with Miramax, Disney, or Dreamworks, the source of megabucks. That may even produce, as it did recently, in *Saving Private Ryan* or *The Thin Red Line*, powerful images of fear and courage at the excruciating limits of performance, where teamwork exists at the edge of the imbecilic. If the harrowing realism of it depends on a prior teamwork of actors, crew, editors, stunt men, and wizards of special effects, what is achieved by camera and cutting is unavailable to the theater, whose teamwork always returns to the susceptible thing itself, the unaccommodated body that at any performative moment may really lose control, as in something so elemental as a case of stage fright. It should be apparent, though it is not, that while it may be superbly sublimated, stage fright is the latency of any performance, as it is there in the batter's box or down in the sprinter's crouch, or even in the supposed privacy of the analytic encounter, where the patient forgets the dream or stutters through made-up experience or, in a seizure of dislocation, is made speechless by the uncanny. Harrowing as it may be, the symptoms of stage fright, like the blanking out on lines, still occur in a situation that you cannot shoot over again. Laurence Olivier was quite aware of that when, at the height of his career, having made his film of *Hamlet* and played triumphantly as Othello, he was directing the National Theater and about to perform in *The Master Builder*. It was then, after some vague "feelings of misgiving" at an afternoon dress rehearsal, that he experienced "a much-dreaded terror," which he thought of as the punishment his pride always deserved, but "which was, in fact," as he wrote of it in his autobiography, "nothing other than a merciless attack of stage fright with all its usual shattering symptoms."[16] For which, and other reasons, he had entered into analysis.

Meanwhile, the vicissitudes of control are endemic to the art of acting, and in the exacerbation of rehearsal—with its associational process—a director may work on that, escalating a certain danger that, in the reciprocity of actors, may really get out of hand, not only in scenes of violence but, as lyrical or tender as it may be, in a love scene as well: more of that, yes, it's splendid (so the director thinks, sometimes saying it, sometimes not), but if the sensuosity increases, whatever the text says, text or no text, the bodies becoming the book, when do you stop? and why? since the actors are into it now, and then again, if one of them is not, how do you get them to take it a little further? one controlling the situation, one ever so slightly resisting, and if the truth were known, you not sure that it isn't too much already. "Do it again," you say, but the demoralizing thing in rehearsal—what the French call *répétition*—is not really knowing what *it* is, "it all, it all," as Beckett says, the intangible referent that always escapes you, not that, *this,* not this, *that,* nor do you really want to repeat it, not that merely, because it wouldn't be the same if it were only the same, it would be nothing but a repetition, not as right as it was, spontaneous, as when it happened for the first time, because the actors were, as they say, "living the moment," not what was, but what *is,* while the desire to get at it, whatever *it* (again) is, drives the rehearsal even more, sometimes driving it crazy. Which suggests that, at some limit, you are dealing with the impossible, arousing an interior violence, which is the mythic source of theater, if we can believe the canonical drama (which moved into psychoanalysis), back through Oedipus to Dionysus, the root not only insane but insatiable as well. And when there is, indeed, physical violence on a stage (which can neither be achieved, escalated, cut away from as on film), a sword fight, a murder, a rape, Othello smothering Desdemona, you always want more, more, but how far do you go, you wonder, before somebody does get hurt, emotionally or physically, you are not always sure which is worse.

That may become an incessant question when there is a sustained history among the actors, with mixed feelings of attraction and aversion, or along with devotion, inflexions of animosity, intensified by dependence, with the director as shadow ego (or as with the analyst drawn into the "emotional constellation," a kind of "somatic double" [Bollas, 12]), caught up in the displacements and condensations that eventually shadow them all, as intrinsic to what they do as the atmosphere they breathe. What they come to know about each other could naturally be an asset, drawn upon in performance, but it could also be a burden, cutting off surprise. That was certainly our experience at The Actor's Workshop of San Francisco, as it developed from a studio with 8 actors to a company of about 150, at a time in the American theater, through the early fifties into the sixties, when (as I have said) there were no examples of continuity, and almost nothing like a company concept. As a performative proposition, the mixed feelings were addressed, even more intimately, in my work with the KRAKEN group (young people whom I trained, some of them famous now), where no matter what we did, whatever the theme or surface appearance, it was always at some level about relations among the performers and—whether on the brain-struck ramparts of *Elsinore,* a work derived from *Hamlet,* or forced to cannibalism in the Sierras in *The Donner Party, Its Crossing*—the psychic condition of the group, with none of the easy escape routes of therapeutic consciousness-raising.

So it was only to be expected when, at the exhausting limit of one improvisation, which was part of an exhaustive interrogation (some of these went on for hours) of materials resembling *Othello* that, when one of the men in the group started to smother one of the women, there was nothing like the accustomed Desdemona about her, certainly nothing submissive, as she threw him off in a rage, and shouted ceaseless obscenities, every scurrilous word of it meant, what they felt about each other being not merely a subtext, but rather the compulsively abrasive substance of the event. "You bastard, you shit, don't you ever do that

again!" she cried, as he backed away, "you always do that, always!"—
what wasn't entirely clear—"don't you ever put your filthy hands on me
again!" Whereupon he looked at her and said simply, "But I can't help it,
it's written," and started moving toward her, big and powerful, over-
whelmingly so, in a muted rage of his own, and I let him go until he
touched her, because I really *wanted to see it,* you always want to *see* it,
and then had all I could do to stop it—she there flailing, scratching,
cursing when he grabbed her—because they were no longer simply acting and he was almost ready to kill her, and if I hadn't interfered it
would have been something more than a fiction or mimicry of abuse.
And it was something more than that, too, when it was reflected upon,
debated, worked through in other sessions, then displaced to another
context (over the months of analysis) and, in another imagistic form,
dispersed among the actors, entered into the structure of a developing
work, charged as it might not have been if the outbreak had never happened or, since I saw it all coming, if I wasn't entirely sure—in letting it
go the limit, and wanting it to go beyond—that I hadn't, almost, lost
control of the situation.

When you think about it, it is a strange thing that we were doing, but it
may seem even stranger when I say that we were doing it, methodologi-
cally, *in order to think,* as if thought were insufficient unless impassioned,
imperiled, out there on the edge, caught in the awesome drafts of incon-
clusion. When I say, however, that something was debated, that might
be verbally but also ideogrammatically, because the actors had the capacities of gymnasts or acrobats, and could act, literally, standing on their
heads, which was only appropriate because at some limit, however emotionally charged, the work was intensely cerebral, as in a novel of Dostoyevsky, passionately so, to the point of brain fever or phobia, the vital
dehiscence such that—mirror upon mirror mirrored all the show—it
seemed that the mirror had shattered into "the concrete problematic of
the realization of the subject" (Lacan, "Aggressivity," 15).
   But I also mean this, as a reflection on limits, in a particular way.
There is a certain kind of thinking that I associate with the thought of
theater, not only when we think *about* the theater but when we think *as
the theater thinks,* in its incipience, that is, coming into being, as if crossing whatever limit kept it (before) from *being performance,* not as the
word is used today in almost every aspect of experience, or mere charade
or drag or masquerade, or as embraced in identity politics or, through
the play of signifying absences, confused with performativity, the *"styl-*

ized repetition of acts" (Butler, *Gender Trouble,* 140) that is not to be thought of as theater. Which, to be precise, is something else again. I mean, rather, the kind of thought that is deliberately, even relentlessly, subjunctive and provisional, putting out interrogative feelers, often thinking out loud what it does not quite (yet, if ever) understand, self-reflexive, yes, parenthetical, no doubt elusive, or allusive, trying out an idea, taking it back again, saying it another way, not saying it at all, but finding a gesture for it, putting it up for grabs in the exhaustive play of perception that, at some limit approaching meaning, always seems to escape, thus keeping meaning alive. And let me not be misleading, there is nothing loose about it, no slack in the void, there being in all the indeterminacy a pressure toward form, *per*-form, what insists in the end on *being thought,* now you see it now you don't, but even in the slippage nevertheless embodied, obdurately so, inarguably, as I wrote in *Take Up the Bodies,* creating "the terms by which it is perceived, when it becomes its own system of value, when there is nothing *behind* what it is saying, when it certifies and substantiates itself as the sole species of its own genre."[17] That, to me, is the ultimate limit.

If what happens, then, in the theater materializes in the flesh, any way you look at it, the theater is a play of mind, "an abstraction blooded, as a man by thought," as Wallace Stevens wrote in his *Notes toward a Supreme Fiction.* That is what I tried to suggest in the supreme image of Philippe Petit aloft at night between the towers, luminously there like a Platonic Idea. And while it comes with the ecstatic dance of a ritual plenitude, it was a similar sort of abstraction that Artaud defined when—describing the perpetual motion of Balinese drama, the dance of "animated manikins" and "robot squeakings," the flights of elytra and sudden cries, the "strange games of flying hands, like insects in the green air of evening," an ensemble of "explosions, flights, secret streams, detours in every direction of . . . *gestures made to last,"* he spoke of it as "an inexhaustible *mental* ratiocination, like a mind ceaselessly taking its bearings in the maze of the unconscious" (63; emphasis mine).

To be sure, this is not everybody's notion of theater, and the mind needs to take its bearings, too, in the maze of history as it thinks through the politics of the unconscious, which is what we were trying to do, just before my work with KRAKEN stopped, in an extended project called *The Cell,* which moved from the molecular cell to the Maoist cell through various kinds of ideological formation, at that limit of perception where history looks like theater or, like theater, may be defined as "blooded thought."[18] The investigations for this work included a series of exercises that, on the edge of drawing blood, moved the question of limits into the theater of medicine, though that was unexpected. The exercises entailed a fastidious study of the body and selected body parts, from kneecaps and genitals to finger nails, eardrums, eyelids, skin, in an avid repertoire of torture, repellent at first, but eventually performed, as the actors got into it—wanting to see more, more—as a sort of dance, dreamlike, nightmarish, but with such exploratory and ingenious cruelty, each act refined and carried to such an extreme, then various acts together in an appalling ensemble of the utterly perverse, that were you to have come upon a rehearsal you would have found it, if fascinating, wanting to see more, rather hard to take.

It was precisely because of that, however, that when we did a public demonstration—we were in residence at the time at the University of Maryland in Baltimore—I was approached by the chief psychiatrist at the medical school, who was in charge of a new program there in the humanities. He wondered whether we would be interested in developing a workshop for medical students and interns. (When we met to talk about it, I actually had with me a friend of mine, a philosopher, who was then editor of the *Journal of Aesthetics and Art Criticism,* and the discussions did lead to a series of workshops that my group conducted while we were there.) What he wanted us to deal with, by similar exercises (don't think of anything like psychodrama) was not so much the politics of the unconscious but the issue of pain, which at the unbearable limit of medical practice—and somewhere in the genetics of the unconscious, and probably untreatable by psychoanalysis—remains a problem, apparently, for many doctors, unable to work in cancer wards or burn clinics, or do an amputation, because they cannot take the pain.

There is more I could say of that, but if we think of pain in the theater, there is an appalling limit, too, defined by the greatest drama—say, *Oedipus* or *King Lear*—which may test the power of acting by its capacity to deal with it, an experience so unbearable you are tempted to turn away. Maybe in fact you should, but then you could not perform it, and even then, when you think of it—"Is this the promised end?" "Or image of that horror?" (*Lear* 5.3.265–66)—if you didn't lose control, it is probably not enough. "Never, never, never, never, never" (5.3.309). All other limits are subordinate to that, which Freud in his final wisdom seemed to know.

(2000)

Notes

Introduction

1. Herbert Blau, *Blooded Thought: Occasions of Theater* (Baltimore: PAJ/Johns Hopkins, 1982).

2. "What, has this thing appeared again to-night?" (*Hamlet* 1.1.21). Quotations from Shakespeare are mainly from the Pelican editions, in this case *Hamlet, Prince of Denmark*, ed. Willard Farnham (Baltimore: Penguin, 1974).

3. Starting with Artaud's desire for a theater that has yet to exist, Derrida concludes by acceding to what, at "the fatal limit of a cruelty which begins with its own representation," the theater insists on being. The stark conclusion of the final sentences has still not been wholly absorbed, as reality principle, by the desiring machines of cultural critique, or performativity: "To think the closure of representation is to think the tragic: not as the representation of fate, but as the fate of representation. Its gratuitous and baseless necessity. And it is to think why it is *fatal* that, in its closure, representation continues" (Jacques Derrida, "The Theater of Cruelty and the Closure of Representation," in *Writing and Difference* [Chicago: University of Chicago Press, 1978], 250).

4. Judith Butler, *Gender Trouble: Feminism and the Subversion of Identity* (New York/London: Routledge, 1990), 139.

5. Bertolt Brecht, "A Short Organum for the Theater," in *Brecht on Theater: The Development of an Aesthetic*, ed. and trans. John Willett (New York: Hill and Wang, 1964), 189. For an account of the circumstances surrounding my production of *Mother Courage*, and events that specifically determined a revisionist attitude toward *Galileo*, see chapters 4 and 7 of *The Impossible Theater: A Manifesto* (New York: Macmillan, 1964).

6. Gilles Deleuze and Félix Guattari, *Anti-Oedipus: Capitalism and Schizophrenia*, trans. Robert Hurley, Mark Seem, and Helen R. Lane (New York: Viking, 1977), 11.

7. Herbert Blau, *Nothing in Itself: Complexions of Fashion* (Bloomington: Indiana University Press, 1999).

8. For a detailed account of the process of "ghosting," as it emerged, it seemed, from the stagings of the unconscious, to develop not only into a methodology but a virtual metaphysics of performance, see my *Take Up the Bodies: Theater at the Vanishing Point* (Urbana: University of Illinois Press, 1982), chapters 4 and 5.

9. Editorial, *Performing Arts Journal* 16, no. 1 (1994): n.p.

10. This is an issue that I felt compelled to write about in the midst of the student movement of the sixties, when even quite discerning and eminent faculty were put off by calls for relevance, and saw it as a sort of anti-intellectual juggernaut destructive to higher learning. I am not talking of your ordinary backlash know-nothing academics today, like those opposed to cultural studies, but some of the finest scholars in the country, not insensitive to student protest, who were at a conference on "The Future of the Humanities" organized in 1968 by the journal *Daedalus* at the American Academy of Arts and Sciences. What I wrote for that occasion ("Relevance: The Shadow of a Magnitude," *Daedalus* 98, no. 3 [1969]: 654–76) was described by the art historian James Ackerman, who edited the collected papers, as an "apocalyptic message [with] the most radical implications of any in the issue" (Introduction, 609), though if it were included here I might have been inclined to tone down the apocalypse somewhat, and maybe even recant some of what I said. But then, that comes from the sort of retrospective impulse one also has to distrust. Quite frankly, I think I was right on at the time, in understanding historically the urgency of the moment. What the students were doing and demanding was not at all ungrounded, but then the ground began to shift, the necessary or justifiable became excessive, questionable, and through the Days of Rage more than severely so. Which is only to observe again that in the quick warp of history any just claim may become a problem unto itself, and what you supported to begin with, and beyond considerable doubt, is likely to raise unavoidable questions, as certain aspects of affirmative action (which I still support with reservations) are likely to do today. As for the relevance of the essay, if I were to have included in this collection anything from this earlier period, it would have had priority.

11. Herbert Blau, *The Audience* (Baltimore: Johns Hopkins University Press, 1990), 1.

12. Bruce Weber, "A Common Heart and an Uncommon Brain," review of *Proof, New York Times,* 24 May 2000, B3. Coincidentally, *Proof* was directed by Daniel Sullivan, who grew up with our theater in San Francisco and went with us to New York, before he became the director of the Seattle Repertory Theater, where he was for many years before returning to New York.

13. The big issue today for many of these theaters remains what it soon became: how to sustain artistic vision above the bottom line. As nonprofit theaters started sending plays to Broadway, they were eventually caught up in allegiances with commercial producers that, over time, exacerbated old problems. These were debated and publicized back in 1974 at the First Annual Congress of Theater (FACT), a meeting at Princeton of Broadway producers and regional theater directors, with foundation and government

officials; and now a second congress, about to take place at Harvard, in June 2000, seems stuck on the same agenda. "And, of course," as Ben Cameron, executive director of TCG (Theater Communications Group), puts it, "the old familiar questions will arise: Can the commercial theater, driven wholly by earnings, really understand the needs of the nonprofit theater, largely dependent on charitable contributions? How can we collaborate effectively, responsibly, respectfully? . . . Who has the last word about marketing strategies and materials?" ("Finding the Right Way to Cross the Divide," *New York Times*, 4 June 2000, sec. 2, p. 11). Whoever has the last word, marketing strategies would appear to be dominant, accounting for a companion article, "A Vital Movement Has Lost Its Way," by Rocco Landesman, president of Jujamcyn Theaters: "But what happened," he asks, the question and lament familiar, "to what used to be called the resident theater movement? What had been a cause seems now to be mostly a marketing campaign" (16). The instincts that made it such—as I suggested in *The Impossible Theater*, when deeply engaged with the cause—were always already there, even back when there was next to nothing to market. That was true in the emergence of my own theater in San Francisco, where we struggled to contain those instincts, and all the more so with the development of TCG and LORT (the League of Resident Theaters), of which my partner Jules Irving was one of the guiding spirits. As for the National Endowment for the Arts, which came on the scene with the wish-fulfilling promise of somehow financing the cause, it had all it could do to survive the indifference of Congress itself and the disdain of Jesse Helms.

1. Afterthought from the Vanishing Point

1. A planned Festschrift for Ruby Cohn, one of our foremost scholars of modern drama, caused me to revise and elaborate on a keynote talk I had given, in 1993, at a conference on the cultural politics of theater at Lancaster University, England. Completed that same year, the essay was published in *The Theatrical Gamut: Notes for a Post-Beckettian Stage*, ed. Enoch Brater (Ann Arbor: University of Michigan Press, 1995).

2. Walter Benjamin, "Theses on the Philosophy of History," in *Illuminations*, ed. and intro. Hannah Arendt, trans. Harry Zohn (New York: Harcourt, Brace, 1968), 265.

3. See Samuel Beckett, *Footfalls*, in *Collected Shorter Plays* (London: Faber, 1984), 243.

4. Roland Barthes, *Camera Lucida: Reflections on Photography*, trans. Richard Howard (New York: Hill and Wang, 1981), 80.

5. Ruby Cohn, *Samuel Beckett: The Comic Gamut* (New Brunswick, N.J.: Rutgers University Press, 1962), 4.

6. Raymond Williams, *Writing in Society* (London: Verso, n.d.), 19.

7. Quoted by Jim Hoagland, *International Herald Tribune*, 25 February 1993, 4. Here in the United States recent polls show—what once might have been shocking— that Americans are not only jaundiced about their politicians but distrust each other as well.

8. Herbert Blau, *The Audience* (Baltimore: Johns Hopkins University Press, 1990), 1.

9. Sophocles, *Oedipus at Colonus*, ll. 105–6, trans. Robert Fitzgerald, vol. 3 of *The*

Complete Greek Tragedies, ed. David Grene and Richmond Lattimore (New York: The Modern Library, n.d.), 99.

10. Samuel Beckett, *Endgame* (New York: Grove, 1958), 68.

11. Antonin Artaud, *The Theater and Its Double,* trans. Mary Caroline Richards (New York: Grove, 1958), 51.

12. Jacques Derrida, *Speech and Phenomena and Other Essays on Husserl's Theory of Signs,* trans. and intro. David B. Allison, pref. Newton Garver (Evanston: Northwestern University Press, 1973), 76.

13. For a description of this legendary event, and responses to it, see Ruby Cohn, *From Desire to Godot: Pocket Theater of Postwar France* (Berkeley: University of California Press, 1987), 51–63.

2. The Impossible Takes a Little Time

This essay was originally prepared for a gathering, with several American visitors, of British playwrights, directors, and critics at East Anglia in Norwich, England, July 1984. For this meeting I was asked to assess the overall situation of the American theater, as I had done just about twenty years before, in the opening chapters of *The Impossible Theater.*

4. From Red Hill to the Renaissance

This essay was presented at a session on the San Francisco Renaissance, at the MLA conference, in San Francisco, December 1987.

1. Adrian Wilson died in February 1988.

5. A Dove in My Chimney

1. There are allusions, here and elsewhere, to questions or remarks that came in a letter from Marie-Claire Pasquier, who edited the issue of *Revue française d'études américaine* (October 1980) in which these somewhat disjunct responses, by return letter, first appeared.

2. That the dove sounded as it did may also have had something to do with Professor Pasquier's being the foremost authority in France on the writings of Gertrude Stein.

7. Deep Throat

This text was presented at a conference on "Oral Modes in Contemporary Arts and Culture" at the Center for Music Experiment, University of California-San Diego, February 1982. The participants were mainly sound-poets and musicians.

8. A Valediction

These remarks were prompted by a series of questions from the editors of *Performing Arts Journal,* to performers, writers, directors who had worked in the experimental tradition. The responses were published, in 1994, under the title "Ages of the Avant-Garde," with its pun about aging too.

9. The Dubious Spectacle of Collective Identity

This text was presented at a conference of the European Association of American Studies, held in Lisbon, Portugal, in April 1998.

1. Lionel Trilling, "On the Modern Element in Modern Literature," *Literary Modernism,* ed. and intro. Irving Howe (Greenwich, Conn.: Fawcett, 1967), 69.

2. For a useful review of the status of ritual in contemporary thought, see Richard F. Hardin, "'Ritual' in Recent Criticism: The Elusive Sense of Community," *PMLA* 98 (1983): 846–59.

3. Antonin Artaud, quoted by Jacques Derrida, in "The Theater of Cruelty and the Closure of Representation," in *Writing and Difference,* trans. and intro. Alan Bass (Chicago: University of Chicago Press, 1978), 232.

4. René Girard, *Violence and the Sacred,* trans. Patrick Gregory (Baltimore: Johns Hopkins University Press, 1977).

5. Antonin Artaud, *The Theater and Its Double,* trans. Mary Caroline Richards (New York: Grove, 1958), 13.

6. Northrop Frye, *Anatomy of Criticism* (1957; Princeton: Princeton University Press, 1973), 109.

7. Judith Butler, *Gender Trouble: Feminism and the Subversion of Identity* (New York: Routledge, 1990), 140.

8. T. S. Eliot, *Selected Essays,* 3d ed. (London: Faber, 1953), 47.

9. Raymond Williams, "Drama in a Dramatized Society," *Writing in Society* (London: Verso, n.d.), 12.

10. Jean Baudrillard, *Simulations,* trans. Paul Foss, Paul Patton, and Philip Beitchman (New York: Semiotext[e], 1983).

11. Samuel Beckett, *Waiting for Godot* (New York: Grove, 1954), 58.

12. William Butler Yeats, *Essays and Introductions* (New York: Macmillan, 1961), 215.

13. Bertolt Brecht, "Alienation Effects in Chinese Acting," in *Brecht on Theater: The Development of an Aesthetic,* ed. and trans. John Willett (New York: Hill and Wang, 1964), 94.

14. Bertolt Brecht, "A Short Organum for the Theater," in *Brecht on Theater: The Development of an Aesthetic,* ed. and trans. John Willett (New York: Hill and Wang, 1964), 181.

15. Roland Barthes, *Empire of Signs,* trans. Richard Howard (New York: Hill and Wang, 1982), 3–4.

16. Roland Barthes, *Image-Music-Text,* trans. Stephen Heath (New York: Hill and Wang, 1977), 170.

10. Fantasia and Simulacra

1. Robert C. Morgan describes the work of p.u.l.s.e. as more concentrated than the technology movement of the sixties "upon the issues of disjuncture and narrative as related to current issues of deconstruction and appropriation" ("The Spectacle in Time: A New Look at Art and Technology," *Arts Magazine* 61 [October 1987]: 76).

2. Quoted in the *New York Times,* 29 October 1987, 21.

3. Ezra Pound, *Gaudier-Brzeska: A Memoir* (New York: New Directions, 1970), 19.

4. Quoted by Milton Esterow, "Public Art Becomes a Political Hot Potato," *ARTnews* 85 (January 1986): 106.

5. Quoted by Paul Gardner, "Rodney Alan Greenblat's Candy-Colored Cartooni-verse," *ARTnews* 85 (January 1986): 106.

6. Jean Baudrillard, *Simulations,* trans. Paul Foss, Paul Patton, and Philip Beitch-man (New York: Semiotext[e], 1983), 24.

7. Quoted in the *New York Times,* 28 January 1988, 17.

8. Theodor W. Adorno, *Philosophy of Modern Music,* trans. Anne G. Mitchell and Wesley W. Blomster (New York: Continuum, 1985), 14.

9. Bertolt Brecht, "Modern Theater Is Epic Theater," in *Brecht on Theater: The Development of an Aesthetic,* ed. and trans. John Willett (New York: Hill and Wang, 1964), 37.

10. Quoted by John Schaefer, *New Sounds* (New York: Harper and Row, 1987), 252.

11. See Herbert Blau, *Take Up the Bodies: Theater at the Vanishing Point* (Urbana: University of Illinois Press, 1982), 195–247.

11. With Your Permission

This essay was delivered as the keynote address at the first convention of the new Association for Theater in Higher Education in Chicago, August 1987.

1. Bertolt Brecht, *Brecht on Theater: The Development of an Aesthetic* (New York: Hill and Wang, 1964), 34.

2. Antonin Artaud, *The Theater and Its Double,* trans. Mary Caroline Richards (New York: Grove, 1958), 8.

3. Vsevelod Meyerhold, *Meyerhold on Theater,* ed. and trans. Edward Braun (New York: Hill and Wang, 1969), 52.

4. Konstantin Stanislavski, *My Life in Art* (Moscow: Foreign Languages Publishing House, n.d.), 217.

5. Konstantin Stanislavski, *An Actor Prepares,* trans. Elizabeth Reynolds Hapgood (New York: Theater Arts, 1936), 198–99.

12. The Pipe Dreams of O'Neill in the Age of Deconstruction

The occasion for this essay was an international symposium on "Eugene O'Neill as Our Contemporary Dramatist," at Hosei University, Tokyo, in 1988.

13. Readymade Desire

1. Tennessee Williams, "The Catastrophe of Success," in *The Theater of Tennessee Williams,* vol. 1 (New York: New Directions, 1971), 140. The article on success seems to have been of some importance to Williams. Written for the *New York Times* drama section, 30 November 1947, it was first reprinted as the introduction to the Signet edition of *A Streetcar Named Desire* (New York: NAL, 1951).

2. Mary McCarthy, *Theater Chronicle 1937–62* (New York: Farrar, Strauss, 1963), 134.

3. *The Glass Menagerie*, in *The Theater of Tennessee Williams*, vol. 1, 132.

4. Quoted by Ted Kalem, "The Theater: The Angel of the Odd," *Time*, 9 March 1962, 53.

5. See Sidney Olson, "The Movie Hearings," *Life*, 24 November 1947, 137–48.

6. *A Streetcar Named Desire*, in *The Theater of Tennessee Williams*, vol. 1, 239.

7. David Frost, "Will God Talk Back to a Playwright? Tennessee Williams," in *The Americans* (New York: Stein and Day, 1970), 40.

8. The phrase was used by Michel Foucault to describe the performative logic of a phantasmic movement of mind in the discourse of Gilles Deleuze ("Theatrum Philosophicum," in *Language, Counter-Memory, Practice: Selected Essays and Interviews*, ed. Donald F. Bouchard, trans. Bouchard and Sherry Simon [Ithaca: Cornell University Press, 1977], 171).

9. "Old Girl's New Boy," *Time*, 24 November 1947, 26.

14. Water under the Bridge

1. Maria Irene Fornes, *Tango Palace*, in *Promenade and Other Plays*, intro. Richard Gilman (New York: Winter House, 1971), 139.

2. Roland Barthes, *The Pleasure of the Text*, trans. Richard Miller (New York: Hill and Wang, 1975), 17.

3. Garry Kasparov, "IBM Owes Mankind a Rematch," *Time*, 26 May 1997, 66.

4. *Throwing shade* is a phrase used to describe the competitive rituals of drag-ball culture, though vogueing itself is virtually synonymous with throwing shade on the dance floor. The competitive spirit flourishes through the ability to read and expose, through personal insult, a rival's weaknesses or vulnerability.

5. Samuel Beckett, *Waiting for Godot* (New York: Grove, 1954), 7.

6. See Eve Kosofsky Sedgwick, *Epistemology of the Closet* (Berkeley: University of California Press, 1990).

7. Maria Irene Fornes, *Mud*, in *Plays* (New York: PAJ Publications, 1986), 19.

15. Fervently Impossible

This talk was given at a conference, "The Theater of Affirmation," in honor of Harold Clurman, sponsored by the Department of Theater and Film at Hunter College of the City University of New York, November 21, 1993.

17. Flat-Out Vision

1. Quoted by Christopher Phillips, ed., *Photography in the Modern Era: European Documents and Critical Writings, 1913–40* (New York: Metropolitan Museum of Art/ Aperture, 1989), 246.

2. Jacques Lacan, *The Four Fundamental Concepts of Psychoanalysis*, ed. Jacques-Alain Miller, trans. Alan Sheridan (New York: Norton, 1978), 82.

3. Walter Benjamin, "A Short History of Photography," trans. Stanley Mitchell, *Screen* 13 (1972), 7.

4. Henrik Ibsen, *The Wild Duck*, in *Four Great Plays*, trans. R. Farquharson Sharp, intro. John Gassner (New York: Bantam, 1958), 225.

5. Karl Marx, "For a Ruthless Criticism of Everything Existing," trans. Ronald Rogowski, in *The Marx-Engels Reader*, ed. Robert C. Tucker (New York: Norton, 1978), 13. Written as a letter, in 1844, to Arnold Ruge, the article elaborated the idea of criticism into a program for the journal *Deutsch-Französische Jahrbücher*, of which Marx and Ruge were coeditors.

6. Jean Baudrillard, "What Are You Doing after the Orgy?" *Artforum* 22.2 (1983): 42.

7. Roland Barthes, *Camera Lucida: Reflections on Photography*, trans. Richard Howard (New York: Hill and Wang, 1981), 70.

8. Nadar (Gaspard-Felix Tournachon), "My Life as a Photographer," *October* 5 (1978): 9.

9. Rosalind Krauss and Jane Livingston, *L'Amour fou: Photography and Surrealism*, with essay by Dawn Ades (Washington, D.C.: Corcoran Gallery of Art; New York: Abbeville, 1985), 31.

10. Quoted by Beaumont Newhall, *The History of Photography: From 1839 to the Present* (New York: Museum of Modern Art/New York Graphic Society; Boston: Little, Brown, 1988), 69.

11. *Great Photographers* (New York: Time-Life Books, 1971), 217.

12. Walter Benjamin, *The Origin of German Tragic Drama*, trans. John Osborne, intro. George Steiner (London: NLB, 1977), 92.

13. Rosalind Krauss, "Photography's Discursive Spaces," in *The Originality of the Avant-Garde and Other Modernist Myths* (Cambridge: MIT Press, 1985), 149.

14. See Eugène Atget, *Modern Times*, vol. 2, *The Work of Atget*, ed. John Szarkowski and Maria Morris Hambourg (New York: Museum of Modern Art, 1985), 136.

15. John Szarkowski, *Photography Until Now* (New York: Museum of Modern Art, 1989), 143, 161.

16. Abigail Solomon-Godeau, "Living with Contradictions: Critical Practices in the Age of Supply-Side Aesthetics," in *The Critical Image: Essays on Contemporary Photography*, ed. Carol Squiers (Port Townsend, Wash.: Bay Press, 1990), 72.

17. Hal Foster, *Recodings: Art, Spectacle, Cultural Politics* (Port Townsend, Wash.: Bay Press, 1985), 25.

18. Coco Fusco, "Andrés Serrano Shoots the Klan: An Interview," *High Performance* 14.3 (no. 55; 1991): 43.

19. Walter Benjamin, *Illuminations*, ed. Hannah Arendt, trans. Harry Zohn (New York: Schocken, 1977), 225.

20. Allan Sekula, "The Body and the Archives," *October* 39 (1986): 3–64.

21. "The Last Snapshot of the European Intellectuals," in Walter Benjamin, *Reflections: Essays, Aphorisms, Autobiographical Writings*, ed. Peter Demetz, trans. Edmund Jephcott (New York: Harcourt, 1978), 179. It was, too, in the essay on surrealism that

Benjamin issued a premonitory caveat to our cultural critique and, as in Peter Burger, its view of the avant-garde, the new "obligatory misunderstanding of *l'art pour l'art.*" "For art's sake," Benjamin adds, "was scarcely ever to be taken literally; it was always a flag under which sailed a cargo that could not be declared because it still lacked a name" (183–84). If this suggests certain contradictions in the apparent politics of Benjamin, what he had in mind is a project that would illuminate what, in the year of our stock market crash, he considered the crisis of the arts. This project, "written as it demands to be written," would arise not from critique itself, but from "the deeply grounded composition of an individual who, from inner compulsion, portrays less a historical evolution than a constantly renewed, primal upsurge of esoteric poetry—written in such a way that it would be one of those scholarly confessions that can be counted in every century. The last page would have to show an x-ray picture of surrealism" (184), like a rayograph of Man Ray, its precise mystifications, a deposit through light of reality itself, inscribed.

22. Atget, *The Ancien Régime,* vol. 3, *The Work of Atget,* 122–31.

23. Djuna Barnes, *Nightwood,* intro. T. S. Eliot (New York: New Directions, 1937), 34.

24. Jacques Derrida, "Violence and Metaphysics: An Essay on the Thought of Emmanuel Levinas," in *Writing and Difference,* trans. and intro. Alan Bass (Chicago: University of Chicago Press, 1978), 85.

25. Quoted by Guido Bruno, "The Passing of '291,'" *Pearson's Magazine* 38.9 (1918): 402–3; my source for this is Bram Dijkstra, *Cubism, Stieglitz, and the Early Poetry of Williams Carlos Williams: The Hieroglyphics of a New Speech* (Princeton: Princeton University Press, 1969), 12.

18. The Absolved Riddle

1. All quotations from the tragicomedies of John Fletcher are from the texts under the general editorship of Fredson Bowers, *The Dramatic Works in the Beaumont and Fletcher Canon,* vol. 5 (Cambridge: Cambridge University Press, 1982), except for *The Faithful Shepherdess,* which is in vol. 3 (1973).

2. Jonathan Goldberg, *James I and the Politics of Literature: Jonson, Shakespeare, Donne, and Their Contemporaries* (Baltimore: Johns Hopkins University Press, 1983), 79.

3. Quoted by Ian Fletcher, *Beaumont and Fletcher, Writers and Their Work,* no. 199 (London: British Council, National Book League Series, 1967), 12.

4. Michel Foucault, *An Introduction,* vol. 1, *The History of Sexuality,* trans. Robert Hurley (New York: Pantheon, 1978), 48.

5. Michel Foucault, *Power/Knowledge: Selected Interviews and Other Writings, 1972–1977,* ed. Colin Gordon, trans. Gordon et al. (New York: Pantheon, 1980), 190.

6. See Goldberg, *James I and the Politics of Literature,* ch. 2, "State Secrets," 55–112.

7. Walter Benjamin, *The Origin of German Tragic Drama,* trans. John Osborne (London: NLB, 1977), 69–70.

8. John Dryden, *Conquest of Granada, Part I,* in *The Works of John Dryden,* vol. 11 (Berkeley: University of California Press, 1978), 25.

9. See, for example, Eugene Waith, *The Pattern of Tragicomedy in Beaumont and Fletcher* (New Haven: Yale University Press, 1952), 148.

19. "Set Me Where You Stand"

1. The opening paragraph of Mack's essay on "The World of *Hamlet*" reveals an immediate difference in scholarship with another meaning of "the world": "I do not of course mean Denmark, except as Denmark is given a body by the play; and I do not mean Elizabethan England, though this is necessarily close behind the scenes. I mean simply the imaginative environment that the play asks us to enter when we read it or go to see it" (Maynard Mack, *The Yale Review* 41 [1952]: 502).

2. Maynard Mack, *King Lear in Our Time* (Berkeley: University of California Press, 1972); hereafter cited in the text as *KL*.

3. Stephen Greenblatt, "Towards a Poetics of Culture," in *The New Historicism Reader*, ed. H. Aram Veeser (New York/London: Routledge, 1989), 12.

4. Samuel Johnson, "General Observations" on *King Lear* in his edition of Shakespeare (1765), quoted by Mack, *King Lear in Our Time*, 15.

5. William Shakespeare, *King Lear*, ed. Alfred Harbage (Baltimore: Penguin, 1958), 5.3.63–64. All further quotations from Shakespeare are from the Pelican editions (general editor, Harbage) and cited in the text.

6. *Brecht on Theater: The Development of an Aesthetic*, ed. and trans. John Willett (New York: Hill and Wang, 1964), 189; hereafter cited in the text as *BT*.

7. Jonathan Dollimore and Alan Sinfield, eds., "Foreword: Cultural Materialism," in *Political Shakespeare: New Essays in Cultural Materialism* (Ithaca: Cornell University Press, 1985), viii.

8. Stephen Greenblatt, "Invisible Bullets," in Dollimore and Sinfield, eds., *Political Shakespeare*, 45.

9. Herbert Blau, *The Impossible Theater: A Manifesto* (New York: Macmillan, 1964), 3; hereafter cited in the text as *IT*.

10. It should be apparent that distinctions among that older generation of critics still need to be made. As for Winters, he indeed thought he was right, and everybody else dead wrong, but that was a fighting proposition to be proved in every line, against the grain of other readings, without the slightest mystification.

11. Herbert Blau, "A Subtext Based on Nothing," *Tulane Drama Review* (now *TDR*) 8, no. 2 (1963): 122–32. A more extended version of that essay, with more context for the production, can be found in "The Clearest Gods," the last chapter of *The Impossible Theater*, 277–309.

12. That I have never been particularly sanguine about the judgment of an audience can be seen in various passages of *The Impossible Theater*, and, as a theoretical matter, even more extensively in another of my books, *The Audience* (Baltimore: Johns Hopkins University Press, 1992). As to really quite radical depredations upon a text— for instance, a theater piece called *Elsinore*, derived from *Hamlet*, which was developed with the KRAKEN group—I will be describing them briefly later on, but for a detailed ac-

count see chapters 3–5 of my *Take Up the Bodies: Theater at the Vanishing Point* (Urbana: University of Illinois Press, 1982).

13. The liability is, of course, not confined to the English-speaking theater. When at the recent festival of Avignon, the Russian director Anatoli Vassiliev did a version of Molière's *Amphitryon,* in which he dismembered the text, virtually deboned it, and sliced it up into eight pieces of dialogue played and replayed by three men and three women, sometimes mixing their voices, in rasping or guttural sounds or hammered words, he made no apologies to those who wanted what Molière actually wrote, as many still do at the Comédie Française; he assumed they could read that. Nor was he embarrassed by sequences in which the actors were incomprehensible to each other, no less to the audience. What he did was, perhaps, more extreme or even ferocious than what other directors might do to a text, but his view of the matter—actually within a tradition of the Russian avant-garde, stifled by the Soviets when Meyerhold disappeared—is no longer so unusual as it once was, even on the fringes at Avignon. What is somewhat unusual now is to have had a writer like Beckett, once still associated with the avant-garde, being vigilant over his texts, and intervening to stop productions if he heard they were not being faithful, not only to the words but also to the setting as prescribed, and the stage directions.

14. Jonathan Dollimore, "Introduction: Shakespeare, Cultural Materialism and the New Historicism," in Dollimore and Sinfield, eds., *Political Shakespeare,* 9.

15. Marjorie Garber, *Vested Interests: Cross-Dressing and Cultural Anxiety* (New York/London: Routledge, 1992), 35; hereafter cited in text as *VI.*

16. David Scott Kasten and Peter Stalleybrass, eds., introduction to *Staging the Renaissance: Reinterpretations of Elizabethan and Jacobean Drama* (New York/London: Routledge, 1991), 9.

17. Samuel Beckett, *Waiting for Godot* (New York: Grove, 1954), 8, 41.

18. See Sonnet 60, ll. 5–8: "Nativity, once in the main of light, / Crawls to maturity, wherewith being crowned, / Crooked eclipses 'gainst his glory fight, / And Time that gave doth now his gift confound."

19. Judith Butler, "Performative Acts and Gender Constitution: An Essay in Phenomenology and Feminist Theory," in *Performing Feminisms: Feminist Critical Theory and Theater,* ed. Sue-Ellen Case (Baltimore: Johns Hopkins University Press, 1990), 270–71.

20. Stephen Greenblatt, *Renaissance Self-Fashioning: From More to Shakespeare* (Chicago: University of Chicago Press, 1980), 227; hereafter cited in text as *RSF.*

21. The essay in which the linkage is made between empathy and Iago is called "The Improvisation of Power," and Greenblatt is quite sensitive to the careful preparation that improvising requires. Though he does not mention it, he seems to understand with Freud that the instincts are (if a great matter to Falstaff) essentially conservative. Which is why most improvisations in an acting studio (as in a jam session) are usually, at first, full of repetitions, banalities, a tedium of behavioral clichés, until resistances wear off and surprises begin to occur. This in itself requires a kind of discipline, and techniques of improvisation are usually part of a regimen of training. There are, in fact, different

kinds of improvisation, but as Greenblatt says of the movement of the aleatoric toward a novel shape, "We cannot locate a point of pure premeditation or pure randomness." As for the appearance of the impromptu, he points out that Castiglione and others in the Renaissance knew that it is "often a calculated mask" (*Renaissance Self-Fashioning*, 227).

22. The Moscow performance by Mei Lan-Fang was in the spring of 1935, and Willett remarks that the essay induced by it, "Alienation Effects in Chinese Acting," is the first of Brecht's writings to use the term *Verfremdungseffekt* (*Brecht on Theater*, 99).

23. *Life of Galileo*, trans. Wolfgang Sauerlander and Ralph Manheim, in *Brecht: Collected Plays*, vol. 5, ed. Ralph Manheim and John Willett (New York: Vintage, 1972), 50.

24. Walter Benjamin, *The Origin of German Tragic Drama*, trans. John Osborne (London: NLB, 1977), 92.

25. Samuel Beckett, *Endgame* (New York: Grove, 1958), 26–27.

26. Jacques Derrida, "The Theater of Cruelty and the Closure of Representation," in *Writing and Difference*, trans. and intro. Alan Bass (Chicago: University of Chicago Press, 1978), 236.

27. Jacques Derrida, "La parole soufflée," in *Writing and Difference*, 175.

28. Antonin Artaud, "The Alchemical Theater," in *The Theater and Its Double*, trans. Mary Caroline Richards (New York: Grove, 1958), 51–52.

29. See Murray Krieger, *The Institution of Theory* (Baltimore: Johns Hopkins University Press, 1994), 18, and ch. 2.

30. *Roland Barthes by Roland Barthes*, trans. Richard Howard (New York: Hill and Wang, 1977), 53.

31. Michael Foucault, "Theatrum Philosophicum," in *Language, Counter-Memory, Practice: Selected Essays and Interviews*, ed. and intro. Donald F. Bouchard (Ithaca: Cornell University Press, 1977), 171.

32. Roland Barthes, *The Pleasure of the Text*, trans. Richard Miller (New York: Hill and Wang, 1975), 67.

33. Harold Bloom, *Agon: Towards a Theory of Revisionism* (New York: Oxford University Press, 1982), 17.

34. Gilles Deleuze and Félix Guattari, *Anti-Oedipus: Capitalism and Schizophrenia*, trans. Robert Hurley, Mark Seem, and Helen R. Lane (New York: Viking, 1977), 8.

35. Aeschylus, *The Eumenides*, ll. 254–55, in *Oresteia*, trans. and intro. Richmond Lattimore (Chicago: University of Chicago Press, 1953), 144.

36. Ezra Pound, *The Cantos* (1–95) (New York: New Directions, 1956), Canto 2: 6.

20. Limits of Performance

This is a revised and expanded version of a talk given, in May 1999, at the Stanford Presidential Symposium on "Limits of Performance: Sports, Medicine, and the Humanities."

1. Jacques Lacan, "Aggressivity in Psychoanalysis," in *Ecrits: A Selection*, trans. Alan Sheridan (New York: Norton, 1977), 10.

2. Sigmund Freud, "The Disposition to Obsessional Neurosis," in *The Standard Edition of the Complete Psychological Works of Sigmund Freud*, ed. and trans. James

Strachey, 24 vols. (London: Hogarth and Institute of Psycho-analysis, 1953–74), 12: 324; hereafter references will be to this edition, with customary abbreviation *S.E.*

3. Herbert Blau, *The Impossible Theater: A Manifesto* (New York: Macmillan, 1964). The book, which opens with a relentless assault on the state of the art, was started after ten years of trying to create a company with another attitude at The Actor's Workshop of San Francisco. That theater was still a work-in-progress when, shortly after the book was published, I left to become codirector (with Jules Irving) of the Repertory Theater of Lincoln Center in New York.

4. See Judith Butler, *Bodies That Matter: On the Discursive Limits of "Sex"* (New York/London: Routledge, 1993).

5. Jean Baudrillard, *Simulations,* trans. Paul Foss, Paul Patton, and Philip Beitchman (New York: Semiotext[e], 1983), 36.

6. Christopher Bollas, *Cracking Up: The Work of Unconscious Experience* (New York: Hill and Wang, 1995), 12.

7. Henrik Ibsen, *The Master Builder,* Act 1, in vol. 1 of *Four Major Plays,* trans. Rolf Fjelde (New York: Signet, 1990), 331.

8. Jacques Lacan, "The Function and Field of Speech and Language in Psycho-analysis," in *Ecrits,* 45.

9. Judith Butler, *Gender Trouble: Feminism and the Subversion of Identity* (London: Routledge, 1989), 67.

10. See the chapter titled "Ghostings," in my *Take Up the Bodies: Theater at the Vanishing Point* (Urbana: University of Illinois Press, 1982), 195–247.

11. Quotations from Mike Freeman, "A Cycle of Violence, On the Field and Off," *New York Times,* 6 September 1998, 27, 34.

12. Blau, *The Impossible Theater,* 1, 5.

13. "An Interview with Stelarc," *Obsolete Body/Suspensions/Stelarc,* ed. D. Paffrath with Stelarc (Davis, Calif.: JP Publications, 1984), 16–17.

14. Herbert Blau, *The Audience* (Baltimore: Johns Hopkins University Press, 1992), 334.

15. Antonin Artaud, *The Theater and Its Double,* trans. Mary Caroline Richards (New York: Grove, 1958), 36–37.

16. Laurence Olivier, *Confessions of an Actor: An Autobiography* (New York: Simon and Schuster, 1982), 261.

17. Blau, *Take Up the Bodies,* xii.

18. This was how I defined it in a book with that title, *Blooded Thought: Occasions of Theater* (New York: PAJ Publications, 1982), written, like *Take Up the Bodies,* in a kind of theoretical fallout from the work of the KRAKEN group.

Previous Publications

The chapters in this collection were originally published in the following books and journals. I am grateful to the editors and publishers of these publications for permission to reprint these essays.

"Afterthought from the Vanishing Point: Theater at the End of the Real," in *The Theatrical Gamut: Notes from a Post-Beckettian Stage,* ed. Enoch Brater (Ann Arbor: University of Michigan Press, 1995), 279–98.

"The Impossible Takes a Little Time," *Performing Arts Journal* 8, no. 3 (1984): 29–42.

"Spacing Out in the American Theater," *Kenyon Review* 14, no. 2 (1993): 27–39.

"From Red Hill to the Renaissance: Rehearsing the Resistance," *The Literary Review* 32, no. 1 (1988): 21–28.

"A Dove in My Chimney," *Revue française études americaines* 10 (1980): 209–16.

"*Elsinore*: An Analytic Scenario," *Cream City Review* 6, no. 2 (1981): 56–99.

"Deep Throat: The Grail of the Voice," *New Wilderness Letter* 11 (1982): 68–76.

"A Valediction: Chills and Fever, Mourning, and the Vanities of the Sublime," *Performing Arts Journal* 16, no. 1 (1994): 41–44.

"The Dubious Spectacle of Collective Identity," in *Ceremonies and Spectacles: Performing American Culture,* ed. Teresa Alves, Teresa Cid, and Heinz Ickstadt (Amsterdam: VU University Press, 2000), 21–37.

"Fantasia and Simulacra: Subtext of a Syllabus for the Arts in America," *Kenyon Review* 16, no. 2 (1994): 99–118.

"With Your Permission: Educating the American Theater," *Theater Journal* 40, no. 1 (1988): 5–11.

"Readymade Desire," in *Confronting Tennessee Williams' "A Streetcar Named Desire": Essays in Critical Pluralism,* ed. Philip C. Kolin (Westport, Conn.: Greenwood Press, 1993), 19–26.

"Water under the Bridge: From *Tango Palace* to *Mud,*" in *The Theater of Maria Irene Fornes,* ed. Marc Robinson (Baltimore: PAJ/Johns Hopkins University Press, 1999), 76–84.

"Fervently Impossible: The Group Idea and Its Legacy," *Performing Arts Journal* 17, no. 1 (1995): 1–12.

"Noise, Musication, Beethoven, and Solid Sound: New Music and Theater" was published as "New Music and Theater" in *Raritan* 8, no. 2 (1988): 117–35.

"Flat-Out Vision," in *Fugitive Images: From Photography to Video,* ed. Patrice Petro (Bloomington: Indiana University Press, 1995), 245–64.

"The Absolved Riddle: Sovereign Pleasure and the Baroque Subject in the Tragicomedies of John Fletcher," *New Literary History* 17, no. 3 (1986): 539–54.

"'Set Me Where You Stand': Revising the Abyss," *New Literary History* 29, no. 2 (1998): 247–72.

"Limits of Performance: The Insane Root," in *Psychoanalysis and Performance,* ed. Patrick Campbell and Adrian Kear (London/New York: Routledge, 2001), 21–33.

Index

Abramović, Marina, 14, 172
Acconci, Vito, 13, 26; and *Seedbed,* 121
Acker, Kathy, 173
Acting: in act of fear, 72; and adherence
to text, 301–3; and Alienation effect,
122; and all its imaginable forms, 35,
117; and Artaud, 314–15, 319; as
body of thought, 66, 310–11; and
breathing, 50–51; and Brecht on
Chinese, 148–50, 155, 293; coming
from who knows where, 289; and
emotion, 293–94; and Freud, 310;
and improvisation, 331; the insane
root of, 312, 317–18, 320; and
KRAKEN, 70–72, 175, 221; and the
Method, 122, 148, 217–18, 221–22,
293, 299; and Meyerhold, 185–88;
and pain, 320; and perception of
process, 78–79, 80; and problem of
referent, 300, 316; quality of, in alternative theater, 221–22; radical recon-
ception of, 286–88; and repertoire
of rehearsal, 289, 307, 311, 315–16;
and stage fright, 316; and Stanislavski,
177, 185–88; and training programs,
166; and vicissitudes of control,
311–12, 316–18, 320; as vocation

of otherness, 291–92; as way of life,
177; for whom? where? why?, xvi, 63,
175, 182
Actors, 57, 59, 64, 66, 121, 123–24, 125,
185, 288; and aging, 133–34; and
becoming the other, 121; and bodies
as architecture, 50; and breathing,
50–51; difficulties of training, 159,
166; and disappearance, 68; giving
birth astride a grave, 51; and legacy
of subservience, 58; metamorphosed
to "performers," 11, 286; and reclaim-
ing the text, 19; relations, in KRAKEN,
317; as shamanistic, 124; splendid isolation of, in Brecht, 148; as thinkers,
18; and voice, 118–31
Actor's Studio, 120–21, 124
Actor's Workshop of San Francisco, xxi,
xxii, 28, 35, 40–41, 46, 48–50, 53–61,
67, 164; and the Group, 224–29; as
notorious, xix; and playing spaces,
xv, 48–50. Productions: *The Balcony,*
304; *Cock-a-Doodle-Dandy,* 226; *The
Crucible,* 61; *Endgame,* 56, 224, 226;
Galileo, xi, 56, 58, 302; *King Lear,* 56,
67, 123, 224, 234, 281–306; *Mother
Courage,* 60, 141, 226, 257–58, 301;

337

Ulay (Uwe Laysiepen), 14

Vasulka, Steina, 134
Vasulka, Woody, 134
Venturi, Robert, 169
Vilar, Jean, 60, 132, 226, 228
Vision: and duplicity, 289; and gaze of high fashion, 4; in Lacan, 247; and ocular site of "blooded thought," 51; and photography, 246–64; in *Play* and *Film* (Beckett), 4; and proliferous spectacle, 248; and reluctant gaze at Stelarc, 13; and ritual, 140; and Stieglitz, 264; as surveillance by media, 39; and theater too painful to watch, 12; and time, 249; and voracity of the eye, 66, 263. *See also* Illusion; Representation
Voice, the: and actors' incapacities, 122–24; in Artaud, 118, 119, 122–123, 122–23, 125, 126; in Barthes, 119, 130, 131; and Dada, 119; and KRAKEN, 125–30; in "La parole soufflée" (Derrida), 122–23, 130; and the Method, 120–21; as scream, 29, 125, 129; in *Sonnets*, 120; training in, 124–125

Warhol, Andy, 160, 165, 186, 202, 203, 218, 257
Wasserstein, Wendy, 34
Watergate, 42, 158
Weill, Kurt, 235, 239
Wellman, Mac, 45
Whitehead, Robert, 228
Wilder, Thornton, 27; *Our Town*, 21, 22, 25

Williams, Raymond, 4, 142, 284; and leftist politics, 200–201
Williams, Tennessee, 199–205; and Brecht, 200; early work of, 200–201; and homosexuality, 201; Works: *Camino Real*, xx; *Candles to the Sun*, 200; *The Glass Menagerie*, 199, 200, 201; *A Streetcar Named Desire*, 199–205; *Suddenly Last Summer*, xx
Williams, William Carlos, 131, 160
Wilson, Adrian, 56
Wilson, Robert, xv, 12, 24, 46, 64, 66, 133; and the edge of trance, 23, 147–48, 233; and Theater of Images, 68, 221
Winters, Yvor, xxi, 284
Wittgenstein, Ludwig, 130
Wobblies (International Workers of the World), 54, 196
Woolf, Virginia, 10, 248
Wooster Group, 21–26, 217; and *The Cocktail Party*, 25; and *Route 1 and 9*, 21–22, 24–25, 27
Wright, Frank Lloyd, 44
Wuorinen, Charles, 166

Yeats, William Butler, 23, 127, 193, 251; and cultural unity, 141; and sanctification of art, 147–48; on symbolism, 139, 141, 147–48
Yeltsin, Boris, 16
Yoneyama, Mamako, 174
Young, La Monte, 166, 237

Zadek, Peter, 20
Zeami, Motokiyo, 177
Zorn, John, 166

Herbert Blau is the Byron W. and Alice L. Lockwood Professor of the Humanities at the University of Washington. He has had a long and distinguished career in theater as cofounder (with Jules Irving) of The Actor's Workshop of San Francisco, codirector of the Repertory Theater at Lincoln Center in New York, and artistic director of the experimental group KRAKEN. The work of KRAKEN was first prepared at California Institute of the Arts, where Blau was the founding provost and dean of the School of Theater and Dance. His numerous books include *Take Up the Bodies: Theater at the Vanishing Point, The Audience, To All Appearances: Ideology and Performance,* and, most recently, *Nothing in Itself: Complexions of Fashion* and *Sails of the Herring Fleet: Essays on Beckett.*